Global Environment of Policing

International Police Executive Symposium Co-Publications

Dilip K. Das, *Founding President-IPES*

PUBLISHED

Global Trafficking in Women and Children
By Obi N.I. Ebbe and Dilip K. Das, ISBN: 978-1-4200-5943-4

Contemporary Issues in Law Enforcement and Policing
By Andrew Millie and Dilip K. Das, ISBN: 978-1-4200-7215-0

Trends in Policing: Interviews with Police Leaders Across the Globe, Volume Two
By Dilip K. Das and Otwin Marenin, ISBN: 978-1-4200-7520-5

Criminal Abuse of Women and Children: An International Perspective
By Obi N.I. Ebbe and Dilip K. Das, ISBN: 978-1-4200-8803-8

Urbanization, Policing, and Security: Global Perspectives
By Gary Cordner, AnnMarie Cordner and Dilip K. Das, ISBN: 978-1-4200-8557-0

Global Environment of Policing
By Dilip K. Das, Darren Palmer, and Michael M. Berlin, ISBN: 978-1-4200-6590-9

Trends in Policing: Interviews with Police Leaders Across the Globe, Volume Three
By Otwin Marenin and Dilip K. Das, ISBN: 978-1-4398-1924-1

Police Without Borders: The Fading Distinction between Local and Global
By Cliff Roberson, Dilip K. Das, and Jennie K. Singer, ISBN: 978-1-4398-0501-5

Effective Crime Reduction Strategies: International Perspectives Enhancing Law Enforcement Profesionalism, Effectiveness and Leadership in the 21st Century
By James F. Albrecht and Dilip K. Das, ISBN: 978-1-4200-7838-1

Strategic Responses to Crime: Thinking Locally, Acting Globally
By Melchor de Guzman, Aieteo Mintie Das, and Dilip K. Das, ISBN: 978-1-4200-7669-1

FORTHCOMING

Policing Neoliberal Societies
By Allison Wakefield, Bankole Cole, and Dilip K. Das, ISBN: 978-1-4398-4135-8

Terrorism, Counterterrorism, and Internal Wars: Examining International Political Violence
By Austin Turk, Dilip K. Das, and James Ross, ISBN: 978-1-4398-2104-6

Justices of the World: Their Views, Opinions and Perspectives
By Chandrika M. Kelso and Dilip K. Das, ISBN: 978-1-4200-9978-2

Cross Cultural Profiles of Policing
By Dilip K. Das, Osman Dolu, and Bonnie Mihalka, ISBN: 978-1-4200-7014-9

International Police Executive Symposium Co-Publications

Dilip K. Das, *Founding President-IPES*

Interviews with Global Leaders in Policing, Prisons, and Courts Series

PUBLISHED

Trends in Policing: Interviews with Police Leaders Across the Globe, Volume Three
By Otwin Marenin and Dilip K. Das, ISBN: 978-1-4398-1924-1

Justices of the World: Their Views, Opinions, and Perspectives
By Chandrika M. Kelso and Dilip K. Das, ISBN: 978-1-4200-9978-2

FORTHCOMING

Trends in Corrections: Interviews with Corrections Leaders Around the World
By Jennie K. Singer and Dilip K. Das, ISBN: 978-1-4398-3578-4

Trends in Policing: Interviews with Police Leaders Across the Globe, Volume Three
By Bruce F. Baker and Dilip K. Das, ISBN: 978-1-4398-8073-9

Global Environment of Policing

Edited by

Darren Palmer • Michael M. Berlin • Dilip K. Das

International Police Executive Symposium Co-Publication

CRC Press
Taylor & Francis Group
Boca Raton London New York

CRC Press is an imprint of the
Taylor & Francis Group, an **informa** business

CRC Press
Taylor & Francis Group
6000 Broken Sound Parkway NW, Suite 300
Boca Raton, FL 33487-2742

Printed in the United States of America on acid-free paper
Version Date: 20111213

International Standard Book Number: 978-1-4200-6590-9 (Hardback)

Library of Congress Cataloging-in-Publication Data

Palmer, Darren.
Global environment of policing / Darren Palmer, Michael M. Berlin, and Dilip K. Das.
p. cm.
Includes bibliographical references and index.
ISBN 978-1-4200-6590-9
1. Police. 2. Law enforcement. 3. Community policing. 4. Police administration. I. Berlin, Michael M., 1954- II. Das, Dilip K., 1941- III. Title.

HV7921.P3153 2012
363.2'3--dc23 2011048930

Visit the Taylor & Francis Web site at
http://www.taylorandfrancis.com

and the CRC Press Web site at
http://www.crcpress.com

Contents

Section IV

POLICE LEADERSHIP, MANAGEMENT, EDUCATION AND ORGANIZATION: ISSUES AND TRENDS

Preface

The *International Police Executive Symposium* (IPES) was founded in 1994 to address one major challenge i.e., the two worlds of research and practice remain disconnected even though cooperation between the two is growing. A major reason is that the two groups speak in different languages. The research is published in hard to access journals and presented in a manner that is difficult for some to comprehend. On the other hand police practitioners tend not to mix with researchers and remain secretive about their work. Consequently there is little dialogue between the two and almost no attempt to learn from one another. The global dialog among police researchers and practitioners is limited. True, the literature on the police is growing exponentially. But its impact upon day-to-day policing, however, is negligible.

The aims and objectives of the IPES are to provide a forum to foster closer relationships among police researchers and practitioners on a global scale, to facilitate cross-cultural, international and interdisciplinary exchanges for the enrichment of the law enforcement profession, to encourage discussion, and to publish research on challenging and contemporary problems facing the policing profession. One of the most important activities of the IPES is the organization of an annual meeting under the auspices of a police agency or an educational institution. Now in its 17th year the annual meeting, a five-day initiative on specific issues relevant to the policing profession, brings together ministers of interior and justice, police commissioners and chiefs, members of academia representing world-renown institutions, and many more criminal justice elite from over 60 countries. It facilitates interaction and the exchange of ideas and opinions on all aspects of policing. The agenda is structured to encourage dialog in both formal and informal settings.

Another important aspect of the meeting is the publication of the best papers presented edited by well known criminal justice scholars and police professionals who attend the meetings. The best papers are selected, thoroughly revised, fully updated, meticulously edited, and published as books based upon the theme of each meeting. This repository of knowledge under the co-publication imprint of IPES and CRC Press–Taylor & Francis Group chronicles the important contributions of the International Police Executive Symposium over the last two decades. As a result in 2011 the United Nations awarded IPES a *Special Consultative Status* for the Economic and Social Council (ECSOC) honoring its importance in the global security community.

In addition to this book series, the IPES also has a research journal, *Police Practices and Research: An International Journal* (PPR). The PPR contains research articles on police issues from practitioners and researchers. It is an international journal in true sense of the term and is distributed worldwide. For more information on the PPR visit http://www.tandf.co.uk/journals/GPPR.

The Global Environment of Policing combines historical and contemporary analyses of the development of policing and the challenges that have confronted and shaped police institutional arrangements and policing practice in the 21st Century. One of the key features of this book is that the content is not limited to a global view from the desks and screens of the western academics, avoided in this instance through two means: the incorporation of scholarship from outside the west, and equally important the inclusion of chapters from practitioners.

IPES advocates, promotes and propagates that POLICING is one of the most basic and essential avenues for improving the quality of life in all nations; rich and poor; modern and traditional; large and small; as well as peaceful and strife-ridden. IPES actively works to drive home to all its office bearers, supporters and admirers that, in order to reach its full potential as an instrument of service to humanity, POLICING must be fully and enthusiastically open to collaboration between research and practice, global exchange of information between police practitioners and academics, universal disseminations and sharing of best practices, generating thinking police leaders and followers, as well as reflecting and writing on the issues challenging to the profession.

Through its annual meetings, hosts, institutional supporters, and publications, IPES reaffirms that POLICING is a moral profession with unflinching adherence to the rule of law and human rights as the embodiment of humane values.

Dilip K. Das
Founding President,
International Police Executive Symposium, www.ipes.info

Book Series Editor for *Advances in Police Theory and Practice*
CRC Press, Taylor and Francis Group

Book Series Editor for *Interviews With Global Leaders in Criminal Justice*
CRC Press. Taylor and Francis Group

Book Series Editor, PPR Special Issues as Books
Routledge, Taylor and Francis Group

Founding Editor-in chief
Police Practice and Research: An International Journal, PPR,
http://www.tandf.co.uk/journals/GPPR

International Police Executive Symposium

Police Practice & Research
An International Journal

Foreword

Tapestries of Policing

It is indeed a pleasure for me to see this volume on the *Global Environment of Policing* come to fruition. The chapters that make it up provide a very welcome window through which readers are invited to explore policing within different geographic locations through the eyes of both practitioners and academics.

Both of these elements reflect, and cement, two important developments in policing studies. The first of these developments is the fact that policing studies have become progressively global. This is true not simply because studies of policing are today being carried out in more and more parts of the world, but because this has enabled the emergence of more comparative scholarship than was hitherto the case. While the effects of this globalization of policing research are still in their infancy, the existence of a comparative database on policing is slowly, but surely, reshaping our understandings of policing. Today, policing scholarship is gradually painting a rich tapestry of intricately interwoven colors—colors drawn from across the public–private spectrum of "auspices" and "providers" of policing (Bayley & Shearing, 2001).

The second of these developments is one that is progressively undermining the persistent divide, so long characteristic of policing studies, which has seen practitioners identified as the objects of research undertaken by academics. This "dialogue of the deaf" has been increasingly replaced by a "dialogue of listening" (Johnston & Shearing, 2009) in which the voices of practitioners, often as sensitive ethnographers of their trade, have progressively become a characteristic feature of the policing studies literature. This is, of course, not new, as there was most certainly a period, especially during the early years of policing, when state police practitioners were active sources of scholarly thinking, for example, August Vollmer (see Vollmer, 1936) and his protégé, Orlando W. Wilson (1950).

The editors of this volume note that this is an "eclectic collection of articles." This is indeed true. However, there is more unity, albeit in the shadows, within this collection than is at first apparent. This unity lies less with the explicit focus of the papers, which the editors correctly note is "state police and policing," and more with the context within which state police operate.

Marc Galanter (1981), in a paper published exactly 30 years ago on legal pluralism, drew attention to this idea of a backstage that is present, but is not an explicit object of attention. He noted that when "private ordering," which includes what we now often think about as private or nonstate policing, takes place, it does so within the context of the ordering of state auspices of governance. Galanter termed this context, following Mnookin (1979), "the shadow of the law."

In his paper, Galanter draws attention to a "legal centralism," that like what might be thought of as "state police centralism," assumes that "remedies [should be] dispensed by experts who operate under the auspices of the state" (Galanter, 1981, p. 1). In his analysis, Galanter uses the notion of the shadow of the law to temper critics of legal centralism who are too quick to imagine a realm that lies entirely outside of state law. The shadow of the law, and especially that of state courts, is, he argues, a long one that colors what happens outside of state processes. Galanter's point, in this discussion, is that we should be careful not to bifurcate the world into state and nonstate spheres in ways that do not appreciate the shadow that states cast over the nonstate actors and their terrains of action.

In developing his argument, Galanter writes

> ... [d]iscussions of private as opposed to public legal systems contain valuable insights, but the public–private distinction invites us to categorize where we need to measure variation. (Galanter, 1981, note 27)

This critique of the private–public distinction, which insists that the public and the private spheres should be understood as part of a single, rich tapestry, does not only apply to attempts to lift the private out of, and away from, the public, but applies equally (as Ayling, Grabosky, and Shearing (2009) have recently argued) to attempts to extract the public from the private. Within a nodal conception of ordering, the public sphere, by definition, exists in the shadow of private auspices and providers in precisely the same way as the private exists within the shadow of states.

There is a normative question that this shadow of the private raises. Although this feature is typically barely recognized within policing studies, it is becoming progressively more and more apparent within the strategic thinking of state police organizations. This normative question being posed by police organizations, in a variety of different ways, is: Who should the police be within an era in which the tapestry of policing has become so completely enmeshed with the colors of private auspices and providers of security governance? (Marks, Shearing, & Wood, 2009).

While this question has, to date, rarely been asked explicitly (exceptions include Ian Blair (1998), the former Commissioner of the London Metropolitan Police when he was the Chief of Police of Sussex and the Patten

Commission (Independent Commission on Policing for Northern Ireland, 1999)), it is one that is coming increasingly to the fore as police organizations, across the world, have been compelled to accept, albeit reluctantly, the enormous extent of private ordering processes and to locate themselves in relation to them.

While this question is not one that has been raised explicitly in this volume, it casts a shadow that can be glimpsed between its lines—whether this glimpse be the impact of neo-liberal thinking, illegal forms of ordering, private security, the impact of social change on policing reform, a recognition that police cannot alone solve crime, the importance of the local or the limits of crime fighting. Perhaps it is this shadow of the nonstate, that Brodeur (2010) has been so careful to highlight, which unifies this eclectic set of chapters.

Clifford Shearing
University of Cape Town

References

Ayling, J., Grabosky, P., & Shearing, C. (2009). *Lengthening the arm of the law: Enhancing police resources in the twenty-first century.* Cambridge, U.K.: Cambridge University Press.

Bayley, D., & Shearing, C. (2001). *The new structure of policing: Description, conceptualization, and research agenda.* Washington, D.C.: National Institute of Justice.

Blair, I. (1998, June). *The governance of security: Where do the police fit into policing?* A draft discussion paper by Ian Blair, Chief Constable of Surrey Police, United Kingdom.

Brodeur, J-P. (2010). *The policing web.* Oxford: Oxford University Press.

Galanter, M. (1981). Justice in many rooms: Courts, private ordering and indigenous law. *Journal of Legal Pluralism, 19,* 1–47.

Independent Commission on Policing for Northern Ireland. (1999). *A new beginning: Policing in Northern Ireland.* Report of the Independent Commission on Policing for Northern Ireland. Norwich: HMSO.

Johnston, L., & Shearing, C. (2009). From a 'dialogue of the deaf' to a 'dialogue of listening': Towards a new methodology of policing research and practice. *Police Practice and Research, 10*(5), 415–422.

Marks, M., Shearing, C., & Wood, J. (2009). Who should the police be? Finding a new narrative for community policing in South Africa. *Police Practice and Research: An International Journal, 10*(2), 145–157.

Mnookin, R. H. (1979). *Bargaining in the shadow of the law: The case of divorce.* (Working paper No. 3). Oxford, U.K.: Centre for Socio-Legal Studies, Wolfson College.

Vollmer, A. (1936). *The police and modern society: Plain talk based on practical experience.* Berkeley, CA: University of California Press.

Wilson, O. W. (1950). *Police administration.* New York: McGraw-Hill.

Introduction

The Global Environment of Policing is an eclectic collection of articles that combine historical and contemporary analyses of the development of policing and the challenges that have confronted and shaped police institutional arrangements and policing practice in the 21st century. One of the key features of this book is that we have worked assiduously to ensure that the content is not limited to a global view from the desks and screens of the western academics, avoided in this instance through two means: the incorporation of scholarship from outside the West, and, equally important, the inclusion of chapters from practitioners. We do not want to overstate these dual divides—between the West and the "other" or between the academic and the police practitioner—but rather and more straightforwardly note the importance of the incorporation of a range of perspectives to inform the reader of the developments within the global environment of policing. It also must be said at the outset that this collection is, for the most part, focused directly on state police or policing under the auspices of the state rather than the diverse range of policing providers or organizations that exist (Bayley & Shearing, 2001) and the various relations or networks (Fleming & Wood, 2006) across policing providers, auspices, and nodes (Shearing, 2001). More specifically, though to varying degrees, the chapters that follow explore key questions such as: What factors in different contexts or places and spaces have shaped policing historically and contemporaneously? Are there particular policing "paradigms" or models that have recently held particular sway over the transformations in policing?

This last question is a pointer to the manner in which the ideas shaping state policing are increasingly drawn from the global environment. Yet, it would be too much to say that this is all new and/or that the local context dissipates in the face of global forces. As Suzanne Karstedt makes clear in her chapter (10), the global is always necessarily played out in local contexts.

The book is divided into four sections. The first of these, Policing, Crime Control, and the Community, begins our inquiry into how ideas of different models of policing have traversed Latin and North America and more generally democratic countries. Hugo Frühling begins this section by examining the dispersion of community policing in Latin America through exemplars of four case studies—São Paulo, Brazil; Villa Nueva, Guatemala; Bogotá, Colombia; and Belo Horizonte, Brazil. According to this account, at the macro level, the 1990s represented significant shifts toward democratic polities, which in turn shaped a process of "de-militarizing" of the police in several countries. Such significant *political* changes, and equally significant *police* changes, created the space for a radical rethinking of police arrangements and orientations, shaped further by a range of key international institutions as well as governments. As Frühling argues, community policing cannot be reduced to a single essence, such as improving relations between police and local communities, but rather has many dimensions, such as seeking to effect crime rates (down), enhancing police accountability (up), including lessening the extent of police violence and corruption (down). In addition, Frühling documents how such reform strategies have to adapt to local contexts, in particular local police institutional structures and practices, and are in a sense always falling short of the broader aspirations for more democratic policing. The particular contexts in Latin America were not only the broad democratization of the state, but also additional specific features intertwined with this process, most notably the high levels of crime and corruption. In addition, Latin America was undergoing broader state reforms demanding a "smaller state" and devolution of authority. The key point arising from this analysis concerns the need to develop a detailed understanding of the local context shaping police reform.

Michael Berlin's chapter (2) examines the "community policing" revolution in the United States over the past three decades. He begins by focusing on the origins of community policing in the early 1980s, its growth and development over the next 15 years, subsequent decline from the late 1990s to the mid-2000s, and nascent transformation in recent years. He suggests that rising crime and increasing complaints against the police led to implementation of community policing but that even 30 years later there is no common definition of community policing. Berlin sets forth his own framework for defining community policing based upon an extensive review of the literature and argues that application of the framework clearly explains the mechanism by which community policing is intended to improve police–community relationships, but that the specific mechanisms by which community policing would reduce crime are not clear.

For Berlin, the decline of community policing is tied, at least in part, to its apparent inability to reduce crime in many jurisdictions. The explosive growth of Compstat (COMParative (or COMPuter) STATistics), zero tolerance, and aggressive enforcement approaches and their apparent success in reducing crime in New York City and elsewhere coincided with the decline of community policing. However, in response to increasing community complaints to broad application of zero-tolerance strategies coupled with greater recognition of the need for intelligence to combat crime and terrorism, he indicates that there appears to be a growing movement to integrate community policing, Compstat, and antiterrorism approaches. While he recognizes that there are significant barriers to integrating these seemingly divergent strategies, he is cautiously optimistic that this is a viable approach and expects to see substantial differences between jurisdictions given the broad diversity of American communities and the U.S. model of local control.

The following chapter (3) by John Eterno focuses more specifically on one of the key "alternatives" to community policing discussed by Berlin, "zero tolerance" policing. Eterno's chapter examines the extent to which zero-tolerance policing has been a "success," arguing that any account of zero tolerance or "aggressive policing" or crime fighting must also place on the ledger the impact on police complaints and police misconduct. Eterno locates this need within the traditional debates concerning "crime control" versus "due process." What was evident from the New York City "experiment" was the dramatic increases in complaints against police that accompanied aggressive quality of life policing that is zero tolerance. However, Eterno argues that this "dilemma" of successful crime fighting threatens democratic policing, as "abuse of authority is the antithesis of policing in a democracy." He goes on to explore how this was addressed in New York City, most particularly New York City Police Department's (NYCPD) Courtesy, Professionalism, and Respect program. Whether this overcomes concerns that decreases in crime necessarily require aggressive policing tactics (other cities had similar decreases) and that internal programs of professionalism can maintain lower and, hopefully, lowering police complaints due to less reasons to complain, remains to be seen.

The notion of democratic policing practice is then subject to an historical case study of the development of policing in Portugal. Luis Fernandes charts the early "premodern" development of policing in Portugal. From the outset, Fernandes approaches the development of Portuguese policing in terms of a "long evolution" beginning in September 1383 via the formation by Royal Charter of the *quadrilheiros* (gang members) of Lisbon. For some scholars of policing historiography, this would be interpreted as a signal that the approach taken fits within the "orthodox" or "conservative" approach to policing histories (see Reiner, 1985, Chapter 1). However, Fernandes questions the underlying power shifts effecting police, thus extending beyond the traditional orthodox approaches. Indeed, rather than a unilinear path toward democratic policing and the teleological fit between the demand for order and the supply of "the" appropriate model of modern policing, Fernandes leaves us with a sense of ongoing tension on policing arrangements in Portugal. As he suggests, contemporary Portuguese policing is fragmented (a multiplicity of police bodies with national jurisdiction), has a multiplicity of auspices within and across the state, has concurrent or overlapping legal jurisdictions (the National Republican Guard and the Public Security Police), and tension remains between centralized command and operational decentralization. This last point highlights the local–national interplay, which plays upon and shapes the other key tension between military and civilian personnel and control, which remains an important tension in many countries. Perhaps a question left to ask is the extent that states that maintain inquisitorial-oriented legal systems find stronger practices, or remnants of the military in (at least some parts of) civil policing arrangements? In turn, this is also suggestive of another question for all policing scholars and practitioners: Is the tension between military and civil policing one of degrees or, more specifically, a matter of an ongoing dynamic particularly evident in the literature pointing to the "paramilitarization" of police?

Fernandes suggests that democratic reform to Portuguese policing only really began in the mid-1980s and particularly from the mid-1990s following two key developments. The first of these involved the introduction of external oversight of the police through the General Inspectorate of Internal Administration (GIIA). The second was internal to the police as they moved toward community policing in the form of the "*policiamento de proximidade*" (proximity policing) in the mid-1990s and the subsequent 2006 Integrated Proximity Policing Program (*Programa Integrado de Policiamento de Proximidade*). Democratic reform is thereby linked to a dyad of external and internal change—the introduction of "audit" via the Inspectorate and the move toward community policing. Of comparative interest is the extent that countries with claims to longstanding democratic policing traditions have also undergone similar changes over the past two to three decades regarding both internal "models" of policing, such as community policing and more robust forms of external oversight, audit, and investigation. This chapter, and several that follow concerns the shift from what Brogden and Nijhar (2005) refer to as a move from "regime policing" to "democratic policing.'

The second section of the book, Policing, Politics, and Democracy, takes up where Fernandes left off with a more focused discussion of challenges for democratic policing and the mechanism used to develop, enhance, and embed democratic policing. Emilio E. Dellasoppa starts with a broad review of the challenges confronting developing countries, with a particular focus on utilizing the experiences of Brazil as a kind of "heuristic device" to understand these challenges. Dellasoppa identifies an important starting point when considering developing countries (though one also could suggest the same might apply to some groups of or locations within developed countries): "... public opinion sees police as a part of the violence and insecurity problem, and not part of the solution." To further this discussion, Dellasoppa puts forward seven hypotheses regarding police–community relations applicable to democracy in developing countries.

The task of policing in Brazil is generally one of confronting high rates of crime and, more specifically, high rates of violent crime, a context that would challenge even the most highly resourced and effective and efficient police agencies. However, Dellasoppa highlights the difficulties of ensuring democratic policing in the context of general weak democratic structures including a fragile judiciary, significant economic challenges and a residual and growing penal population of the poor and illiterate. This reiterates a longstanding truism of police scholarship, quite often misstated by police leaders: It is not that police alone cannot prevent and solve crime, as if with the latest model and community support crime can be eradicated. Rather, it is a case of how the social, political, and economic conditions shape social order and disorder, and then how the police are then differentially organized and deployed to respond to various breaches of the social order. Where the police focus, how resources are allocated, and what drives police sense of self are shaped by as well as shape these processes. However, without a "foundational order" where police can operate within conditions where generally they can expect a good degree of law-abiding behavior and not outright hostility to their existence, is an issue discussed at length in Brodeur's (2010) recent "theory of policing."

K. S. Dhillon provides an account of the development of police accountability mechanisms in India. In a strongly polemical account of police reform, Dhillon writes with some urgency about the threat to police accountability, most notably through the twin forces of increasing complexity in policing work, and what he refers to as the growing politicization of policing, which, in turn, threatens not only the capacity of the police to ensure equitable justice, but also threatens the very fabric of Indian social order. This is an important intervention in the politics of police reform in India as Dhillon has served previously as Director General of Police, Punjab and Madhya Pradesh. Traversing the country, Dhillon points to selective law enforcement and what he argues to be a dangerous trend toward the "communalization" of policing. Dhillon uses the 1977 National Police Commission (NPC) review of police as the benchmark for reform, arguing its recommendations offered a strong platform for much-needed reform. Unfortunately, the reform process has since stalled under whatever political party has been in power, in contrast to Pakistan that, according to Dhillon, used the Indian NPC as a model to reform the 1861 Police Act. Though overlooking the recent Public Interest Litigation undertaken by another ex-Director General of Police, and forcing the Supreme Court to intervene in police reform, Dhillon focuses on the need to ensure police accountability is enhanced across the three areas of popular accountability (to the people), legal accountability (to the law), and functional transparency. In sum, Dhillon is seeking a movement away from the time-honored focus on crime fighting (as enshrined in the outdated 1861 Police Act) toward a broader agenda that not only addresses "models of policing" (itself too often clothed in foundational democratic aspirations, but most often only limited internal bureaucratic changes), but also and fundamentally how policing reform must be directed at and be part of social change. And, to achieve this necessarily demands far more of the internal checks and balances against police malpractice as well as the need for stronger external oversight and transparency, views that sit comfortably alongside P. Manning's recent stimulating foray into reviewing what democratic policing might mean in a (rapidly) changing world (Manning, 2010).

In the final chapter of this section, Michael Kempa takes up these concerns regarding the democratization of policing and places them within the more recent police theorizing concerning the multiplicity of the auspices and providers of policing services (this chapter does seek to understand *policing*, or, more specifically, the governance of policing rather than only the state police). For Kempa, the acknowledgment that throughout history policing has always been more or less "plural," the recent growth of nonstate and hybrid policing forms demands a need to search for new ways of making *policing* accountable. To explore these issues, Kempa examines the Independent Commission on Policing in Northern Ireland (the Patten Commission) (Independent Commission on Policing for Northern Ireland, 1999).

Kempa points to the more expansive view of policing within the Patten Commission and the, therefore, broader sensibilities to governance needs that extend beyond the state police. While the political response to Patten was not the wholesale embracement of all recommendations and reforms, it is nonetheless important to grasp the way Patten was concerned with a broader sense of both *how* you might *govern police work* and who does this *policing*.

Section 3, Policing: Global Challenges, takes us to a consideration of a range of contemporary issues within the policing environment. In the first chapter, David Wall examines the issue of policing cyberspace, how this new domain of activity gives rise to new policing challenges where "old" offenses can occur in new ways, or new offenses are created. In terms of policing it is not simply the new volume of crimes that might be facilitated in cyberspace, but the ways in which this space demands how police, government, and communities need to think about the different ways in which policing can be provided and practiced. In other words, just as Dellasoppa earlier raised concerns about the police self-image as crime fighters, Wall is alerting us to the dangers, or more accurately the limits, of thinking in this way when contemplating the provision of order and security in cyberspace.

A good part of these changing dynamics of police and policing takes us back to a central issue for any policing agency—the need to establish and maintain legitimacy. Much of the recent literature concerning police has been shaped by the concerns with procedural justice (unfortunately too much of it bypasses substantive justice issues). Palmer takes up the issue of legitimacy through alternative means, exploring the introduction of memorials for state police agencies, suggesting that memorials can be seen as a means of garnering community support and sympathy. Memorials stress the "ultimate sacrifice" made by police who lost their lives "in the line of duty." As Palmer points out, it is quite remarkable that such a "global" development, albeit uneven in time and diverse in approaches, has developed with scant analytical attention despite police legitimacy being a foundation of policing studies and the politics of policing. His central argument is that police legitimacy is shaped in various ways, but policing scholarship can benefit significantly by looking at the multiple of ways this can be achieved, and can do so in this area by borrowing from and reinterpreting the extensive literature on war memorials concerning different forms, different reasons for their introduction, the different uses of memorials and associated spaces, and the importance of memorials for garnering community support.

Suzanne Karstedt makes the global processes referred to by Palmer more explicit, examining how policies travel. Karstedt cautions against writing off developments as inevitable, highlighting the need to understand the process of interaction between, and reinterpretation of, different ideas and policies as part of an interplay between the local and the global. While there is now a veritable industry involved in "policy transfer" and implementation of "best practice" that emanates within and beyond western societies in policing and crime prevention and control (as well as beyond these fields), Karstedt builds upon Cohen's (1982) earlier caution against the potential "iatronic" effects of such impositions or adoption of abstract policy ideas created from the "center" without understanding the local in the global, how actual practice is always inherently local and, thus, needs to work through the local context and institutions. As Karstedt suggests, while developing countries were attempting to displace local, communal mechanisms of control and ordering through "modernization" via models from developed countries, the latter were simultaneously seeking to revert to more community-oriented crime prevention practices.

Karstedt stresses the need to focus on "the 'local' and 'particular,' in contrast to the global and universal," stressing that it is "the cultural, sociopolitical, and, in particular, institutional context at the receiving end [which] is decisive for the success and impact of such transfers." It is not that the models have not worked in their originating context, but rather that they might turn out to fail due to being "cultural, structural, and institutional 'misfits.'"

The final chapter in this section is focused on the important issues of organized crime and people smuggling. Arije Antinori locates these issues within the changing practices of the Italian mafia, particularly from the 1960s as 'Ndrangheta empowerment, strengthening, and expansion occurred in Northern Italy. Apart from the litany of violence involved in this expansion, there was also a growing involvement with illegal migration, first to exploit illegal migrants and later to be active agents in illegal people smuggling. Antinori uses the recent 2010 Leone police operation to highlight this transformation, detailing a national network of illegal people smuggling uncovered by police. However, in recent years serious conflict has emerged between mafia groups and people from African backgrounds with four key conflicts documented by Antinori. While he documents the partial success of police operations, the tone generally is one of pessimism with the suggestion that mafia groups have become deeply ingrained in Italian life in ways that fundamentally undermine the state, create a crisis on values, and a bleak future.

The final section of the book, Section 4: Police Leadership, Management, Education, and Organization, brings together a collection of chapters reflecting upon the ongoing issue of police reform, a staple of police scholarship and police practice. Pat O'Malley and Steven Hutchinson examine the intersections between public and private policing and, in particular, the infusion of private sector thinking into state police organizations. But, rather than limiting their argument to how these corporate modes of thinking have influenced and shaped state-based police, their analysis ties such developments to broader governing mentalities, in this case, neo-liberalism. Is it now the case that we should be approaching our analysis of policing as that concerned with a broader policing industry rather than be tied to the ongoing documentation and debates regarding how big the private policing sector has become, the ratio between state and nonstate policing, and the "loss" of public sector monopoly (not a point they make, but one often assumed but surely never the case since the advent of the "new police"). What is of particular interest is that state-based policing is heavily unionized, whereas traditionally the private sector has involved a considerable proportion of nonunion labor. O'Malley and Hutchinson seek to shift the focus away from the traditional interpretation of this being a clash between the "streets" and the "suites" (or the clash street and management cultures, cf. Reuss-Ianni, 1983).

Police unions have been quite successful in negotiating the ongoing reforms to policing, including the delineation between what is "properly" the domain of state-based policing and that which is open to market competition. In other words, state police unions are a key site for the negotiation of the march of neo-liberal governing techniques, in particular, new managerial principles applying across the "new policing industry," or, as Brodeur (2010) calls it, the "police–industrial complex" (drawing upon a longstanding use of the "military–industrial complex").

O'Malley and Hutchinson suggest that the clashes that have become common within state police organizations over managerial innovations should perhaps not be understood as a conflict at a cultural level—between a canteen and a management culture—but, rather as a labor–management clash. The differences in the prominence of unions across the policing industry, they argue, may have less to do with differences between its public and private sectors and more to do with differences in the ability of management to manage unionism.

The success of public sector unions, they argue, has been a determining factor in structuring the market share of public and private sector organizations within the policing industry. This, along with shifts in recruitment practices by state police organizations that are producing better educated state police organizations, may now be facilitating a rapprochement between management and unions within the industry's public sector that may bring about a renewed solidarity across the ranks. They add that ironically, unionism "may be [becoming] a medium for change," resulting in perhaps a greater convergence of public and private policing.

While police unions are relatively strong in Anglo-American contexts, in other societies where unionism is generally less prevalent and/or effective, police unionism is a limited presence on the process of police reform. In such contexts, other levers of authority are needed to promote police reforms. In the case of Ghana, police managers have been testing new motivational tools to seek to enhance police performance. In this chapter, Gerald Gyamfi reports on a small-scale study to test the level of satisfaction with incentives amongst police personnel. The results are sobering as police personnel indicate dissatisfaction across key areas of incentives including remuneration, accommodation, and training. This leads Gyamfi to arguing the case for a more fundamental shift in the delivery of incentives and (though, he does not say it in these words) a shift from seniority to merit-based performance and rewards.

The following chapter takes up one of the key areas identified by Gyamfi as in need of reform: training, or more specifically, police education. In his Australian case study of police education, David Bradley argues the case for policing as an emergent profession where there is a need to embed police education within the university sector. He comes to this point by reviewing critiques of police education and providing an overview of government responses to these critiques. In doing so, he highlights the limited responses of state governments to a range of inquiries demanding changes to police training and education. Too often the responses were at best partial in introducing reforms, limited in their time span and often not practical in their arrangements. He then contrasts two models for delivering police education—the University model and the Registered Training Organization (RTO) model (effectively police training academies qualifying as training authorities)—across three dimensions. These are "managing recruitment targets," "costs," and "quality assurance." For Bradley, the University model provides the best pathway for the future of the police profession. Bradley has substantial personal experience to draw upon as he was involved in reviews of police training and education in Britain and Australia and a key driver of reforms. In New South Wales, where he first served as a police education reformer, the police entered into the University model. In his subsequent appointment in Victoria, which he recently left, the RTO model became the default arrangement.

Chapter 15, by Taptun Nasreen, examines police accountability in Bangladesh. Representative of the possibilities of taking a global approach to local issues and the importance of including police practitioners as active participants in the dialogue of policing reform, Nasreen seeks to identify the key features of an effective oversight framework for law enforcement agencies by utilizing Transparency International's graphical metaphor of the Greek temple model to explain oversight mechanisms within a national integrity system. Nasreen makes a similar point to several of the chapters, whereby "networked governance" (or "cooperation from all stakeholders" in Nasreen's terms) is required for the effectiveness of the agency. It is not simply a matter of introducing a new accountability agency, but also involves a broader reform program of community policing, raising, again, the issues discussed in the first section of this book. While Bangladesh is in transition from a repressive police apparatus with significant political interference in policing, Nasreen is optimistic about the possibilities arising from the combination of "the new accountability" embracing both anticorruption measures as well as broader cultural change through community policing. It is not the full "external accountability" model, but rather a work in progress and one Nasreen, who is a senior police officer with experience working within the United Nations Peacekeeping domain, believes might significantly change policing in Bangladesh. However, her final caution is one that applies to all aspects of policing, including police accountability mechanisms (whether internal, external, or a mix of both); the need for "appropriate resources." Of course, just what this might mean, how appropriateness can be determined, and how effectiveness is operationalized has troubled many countries with considerably more economic resources than Bangladesh. Finally, it is appropriate to end the substantive chapters with Nasreen's account because it raises key issues central to this book. It is translating the global to the local, using a global tool from a global nongovernmental organization (NGO) to explore local issues; it is an account from a "reflexive practitioner"; the practitioner is female in what remains a male-dominated upper echelon of police officers; and, finally, the chapter provides a blend of cautious optimism that change is occurring but never guaranteed. In the "global environment of policing," we can never assume that things are fixed, that the trajectory of reform is unidirectional toward greater and more effective police accountability, or that global factors might not contribute to shaping better local policing.

Darren Palmer
Michael Berlin
Dilip Das

References

Bayley, D., & Shearing, C. (2001). *The new structure of policing: Description, conceptualization, and research agenda.* Washington, D.C.: National Institute of Justice.

Brodeur, J. P. (2010). *The policing web.* New York: Oxford University Press.

Brogden, M., & Nijhar, P. (2005). *Community policing: National and international models and approaches.* Portland, OR: Willan Publishing.

Cohen, S. (1982). Western crime control models in the third world: Benign or malignant? *Research in Law, Deviance and Social Control, 4,* 85–119.

Fleming, J., & Wood, J. (Eds.). (2006). *Fighting crime together: The challenges of policing and security networks.* Sydney: University of New South Wales Press.

Independent Commission on Policing for Northern Ireland. (1999). *A new beginning: Policing in Northern Ireland: The report of the Independent Commission on Policing for Northern Ireland.* Norwich: Independent Commission on Policing for Northern Ireland.

Manning, P. (2010). *A review of policing in a changing world.* Boulder, CO: Paradigm Press.

Reiner, R. (1985). *The politics of the police.* Brighton, U.K.: Wheatsheaf Books.

Reuss-Ianni, E. (1983). *The two cultures of policing: Street cops and management cops.* London: Transaction Books.

Shearing, C. (2001). A nodal conception of governance: Thoughts on a policing commission. *Policing and Society, 11,* 259–272.

Policing, Crime Control and the Community

I

1

The Impact of International Models of Policing in Latin America
The Case of Community Policing

HUGO FRÜHLING

Contents

The rise in crime in Latin America has influenced a number of institutional changes, ranging from efforts to reform the criminal justice procedure to developing adversarial and oral procedures to mobilizing the population to protect itself to, finally, community policing pilot projects. Community policing efforts began in the early 1990s in Copacabana, Rio de Janeiro. Other implementation efforts have followed in other parts of Latin America. These experiences have been promoted and supported by international agencies and governments interested in achieving a reduction of crime and violence, including high levels of police violence as well as enhanced police accountability to the public. They have contributed to the predominance of a new discourse promoted by policymakers and police officers that voices support for popular participation in crime prevention schemes, partnerships at the local level, and public accountability.

This chapter examines some of the existing experiences, their shortcomings as well as their achievements. It analyzes the type of difficulties that confront the implementation of the community policing model in the region, as well as some realistic objectives that it can achieve, but that will be far more limited than those initially planned.

Introduction

During the decade that began in 1991, efforts to reform the police forces multiplied in Latin America. One factor that motivated these efforts was the signing of peace accords between the government and representatives of the armed opposition in El Salvador and Guatemala in 1991 and 1996, respectively. In both cases, the peace accords stipulated the creation of new civilian police forces to replace the former police that had operated under the auspices of the military. These reforms involved a variety of international actors and were carried out in parallel with institutional changes that affected the criminal justice system via the introduction of oral trials and accusatory procedural systems (Stanley, 1999, p. 113–134; see also Neild, 2002).

In the years that followed, initiatives of police reform extended throughout the rest of the region. The processes were influenced by the model of community policing developed in North America and Europe during the 1980s and were strongly supported by multilateral institutions, such as the Inter-American Development Bank, which saw the changes as an appropriate path toward more democratic policing (Frühling, 2004). The attempts to implement programs of community policing have also often enjoyed technical or financial support from governments, foundations, and study centers outside the region.

The following article analyzes the origins of the process of police reform in Latin America, as well as the reasons why community policing has been the focus of many of these processes. Four cases studies of community policing in São Paulo, Brazil; Villa Nueva, Guatemala; Bogotá, Colombia; and Belo Horizonte, Brazil, provide useful examples for a debate on the difficulties that must be confronted in the introduction of this foreign model in the Latin American context as well as the positive effects that, nonetheless, may be achieved through community policing.

Origins of Police Reform

The police reform initiatives to which this article refers are influenced by three factors that influence their characteristics and contents. The first of these is the process of democratization that took place during the 1980s and 1990s in many countries in the region. This process drew attention to the incompatibility between the norms of democracy and human rights and the actions of Latin American police forces. Second, the significant rise in crime in almost all Latin American countries has been accompanied by the visible presence of the issue of crime as an urgent problem that needs to be resolved by public authorities. This sentiment amongst citizens, evident in various opinion polls, led to attempts to transform the police forces that were considered inefficient or corrupt. A final factor influencing police reform has been the context of state reform, widespread in recent years in Latin America as well as the rest of the world. These reforms are characterized by dramatic reductions in size of the state apparatus, the privatization of certain government functions, the decentralization of other functions to local and regional governments, and the search of mechanisms of accountability to ensure the efficiency and effectiveness of government agencies (Bresser Pereira, 1999, pp. 1–13). In light of these changes, the serious deficiencies of the national law enforcement agencies became increasingly evident.

Impact of Democratization in Latin America

The establishment of new democratic governments in Latin America during the 1980s and 1990s allowed for the expression of criticism regarding police abuse that had been pervasive under the preceding authoritarian regimes. For example, an analysis of the use of violence by the civil police, based on denunciations presented to the Internal Affairs Department of the Civilian Police of Bahia (Brazil), reveals troubling results: Of a total of 1,140 complaints of violence by this police force during 1993 to 1997, 24.12% of complaints alleged torture, 5.61% reported battery of citizens, 6.84% death threats, and 2.8% murder, a total of 40% of all the complaints of violence for that period. The overwhelming majority of these complaints were either filed away with no action taken or they resulted in mere recommendations of administrative sanction (Lemos-Nelson, 2001). This situation is not only indicative of the seriousness of the infractions presumably committed by the police, but also reflects the absence of internal administrative control over police conduct.

The São Paulo police have presented similar flaws, and the mass media has avidly covered up incidents of police brutality in this Brazilian state. In 1991, 1,056 civilians were killed by the Military Police and, in 1992, this number rose to 1,421. However, in 1995, 592 civilians were killed by the police, 368 in 1996, and 405 in 1997 (online at: www.ouvidoria-policia.sp.gov.br/pages/Tabelas.htm). This decline may be due in part to the criticism of police practices.

In Bogotá, Colombia, a series of serious crimes committed by police were brought to light in February 1993. Due to the low level of credibility of the police forces, a reform process was undertaken to redeem an institution viewed as corrupt, inefficient, and infiltrated by drug trafficking. By resolution of then Minister of Defense Pardo Rueda, the process began the same year with two commissions charged with evaluating the situation and developing a set of proposals to transform the police. The efforts of these two commissions led to Law 62 of 1993. The reforms began with the naming of Major General Serrano as Chief of the National Police of Colombia in 1994. Major General Serrano was granted special powers by Congress to dismiss officers on well-founded charges of involvement in corruption. Some 7,000 police officers were fired. Unlike other processes of "purging the ranks," this initiative was perceived as credible and affected all levels, not only the lower ranks.

The abuses may be explained in part by the widespread acceptance of institutional violence in society, even when this violence is not legitimate. Cultural acceptance of violence appears even stronger during times in which civil guarantees are suspended (Lemos-Nelson, 2001). At the same time, the systems of internal and external control of police conduct are inadequate, even where there is a will to correct illegal actions (Palmieri, Martínez, Sozzo, & Thomas, 2001, p. 177–220).

Rise in Crime in Latin America

A second factor that influences initiatives to transform the police in Latin America is the increase in crime that has occurred in almost the entire region in recent years. According to the Pan American Health Organization, in 1998, Colombia had a homicide rate of 54 murders per 100,000 inhabitants; Venezuela, 20 (which rose to 33 in 2000); Ecuador, 15.1; Brazil, 26; and Mexico, 15.7 (online at: www.paho.org/English/HCP/HCN/VIO/violence-graphs.htm). Additionally, some of the cities in these countries have homicide rates that are significantly higher than their country average. For example, the homicide rate in Cali, Colombia, is 94 per 100,000 inhabitants, and, in Caracas, Venezuela, the rate is 71 per 100,000 inhabitants. With regard to other crimes, even countries with low homicide rates reveal increased rates of victimization resulting from the commission of other offenses. For example, a recent comparison among several countries reveals that Chile has a high percentage of victimization occurring in the commission of robberies (see the Urban National Victimization Survey 2003 and, in particular, the Annex with international comparisons at www.seguridadciudadana.gob.cl).

This rise in crime has led to a parallel increase of distrust in the police and fairly widespread feelings of insecurity. With regard to Argentina, Dammert and Malone (2002, p. 285) argue that mistrust of police is one of the factors most responsible for the prevalent feelings of insecurity within the community.

In the face of increased crime levels, the need to have better trained and more accountable police forces and to make changes in the strategies of law enforcement were publicly debated. While one position emphasized the need to increase the police forces' functions and powers of control, the other proposed the need to generate channels of citizen participation that would encourage law enforcement accountability to the community with regard to the effectiveness of their policing.

In addition, the progressive application of community policing programs was also in keeping with the principles of the process of state reform in Latin America. In other words, economic and political factors led to changes in the administration of the state that would make the government more accountable and bring public services closer to the citizenry. This reform process emphasized the decentralization of functions to local government and increased the flexibility of the principles of state administration. When applied to the police, these changes were in keeping with some concepts embodied in community policing.

Decentralization and State Reform

During the 1980s and 1990s, interest in state reform increased in Latin America. To a large extent, these reforms were spurred by the economic crisis that urged the reduction of the state apparatus, the effective accountability of public institutions to the citizenry, and the delegation of functions to regional and local governments in an effort to reduce costs, bring public services closer to the citizenry, and reduce the size of the institutions providing these services (Bresser Pereira, 1999, pp. 2–9).

In some cases, this process was encouraged by political factors. Decentralization in Venezuela was due in part to the discrediting of the political parties that had alternately held power. This situation led to the creation of a commission for state reform and municipal and state elections in 1989. In Chile, under the military regime, the administration of public education and primary healthcare was handed over to municipalities, which increased the functions, budgets, and visibility of local government. With the return to democracy, municipal elections were resumed in 1992, and the new mayors became significant political players.

Decentralization and the reform of the state have also had an impact on police forces. As a result of decentralization, some local and regional authorities have displayed an interest in developing programs for citizen security, which may compete with those developed by the central government. In Chile, for example, the mayor of Las Condes initiated preventive patrolling using municipal guards and vehicles that was, to some extent, an alternative to police forces (Sandoval, 2001, p. 66). Municipal police were established in cities of Brazil, Ecuador, and Guatemala. These initiatives have encouraged law enforcement to pay more attention to local officials and local realities, which sometimes contribute to the financing of the police.

At the same time, the state reforms were founded on a new concept of public administration. Public institutions increasingly focused on providing services to consumers, with attention to the values and expectations of the citizenry, the evaluation of the quality of the services, and the integration and participation of the consumer/citizen in the formulation, implementation, and evaluation of the actions of the institution (Mesquita Neto, 2004).

The processes of administrative decentralization and privatization introduced new actors to the scene of citizen security that, combined with increased demand for more democratic policing, led to the implementation of community policing programs or other efforts that were less systematic, but which aimed to improve relations with the public.

Community Policing in Latin America

The North American model of community policing that has taken center stage in the debate on policing in recent years has several essential elements:

- An emphasis on preventive policing focused on the neighborhood.
- The cultivation of a close relationship with the community and consultation with the citizenry in order to ensure that the police take into account the community's perspective (Sherman, 1995, pp. 327–348).
- A focus on resolving concrete security problems that affect the members of the community and on preventing crime rather than merely reacting to calls for help.
- An emphasis on policing that deals with citizens' subjective fears, revising law enforcement priorities, and recognizing that the community (however it is defined) plays a central role in resolving the neighborhood's problems.
- The recognition that police forces must decentralize in order to meet the demands of this strategy (Rosenbaum, 1998, p. 7).

The role of the community is fundamental in this model not only in terms of crime prevention, but also for strengthening the mechanism through which the police account for their actions. The community policing model is based on the police being in constant consultation with the community in order to fulfill three primary functions: (1) it allows the police to learn about local interests and needs, (2) it provides the police with an opportunity for educating the citizenry regarding behavior that can help prevent crime, and (3) it opens a space for citizens to express their complaints as well as providing a public mechanism for the immediate evaluation of policing (Bayley, 1994, pp. 105–120).

By contrast, the processes of police reform underway today in Latin America display considerable variety. Some seek closer involvement with the community, but are not called "community policing," apparently because the institutions involved do not accept all the premises promoted by this model. At the other end of the spectrum are those community-based programs that seek to transform law enforcement in its entirety. Police agencies with higher levels of professionalization will be more likely to make the shift to community policing. But, while law enforcement institutions in Latin America will experience tremendous change, the resistance to this transformation will be much greater than in more developed countries.

While the North American model places an emphasis on the role and responsibility of the police officer on the street and enables officers to acquire skills and abilities through the training process, the police force as an institution is very resistant to change in any context and this change in the organizational paradigm is especially difficult in those Latin American countries where members of the police lack quality training, are poorly paid, lack motivation, and endure serious management problems.

The first formally evaluated experience in Latin America took place in Copacabana, Rio de Janeiro, in 1994. While this initiative was short-lived, it was followed by similar programs in many other cities throughout Brazil (Muniz, Larvie, Musumeci, & Freire, 1997, pp. 197–214). This experiment and the ones that followed confronted similar obstacles. First, the demand for crime control and the parallel call for a drastic reduction in police abuse have been perceived as somewhat contradictory by significant sectors of public opinion, which brought about an early end to many of the reform initiatives (Frühling, 2001). Second, increased crime and fear place pressure on the police to show short-term results in circumstances that require long-range efforts. Finally, the institutional modernization that is required faces significant obstacles within the police given the large numbers of police members involved, serious financial difficulties, and a highly regulated, centralized administration. For example, Peru's National Police are composed of some 100,000 police officers, but, the 2002 Report of the Special Commission for the Restructuring of the National Police of Peru states, "[t]he police was neither a political nor budgetary priority in the 1990s. For this reason, the infrastructure dedicated to citizen security and public order is profoundly deteriorated. . . ."

The following four examples of community policing lead to some useful conclusions regarding the design and execution of projects of this kind, which influence their impact on the institution as a whole. The projects were chosen because of the length of time for which they had been in effect and the considerable volume of information available regarding these projects, which provided a basis for the evaluation of these experiences (Frühling, 2004).

The Community Policing Program of São Paulo's Military Police

During the 1980s, the state of São Paulo, along with the rest of Brazil experienced a dramatic upsurge in crime. According to the country's Ministry of Health, the number of homicides and other deaths resulting from intentional injuries increased from 3,452 in 1980 to 12,350 in 1996, resulting in a murder rate of 36.20 per 100,000 inhabitants (Mesquita Neto, 2004). Law enforcement responses to this situation reveal a series of shortcomings, and levels of public distrust of the police were high.

In 1997, the head of the Military Police, responsible for public security as well as crime prevention, officially adopted community policing as an operational strategy and philosophy. The implementation of community policing included the creation of an Advisory Commission. In the case of São Paulo, the Advisory Commission for the Implementation of Community Policing is primarily responsible for examining and analyzing the execution of the community policing program. This commission has no set number of members; in August 1998, the Advisory Commission included representatives from human rights nongovernmental organizations (NGOs), community councils, the State Federation of Industries, the Business Councils, the São Paulo Association of Prosecutors, and the United Nations Latin American Institute for the Prevention of Crime and the Treatment of Delinquents, among other organizations.

This commission debated security problems affecting the population and determined the priorities and solutions that led to the definition of police goals and objectives, including the incorporation of democratic values and respect for human rights that had never before formed part of the doctrine of the Military Police. The goals formulated were

- to promote the model of community police as an organizational strategy of the Military Police,
- to improve the quality of police training and education,
- to improve the quality of the system of recruiting and promotion within the police forces,
- to integrate the police with other public institutions, and
- to improve the public standing and rights of the police force (Mesquita Neto, 2004).

Initially, the Military Police selected 41 zones of the region for the implementation of the project, which included beat cops, traffic police, rail police, forest rangers, and firefighters. The company commanders (in charge of police units composed of between 100 and 300 officers) chose the neighborhoods in which the project would be implemented. Between December 1997 and July 2001, the community policing program was put into practice in 199 of the 386 police companies of the state's Military Police, some 50% of all companies (Mesquita Neto, 2004). From September 1997 to May 2000, 239 community police stations were established and nearly 16,000 police officers successfully completed specialized courses on community policing (Kahn, 2003).

Together with the police, the Advisory Commission for the Implementation of Community Policing evaluated the problems that arose during the implementation of this model. While the community policing program was a considerable achievement, the relationship between the representatives of civil society and the police was by no means smooth (Mesquita Neto, 2004). In these meetings, the police made note of problems, but rigorous follow-up of the measures taken to resolve these concerns was rare.

Pilot Project in Villa Nueva, Guatemala

The program of community policing in Villa Nueva, Guatemala, was developed as part of an international project undertaken by the Inter-American Institute of Human Rights (IIHR). Implemented in Belize, Costa Rica, El Salvador, Guatemala, Honduras, and Nicaragua, the IIHR project, "Citizen Security in Central America," encouraged the police forces to take up a community approach and to emphasize conflict resolution.

Villa Nueva is a municipality of 192,000 inhabitants located in the Department of Guatemala, a central province of Guatemala, also home to the country's capital. Villa Nueva was selected as the pilot municipality by government officials and not by the police. The program did not make organizational changes in the police force as a whole. As with any internationally promoted pilot program, considerable international cooperation supported the program's implementation. Nonetheless, it was clear that when this support ceased, the program's sustainability would be tested in truth.

The project focused on the National Civil Police (PNC) created following the peace accords between the government and the guerrillas. While the old security forces were replaced by this new police force, the composition and preparation of the police far from fulfilled the expectations of the citizenry (Chinchilla, 2004).

The Villa Nueva project began with a series of preparatory activities, which included an evaluation based on the compilation and analysis of crime statistics in the zone and other significant characteristics of the area as well as the first public opinion poll on victimization. This first stage was followed by the creation of a Municipal Citizen Security Council (MCSC), which included representatives from all the institutions interested and involved in the issue. The objective of the MCSC was to coordinate the different activities of crime prevention and control that would later be implemented in the Villa Nueva municipality. The police forces would focus on patrolling areas in which there was a greater incidence of crime with an emphasis on the illegal sale of alcohol, particularly near schools and parks. Meetings were also held with police, judges, public prosecutors, and public defenders in order to increase the efficiency of coordinated action among these institutions. Community leaders, teachers, and members of the PNC made contact with youth gangs with the objective of encouraging the reintegration into society of gang members implicated in criminal activities.

Community Policing in Bogotá, Colombia: A Process of Reform

Unlike the project in Villa Nueva, the community policing program in Bogotá was the result of a decision made by the police forces themselves, although the model adopted and the training program provided for the participating officers did indeed have a strong international component.

In the early 1990s, the Colombian police were strongly criticized for their lack of effectiveness, cases of corruption, and the participation of the police in the murder of delinquents, prostitutes, and mentally ill in several cities throughout the country. In response to this criticism, a reform process began in 1993. The first stage of this two-phase process strengthened the civilian nature of the police, even though they continued under the command of the Ministry of Defense. Secondly, in 1995, a process of "internal cleansing" was carried out by the police themselves, which included all police ranks.

The transformation of the internal culture of the police force was measured in part through of a series of surveys. The results of one such survey, undertaken in Bogotá in 1996 on the public's expectations of the police, suggested that a program of community policing could meet the demands of the citizenry. In 1998, the head of Bogotá's Police Department adopted the model of community policing, identifying this endeavor as the department's most important program. The national government, in turn, adopted the community model as a central policy for the promotion of citizen security to be implemented by police throughout the country.

The primary manifestations of these community initiatives were the involvement of the police in Citizen Security courses that train local leaders to promote citizen security, and Local Security Fronts, which are neighborhood support networks that collaborate with the police. Organized by neighborhood blocks or sectors, the members of the Fronts carry out informal patrolling and provide aid to their neighbors in the event of suspicious activity. To this end, the neighbors exchange phone numbers and install neighborhood alarms (Llorente, 2004). There are some 5,400 Fronts in operation in the city of Bogotá, which account for 13% of the residential areas of the city (Llorente, 2004).

For the development of the community policing model, 1,000 police officers were selected based on characteristics that made them particularly suited for the project and received training on the model. They formed a special branch of Bogotá's police that includes officers performing random patrolling as well as community police officers who are assigned specific, permanent beats.

Belo Horizonte, Brazil: Result-Oriented Policing

In the case of Belo Horizonte, the current program finds its immediate forerunner in a previous project undertaken in some of the city's neighborhoods in 1993. A recent evaluation deemed this experience a failure due to the police forces' lack of preparation and the fact that the program was perceived by the public as a way for the police to tap community resources for their own specific projects (Souza, 1999).

In 1999, the command of the Minas Gerais Military Police launched a broader program known as "result-oriented policing," which focused on deploying police to geographical areas based on information about local criminal activity. The other central element of this program was the creation of Community Security Councils, which collaborated with the police in planning strategies for crime prevention in keeping with the security needs of each area (Beato, 2004).

The impetus for this program came primarily from the Military Police with the support of the Universidad Federal de Minas Gerais in the development of training courses for the members of the Community Councils as well as police officers.

The central objective of the Councils is the development of crime prevention programs with community participation. There is one Council for each of the 25 police companies. The Council members include the company commanders, representatives from the Office of the Mayor, and members of other associations and institutions. The goals of the Councils are to train the police in community policing and problem solving, to encourage increased membership, to promote programs that encourage communities' self-defense, and to gather information regarding the service provided by the police to the citizens (Beato, 2004).

As a result of the creation of these Community Councils, there have been some examples of joint efforts with the police to confront urgent problems of public security. However, it appears that in areas with greater levels of violent crime, these community institutions are much less active (Beato, 2004).

Challenges Facing Institutional Change Within the Police

Community policing programs in Latin America confront serious internal and external challenges. As a result, the impact of these programs must be measured not only in terms of their ability to reduce fear of crime and levels of victimization, but also their ability to produce significant changes within the police.

Among other difficulties, the programs described above face problems in relation to resources, the fear of radical institutional transformation on the part of police leadership, and the characteristics of the dominant police subculture under which the programs operate.

Community policing requires enough officers to manage relations with the neighbors, to "cover the beat" by patrolling the area on foot and to hold regular meetings with the members of the community. Sufficient personnel are rarely available to carry out the initiatives in accordance with the premises described above. The pilot program of Villa Nueva, for example, was not intended to have an immediate impact on the entire force and, for this reason, the changes were made at the local level. At the beginning of the project, only 117 officers were assigned to Villa Nueva, a woefully insufficient number for the purposes of the program (Chinchilla, 2004). To correct this situation, the project was assigned an additional group of 80 officers who had served in the previous National Police. Despite this attempt, the number of police officers continued to be low and when the participation of the Inter-American Institute of Human Rights in the project ended, this number returned to nearly the same level as prior to the pilot project.

Limited numbers of officers and general instability in the area of human resources resulted in shifts as long as 12 hours, which, combined with requirements of more intense patrolling, and on foot, gave rise to numerous police complaints (Chinchilla, 2004). At the same time, despite the changes promoted by the project, the lower-ranking officers continued to be treated in a rigid and authoritarian fashion, following police tradition.

In Bogotá, only 6% of the officers of the Police Department were assigned to community policing, which is equivalent to 15% of all law enforcement personnel involved in preventive patrolling. Clearly, the emphasis continues to be placed on reacting to crime and random preventive patrolling.

As in Villa Nueva, the community policing service covers a considerable urban area, but the ratio of police to inhabitants is insufficient. While in theory the service covers a series of neighborhoods that are home to 3 million people, or 42% of the entire population of Bogotá, the low number of police officers assigned to the service has led to only 13% of homes and 16% of businesses reporting that community policing occurs in their neighborhood (Llorente, 2004).

In São Paulo, both human and material resources appear scarce. During 1998 and 1999, the police invested very limited resources in the implementation of community policing programs. At this time, no officers of the Military Police were exclusively dedicated to carrying out community policing initiatives at either the state or local level. As a result, the police had to attend neighborhood meetings or make contact with members of the local community in their own time. Generally, these meetings were held after regular working hours (Mesquita Neto, 2004). Only in 2000 did the Military Police establish the Department of Community Policing and Human Rights. The fundamental role of this department is to plan and coordinate the implementation of the community policing program, and a significant portion of the department's budget is allocated to training police officers and neighborhood leaders.

In addition to the issues described above, community policing in Latin America also faces a related difficulty of ensuring continuity in personnel assigned to particular neighborhoods. Constant movement of police officers is very common, whether due to demand for officers in crisis situations in other areas, processes of promotion and relocation, or requests for transfer from the officers themselves.

A third concern has to do with the existence of a police subculture that is reluctant to believe that community policing programs really can have an impact on crime. As a result, not all of the principles of community policing are applied in full. This type of resistance also has occurred in programs implemented elsewhere, but it would come as no surprise if this recalcitrant attitude was even greater in extremely hierarchical and centralized institutions functioning in societies with weak democratic beliefs. In such settings, the prevalent idea is that the strict application of the law should be enough to control crime.

For example, a survey of 1,200 police officers in the city of Belo Horizonte carried out by the Center for Research on Public Security (CRISP) at the Universidad Federal de Minas Gerais indicated that 46.1% of those officers surveyed thought that the most important crime control measures were the increase of material and human resources within the police forces and increased police salaries. In addition, 58.7% of those surveyed agreed totally or partly with the statement: "Only other police can really evaluate police work." This clearly calls into question the emphasis on accountability to the public that community policing programs defend. It should also be noted that 44.7% of the police surveyed maintained that organizations defending human rights are the greatest obstacle to the public's understanding of police work (Beato, 2004).

A survey of the Military Police in São Paulo by the United Nations Latin American Institute for Crime Prevention reveals a generally positive opinion of the community policing program. However, when the officers were asked if community policing was more efficient in confronting crime, only 21.4% of the police involved in the initiative agreed (Kahn, 2003). Even more troubling is the fact that 66.3% of the community police interviewed maintained that community policing is a public relations tactic to improve the image of the police forces (Kahn, 2003).

Finally, another serious obstacle to the successful implementation of community policing programs is the fact that lower-ranking officers do not readily identify with these programs and that they lack the appropriate training to confront the challenges of problem solving. In the case of Belo Horizonte, senior officers are well prepared for the requirements of community policing, but the officers on the street have very little understanding of the program. Evaluations of this program revealed significant differences between senior and subordinate officers regarding their knowledge of the community policing program and, particularly, the role of the Community Councils (Beato, 2004). The United Nations Latin American Institute for Crime Prevention survey, described above, indicated that the idea of community policing is clearly shared by the high-ranking officers and sergeants of the São Paulo Military Police, but there is resistance to the program on the part of corporals and privates. Thus, while 36.2% of the ranking officers surveyed stated that community policing is more efficient in crime fighting, only 17.8% of their subordinates agreed with this assertion. At the same time, 66.6% of the lower-ranking police believe that community policing is a public relations tactic to improve the image of the police forces, an opinion shared by only 43.5% of the higher-ranking officers (Kahn, 2003).

The Relationship Between the Police and the Community

The community policing programs examined in this chapter reveal that, in Latin America, citizen participation does not define policing priorities, and that citizens are poorly prepared to interact with the police and to take action to resolve the security issues that affect them.

In this regard, there are three possible models for the organization of the relationship between the police and the citizenry. The first emphasizes the existence of a central Commission that assumes a partnership role in ensuring security in a given area. The members of such Commissions come from a range of sectors, generally government institutions and nongovernmental organizations as well as representatives from the police itself. Such commissions generate opportunities for debate and reflection and are only rarely authorized to make binding decisions. In the event of a mixed model, neighborhood commissions may complement the central commission. A third possibility is that police and community relations are totally decentralized, and the police themselves promote the formation of prevention committees in the jurisdictions corresponding to the respective police stations.

The experience in Villa Nueva is an example of the first model. At the beginning of the project, a Municipal Citizen Security Council was created with representatives of all the institutions and agencies involved and interested in the issue. The objective of the Council was the coordination of crime control and prevention activities. The Council designated an Executive Committee responsible for carrying out the actions agreed upon by the Council. This Committee met at least once a week until late 2000, in addition to the time the committee members dedicated to overseeing all the different activities proposed in the plan of action. The Executive Committee contributed significantly to cooperation among the police, government institutions, and private businesses (Chinchilla, 2004).

In São Paulo, a mixed model was introduced because the program began by creating a central commission called the Advisory Commission on Community Policing established by the police. This Commission has provided the principal arena for community representatives and police to discuss the program. The Commission members play an advisory role only, but their opinions have been taken up in official documents concerning the implementation of the new strategy. This state-level consultation has been complemented at the local level by numerous community public security councils and community fora, which organize events in collaboration with the police.

The network of local organizations has been mobilized to support the Military Police. One of the most notable expressions of this support is the provision of financial contributions to the police as well as the work of volunteers in the small neighborhood police stations. The members of the communities also organize neighborhood citizen security groups through which they collaborate by disseminating information on suspicious individuals in the sector.

Training the citizens who participate in the local committees is essential in order for citizen participation to go beyond merely complaining that "the police do nothing" to effectively collaborate in the design of measures to solve existing security problems. In Bogotá, the National Police collaborate with the Local Security Fronts and the Citizen Security courses. The Local Security Fronts incorporate the neighbors of a given area in networks to collaborate with and support the police. The leaders are volunteers and they set up telephone trees and other mechanisms of coordination among neighbors in order to help each other in emergency situations. The Citizen Security courses train promoters of order and community harmony. These courses explain the current penal code, the organization and functions of the police, and crime prevention actions that citizens can take.

One of the few evaluations regarding the functioning of the community councils of which we are aware was that undertaken by CRISP at the

Universidad Federal de Minas Gerais. The variables analyzed in this evaluation were classified as nonexistent, low, medium, and high. According to this evaluation, all the Councils were functioning one year after they had begun, most in the middle range and a few, very well. Levels of representation in most of the Councils were rated as low and medium, despite the efforts undertaken to attract new members. Representation is lower in those areas with more significant levels of violence and in those areas where there is a greater heterogeneity of social classes. Most of the Councils' capacity to monitor police work was evaluated as low. Participation in the meetings was rated as low or medium, but there is at least some level of participation. In the community policing model, citizen participation should be autonomous from the police so that citizens can supervise law enforcement efforts and represent the public's perspectives and priorities. Nonetheless, the level of autonomy with regard to the local commanders is low or nonexistent in 11 cases, medium in 8, and high in only one Council. Finally, the higher-ranking police officers participating in the Councils demonstrated a high level of support for the programs of community participation, while the lower-ranking police showed less understanding of the Councils (CRISP, 2000, cited in Beato, 2004).

As previously stated, one of the principal factors that impacts on the functioning of the councils appears to be the level of crime predominant in a given area. In neighborhoods with higher rates of crime, there is an understandable reluctance to collaborate with police. There is also more support for the Councils from police commands in areas with lower levels of crime, while in the more violent areas the higher-ranking officers prefer the use of more coercive methods of intervention.

The Relationship Between the Police and Other Public Agencies

The population's objective and subjective security does not depend solely on policing and, thus, the community model assumes the need for the police to collaborate on resolving security issues that affect citizens by effectively coordinating with other public agencies.

In the Villa Nueva project, the creation of the Municipal Citizen Security Council encouraged a set of initiatives that required coordination between the police, the municipality, public prosecutors, judges, and public defenders. In particular, the establishment of the Council allowed for the proposal and implementation of solutions such as improvement of public lighting. Police cooperation with judges allowed the judiciary to make declarations more quickly, decreasing overcrowding in police detention cells and improving the use of resources (Chinchilla, 2004).

The urgent problem of public security has led to the municipalities in Minas Gerais contributing financially to the police forces. The mayor of Belo Horizonte made an election year announcement that $2 million would be invested in the purchase of police patrol cars, police armament, and for the organization of Community Council databases. Nonetheless, a lack of organic coordination between the police and local government means that these resources are used to support traditional, reactive strategies, most likely due to the fact that the police prefer this type of policing. Organic coordination supposes that local government enjoys explicit powers with regard to security and that the police are bound to take into account local priorities when they plan their actions. The municipalities' lack of explicit powers complicates coordination between the local government and the police.

In most of Latin America, the police fall under the aegis of the central or regional government, quite different from the situation in North America where close ties between the community and local government occur in a context in which the police forces are also local and completely decentralized. If efforts at institutional collaboration between the police and other public agencies in Latin America are not as systematic as could be expected, this is also due to the fact that the police do not wish to take responsibility for demands for urban and social measures they feel to be well outside their bailiwick.

Results from the Community Policing Programs

Measurements of the impact of community policing programs on the levels of fear amongst the population and on the crime rate are not entirely trustworthy because there are no comparisons between areas with community policing and those with traditional patrolling in any of the cases. In addition, Villa Nueva was the only project to carry out victimization surveys before and after the program's implementation. In the other three cases, we must rely on the police data of reported crimes.

In the case of Villa Nueva, two victimization surveys were undertaken. The first survey was carried out prior to the project's initiation in 1998, while the second was conducted in 2000. The latter survey revealed a 10% reduction in the number of individuals who reported being victims of crime in recent months, dropping from 34% to 23.8% (Instituto Interamericano de Derechos Humanos, 2000). This drop in crime may be the result of increased police patrolling and police monitoring of businesses that sell alcoholic beverages illegally (Chinchilla, 2004).

It is also important to stress that the interviews held in March 2000 widely approved of the community policing project and stated a desire for the project to continue. Nonetheless, those interviewed in August 2001 were unanimous in their criticism of the lack of follow-up on the project and its ostensible weakening with the end of the financial support from the Inter-American Institute of Human Rights.

In the case of São Paulo, the evaluation of the program's impact has been measured through public opinion polls carried out throughout the state and other surveys of specific locales. The statewide surveys show that public opinion of the police has tended to improve throughout the state, but due to the broad nature of the survey and the lack of sufficiently disaggregated data, it is unclear whether or not this is a direct consequence of the community policing program. Surveys undertaken by the polling service of a São Paulo newspaper reveal that in 1997, 74% of the population was more fearful of the police than trusting. This percentage decreased to 66% in 1999. In addition, in 1997, 73% of the population felt that the police used excessive force in the fulfillment of duty, a figure that fell to 49% in 1999. Despite this, the percentage of the population that viewed the police as inefficient increased from 22% in 1995 to 43% in 1999 (Folha de São Paulo, 2000).

However, the only way to determine whether or not changes in public opinion regarding the police and levels of fear are the result of the application of the community model is to focus these surveys on the areas in which this policing model is applied. Two such studies have been carried out. The first was undertaken by the *Fórum em Defesa da Vida* (Forum for the Defense of Life) in Jardim Ângela, one of the more violent districts of the city of São Paulo. This survey polled 945 residents and businesspersons regarding their perception of the community policing program. Those who lived or worked less than a kilometer away from the small neighborhood police stations had a better perception of community policing, its impact on citizen security, and with regard to the treatment of citizens than those who lived or worked farther from the stations. This suggests that the model is not extensive enough and that it does not reach all the citizens of the area.

A 2000 study by the United Nations Latin American Institute for Crime Prevention focused on 23 neighborhoods with community policing stations and 23 neighborhoods without these stations. The results of this study are similar to the survey cited above. In those areas where a community policing program exists and is known to residents, levels of fear are lower, there is a better opinion of the police, and there is more support for community policing than those neighborhoods in which the program exists, but is not known or where there is no program at all (Kahn, 2003).

The results of both surveys appear to suggest that the impact of community policing on feelings of insecurity requires a combination of personal contact and media campaigns to promote awareness of the program and its benefits. But, they also suggest that the effects of the program are very dependent upon the physical presence of the police. Whether due to lack of personnel or lack of initiatives to promote closer contact between citizens and the police, not all neighbors are aware of the presence of the community policing program.

However, both surveys provide disheartening results regarding crime control. In the case of Jardim Ângela, most of the population still think that the police do very little about drug trafficking or even suggest that the police participate in this crime. The United Nations Latin American Institute for Crime Prevention survey shows that the presence of small community police stations has had no impact on levels of victimization (Kahn, 2003). These results are mirrored to some extent in the official crime rates registered by the police. Indeed, as Mesquita Neto (2004) points out, in the year 2000, rates of homicide, robbery, and theft decreased in the metropolitan region, but not in the interior of the state, the location of most of the small police stations that provide the bases for the community patrols.

Conclusion

As Davis, Henderson, and Merrick (2003) argue, the introduction of community policing faces significant difficulties in developing countries whose police forces have limited experience with democratic practices. Evaluations of community policing programs undertaken in developed democratic countries reveal that police forces have had to undergo a series of rigorous transformations. Community policing has introduced a new system of internal values, narrowed considerably the gaps between officer ranks, and encouraged innovation and individual responsibility among officers in lieu of centralized disciplinary control by central management. The model of community policing seeks to transform the police officer into a law enforcement professional who designs strategic solutions to meet citizens' demands and to confront crime trends or patterns. Clearly, the human, material, and organizational resources of Latin American police and the organizational structure of law enforcement in the region are quite different, and moving forward in this direction is difficult. In this chapter, we have hinted at the cultural skepticism regarding these programs that exists among the lower ranks of the police and their lack of training in problem solving, as well as the logistical and financial deficits faced by police forces in the region, which limit the expansion of these programs beyond the pilot stage.

A more precise evaluation of Latin American community policing requires that we address three aspects: firstly, the immediate effects of the community policing programs in existence; secondly, the capacity of these programs to produce more complex, long-lasting transformations in the police; and finally, the recommendations that stem from the implementation of these programs.

The different programs described here do share some similarities—they bring the communities and the police closer together, with some benefits, but they do not, in and of themselves, bring about a transformation of the police institution. As we previously observed, there are significant difficulties inherent in any attempt to change highly centralized institutions, particularly those that face the problems described above.

This does not mean, however, that these programs are entirely without merit. There are benefits for the police as well as the public users of the police services. Community policing programs are strongly supported by the population, and citizens support the continuation of these projects. These initiatives also improve the public image of the police. Moreover, when the citizens know that such programs are in operation, their levels of fear are reduced. Community action alone does not reduce public fear; this requires intense, well-understood, rigorously applied patterns of interaction and adequate communication with the population. In this relationship with the community, particular attention should be paid to cultivating relationships with the poorer sectors. There is a very real possibility that community outreach may favor wealthier sectors that already have access to private security.

The results are inconclusive with regard to the impact of these programs on the crime rate. The drop in crime in Villa Nueva, for instance, could very well be due to an increase in patrolling and spot checks and may not necessarily stem from the community-related aspects of the new strategies.

Whether or not these programs bring about a general decrease in police abuse is also unclear, although they do appear to be a significant step in the right direction. They should be complemented by programs to retrain police who display proclivities toward abuse and the establishment of an early warning system in the case of repeated incidents of abuse by the same officers, among other measures (Frühling, 2002).

It is possible that the difficulties facing the community policing programs are due, at least in part, to deficiencies in their processes of implementation. For example, not all of the community policing programs described above have been preceded by careful planning to maximize their impact and usefulness. The implementation of these programs must follow a carefully designed, sufficiently financed plan that targets areas for the program's application in agreement with strategic criteria that allow for the progressive implementation of the project and an independent, on-going evaluation. The community policing programs also require good working relationships with local government and citizens' associations as partners with the police in debate, in collaboration, and in the evaluation of the strategies being implemented.

The management of community policing programs should be adequately communicated within the police and paralleled by the incorporation of courses on community policing into the regular training curriculum, with targeted courses for officers of various ranks. These training programs should be based on case studies because most of the police have no direct experience with community policing and the predominant subculture within the police privileges a traditional approach to security problems.

The police leadership must bear in mind a number of aspects when planning a community policing program. Above all, visible police presence in the form of police patrols on foot is needed for citizens to realize that the program exists. Officers must also have time to attend public meetings or to make contact with the community on the street. Resources are required for the design and execution of new police training programs and programs to train citizens as well as for the printing and distribution of appropriate information on the program. It is essential that the budget allow for on-going evaluation of the project implementation and results by an academic institution unrelated to the police.

The program design must also ensure that the officers assigned to a given geographical area remain in this location for a relatively long time, in order to guarantee their stable and close contact with citizens. This may require changes in the personnel policies of the police.

In most cases, the police, local government, and citizens' crime prevention associations do not coordinate their actions or work together closely enough. While there can be no community policing program without police participation, these endeavors also require the participation of the community and local government agencies that can offer crime prevention programs to complement police work. In Latin America, the governments often take responsibility for community programs, while the police carry out parallel initiatives that are not closely coordinated with the community (Dammert, 2001). This problem is partly due to the fact that the municipal governments have only recently begun focusing on community safety issues and their agenda is still unclear. On the other hand, the police are dependent upon state or national governments and, thus, the mechanisms that guide their interaction with local government are either unclear or nonexistent. This situation reveals a need to coordinate agendas and interests among institutions with different sources of legitimacy and authority.

In sum, the programs of community policing currently underway in Latin America should be viewed as a step toward improving the citizen access to the police as well as enhancing public trust in the police. Nonetheless, it is too much to expect these programs to produce the degree of institutional transformation generated in the context of developed, democratic countries. Community policing in Latin America to date has not failed, but its impact is more limited than initially expected by its advocates.

References

Bayley, D. (1994). *Police for the future.* New York: Oxford University Press.

Beato, C. C. (2004). Reinventar la polícia: La experiencia de Belo Horizonte. In H. Frühling (Ed.), *Calles más seguras. Estudios de policía comunitaria en América Latina* (pp. 139–175). Washington, D.C.: Inter-American Development Bank.

Bresser Pereira, L. C. (1999). Managerial public administration: Strategy and structure for a new state. In L. C. Pereira & P. Spink (Eds.), *Managerial public administration in Latin America* (pp. 1–13). Boulder, CO: Lynne Rienner Publishers.

Chinchilla, L. M. (2004). El caso del municipio de Villa Nueva, Guatemala. In H. Frühling (Ed.), *Calles más seguras. Estudios de policía comunitaria en América Latina* (pp. 39–64). Washington, D.C.: Inter-American Development Bank.

CRISP. (2000). *Avaliacão e Acompanhamento dos Conselhos Comunitários de Segurança em Belo Horizonte*. Mimeograph.

Dammert, L. (2001). *Participación comunitaria en la prevención del delito en América Latina ¿De qué participación hablamos? Cuadernos del CED*. Santiago: Centro de Estudios para el Desarrollo.

Dammert, L. & Malone, M. F. T. (2002). Inseguridad y temor en la Argentina: El impacto de la confianza en la policía y la corrupción sobre la percepción ciudadana del crimen. *Desarrollo Económico, 42*(166), 285–301.

Davis, R. C., Henderson, N. J., & Merrick, C. (2003). Community policing: Variations on the western model in the developing world. *Police Practice and Research, 4*(3), 285–300.

Folha de São Paulo. (2000, February). Cited in P. Mesquita Neto. (2004). La policía comunitaria en São Paulo: Problemas de implementación y consolidación. In H. Frühling (Ed.), *Calles más seguras. Estudios de policía comunitaria en América Latina* (pp. 109–137). Washington, D.C.: Inter-American Development Bank.

Frühling, H. (2001). *La reforma policial y el proceso de democratización en América Latina*. Santiago: Centro de Estudios para el Desarrollo.

Frühling, H. (2002). Policía y sociedad. Tres experiencias sudamericanas. *Renglones, 51*, 23–35.

Frühling, H. (Ed.). (2004). *Calles más seguras. Estudios de policía comunitaria en América Latina*. Washington, D.C.: Inter-American Development Bank.

Instituto Interamericano de Derechos Humanos. (2000). *Encuesta de opinión pública, municipio de Villa Nueva, septiembre 1998 y marzo 2000*. Villa Nueva: Instituto Interamericano de Derechos Humanos.

Kahn, T. (2003). *Policía comunitaria: Evaluando la experiencia de Sao Paulo. Cuadernos del CED*. Santiago: Centro de Estudios para el Desarrollo.

Lemos-Nelson, A. T. (2001, September). *Police criminality, citizenship and the (un) rule-of-law*. Paper presented at the Conference of the Latin American Studies Association, Washington D.C.

Llorente, M. V. (2004). La experiencia de Bogotá: Contexto y balance. In H. Frühling (Ed.), *Calles más seguras. Estudios de policía comunitaria en América Latina* (pp. 65–108). Washington, D.C.: Inter-American Development Bank.

Mesquita Neto, P. (2004). La policía comunitaria en São Paulo: Problemas de implementación y consolidación. In H. Frühling (Ed.), *Calles más seguras. Estudios de policía comunitaria en América Latina* (pp. 109–137). Washington, D.C.: Inter-American Development Bank.

Muniz, J., Larvie, S. P., Musumeci, L., & Freire, B. (1997). Resistencias e dificuldades de um programa de policiamento comunitário. *Tempo Social, 9*(1), 197–214.

Neild, R. (2002). *Sustaining reform: Democratic policing in Central America*. Washington, D.C.: Washington Office on Latin America.

Palmieri, G., Martínez, J., Sozzo, M., & Thomas, H. (2001). Mecanismos de control interno e iniciativas de reforma en las instituciones policiales Argentinas. Los Casos de la Policía Federal Argentina, la Policía de la Provincia de Santa Fé, y la Policía de la Provincia de Buenos Aires. In H. Frühling & A. Candina (Eds.), *Policía, sociedad y estado: Modernización y reforma policial en América del Sur* (pp. 177–220). Santiago: Centro de Estudios para el Desarrollo.

Rosenbaum, D. P. (1998). The changing role of the police: Assessing the current transition to community policing. In J-P. Brodeur (Ed.), *How to recognize good policing. Problems and issues* (pp. 3–29). Washington, D.C.: Police Executive Research Forum.

Sandoval, L. (2001). Prevención local de la Delincuencia en Santiago de Chile. In H. Frühling & A. Candina (Eds.), *Policía, sociedad y estado: Modernización y reforma policial en América del Sur* (pp. 57–83). Santiago: Centro de Estudios para el Desarrollo.

Sherman, L. W. (1995). The police. In J. Q. Wilson & J. Petersilia (Eds.), *Crime* (pp. 327–48). San Francisco: Center for Self-Governance.

Souza, E. (1999). *Avaliacão do policiamento comunitário em Belo Horizonte.* (Unpublished master's thesis). Universidad Federal de Minas Gerais, Brazil.

Stanley, W. (1999). Building new police forces in El Salvador and Guatemala: Learning and counter-learning. *International Peace Keeping*, *6*(4), 113–134.

Urban National Victimization Survey. (2003). Annex with international comparisons. Retrieved from: www.seguridadciudadana.gob.cl

The Evolution, Decline, and Nascent Transformation of Community Policing in the United States 1980–2010

2

MICHAEL M. BERLIN

Contents

The development, decline, and transformation of community policing in the United States occurs within the broader context of the evolution of policing in this country and America's unique government structure, which provides for local control of policing. After addressing these broad contextual issues, I focus on the origins, development, and definitions of community policing in the United States. I then analyze the growth of the theory and practice of Compstat (COMParative (or COMPuter) STATistics), which coincides with the apparent decline of community policing. I also briefly examine the impact of the terrorist attacks of September 11, 2001, on local law enforcement, the increase in local law enforcement attention to homeland security, and the recent focus on intelligence-led policing. I explore the compatibility of community policing, Compstat and intelligence-led policing, and the nascent transformation of community policing in the United States.

In order to understand the evolution of community policing, it is important to look to the historical context in which community policing developed and is practiced in the United States. First, the vast majority of policing in the United States is local. There are approximately 12,700 local police departments at the city, county, or town level in the country (Schmalleger, 2007). In addition, there are approximately 3,100 sheriffs departments (Schmalleger, 2007), some of which are full-service law enforcement agencies, frequently found in rural and some suburban jurisdictions, others of which are primarily responsible for providing courthouse security, staffing local jails or detention centers, and service of warrants and court documents, typically found in urban jurisdictions. Local control of policing is ensured through the appointment of the police chief by elected local government leaders, typically mayors or county executives. In some instances, local legislative bodies, city or county councils, may control the appointment process. Sheriffs are elected public officials. As a result of their appointment powers, local, politically elected officials often play a critical role in the decision to implement community policing, an issue which I explore later.

Many of the seminal works on community policing address the historical evolution of policing in order to provide a framework for understanding community policing. Kelling and Moore (1988) provide a context for practitioners and academics in their widely cited article, "The Evolving Strategy of Policing." They distinguish between and summarize salient features of three "eras" of policing: the political era, the reform era, and the era of community policing/problem solving. Each era of policing is characterized by differences in public perception of the primary sources of police legitimacy and authority, view of the police function, organizational design, external relationships between the police and the community, demand management (how police are summoned and the police resources allocated), principal programs and technologies, and measures of success.

The political era dates from the introduction of municipal police forces in the 1840s and continued until the early 1900s. Prior to this, many colonial cities had a night watch system, an outgrowth of the English pledge system. The political era was characterized by close ties between police and politics. Local police commanders had frequent contact and communication with political leaders and ward bosses. Police priorities were set in conjunction with these political figures. It has been argued that the close relationship between police and local politicians increased police legitimacy and responsiveness to the community (Wilson & Kelling, 1982). However, it has also been argued local politicians and ward bosses often acted in their own rather than the public interest and that this era of policing was characterized by corruption and discrimination against minorities (Walker, 1984).

The reform era took hold in the 1930s, reached its peak in the 1950s and 1960s, and began its decline in the 1970s. August Vollmer, a former police chief and first professor of Police Administration at the University of California at Berkeley, was one of the first advocates of the reform era. The reform era was characterized by a "professional crime-fighting" approach, relying upon routine patrol, quick response to calls for service, and criminal investigations. The reform era is said to be both a reaction to the corruption of the political era and in keeping with the growing trend toward scientific management (Kelling & Moore, 1988). Policing is generally viewed as having become far more professional and police organizations far more sophisticated during this era.

Comparison of the characteristics of the eras of policing, according to the criteria established by Kelling and Moore (1988), provides the context for key aspects of community policing. For example, while the police functions during the political era included crime control, order maintenance, and broad social services, the focus shifted primarily to crime control during the reform era of traditional policing and expanded to include prevention and problem solving, as well as crime control, during the community policing/problem-solving era. Similarly, while police success during the political era was measured in terms of citizen and political satisfaction, the focus shifted to crime control as reflected by Uniform Crime Report data (criminal justice statistics compiled by the U.S. Department of Justice, Federal Bureau of Investigation (FBI) based upon voluntary reporting by state and local jurisdictions) during the reform era, and returned to citizen satisfaction and quality of life during the community policing/problem-solving era. The perceived authority and legitimacy of the police, based on law and police professionalism developed during the reform era, was, in part, a response to the corruption of the political era, and expanded to include community support during the community policing/problem-solving era.

It is generally agreed among scholars and practitioners that the community policing/problem-solving era began in the late 1970s or early 1980s following the Kansas City Preventative Patrol Experiment and team policing projects of the 1970s. The Kansas City Preventative Patrol Experiment was designed to measure the impact of routine preventative patrol on crime and fear of crime. The Kansas City, Missouri Police Department conducted the study in conjunction with the Washington, D.C.-based Police Foundation between 1972 and 1973 and found that routine preventative patrol did not have a significant impact on crime or fear of crime. (Kelling, Pate, Dieckman & Brown, 1974). Community policing developed over the past two decades and continues through the present day, albeit, in a very different form from its origins (Oliver, 2001). The community policing era is characterized by close working relationships between the police and the community, attention to quality of life, and problem solving (Kelling & Moore, 1988). Policing is generally viewed to have become far more attentive to community concerns during this period and police organizations became more decentralized.

While there is not complete agreement among scholars with regard to all aspects of Kelling and Moore's eras of policing (see Palmiotto, 2000) and criticize their failure to discuss the crime prevention model that was in vogue between 1910 and 1940, there appears to be significant consensus with regard to much of the historical model. The model provides an excellent context in which to understand key features of community policing.

Community policing was implemented to prevent and reduce crime and improve relationships between police and citizens. The early community policing literature argued that community policing had the potential to prevent and reduce crime and disorder, curb growing violence, and alleviate fear of crime and disorder. It also posited that community policing could reverse the growing distance and isolation of the police from the public and reduce citizen complaints of brutality and indifference. Skolnick and Bayley (1988, p. 1) indicated that the focus of their study of police innovation in six cities was "coping with the urban crime problem" and that their central question was what the police could do to reduce crime and the paralyzing fear of crime. Given that the research repeatedly demonstrated that traditional police strategies, including random motorized patrol, saturation patrol, rapid response to emergency calls, criminal investigations, and increased police personnel were not effective, they examined promising crime control strategies in U.S. cities and concluded that community-oriented policing, involving the community in crime prevention and enlisting their assistance in the apprehension and prosecution of offenders was essential to reducing crime. Skolnick and Bayley (1988, p. 6) cite "Community-based crime prevention is [as] the ultimate goal and centerpiece of community-oriented policing." Skolnick and Fyfe (1994) argued that community policing offers new hope for coping with and preventing crime and disorder and the growing fear of crime and disorder.

The Uniform Crime Reports (UCR) indicate dramatic increases in crime rates between 1960 and the early 1990s (Schmalleger, 2007).* Schmalleger (p. 39) indicates that "from 1960 to 1980, crime rates rose from 1,887 offenses to 5,950 offenses per every 100,000 U.S. residents." National Crime Surveys indicate that the incidence of crime is even higher than that reflected by the Uniform Crime Reports (Schmalleger, 2007).

Suggested reasons for the increase include demographic shifts, baby boomers entering their teenage years, increasing professionalization and better reporting by many police departments, changing social norms, and decreased group controls over individual behavior. The mid-1980s brought further increases in crime, particularly violent crime, often linked to drug-related criminal activity (Schmalleger, 2007). Inner-city violence, particularly homicides involving young African American men, captured headlines across urban America. The criminal justice and social science literature suggests that as a result of the substantial increases in crime over the past several decades, there has been a deterioration in the quality of life in U.S. cities.

* The Uniform Crime Reports consider murder, manslaughter, forcible rape, robbery, aggravated assault, arson, burglary, larceny/theft, and motor vehicle theft as part 1 or index crimes. Other nonpart 1 crimes are reported by local jurisdictions and recorded, as well. These crimes have also risen substantially. Despite reporting difficulties and the fact the UCR is believed to underestimate the actual incidence of crime, the data clearly suggest substantial increases in Part 1 and other crimes since the 1960s.

Public and political pressure to reduce crime mounted. Traditional police tactics were perceived as ineffective in reducing the rising tide of crime. Police leaders, politicians, and academics were searching for solutions to the crime problems. Skolnick and Fyfe (1994, p. 251) indicated that "community policing has become widespread, prevalent, and fashionable not because it has been proven to work, but that the alternatives to it have proved to fail."

Schmalleger (2007) notes the development of a new trend toward decreasing crime beginning in the early 1990s. He states that between 1991 and 2004, the crime index dropped from 5,897 to 3,982 offenses per 100,000 residents and indicates that the new crime rates are comparable to those of the mid-1970s. Despite the substantial decline, these rates remain far higher than the rates of the 1940s and 1950s. The reasons for the recent declines are not clear. Suggested reasons include: community policing, aggressive enforcement, harsher sentencing, increased incarceration, and advances in technology, among others (Schmalleger, 2007).

In addition to rising crime, the growing isolation of the police from the community (Trojanowicz & Bucquerox, 1990) and complaints of police brutality and indifference (Skolnick & Fyfe, 1994), especially in minority communities (Bayley & Mendelsohn, 1969), are also well documented in the literature and contributed to the development of community policing. Included among the primary reasons for the growing isolation of the police from the public are the emphasis on police as crime control professionals and the reliance on routine automotive patrol (Kelling & Moore, 1988; Barnett & Bowers, 1990). As a result of the growing focus on enforcement and reliance upon automotive patrol, informal contacts between police and citizens were reduced and the bond between police and citizens weakened (Kelling & Moore, 1988). At the same time, aggressive patrol tactics adopted in response to rising crime and civil disobedience increased the likelihood of hostile confrontations between police and citizens and contributed to increasing complaints against the police (Miller & Hess, 1998; Radalet & Carter, 1994).

Although community policing appeared to be widely accepted in U.S. police departments by the early 1990s, a commonly accepted definition of community policing does not exist (Palmiotto, 2000, p. 200). Indeed, the concept of community policing is subject to widely varying definitions. According to Roberg and Kuykendall, "... almost any program that attempts to bring the community and the police into closer contact has been labeled as community policing" (1993, p 110). In an effort to define community policing, Skolnick and Bayley (1988) argue that "community policing should be said to exist only when new programs are undertaken that raise the level of public participation in the maintenance of public order" (p. 4). They also point out:

> ... when police departments act rather than just talk about community policing, they tend to do four things: (1) organize community-based crime prevention; (2) reorient patrol activities to emphasize nonemergency servicing; (3) increase accountability to local communities; and (4) decentralize command. (p. 4)

Most academics and experienced practitioners agree that the broad range of concepts and activities associated with community policing require that it be defined on multiple levels. For example, Manning (1989) developed a four-level conceptual framework that includes (a) an ideological system of beliefs, (b) a programmatic series of proactive activities, (c) a pragmatic approach, and (d) a set of programmatic elements and organizational structures. Cordner's (1995; 2001) model also sets forth four dimensions: (a) a philosophical dimension, (b) a strategic dimension, (c) a tactical dimension, and (d) an organizational dimension.

It is odd that despite the fact that community policing has been in existence for over 30 years and has been described as "the most serious and sustained attempt to reformulate the purpose and practice of policing since the development of the 'professional model' in the mid-20th century" (Bayley, 1994, p. 104), there is still no commonly accepted definition. It has been argued that because community policing "is one of those terms that simultaneously suggests so much that is general and so little that is specific that it risks being a barrier rather than a bridge to discourse about development in policing" (Wycoff, 1988, p. 104). On the other hand, Oliver (1992, p. 46) indicates that community policing is an intangible term based upon an intangible ideas "[it] is an all-encompassing idea that focuses on a single goal: reducing crime and public fear." Miller and Hess (1998, p. 19) state the obvious when they indicate "[that] community policing is many different things to many different people." My research suggests that one of the reasons for the lack of a common definition is that the features of community policing in a specific police department are shaped, at least in part, by forces within that jurisdiction and related to local history, concerns, politics, and real or perceived problems.

Manning (1989), Skolnick and Bayley (1988), Trojanowicz and Bucqueroux (1990), Barnett and Bowers (1990), Kelling and Moore (1988), and Eck and Spelman (1989) all propose their own definitions of community policing. Stipak (1994, p. 115) defines community policing as a "management strategy that promotes the joint responsibility of citizens and police for community safety, through working partnerships and interpersonal contacts." While all of the definitions emphasize somewhat different aspects of community policing, common themes emerge. These themes address philosophical, operational, and organizational characteristics of community policing and are echoed in other definitions as well.

Cordner (2001) defines community policing in terms of multiple dimensions, which are similar to Manning's (1989) levels of meaning. Cordner's (2001) four dimensions include the philosophical dimension, the strategic dimension, the tactical dimension, and the organizational dimension. The philosophical dimension addresses central ideas and beliefs underlying community policing and parallels Manning's ideological level. Cordner's strategic dimension addresses key "operational concepts" that link the philosophy of community policing to specific programs and practices, and parallels Manning's programmatic elements. The tactical dimension focuses upon creating "concrete programs, practices, and behaviors" based upon the philosophy of community policing and parallels Manning's pragramatic approach. Finally, Cordner views the organizational dimension as critical to successful implementation of community policing and addresses structural, management, and informational issues. Cordner's organizational dimension parallels Manning's organizational structures.

Brown (1989) does not identify levels of meaning, per se, but a series of components that can easily be placed in Cordner's (2001) dimensions and Manning's (1989) levels of meaning. Brown's (1989) components include a problem-solving, results-oriented approach; articulation of police values that incorporate citizen involvement; accountability of the police to each neighborhood; decentralization of authority; police community partnership and sharing of power; beat boundaries that correspond to neighborhood boundaries; permanent assignment of patrol officers; empowerment of patrol officers to show initiative; coordination of investigations at both neighborhood and citywide levels; new roles for supervisors and managers as supporters rather than evaluators of patrol officers; and changes in training, new systems of performance evaluations, and new approaches to "demand management."

One theme emerging from the literature is that community policing is more than simply a range of programs, one or more of which may be applied at any given time. Community policing involves a significant ideological or philosophical component. Trojanowicz and Bucqueroux (1990, p. xiii) argue that community policing is "both a philosophy and an organizational strategy that allows the police and community residents to work closely together in new ways to solve the problems of crime, fear of crime, physical and social disorder, and neighborhood decay." They state that "a philosophy is defined as what you think and believe" and that "the philosophy [of community policing] rests upon the belief that law-abiding people in the community deserve input into the police process, in exchange for their participation and support..." (1990, p. xiii). Similarly, Skolnick and Bayley (1988, p. 3) argue that the "central premise of community policing is that the public should play a more active and coordinated part in enhancing safety [and that] the public should be seen as 'co-producers' with the police of safety and order."

Manning indicates that at the ideological level, community policing is a system of beliefs premised on the recognition that in previous times communities were more unitary, police more legitimate and accepted, and social control tighter, more coherent, and pervasive (1989).

In addition to partnership, problem solving, and quality of life, several additional principles and values are said to be fundamental to community policing. These values include: citizen satisfaction, sensitivity and respect (Barnett & Bowers 1990; Kelling & Moore 1988). Citizen satisfaction, sensitivity, and respect are reminiscent of the values associated with a police "service" orientation.* Indeed, Roberg and Kuykendall (1993) indicate that the service model is similar to community policing. Patrick Murphy, former Police Commissioner of New York City, has observed that "at its core, community policing is the service model applied to minorities and the poor" (Skolnick & Bayley, 1988, p. 86).

The service model recognizes that many tasks performed by police officers do not involve enforcement of criminal laws, i.e., detection, apprehension, arrest, and prosecution of alleged offenders (Norris, 1973; Reiss, 1971). Service-related tasks, which frequently involve 50% or more of police officers' duties, include dispute resolution; social service-related activities, such as informal counseling and referral; informational functions; and a variety of other activities. Moreover, the service model emphasizes the importance of respect, sensitivity, citizen satisfaction and the appropriate treatment of citizens by police officers while performing both enforcement and service functions (Skolnick & Bayley, 1988).

Definitional issues notwithstanding, there was clearly a growing trend toward adoption of community policing by local police departments. Zhao, Lovrich, and Thurman (1999) trace the origins of community policing back to the 1970s, and analyze its development through a "period of promises and challenges" in the 1980s and "widespread awareness and adoption" in the 1990s. Oliver (2001) describes a similar progression from an idea to the "viable but crude methods" of the 1980s to "successful and detailed practices of the 1990s" to "institutionalization by the turn of the century."

Oliver (2004) categorizes the new era of community policing as falling within three "generations:" innovation (1979–1986), diffusion (1987–1994), and institutionalization (1995–present) (pp. 16–18). Oliver argues that the "innovation generation" began during the 1970s after certain long-held beliefs in the law enforcement community, such as the effectiveness of routine

* Law enforcement literature makes the distinction between a "service" and "enforcement" orientation. Police departments have been categorized as to whether they emphasize the service or enforcement aspects of police work. Traditional departments emphasized enforcement while the more modern approach was to emphasize service (Norris, 1973). Clearly all departments perform a combination of enforcement and service related tasks. The issue is one of emphasis.

preventative patrol, were debunked, sparking a search for "what works in policing." This first stage included Goldstein's (1990) early work on problem-oriented policing and Wilson and Kelling's (1982) "Broken Windows" theory, which focused on dealing with neighborhood disorder, drunks, disorderlies, panhandling, prostitution, and other urban quality-of-life offenses as a means of reducing crime and citizen fear. Community policing experiments, test sites, and demonstration projects implemented during this phase focused on major urban areas and were generally grant funded and typically involved a single intervention. The most widely publicized of these early efforts include: the Newark, New Jersey, and Flint, Michigan, foot patrol experiments; the Houston, Texas, Neighborhood Oriented Policing Project; and the Newport News, Virginia, Problem-Oriented Policing effort.

Early community policing efforts and experiments involved strong emphasis on foot patrol. Two well-known experiments occurred in Newark, New Jersey, and Flint, Michigan. Friedman (1992) reported that for both of these cities the terms *foot patrol* and *community policing* were interchangeable. The Newark experiment hypothesized that increased foot patrol would lead to reduced fear of crime, reduced reporting of crime, and reduced victimization; a larger percentage of arrest rates in the foot patrol areas; increased police officer job satisfaction; and improved citizen relations in foot patrol areas (Pate, 1981). The Newark experiment found that "residents were aware of the different patrol levels in their neighborhoods" and that police patrols were "overwhelmingly popular." The hypotheses that foot patrol would lead to a reduction in crime and victimization were not supported by the findings of the Newark experiment. However, the experiment did produce findings of decreased citizen fear and increased officer job satisfaction (Friedman, 1992).

The Flint foot patrol program is said to "have demonstrated both the efficiency and effectiveness of foot patrol officers" (Friedman, 1992). "Foot patrol officers were judged to be able to carry out a wide range of activities as community organizers, dispute mediators, and service brokers" and "there were indications that mutual respect between police officers and the community was growing" (Trojanowicz, 1983; 1986). It appears that these results were achieved as a combination of the technology of foot patrol that encouraged far more officer-initiated activities, such as home and business visits (Miller & Hess, 1994) and instruction with regard to community organizing, leadership, and problem solving (Radalet & Carter, 1994). Officers were given broad flexibility to carry out their tasks, encouraged to be creative, and take "ownership" of their patrol beats (Radalet & Carter, 1994).

Houston, Texas, experimented with Directed Area Response Teams (D.A.R.T.) to increase positive interaction between police and communities during this early phase of community policing. It also implemented Project Oasis, which involved strategies aimed at reducing fear and encouraging community revitalization before eventually selecting Neighborhood-Oriented Policing (NOP) as its new policing style. NOP facilitated interaction between officers and citizens for the purpose of identifying crime and noncrime problems. It incorporated both a managerial philosophy and operational approach (Wycoff & Oettmeier, 1994). Officers were relieved of general patrol responsibilities and assigned to work with citizens, community associations, and businesses in designated neighborhoods. However, NOP was so poorly received by patrol officers that the acronym was dropped although the elements of the program continued for a time (Sadd & Grinc, 1994).

Newport News, Virginia, implemented problem-oriented policing during this period (Eck & Spelman, 1989). Problem-oriented policing, a technique introduced by Goldstein (1990) is sometimes considered a precursor to or a subset of community policing.* According to Eck and Spelman (p. 425), "problem-oriented policing is a department-wide strategy aimed at solving persistent community problems. Police identify, analyze, and respond to the underlying circumstances that create incidents." Problem-oriented policing involves scanning, analysis, response, and assessment. The Newport News, Virginia, community policing experiment demonstrated that police officers could learn and apply problem-oriented policing techniques to their daily routines and through them enhance cooperation between them, the public, and other agencies (Eck & Spelman, 1989).

The next generation of community policing, the diffusion generation, began in the mid-to-late 1980s and continued through the early-to-mid-1990s. It was marked by the diffusion of community policing to medium and large metropolitan law enforcement agencies throughout the United States (Oliver, 2001). Community policing efforts during this period were generally, although not always grant funded, and involved multiple components, such as specialized units, foot patrol, partnership efforts, and problem solving. New York City's Community Police Officer Program (CROP); Baltimore County, Maryland's, Community-Oriented Police Enforcement (COPE) program; Hartford, Connecticut's, Cartographic-Oriented Management Program for Abatement of Street Sales (COMPASS); and Hayward, California's, Community Police Officer Program (CPOP) are some of the better known examples of community policing programs that were implemented during this stage.

Citizen-oriented police enforcement (COPE), a variation of problem-oriented policing was implemented in Baltimore County, Maryland (Behan,

* Although problem-oriented and community policing share several common characteristics (Trojanowicz & Moore, 1988), it remains a matter of some debate whether the former represents a precursor to, a subset of, or a different strategy altogether (Roberg & Kuykendall, 1993).

1986). Madison, Wisconsin also implemented and experimented with community policing in the late 1980s and early 1990s, focusing on changes in management and organizational structure to facilitate successful implementation (Wycoff & Skogan, 1993). COPE teams worked with local patrol officers to "pinpoint ongoing conditions that were not responding to usual patrol mobilization, but might yield to low-cost coordination of resources among government agencies." COPE had the full support of Baltimore County's Police Chief, Cornelius Behan. COPE teams had extensive contact with residents and were well aware of the importance of fear reduction (Skolnick & Bayley, 1988; Friedman, 1992). COPE was generally viewed as a success and led to the development of Community Foot Patrol Officers (CFPOs).

New York City's Community Police Officer Program (CROP), instituted in 1984, included elements similar to the Baltimore County COPE program. CROP officers were permanently assigned to beats covering approximately 18 city blocks. They were responsible for getting to know the community, uncovering problems, facilitating solutions, and increasing the reciprocal flow of information between the police and the public. The CROP program was subsequently expanded on a citywide basis.

The present generation of community policing began in the mid-1990s and is characterized by the institutionalization of community policing and its spread to small town and rural police agencies. Community policing efforts during this period were widespread; tended to involve multiple strategies, such as improved police–citizen communication and community partnerships; increased attention to quality of life offenses; and targeted enforcement of violent drug offenders. They are marked by increasing sophistication. The Crime Bill of 1994 and extensive federal spending facilitated the institutionalization of community policing on a large scale.

Zhao et al. (1999) indicate that "community policing has become the dominant theme of contemporary police reform in America" (p. 80). They compare the 1993 and 1996 Washington State University Division of Governmental Studies and Services (DGSS) survey results from a representative sample of 201 police agencies and find that there has been a noticeable increase in community policing programs and practices during that three-year period. They indicate that 86.6% of police agencies reported an increase in community policing implementation between 1993 and 1996 and that 80.6% of police agencies participating in the survey rated community policing as "highly valuable" to them. Oliver (2004, p. xiii) indicates that "community-oriented policing is truly an idea whose time has come."

However, despite clear evidence of extensive implementation of community policing over a 20-year period, "the ultimate and widespread institutionalization of community policing still remains somewhat uncertain" (Zhao et al., 1999, p. 89). Barriers to implementation of community policing have been well documented and include rank-and-file resistance to community policing; leadership, management, and organizational issues; and uncertainty concerning the ability of community policing to achieve its stated goals, particularly crime prevention and reduction.

The literature concerning rank-and-file attitudes toward community policing is mixed and reaches seemingly different conclusions. While Sadd and Grinc (1994) found substantial resistance to community policing in the eight Innovative Neighborhood Oriented Policing (INOP) cities they studied, Lurigio and Rosenbaum's (1994) review of the literature with regard to "The Impact of Community Policing on Police Personnel" found positive attitudes toward community policing among those assigned to community policing tasks. Lurigio and Rosenbaum were far more optimistic with regard to the positive impact of community policing on police officers.

Differences in their findings are likely due to differences in the emphasis of the studies and differences between community policing in the jurisdictions studied. While Sadd and Grinc (1994) focused on police officers generally, Lurigio and Rosenbaum (1994) focused on the impact of community policing on officers assigned to and involved with specialized community policing units, often comparing these units to patrol officers generally. In essence, Lurigio and Rosenbaum found those who participated in community policing programs had more favorable attitudes toward community policing and were more supportive of it. Findings from recent studies follow a similar pattern to those described by Sadd and Grinc (1994) and Lurigio and Rosenbaum (1994) and offer few surprises.

Adams, Rohe, & Arcury's (2002) conclusion that officers assigned to community-oriented policing (COP) duties were more supportive of community-oriented policing is entirely consistent with Lurigio and Rosenbaum (1994). Also, their finding that those who received COP training, regardless of assignment, also tended to be more supportive of community-oriented policing is consistent with Sadd and Grinc's (1994) finding that officers in the cities they studied generally had little knowledge or information of the pilot projects being undertaken in their cities or community policing. In addition, Adams et al. (2002) found that officers who perceived that their agency had a "participatory management style" were more supportive of community-oriented policing.

Several common themes emerge concerning rank-and-file acceptance of community policing. These themes are present in the earlier and more recent community policing literature concerning officers' attitudes toward community policing. First, participation in community policing programs and activities tends to have positive influence on officer attitudes toward community policing. Next, departmental preparedness and readiness for change, including adequate training, information, planning, support, and resources for community policing are essential to successful implementation of community policing and improved rank-and-file attitudes toward community policing. Participatory management also appears to contribute to improved officer awareness. Individual differences, such as race, gender, years of service, age, or educational level, may influence rank-and-file awareness and adoption of the principles and values of community policing. However, the research concerning the impact of demographic characteristics is mixed. Finally, there may be an interaction between global perspectives raised by Schafer (2002) and the agency-specific issues raised by Cochran, Bromley, & Swando (2002) and others.

Even more significant barriers than rank-and-file acceptance and organizational readiness is the fundamental question of whether community policing has been able to achieve its stated goals: crime prevention and reduction, reduced fear and disorder, increased quality of life, and improved police–community relationships. Here again, the results are mixed. Approaches to community policing vary significantly between jurisdiction as did police and political leadership, local history, culture and conditions, and available resources. The mechanisms by which community policing could improve police–community relationships are straightforward. Committed police leadership coupled with appropriate implementation of police–citizen communications programs, such as community councils, police–community management teams, liaisons, and foot patrol, tended to be successful in facilitating police–citizen communication, building trust, and improving police–community relationships. Similarly, foot patrol and attention to disorder and quality of life issues tended to reduce fear. However, the mechanisms by which community policing would prevent and reduce crime was not clearly defined or addressed in detail. The paradigm shift suggested by Skolnick and Bayley (1988, p. 3), the "central premise of community policing is that the public should play a more active and coordinated part in enhancing safety [and that] the public should be seen as 'co-producers' with the police of safety and order" did not appear to have occurred (Berlin, 2006).

Just as community policing was reaching its zenith in the mid-1990s after 15 years of gradual expansion, a new movement, Compstat, was rapidly developing and expanding. The origins of Compstat date back to the early 1990s. Jack Maple, a lieutenant in the New York Transit Police, "mapped every train station and train in New York City on 55 feet of wall space ... [and] mark[ed] every violent crime, robbery, and grand larceny that had occurred ... solved versus the unsolved" (Dussault, 1999). Following William Bratton's appointment as Chief of the Transit Police, "Maple showed him the charts and, between 1990 and 1992, they cut felonies in the 'caves' by 27% and robberies by a third." When Bratton was subsequently appointed Chief of the New York City Police Department by Mayor Rudolph Guiliani in 1994, he named Maple his second in command. Crime fell dramatically during the following decade. Maple went on to a lucrative consulting practice with partner, John Linder, and assisted in the implementation of Compstat in numerous U.S.

cities, including, but not limited to, New Orleans; Birmingham, Alabama; Philadelphia; Newark, New Jersey; and Jackson, Mississippi.

Compstat, an acronym for the computer-driven statistics, is a management process that consists of five basic elements: (a) specific objectives, (b) accurate and timely intelligence, (c) effective tactics, (d) rapid deployment of personnel and resources, and (e) relentless assessment and follow-up (McDonald, 2001, p. 263)

Specific objectives are intended to guide the actions of the agency. They are "achievement" or "impact" statements, focusing on desired outcomes, not enabling or process objectives focusing on strategies and tactics. The New York Transit Police objectives were based on the three most serious problems facing the Transit Authority: robbery, fear of crime, and fare evasion. The New York City Police Department under Chief Bratton objectives were: (a) get guns off the streets, (b) curb youth violence, (c) drive drug dealers out of New York, (d) break the cycle of domestic violence, (e) reclaim public spaces, (f) reduce auto-related crime, (g) root out corruption and build integrity in the NYPD (McDonald, 2001; 2002).

The second element, accurate and timely intelligence, consists primarily of crime analysis data obtained from police department management information system records (911 calls for service, computer-aided dispatch, police reports and records) and other sources. The data are geo (geographic) mapped to identify hot spots and crime patterns. Additional sources of information beyond departmental management information system records include information from the public; police investigation and intelligence; other federal, state, and local criminal justice agencies; private security; and community sources. However, collection, storage, retrieval, and mapping of this information is considerably more difficult than that obtained from police department management information systems, which is typically available electronically in-house. Accurate and timely intelligence drives operational changes designed to reduce crime. Police executives use crime data to hold commanders accountable.

Once crime has been identified, analyzed, and mapped, effective tactics are designed and developed to reduce it. In theory, these tactics are developed cooperatively during the course of Compstat meetings for immediate implementation. They are intended to be "comprehensive, flexible, and adaptable." Oliver (2004) incorporates a number of these tactics, including saturation patrol, directed patrol, use of plainclothes officers, and sting operations under the rubric of "Strategic-Oriented Policing."

Immediate implementation requires rapid deployment of personnel and resources. This typically requires a coordinated effort of personnel from different units working together as a team to address the problem. This is achieved through command accountability instilled through the Compstat process and reinforced through regular meetings involving top police personnel, precinct commanders, and commanders of special units. Commanders are expected to "exhibit interest, urgency, dedication to detail, and an ability to coordinate and lead groups of personnel to develop and implement workable solutions" (McDonald, 2001 p. 267).

Relentless follow-up and assessment is the fifth and final element of Compstat. It is the evaluation component of problem solving to ensure that tactical interventions have produced the desired result. Precinct commanders typically report on their application of tactics and results at the next Compstat meeting following implementation. Relentless follow-up and assessment involves detailed analysis of which elements of tactical responses worked best on what problems. Assessments inform future responses to similar problems.

Weisburd, Mastrofski, Greenspan, and Willis (2004) traced the growth and development of Compstat, surveyed all large police agencies with 100 or more sworn officers and a sample of midsize police agencies and found extensive adoption of Compstat-like programs in police agencies across the United States within several years of its introduction in New York City. By 1999, 32.6% of all large police agencies indicated that they had implemented Compstat. Another 25.6% of large police agencies indicated that they were planning to implement a Compstat-like program. Only 41.8% had no immediate plans to implement Compstat. Weisburd et al. (2004, p. 15) indicate that compared with other social and technological innovations, the diffusion of Compstat was rapid and concluded that "Compstat has literally burst onto the American police scene." Additional findings from the study include that larger police agencies were more likely to adopt Compstat than smaller agencies, that the primary motivation to implement Compstat was reduction of serious crime followed by a desire to increase police managers' control over field operations, and that the New York Compstat model strongly influenced adoption elsewhere. Agencies that implemented Compstat were much less likely to focus on improving skills and morale of street-level officers.

The rapid growth and development of Compstat, particularly as compared to the gradual and evolutionary growth of community policing is striking. One likely explanation for this is the fact that Compstat is largely consistent with the existing police culture including its focus on crime control and traditional top-down hierarchy. Other possible explanations include the fact that Compstat was designed, developed, and implemented from within police agencies, whereas community policing originated from within the academic community. However, politics played a role in the implementation of both strategies. External political figures, mayors and city managers, played a critical role in the decision to implement community policing in an effort to reduce crime and improve police–community relationships (Berlin, 2006). They exercised their appointment powers to select new chiefs favorable to community policing. Similarly, Compstat also appears to reflect the importance of politics in the selection of police leaders committed to Compstat. Political influences on both community policing and Compstat extended beyond the selection of the chief. Local politics, personalities, history, and culture impacted strategies and tactics and other aspects of policing (Berlin, 2006).

There was general agreement in the community policing literature that community policing represented a fundamentally new approach to policing, a paradigm shift in the relationship between police and citizens, which offered hope in reducing crime and improved relationships. Trojanowicz and Bucqueroux (1990) argued that community policing was the most influential development in the delivery of police services since the early 1900s and the professional reform movement. Zhao et al. (1999) and others conclude that community policing is similar in significance to the paradigmatic shift that marked the end of the political era of policing in the early 1900s, and the onset of the reform era that dominated much of the rest of the century.

A debate exists within the literature whether Compstat is a paradigm shift representing a new era of policing (Walsh, 2001) or an administrative tool or innovation (Moore, 2003). Walsh (2001) argues that Compstat represents a paradigm shift supplanting the traditional bureaucratic professional model of the reform era and the community policing model which preceded it. Walsh (2001) advocates that the new era is based upon the belief that crime prevention, order maintenance, and community safety are the products of integrated problem solving, strategy development, and intense managerial oversight of the entire organizational process. Walsh (2001, p. 206) describes Compstat as a "goal-oriented, strategic management process that builds upon police organizational paradigms of the past and blends them with strategic management fundamentals of the private sector." The core of Compstat is an executive team using information gathering, processing and mapping technology, flexible operational strategies, and managerial accountability to prevent and control crime.

Moore (2003), on the other hand, views Compstat as a technical and managerial system. He argues that the technical system collects and distributes performance information within a broader managerial system designed to focus the organization as a whole and managers who are relied on to exercise leadership to meet the organization's objectives and accomplish its tasks. Moore rejects arguments that Compstat is purely a technical system, that it is simply a return to an old top-down management style, or management strategy focused only on crime reduction. He views Compstat primarily as an administrative innovation, how the police manage themselves, not a strategic innovation, which would involve changes to the overall purposes of the police, the principal means by which they accomplish their objectives, and important internal and external working relationships in the organization. According to Moore (2003), Compstat does not broaden or change the mission and goals of police departments nor does it transform the principal operational methods that police typically rely upon to achieve their objectives. In fact, it emphasizes the crime-fighting image of police departments and tends to encourage "aggressive, preventative patrol" style tactics and disorder arrests, well documented, and sometimes problematic, in past decades.

Criticisms of Compstat concern negative impacts on external police–community relationships as well as internal police management issues and alleged falsifying of data. Perhaps, the most controversial aspect of Compstat is "zero-tolerance" policing, typically involving aggressive enforcement of "minor" offenses, such as disorderly conduct, drinking or urinating in public, graffiti, and other "quality of life" offenses. Ironically, the origins of "quality of life" policing date back to the early years of community policing and Wilson and Kelling's (1982) "Broken Windows" article and theory set forth in *Atlantic Monthly.* Community policing recognized the importance of quality of life issues to neighborhood residents and made improved quality of life a police priority. However, community policing focused first on abating quality of life issues and problems. Only when abatement was not successful did the police turn to enforcement, arrest, and citation. In fact, the New Haven (Connecticut) Department of Police Services implemented a Training Bulletin that set forth a multistep process to address quality of life issues beginning with officers' "presence" as a means to resolve quality of life issues and ending in arrest if all else was unsuccessful in resolving the problem (Berlin, 2006). Zero tolerance has been the subject of criticism in Australia (Dixon, 1999), the United Kingdom and the Netherlands (Punch, 2007) as well as other nations.

Internal complaints concerning Compstat come from police managers and unions or associations representing rank-and-file officers. John Eterno, a retired New York City Police Department Captain and Molloy College professor, and Eli Silverman, a former John Jay College of Criminal Justice professor, both early proponents of Compstat, surveyed several hundred retired NYPD commanders concerning the integrity of crime date, management climate, and other issues (Eterno & Silverman, 2010). Rank-and-file officers, typically through their unions or associations, have also voiced concerns and complaints about Compstat with regard to pressuring victims not to report crime, downgrading crime from felonies to misdemeanors or lost property, and pressure to cite or arrest "quality of life" offenders. See, for example, Zink (2004), New York Police Benevolent Association Recording Secretary. Weisburd et al., 2003 address related issues as well. It is important to bear in mind, that like community policing, significant variations exist between Compstat in different jurisdictions (Willis, Mastrofski, & Weisburd, 2003).

Central questions remain concerning the extent to which community policing and Compstat are compatible. These questions are both theoretical and practical. Examination of the five key elements of Compstat is revealing in that nowhere are police–community relationships addressed. Nevertheless, many proponents of Compstat argue that the two approaches are not mutually exclusive and can be implemented simultaneously. There is evidence to suggest co-implementation, that both strategies have been implemented independent of each other and operate on parallel tracks within the same jurisdiction (Willis, Kochel, & Mastrofski, 2010b). In fact, based on their findings, Willis, Kochel, & Mastrofski (2010a) argue that "maximizing the benefits of reform ... [requires] ... integrating Compstat and community policing and make recommendations toward this end." These recommendations include: (a) harnessing community policing values, goals, and practices in Compstat; (b) increasing accountability down the chain of command; (c) changing Compstat meetings to operate more strategically; and (d) committing substantial resources to crime analysis, training in problem-oriented policing, problem solving, and building partnerships. Boba et al. (2009) suggests an integrated problem-solving approach as a way to involve officers in street-level problem solving while commanders address more complex issues.

Ironically, increased homeland security and antiterrorism-related responsibilities assumed by local police since September 11, 2001, suggest a potentially workable approach toward integrating community policing and Compstat. It is generally accepted by law enforcement and homeland security officials that intelligence is the key to preventing and disrupting terrorist activities. There is growing attention to a new approach in policing, "intelligence-led policing" (Peterson, 2005). In essence, intelligence-led policing employs a problem-solving approach based upon the "intelligence cycle" to identify and target threats. By targeting enforcement toward specific individuals engaged in serious criminal activity based upon specific information and intelligence, it is possible to avoid broad use of aggressive patrol tactics. Overuse of these tactics contributed to complaints resulting in the birth of community policing as well as recent complaints against Compstat.

In theory, with the probable exception of a jurisdiction-wide, zero-tolerance approach, strong arguments can be made that community policing and Compstat can work in concert to reduce crime and improve community relationships, particularly in the context of an intelligence-led policing approach. To a certain extent, police leaders have always had to balance conflicting priorities: enforcement, service, and order maintenance. In practice, the issues are quite complex. Is it possible for leadership to have two equally important priorities: crime reduction and improved police–citizen relationships? Are leadership styles for community policing and Compstat compatible or do they require different approaches? Can the police aggressively enforce the law, reduce crime, and enjoy good police–community relationships? These are all issues that require further research.

References

Adams, R. E., Rohe, W. M., & Arcury, T. A. (2002). Implementing community-oriented policing: Organizational change and street officer attitudes. *Crime & Delinquency, 48*(3), 399–430.

Barnett, C. C., & Bowers, R. A. (1990). Community policing, the new model for the way the police do their job. *Public Management, 72*, 2–6.

Bayley, D. H. (1994). Community policing: A report from the devil's advocate. In D. P. Rosenbaum (Ed.), *The challenge of community policy: Testing the promises* (pp. 225–237). Thousand Oaks, CA: Sage Publications.

Bayley, D. H., & Mendelsohn, H. (1969). *Minorities and the police: Confrontaton in America.* New York: The Free Press.

Behan, C. (1986). Fighting fear in Baltimore county. The COPE Project. *FBI Law Enforcement Bulletin, 11*, 12–15

Berlin, M. M. (2006). *Implementing community policing: Case studies of New Haven, Connecticut and Richmond, Virginia.* (Unpublished doctoral dissertation). University of Maryland Baltimore County, Baltimore, Maryland.

Boba, R., Wycoff, L., & Santos, R. (2009). Advancing CompStat practices: The stratified model of problem solving, analysis, and accountability. In *Implementing and institutionalizing CompStat in Maryland.* College Park, MD: Institute for Governmental Service and Research.

Brown, L. P. (1989). Community policing: A practical guide for police officials. *Perspectives on Policing, 12* (No. NCJ 118001). Washington, D.C.: National Institute of Justice, U.S. Department of Justice and the Program in Criminal Justice Policy and Management, John F. Kennedy School of Government, Harvard University.

Cochran, J. K., Bromley, M. L., & Swando, M .J. (2002). Sheriff's deputies' receptivity to organizational change. *Policing: An International Journal of Police Strategies & Management, 25*(3), 507–529.

Cordner, G. W. (1995). Community policing: Elements and effects. *Police Forum 5,* 1–8.

Cordner, G. W. (2001). Community policing: Elements and effects. In R. G. Dunham & G. P. Alpert (Eds.), *Critical issues in policing: Contemporary readings* (pp. 493–510). Prospect Heights, IL: Waveland Press.

Dixon, D. (1999). Beyond zero tolerance. In T. Newburn (Ed.), *Policing key readings.* Devon, U.K.: Willan Publishing.

Dussault, R. (1999, March 1). Jack Maple: Betting on Intelligence. [Electronic version]. *Government Technology.*

Eck, J. E., & Spelman, W. (1989). Problem-solving, problem-oriented policing in Newport News. In R. G. Durham & G. P. Alpert (Eds.), *Critical issues in policing: Contemporary readings* (pp. 489–503). Prospects Heights, IL: Waveland Press.

Eterno, J., & Silverman, E. (2010, February 15). The trouble with Compstat: Pressure on NYPD commanders endangered the integrity of crime stats. [Electronic version]. *New York Daily News.* (http://articles.nydailynews.com/2010-02-15/news/27056291_1_compstat-crime-reports-commanders)

Friedman, R. R. (1992). *Community policing: Comparative perspectives and prospects.* New York: St. Martin's Press.

Kelling, G. L., & Moore, M. H. (1988). The evolving strategy of policing. *Perspectives on Policing, 4* (No. NCJ 114213). Washington, D.C.: National Institute of Justice, U.S. Department of Justice, and the Program in Criminal Justice Policy and Management, John F. Kennedy School of Government, Harvard University.

Kelling, G. L., Pate, T., Dieckman, D., & Brown, C. (1974). The Kansas City preventative patrol experiment a summary report. Washington, D.C.: Police Foundation.

Lurigio, A. J., & Rosenbaum, D. P. (1994). The impact of community policing on police personnel: A review of the literature. In D. P. Rosenbaum (Ed.), *The challenge of community policy: Testing the promises* (pp. 147–163). Thousand Oaks, CA: Sage Publications.

Manning, P. K. (1989). Community policing. In R. G. Durham & G. P. Alpert (Eds.), *Critical issues in policing: Contemporary readings* (pp. 451–468). Prospect Heights, IL: Waveland Press.

McDonald, P. (2001). COP. COMPSTAT, and the new professionalism mutual support or counterproductivity. In R. G. Dunham & G. P. Alpert (Eds.), *Critical issues in policing: Contemporary readings*, 4th ed. Prospect Heights, IL: Waveland Press.

McDonald, P. (2002). *Managing police operations: Implementing the New York crime control model–CompStat*. Belmont, CA: Wadsworth/Thompson Learning.

Miller, L. S., & Hess, K. M. (1994). *Community policing: Theory and practice*. St. Paul, MN: West Publishing Co.

Miller, L. S., & Hess, K. M. (1998). *The police in the community: Strategies for the 21*st *Century*, 2nd ed. Belmont, CA: Wadsworth Publishing Company.

Moore, M. (2003). Sizing up COMPSTAT: An important administrative innovation in policing. In T. Newburn (Ed.), *Policing key readings*. Devon, U.K.: Willan Publishing.

Norris, D. F. (1973). *Police–community relations*. Lexington, MA: Lexington Books.

Oliver, W. M. (1992, August). Community policing defined. *Law and Order, 40*(8), 46–58.

Oliver, W. M. (2001). *Community-oriented policing: A systemic approach to policing*, 2nd ed. Upper Saddle River, NJ: Pearson Prentice Hall.

Oliver, W. M. (2004). *Community-oriented policing: A systemic approach to policing*, 3rd ed. Upper Saddle River, NJ: Pearson Prentice Hall.

Palmiotto, M. J. (2000). *Community policing: A policing strategy for the 21*st *century*. Gaithersburg, MD: Aspen Publisher, Inc.

Peterson, M. (2005*). Intelligence-Led Policing: The new intelligence architecture*. (No. NCJ 210681). Washington, D.C.: U.S. Department of Justice, Office of Justice Programs, Bureau of Justice Assistance and the International Association of Chief's of Police.

Punch, M. (2007*). Zero tolerance policing*. Bristol, U.K.: The Policy Press.

Radelet, L. A., & Carter, D. L. (1994). *The police and the community* (5th ed.). Englewood Cliffs, NJ: Prentice Hall.

Reiss, A. J., Jr. (1971). *The police and the public*. New Haven, CT: Yale University Press.

Roberg, R. R., & Kuykendall, J. (1993). *Police & society*. Belmont CA: Wadsworth Publishing Company.

Sadd, S., & Grinc, R. (1994). Innovative neighborhood oriented policing: An evaluation of community police programs in eight cities. In D .P. Rosenbaum (Ed.), *The challenge of community policing: Testing the promises* (pp. 27–52). Thousand Oaks, CA: Sage Publications.

Schafer, J. A. (2002). "I'm not against it in theory…": Global and specific community policing attitudes. *Policing: An International Journal of Police Strategies and Management, 25*(4), 669–685.

Schmalleger, F. (2007). *Criminal justice today: An introductory text for the 21*st *century,* 9th ed. Upper Saddler River, N.J.: Pearson Prentice Hall.

Skolnick, J. H., & Bayley, D. H. (1988). *Community policing: Issues and practices around the world.* Washington, D.C.: U.S. Department of Justice.

Skolnick, J. H., & Fyfe, J. J. (1994). *Above the law police and the excessive use of force.* New York: Free Press.

Stipak, B. (1994, October). Are you really doing community policing? *Police Chief. 16*(61), 115–123.

Trojanowicz, R. C. (1983). An evaluation of a neighborhood foot patrol. *Journal of Police Science and Administration, 11*(4), 410–419.

Trojanowicz, R. C. (1986). Evaluating a neighborhood foot patrol program: The Flint Michigan project. In D. P. Rosenbaum (Ed.), *Community crime prevention* (pp. 258–262). Beverly Hills, CA: Sage Publications.

Trojanowicz, R. C., & Bucqueroux, B. (1990). *Community policing: A contemporary perspective.* Cincinnati, OH: Anderson.

Trojanowicz, R. C., & Moore, M. H. (1988). *The meaning of community policing.* East Lansing, MI: The National Neighborhood Foot Patrol Center, Michigan State University.

Walker, S. (1984). Broken windows and fractured history: The use and misuse of history in recent patrol analysis. *Justice Quarterly, 1,* 57–90.

Walsh, W. (2001). Compstat: An analysis of an emerging paradigm. In R. G. Dunham & G. P. Alpert (Eds.), *Critical issues in policing: Contemporary readings,* 5th ed. Longrove, IL: Waveland Press.

Weisburd, D., Mastrofski, S., Greenspan, R., & Willis, J. (2004). *The growth of Compstat in American policing.* Washington, D.C.: Police Foundation.

Weisburd, D., Mastrofski, S., McNally, A., Greenspan, R., & Willis, J. (2003). Reforming to preserve: Compstat and strategic problem solving in American policing. In T. Newburn (Ed.), *Policing key readings.* Devon, U.K.: Willan Publishing.

Willis, J., Mastrofski, S., & Kochel, T. (2010a). *Maximizing the benefits of reform: Integrating Compstat and community policing in America.* Washington, D.C.: Office of Community Oriented Policing Services, U.S. Department of Justice.

Willis, J., Kochel, T., & Mastrofski, S. (2010b). *The co-implementation of Compstat and community policing: A national assessment.* Washington, D.C.: Office of Community Oriented Policing Services, U.S. Department of Justice.

Willis, J., Mastrofski, S., & Weisburd, D. (2003). *Compstat in practice: An in-depth analysis of three cities.* Washington, D.C.: Police Foundation.

Wilson, J. Q., & Kelling, G. L. (1982). Broken windows: The police and neighborhood safety. *Atlantic Monthly*, 29–38.

Wycoff, M. A. (1988). The benefits of community policing: evidence and conjecture. In J. R. Greene & S. D. Mastrofski (Eds.). *Community policing: Rhetoric or reality.* New York, NY: Praeger.

Wycoff, M. A., & Oettmeier, T. N. (1994). *Evaluating patrol officer performance under community policing.* Washington, DC: National Institute of Justice.

Wycoff, M., & Skogan, W. (1993). *Community policing in Madison: Quality from the inside out. An evaluation of implementation and impact. Research report.* Washington, DC: National Institute of Justice, U.S. Department of Justice.

Wycoff, M. A., & Skogan, W. K. (1994). The effect of a community policing management style on officers' attitudes. *Crime and Delinquency, 40*(3), 371–383.

Zhao, J., Lovrich, N. P., & Thurman, Q. (1999). The status of community policing in American cities: Facilitators and impediments revisited. *Policing: An International Journal of Police Strategies & Management, 22*(1), 74–92.

Zink, R. (2004). The trouble with Compstat. *The PBA Magazine.* Retrieved October 12, 2010, from: www.nycpba.org/publications/mag-04summer/compstat

Zero Tolerance Policing in Democracies

The Dilemma of Controlling Crime Without Increasing Police Abuse of Power

3

JOHN A. ETERNO

Contents

According to some politicians, policing experts, and other pundits, the success of zero tolerance policing programs has been established through reductions in the number of recorded offenses. However, there may be adverse side effects that accompany these crime-fighting programs including the possibility of increased officer misconduct (e.g., illegal searches). A theoretical framework is outlined and evidence is gathered (utilizing both official data and self reports) to analyze the extent to which aggressive crime control policies influence officers. Results indicate that zero tolerance initiatives can lead to increased officer misconduct. Specific strategies for policymakers to cope with these results are discussed.

Introduction

The term *zero tolerance* has been used to describe numerous policing programs. One common aspect of these programs is their almost exclusive focus on aggressive crime control. In fact, police departments and city managers generally claim that these programs are highly successful by pointing to spectacular reductions in the number of offenses reported. The current work applauds such efforts, but, at the same time, also suggests that zero tolerance strategies need to be implemented with extreme care.[1] In particular, this work suggests that proactive strategies that prevent police misconduct should be developed and deployed along with zero tolerance efforts. To that end, the New York City Police Department's (NYCPD) Courtesy, Professionalism, and Respect program is outlined.

For the purposes of this chapter, "zero tolerance policing" refers to aggressive proactive law enforcement, such as stopping cars, running warrants, suppressing quality of life offenses, and similar actions, utilized with the aim of reducing the occurrence of crime (i.e., crime-fighting activities).[2] The current study will focus on the practices of the Police Department of the City of New York. This city has seen an enormous drop in crime.[3] According to NYCPD statistics (which are supplied to the Federal Bureau of Investigation for the Uniform Crime Reports), New York City has seen a drop in crime every year from 1992 through 1998.[4] The most precipitous drops occurred in 1995 (–16.1%) and 1996 (–14%).[5] In fact, this huge decrease was responsible for much of the nation's decrease in crime during the same period (Silverman, 1999).[6]

Aggressive crime fighting (zero tolerance) has been predominant policing style in New York City for the past several years.[7] The lynchpin of this aggressive crime-fighting method is a program called Compstat (COMParative (COMPuter) STATistics), which was unveiled in April 1994, just before the large decreases in crime. The Compstat process is founded on the principle of ensuring that precinct commanders act immediately to attack the crime that occurs within their area of assignment. As Silverman (1997) explains this process, Compstat's twice weekly crime strategy meetings provide a venue in which the new strategies are developed and accountability for precinct and borough decision making is ensured. As part of the Compstat process, four specific steps are outlined by the NYCPD to reduce crime: accurate and timely intelligence, effective tactics, rapid deployment, and relentless follow-up and assessment (New York City Police Department, 1998b). In conjunction with the Compstat process, many other crime control-oriented strategies and programs were deployed. These programs generally work with Compstat to fight crime. One example is an aggressive zero tolerance strategy called "Getting Guns Off the Streets of New York" (see, especially, Silverman 1999, pp. 92, 103).

George L. Kelling and Catherine M. Coles point to New York City as a model department. They suggest that reducing the incidence of minor "quality of life" offenses helps restore communities and is the key to the success of the NYCPD. For example, Kelling and Coles (1996, p. 100) write:

> When it comes to index crimes such as homicide, there is growing evidence to suggest that police attention to "quality of life" issues and low-level crimes, making use of tactics significantly at variance with 911 policing, may have a significant impact in lowering incidence rates of index crimes. For example, in New York City, as of June 30, 1995, the rate of reported murders by handgun was down 40.7% from the previous year, largely attributable, according to federal and local officials, to "quality of life" enforcement.

Former New York City Police Commissioner William Bratton (one of the key persons to institute Compstat and other zero tolerance strategies in New York City) also argues that by using appropriate zero tolerance methods, the police generate a marked influence on crime. He (Bratton, 1995, p. 2) writes:

> Better management, better strategies, higher expectations, and more effort on the part of police departments can do far more than just affect crime rates at the margins . . . we can have a swift and decisive impact on crime. If we start to use police resources efficiently, we can cut crime by 20, 30, or even 50% in the space of several years.

It is clear that these policing experts and many others who are attempting to emulate these policies feel that zero tolerance strategies will be successful at reducing crime.[8] However, reducing crime is *not* the only objective of law enforcement. For example, New York City officers are taught four values in the Police Academy. These are (New York City Police Department, 1997b, *Police Student's Guide—Police Science,* pp. 3–6):

1. Protect the lives and property of our fellow citizens and impartially enforce the law.
2. Fight crime both by preventing it and by aggressively pursuing violators of the law.
3. Maintain a higher standard of integrity than is generally expected of others because so much is expected of us.
4. Value human life, respect the dignity of each individual, and render our services with courtesy and civility.

Zero tolerance (i.e., crime fighting) strategies unquestionably address 1 and 2 above, but could jeopardize the application of the other two values taught at the Police Academy.

Another NYCPD program developed by former Police Commissioner Howard Safir is aptly entitled Courtesy, Professionalism, and Respect (CPR). The CPR program is specifically directed at those values not addressed by crime-fighting strategies. The blueprint for this program was released in June of 1996. Its objective, as complicated and as important as reducing crime, is "to promote a culture of professionalism within the New York City Police Department, where the principles of courtesy and respect are consistently applied in our interactions with each other and with the people we serve" (New York City Police Department, 1997a, p. 2). The anticipated results of the CPR program are:

- a more productive relationship between police and citizens,
- improved officer safety through increased public support,
- more success for all crime strategies [by enlisting citizen cooperation],
- an image of members of the service as law enforcement professionals.

The NYCPD developed this strategy by utilizing a complex array of sources. The Department took seriously the suggestions, complaints, and comments of policing experts, politicians, and community members. As the NYCPD (New York City Police Department, 1998a, p. 4) states, the strategy basically involves the following:

> The CPR Strategy is therefore the culmination of internal re-examination, external analysis, and the subsequent recommendations of advisory boards, citizen focus groups, and internal review committees... the following components are key to achieving our stated objective:
>
> - Set Professional Standards
> - Revise Recruitment Criteria
> - Incorporate the Philosophy of CPR in All Facets of Training
> - Implement Comprehensive Performance Monitoring
> - Revise Reward and Discipline Systems to Support CPR Goals
> - Expand Public Involvement

Under the setting professional standards, the NYCPD stresses certain ideals, such as (New York City Police Department, 1997a, p. 2) "acknowledging the rights and dignity of those we come in contact with; acknowledging the diversity, traditions, and cultures of others; being cognizant of the manner in which we speak to others; etc." Recruitment policy focuses on (New York City Police Department, 1997a, p. 4)... "screening in" desirable candidates rather than "screening out" unqualified candidates. Under the recruitment, the CPR program also stresses minimal age and education requirements (candidates must be 22 and have at least 60 college credits or two years of military experience to be hired). All aspects of training focus on CPR as well.

Monitoring programs were also developed to measure CPR's effectiveness including random testing of officers and reviewing the City of New York's Civilian Complaint Review Board (CCRB) statistics at Compstat. Rewards, including public recognition of officers, transfers to desired assignments, and giving career advancement points, were also initiated. Lastly, the public was involved in every aspect of these changes and invited to participate. For example, a CCRB mediation program was put in place (i.e., an attempt to mediate CCRB complaints by engaging voluntary participants in frank discussions of incidents). These components of the CPR program address precisely those values that crime control strategies tend to neglect: integrity, valuing human life, and respect for every person. This strategy, then, complements efforts on crime control.

Given the publicity and emulation of zero tolerance strategies, it seems that departments and municipalities are willing to pay high prices to reduce crime; however, these same agencies seem much less attentive to programs aimed at reducing officer misconduct. This article addresses the issue of why programs, such as CPR, are as essential to policing (especially in a democratic society) as zero tolerance policies. A theoretical basis for these programs is developed and evidence is gathered to support it. This work also suggests that other agencies replicate strategies to prevent police misconduct (e.g., CPR) just as they have emulated crime-fighting strategies (e.g., Compstat).

Theoretical Underpinning for Programs Aimed at Reducing Police Misconduct

Herbert Packer (1966, pp. 238–239) in his discourse on the courts and the police points out "... the kind of criminal process that we have is profoundly affected by a series of competing value choices which, consciously or unconsciously, serve to resolve tensions that arise in the system." He goes on to describe two models of criminal justice programs to which he ascribes different values. First, he describes the Crime Control Model as, "... the efficient, expeditious, and reliable screening and disposition of persons suspected of crime as the central value to be served by the criminal process." The other model he calls the Due Process Model. Packer explains that this model "sees that function [the criminal process] as limited by, and subordinate to, the maintenance of the dignity and autonomy of the individual." Packer points out that these models are "polar extremes which, in real life, are subject to almost infinite modulation."

This dichotomy, crime control versus due process, provides a useful framework for discussion. In today's world of law enforcement, zero tolerance strategies are clearly focused on crime control. For example, the emphasis of Compstat in New York City is on reducing crime. Similar zero tolerance strategies by law enforcement abound with the rhetoric of reducing crime. One simply has to pick up a newspaper to read about quality of life crackdowns for, say, "road rage" or "driving while intoxicated." The ultimate goal of such crackdowns is reducing crime. As stated in the Compstat process, "The success of this strategic control system and our Crime Control and Quality of Life Strategies are evidenced by the tremendous declines in crime we have achieved since 1993" (New York City Police Department, 1998b, p. 1). Even recent titles about police show a focus on crime fighting (e.g., Maple's *The Crime Fighter: Putting the Bad Guys Out of Business* (1999) and Silverman's *NYPD Battles Crime* (1999)). Zero tolerance strategies, then, tend to focus on decreasing crime and have been praised by some as having a significant impact on the number of reported offenses (see, especially, Bratton, 1995; Silverman, 1997; Kelling & Coles, 1996).

Reducing crime is a worthy goal; however, along with decreases in crime may come other, less desirable consequences. An understanding of Packer's dichotomy is helpful in identifying possible areas of trouble that an agency focusing on zero tolerance strategies might have. Because zero tolerance programs initiated by today's police managers are basically targeted at *crime control*, it seems reasonable to hypothesize that if such programs are not carefully implemented, *due process* considerations are likely to suffer. That is, as more emphasis is placed on crime control, there is increased stress on due process.

If we assume the above hypothesis to be true, then an intense focus on crime control may ultimately lead to a decline in the values of police officers associated with the due process model. More specifically, in a crime control (i.e., zero tolerance) environment, the pressure on police officers of every rank is to reduce the number of reported crimes. This pressure may ultimately manifest itself as overzealous enforcement behavior. That is, some officers could be reacting to the unyielding stress to reduce crime by abusing their authority (e.g., conducting illegal searches, stops, arrests, etc.).

This abuse of authority is the antithesis of policing in a democracy. As stated, values such as high integrity, the importance of protecting every human life, and respecting the dignity of each individual, are critical to democratic policing. There is cause for concern when we empower the police without a counterbalance.[9] As former United States Supreme Court Chief Justice Earl Warren (1959, p. 89) stated, "Life and liberty can be as much endangered from illegal methods used to convict those thought to be criminals as from the actual criminals themselves." Policing in a democracy, therefore, should entail both due process and crime control (zero tolerance) policies.

Academicians and others have recognized this dilemma for the police. For example, Herman Goldstein suggests that in some departments the concern for crime control overwhelms due process considerations. He (1977, p. 13) writes:

> The police are not only obligated to exercise their limited authority in conformity with the Constitution and legislatively enacted restrictions, they are obligated as well to see to it that others do not infringe on constitutionally guaranteed rights. These requirements introduce into the police function the unique dimension that make policing in this country such a high calling. One of the consequences of the current situation is that the police in some communities, especially in the congested areas of large cities, place a higher priority on maintaining order than on operating legally.

Even Kelling and Coles (1996, pp. 163, 168–169), staunch proponents of zero tolerance policing, recognize the possible consequences of empowering police to fight crime:

> Whether explicitly or not, libertarians understand that the shift toward community policing, with the accompanying commitment to order maintenance and problem solving, represents a movement toward a far more aggressive and interventionist police strategy [i.e., zero tolerance policing] ... individual rights are on the line when police engage in order maintenance.... The authority accorded police by law and the mandate from the community under which they operate do not constitute a license for them to violate individual rights....

Recently, former Commissioner Bratton, too, has acknowledged some of these possible consequences and the need for administrators to possibly modify their zero tolerance strategies as the implemented crime control policies evolve (see, for example, Henry, 2000).

Hypothetically, then, in a democracy, it is essential to *check and balance* the increased aggressiveness expected of police who employ zero tolerance (crime-fighting) methods with other strategies that emphasize due process considerations (e.g., CPR). The question to consider now is whether there is any evidence to support this hypothesis. To answer this, we turn to official and self-reported data.

Data Supporting the Need for Programs Aimed at Reducing Police Misconduct

The current research was conducted in New York City. It has a population of approximately 7.3 million, covers an area of 322 square miles, has more than

30 million visitors a year, and has a large immigrant population. Therefore, just about every type of situation, individual, or place is represented. New York City is also well suited to this research because the NYCPD is often cited as a model for zero tolerance strategies (see, especially, Kelling & Coles, 1996; and Bratton, 1998) and other departments are emulating these strategies (see Kelling & Coles, 1996 and Silverman, 1999). The NYCPD divides the five boroughs (counties) into eight patrol boroughs: Manhattan South, Manhattan North, the Bronx, Brooklyn South, Brooklyn North, Queens South, Queens North, and Staten Island. There are 76 patrol precincts within the eight borough commands. The department consists of approximately 37,500 uniformed officers. Of these, about 26,500 are at the rank of police officer.

In this section, we will first overview available official data from a number of sources. Next, the methods utilized to administer the survey will be explicated. Lastly, the results from the survey will be reported.

Official Data

Data collected by official sources (i.e., government agencies) indicate that abuse of authority by officers focused on zero tolerance (crime control) efforts was a concern for the NYCPD. For example, Rashbaum (1996, p. 22) points out:

> Civilian complaints against police for allegedly illegal searches skyrocketed by 135% in the first 2 years of Mayor Giuliani's "quality of life" crackdown... Illegal search complaints jumped from 299 in 1993 to 704 in 1995, a 135% increase... Complaints of illegal vehicle searches jumped from 38 in 1993 to 79 last year, a 108% increase. Allegations of illegal apartment searches shot up 179% from 29 in 1993 to 81 last year.

This suggests that as crime control policies increased, so too did abuse of authority.

As can be seen from Table 3.1 below, decreases in crime, which have been associated with zero tolerance methods, have been accompanied in New York City by corresponding increases in civilian complaints for abuse of authority.[10] Examples of abuse of authority complaints include allegations

Table 3.1 Comparison: Civilian Complaints for Abuse of Authority versus Total Index Crimes

	Year					
	1993	1994	1995	1996	1997	1998
Complaints for Abuse	1,236	2,027	2,460	2,828	2,631	2,646
Index Crimes	600,346	530,121	444,758	382,555	355,893	323,192

Source: Data supplied by the City of New York's Civilian Complaint Review Board (CCRB).

of unwarranted or unlawful searches, seizures, stops, threats of force, threats of arrest, etc.

The total number of civilian complaint allegations (which include unnecessary force, discourtesy, and ethnic slur allegations, along with accusations for abuse of authority) followed the same pattern as the abuse of authority complaints alone. That is, dramatic increases from 1994 through 1996 and then a decrease in 1997 and again in 1998.[11] It may be argued that *substantiated* (rather than total number) civilian complaints are better indicators for actual officer behavior. Those figures, based on completed cases, also indicate an enormous rise from 1994 to 1995 (111 to 269, a 142% increase) with the numbers only beginning to decrease substantially in 1998.[12]

Note that, in 1997, civilian complaints for abuse of authority, total civilian complaints, and crime itself, all decreased. This year was the first full year of the CPR program. It is possible that the reduction in civilian complaints was due to the influence of new due process programs instituted by Police Commissioner Howard Safir (e.g., CPR). These programs commenced with his arrival about a year earlier.[13]

Increases in the number of court claims for abuse by officers as well as payments for civil suits against police further indicate that the abuse of authority in the New York City Police Department was a concern. As Purdy (1997, p. A1) writes, "From 1994 to 1996, the city received 8,316 court claims of abuse by officers compared with 5,983 for the three previous years."[14] Also, in FY1995, the city paid $19.5 million in settlements for police misconduct (Sontag & Barry, 1997; Rohde, 1998). Comparing that figure to the 1996 figure of $27.3 million again suggests that there was an increase in abuse of authority in the Police Department (Sontag & Barry, 1997).[15]

Clifford Krauss (1996, p. B1), writing in *The New York Times*, also points out that officers in New York City may have been abusing their authority:

> There are three key elements of Mr. Brattons approach: a relentless focus on attacking so-called quality-of-life offenses as a way to combat more serious crimes; a thorough overhaul of personnel, strategies, and training within the department, and dollops of symbolism and bravado... [However] while the department under Mr. Bratton increased arrests by 25%, there was an increase of more than 50% in civilian complaints about police misconduct and brutality in the minority communities where the drops in violent crime were sharpest. Moreover, the department weathered two major precinct corruption scandals, in which more than 50 officers were charged with crimes ranging from drug dealing to perjury.

Even if we accept the argument that police are responsible for decreases in crime (which is still a debatable issue), there are indications that the policies that may have led to such a decrease are also responsible for an increase in police abuse of authority. Thus, official data, in the form of civilian complaints and civil suits, show a trend indicating that when crime control policies were adopted, contemporaneously due process considerations by police suffered. While these statistics standing alone may not be convincing to some, they certainly suggest the need for further scientific inquiry.

Self-Reported Data From Police Officers

A research study was designed utilizing a different measure of officer behavior in an attempt to determine if officers' acceptance of crime control (i.e., zero tolerance) influenced their due process behavior. This was developed utilizing a questionnaire sent to officers who work in precincts. Although the self-reports are a snapshot of how officers state they will behave, they provide a useful comparison to the official data. Distribution of the questionnaire took place in the early summer of 1997.[16]

Methods

Utilizing the factorial survey method (Rossi & Nock, 1982), officers were asked to judge how they would react (e.g., search a person) in various hypothetical situations.[17] These situations were scientifically designed such that the extent to which officers were likely to remain within legally permissible boundaries in their street decisions could be empirically measured. Vignettes (i.e., hypothetical situations) were administered to a random sample of New York City officers working in precincts (i.e., districts or areas). The instrument was pretested with a small group of 50 officers. The measures used were found to be both reliable and valid.[18] Importantly, in testing the validity of the measures, it was found that officers' field behavior (as measured by supervisors' evaluations) significantly correlated with responses to the instrument.[19]

The dependent variable was an officer's decision to search on a scale of 1 to 8 with 1 meaning "definitely not search" and 8 being "definitely search." The independent variable was the legal situation; there were four hypothetical situations: two of them were clearly legal and two of them clearly illegal. Additionally, a control variable measuring officers' acceptance of zero tolerance (i.e., their attitude toward aggressive crime fighting) policing was examined.[20]

The hypothetical situations were constructed based on court cases. Two court cases were utilized to create both the legal and illegal hypothetical situations. They were *People v. Jackson* [79 NY 2d 907 (1992)] and *People v. Gokey* [469 NYS2d 618 (Ct. Appt. 1983)].[21] Both are New York State Court of Appeals cases (New York's highest court). In *Jackson*, the New York State Court held that a police officer may reach into a vehicle to determine whether an object is a weapon based on reasonable suspicion only if the object is within the defendant's immediate grasp and the defendant is in the car. In *Gokey*, the Court held that a container on a person that is within the immediate control or probable area of a suspect at the time of arrest may not be subjected to a warrantless search incident to arrest, unless the circumstances leading to the arrest support a reasonable belief that the suspect may gain possession of a weapon or be able to destroy evidence located in the bag.

Both an illegal and a legal scenario were created for each of the cases (see Appendix at end of chapter). Illegal and legal hypothetical situations based on the *Jackson* case involved searching for a weapon. The situations based on the *Gokey* case involved searching for marijuana. These scenarios were examined by nine attorneys to ensure that they accurately reflect New York State law.[22]

The type of situation (i.e., weapon or drug, legal or illegal) to be included in a particular questionnaire as well as the officers who were asked to participate were chosen randomly by a computer program. Each officer was given three vignettes on each type of situation.[23] Questionnaires were then distributed to 2,052 officers—27 randomly selected officers from each of the 76 precincts in New York City.[24]

The survey design allowed maximum contact with respondents at minimum expense (see Miller, 1991, p. 141). Of the 2,052 questionnaires sent, 1,259 (61%) usable surveys were returned. For government workers in New York City, a 61% response rate is exceptionally good (see, especially, Miller, 1991). The large sample size is certainly an advantage (at a minimum, it helps with statistical analyses). There were many other advantages to the survey design: subjects (i.e., officers) had time to consider their answers, a sense of privacy was developed (where subjects were more likely to be truthful), and subjects did not have an interviewer (who might negatively influence officers' answers) (see Dillman, 1983).

As with any method, there were difficulties as well. Two of the most important ones will be discussed. First, some might attribute the responses to ignorance or confusion with the law. However, officers in New York City are extensively trained in the law. New York City police officer recruits are given approximately six months of intensive academic training, of which about 172 hours (this includes special training methods, such as workshops, role plays, etc.) are in the law (NYCPD, 1997b). The legal study material for student officers is 57 chapters in length (NYCPD, 1997b). It contains detailed information ranging from Constitutional principles to specific offenses. Prospective officers must attain at least a 70% grade in law and an overall grade of 75% to graduate from the Academy. Additionally, the New York City Police Department has numerous other training sessions (e.g., borough-based training, precinct-level training, etc.) and officers receive updated *Legal Bureau Bulletins* that summarize new laws and cases for them.

Note, too, that the hypothetical situations were designed to be clearly legal or clearly illegal. The situations were not legally ambiguous or meant to *trick or confuse* officers in any way. Therefore, officers should, at a minimum, be aware of the law's requirements and be able to recognize the clearly legal and illegal fact patterns.

Second, an argument can be made that a survey may not capture actual field behavior. However, the work accomplished on validity with this project helps to mitigate this (i.e., face validity and concurrent validity). Further, to capture illegal behavior of the type being studied through observational methods would be extremely difficult. This is because officers are unlikely to behave in illegal ways while being observed. More specifically, observer effect would likely be an obstacle for a study on officers' illegal behavior. Thus, while this method has admitted difficulties, it is appropriate to the issue being studied.

To help minimize the difficulties and maximize advantages, other strategies were used as well. To distribute the questionnaires, precinct training sergeants were utilized. Not only do these officers have a considerable amount of experience in distributing questionnaires for numerous researchers, but they were also given detailed instructions and training on proper methods of distribution for the current project. Above all, anonymity was stressed. Training sergeants were the only persons who knew the identity of those officers chosen randomly by computer to complete the surveys. Subjects were instructed, both in writing and orally, not to put indentifying information on the survey. Two important reasons for stressing anonymity are that it helps to achieve a higher response rate and it encourages truthful responses rather than socially desirable answers (see, e.g., Babbie, 1989, p. 475; Bradburn, 1983, p. 298).[25]

One issue that must be considered when using surveys is whether the returned surveys are representative of the population being studied. That is, response bias may be a problem (see, e.g., Miller, 1991). Based on the self-reported characteristics of those returning the surveys, the sample certainly seems representative of precinct officers who work for the New York City Police Department. The average age of New York City police officers who work in precincts is 32.3 years.[26] The average age of the sample was 31.7 years. The average tenure of New York City police officers who work in precincts is 7.1 years. The average tenure of the sample was 7.6 years. Of particular concern was achieving a representative sample of officers who have no more than a high school education (i.e., no college credit whatsoever). The percentage of officers who work in the precincts with a high school education is 37.2%. The percentage of officers with a high school education in the sample of officers was 31.7%.[27] These statistics certainly suggest that the sample was highly representative of officers who work in precincts.

Results From Questionnaire

For the purposes of this analysis, responses were grouped into three categories: not search, search, and unsure. Officers who responded 1 or 2 on an 8-point scale (where 8 is definitely search and 1 is definitely not search) were categorized as not searching. A response of 7 or 8 indicated that officers would search. Where officers chose 3 to 6 on the 8-point scale, they were classified as unsure or uncertain about how to respond.

Using these categories, we examined the impact of the law on officers' search behavior. Tabular analysis revealed that officers in New York City are indeed influenced by the court cases. A zero-order table (which combined both the weapon and drug situations merely for ease of presentation) revealed that the majority of officers chose not to search when the situation was illegal (53.9%) compared to legal (26.4%) (see Table 3.2).[28] Also, officers, in general, increased their search behavior in legal situations (from 26.4 to 36.5%) and decreased (quite markedly) their search behavior in illegal situations (from 53.9 to 15.6%). This is certainly encouraging given some previous research that suggests that officers were not deterred from conducting illegal searches by court rulings (see, especially, exclusionary rule research, such as Oaks, 1970; Spiotto, 1973; Hirschel, 1997; Heffernan & Lovely, 1991).[29] It is also interesting to note that officers, in general, did not search that much more when it was legal to do so. Thus, other factors may explain why officers do not exercise their right to search in clearly legal situations (e.g., officer attitude to zero tolerance).

Importantly, these results also indicate that a small percentage of officers appear to be willing to violate the court guidelines (15.6%). Furthermore, the current study shows that about 30.5% of officers are somewhat uncertain in their responses in a situation that is clearly illegal. This, of course, means that

Table 3.2 Cross Tabulation: Both Weapon and Drug Situations Combined

			Weapon and Drug Situations		
			1.00 Legal	2.00 Illegal	Total
Category of Judgment	Chose Not to Search (0)	Count	499	988	1487
		% within LEGVILL	26.4%	53.9%	40.0%
	Unsure (1)	Count	700	559	1259
		% within LEGVILL	37.1%	30.5%	33.8%
	Chose to Search (2)	Count	688	286	974
		% within LEGVILL	36.5%	15.6%	26.2%
Total		Count	1887	1833	3720
		% within LEGVILL	100.0%	100.0%	100.0%

Note: Gamma = –.48; $p < .0001$
Pearson's $r = -.30$; $p < .0001$.
LEGVILL = Legal versus Illegal

a total of 46.1% of officers are, at a minimum, not sure whether they would search in a clearly illegal situation. As an explanation, we must consider the pressure on police officers to make arrests, to be aggressive in fighting crime, and to bring down crime statistics. Also, as part of our explanation, we should consider the fact that these scenarios basically involve unsupervised, unwitnessed activities that have very little punishment for failure to obey (punishment may involve courts excluding illegally obtained evidence, civil suits in serious cases, or perhaps a civilian complaint).

Overall, for this model, we are able to explain about 48% of officers' search decisions by the category of the situation (legal vs. illegal). Additionally, this result is not likely to have resulted from chance alone ($p < .0001$). Thus, there is a statistically significant relationship between the legal situation and officers' judgments. The majority of officers follow legal mandates. However, some officers are uncertain and a smaller percentage, about 15%, appears to be violating search guidelines. Further analyses were conducted to more specifically determine to what extent zero tolerance (i.e., crime fighting) orientation of officers explains their judgments. First-order tables controlling for those subjects who identified themselves as aggressive crime control officers were developed. Aggressiveness in crime fighting is a common theme to zero tolerance strategies. In fact, for the purposes of this research, it is the defining quality. Officers were given a separate question measuring aggressiveness (see Appendix for specific wording). They were categorized as aggressive and less aggressive based on their answer to that question.[30]

Table 3.3 shows the results of those analyses (Less Aggressive and Aggressive). In Less Aggressive, we see how less aggressive officers responded to the survey. In general, the responses by less aggressive officers were similar to the results seen in the zero-order table. About 14% of the less aggressive officers stated they would do the search in an illegal situation. Over half (55.1%) said they would not engage in the illegal behavior. Overall, this model allows us to explain 50% of officers' search behavior by knowing the category of the situation (legal vs. illegal) and excluding aggressive officers. Furthermore, this result is not likely to have come from chance alone ($p < .0001$).

The Aggressive section of the table sets out the responses from aggressive officers. As predicted, these aggressive officers are more likely to be illegal (violating due process considerations). In Less Aggressive, we saw about 14% of the less aggressive officers state they would do an illegal search. Contrast this result with the Aggressive section, a first-order part showing the relationship between officers' judgments to legal and illegal scenarios excluding less aggressive officers. The Aggressive area shows that approximately 24% of the aggressive crime control (zero tolerance accepting) officers are likely to conduct an illegal search. Thus, aggressive officers' illegal behavior is about 10% higher than less aggressive officers (24–14%). Moreover, aggressive officers were more likely to search in a legal situation (about 8% higher

Table 3.3 Judgments by Officers on Legal Situations Controlling for Aggressiveness

			Aggressive vs. Less Aggressive Officers					
			Less Aggressive			Aggressive		
			Legal vs. Illegal Behavior			Legal vs. Illegal Behavior		
			Legal	Illegal	Total	Legal	Illegal	Total
Judgments by Officers	Not Do Behavior	Column %	26.1%	55.1%	40.5%	28.6%	46.1%	36.7%
	Unsure Behavior	Column %	38.7%	30.5%	34.6%	28.3%	30.2%	29.2%
	Do Behavior	Column %	35.3%	14.4%	24.9%	43.1%	23.7%	34.1%
Total		Column Count	1604	1588	3192	283	245	528

Note: Less Aggressive—Gamma = .50, $p < .0001$; Pearson's $r = -.315$, $p < .0001$.
Aggressive —Gamma = .350, $p < .0001$; Pearson's $r = -.219$, $p < .0001$.

[43–35%]). Thus, as predicted, zero tolerance-oriented officers search more often in legal as well as illegal situations.

Note that the model in Aggressive allows us to explain 35% of aggressive officers' judgments by knowing the category of the law (legal or illegal). Further, this result is not likely to have occurred by chance alone ($p < .0001$). This indicates an interaction effect in which officers respond differently depending on their aggressiveness. Less aggressive officers respond in a more lawful manner (searching less often) compared to aggressive crime control-oriented officers.[31] Note well, however, that crime control officers are also more likely to search in patently legal situations. One important aspect of this study, then, is to suggest that when there is a need to institute zero tolerance (i.e., aggressive crime control) policies, it is important to attempt to achieve the increase in legal searches as seen in the aggressive officers *but not to get the corresponding increase in illegal searches as seen in the aggressive officers as well.*

These self-report data clearly lend support to the hypothesis that aggressive crime control officers are more likely to violate due process considerations (operationally defined with legal situations in this study). In fact, increased illegal search behavior was demonstrated to occur precisely in those officers who identified themselves as aggressive, zero tolerance, crime fighters. While future study is needed to confirm these findings, there is a strong case to be made that aggressive crime control (i.e., zero tolerance) can have an adverse impact on due process considerations.

Discussion/Suggestions

Based on the information presented, it is suggested that zero tolerance (i.e., crime control) strategies *need to be carefully implemented* considering both crime control and due process values. Evidence for this is indicated by official data and self-reported data. Official data were presented in the form of rising civilian complaints and increasing civil suits. These were complemented with self-reported data. The self-reports suggest that a small minority of officers could be abusing their authority (15%). More importantly, those officers who are most aggressive (i.e., zero tolerance, crime control-oriented) are more likely to be illegal in their behavior (24% compared to 14%).[32]

The previously presented material suggests that administrators need to implement, replicate, and be concerned with programs that focus on due process values as well as crime control-oriented programs (which already seem to be a main concern for agencies). Without this "dual focus," the current study clearly indicates that aggressive, zero tolerance policies will likely lead to increased violation of due process. Again, this does not necessarily mean that administrators should refrain from utilizing zero tolerance strategies. Rather, it is suggested that, by carefully considering and implementing both crime control (zero tolerance) and due process programs, police administrators may be able to achieve the most favorable results, namely, an increase in crime control behaviors without getting the corresponding increase in violating due process behaviors.

Numerous agencies have become involved in zero tolerance strategies and replicated other department's programs on crime control (e.g., Compstat). This has, in general, not been the case with due process strategies. Some police administrators and others may recognize this issue, but may not be as familiar with various due process strategies as they are with crime control strategies. To that end, the following discussion gives some ideas about due process strategies for police administrators and others to consider.

Initially, at the outset of an officer's career, it is important for him/her to understand the full ramifications of the law enforcement officer's role. Police departments, in general, tend to train officers to handle practical situations rather than history and theory. While practical training is critical, it is equally important—*especially at entry level*—for officers to understand their role in the democratic process including their accountability to the public. An understanding of the theoretical basis for an action can assist in practical application. That is, officers who understand *why* they are being told to do (or not do) something may be more likely to follow directions. Regarding legal restrictions, officers must determine for themselves in most situations (due to, for example, the lack of direct supervision) where to draw the line. Fundamental lessons in history, law, and ethics will assist them in making such decisions. After the fundamentals are grasped, other lessons should demonstrate their practical importance (e.g., role plays, street experience with officers willing to show proper methods, etc.).

After officers graduate from the police academy and begin to work on the streets, they need to have those lessons constantly reinforced, both in crime fighting and due process considerations. Regarding crime fighting, officers are often rewarded and made aware of good, quality arrests. However, in general, there tends to be very little done to communicate good or bad due process behavior to field officers.

To help remedy this situation, it is suggested that officers be advised of occurrences farther on in the criminal justice process. For example, in the United States, the specific reasons why evidence was excluded at court would be helpful. As Orfield (1987, p. 1037) states, "although the officers uniformly believed training was important in understanding the law, they also believed that the lessons of training did not firmly take hold until the officers faced real-life situations in the courtroom." Officers today often do not know the outcome of a case due to plea bargaining or legal technicalities that take place without the officer being present. While this certainly saves time, there is a need for other parts of the criminal justice system to communicate to officers pertinent information, such as why a defendant was released (e.g., a bad search because...) Even a quick letter from the prosecutor would suffice. The capabilities are certainly there. It is simply a matter of improving the link between the different agencies involved. Without constant reinforcement by judges, district attorneys, etc., these lessons may not be fully grasped.

There is also a need for in-service training and field supervisors to stress the importance of legal parameters. In particular, front-line supervisors need to set an example. Additionally, based on some of the comments by officers on the survey (if they so desired, officers could make comments at the end of the questionnaire), search and seizure and other legal training should be coupled with tactical training to help officers understand how the situation should be handled in the field.

Thus, a strategy of instruction, which includes theory, history, and ethics is suggested. At first, these lessons should be theoretical. At a later stage, concrete examples stressing practical law enforcement situations would help to strengthen officers' abilities to apply the theory. After graduation, the lessons must be reinforced by in-service training, supervisors, and from input by other criminal justice agencies (e.g., prosecutors informing departments when officers had evidence excluded). Police departments need to use the information from other agencies to focus on training needs, inform individual officers of mistakes, and to discipline officer for misconduct where appropriate. Note, however, that positive reinforcement is more likely than discipline to change behavior (rewards, including higher pay, would likely contribute to street officers following these initiatives).[33]

Many of these recommendations are incorporated into the NYCPD's current CPR program.[34] Furthermore, the program specifically addresses many of the issues cited in this work. For example, one of the objectives of this program is improved field performance, including reducing civilian complaints (New York City Police Department, 1997a). In fact, since the CPR program was initiated, the number of civilian complaints has fallen. In 1997, total complaints decreased 13.2% (4,816) (see New York City Civilian Complaint Review Board Semiannual Status Report, 1997). Crime was also reduced during this same period by 7% (total index crimes 355,893). It is not claimed that this is proof of the success of this program, but rather it is suggested that CPR is one of many possible programs that complement crime-fighting strategies by focusing on due process considerations. Therefore, CPR, as well as the other recommendations contained herein, should be considered by those implementing crime-fighting (i.e., zero tolerance) programs to help minimize the possible negative impact of crime control policies (e.g., illegal activities by aggressive officers) as discussed in this chapter.

This work also describes the importance of due process policies in an environment of zero tolerance policing. This is accomplished by providing a theoretical framework to better understand the effects of zero tolerance initiatives. Data are collected and analyzed which supports this framework. Lastly, this chapter outlines specific strategies to help policymakers properly control crime without increasing police abuses of power. This chapter, however, is not meant as a complete answer to the issue of balancing zero tolerance policies with due process considerations. That is well beyond its scope. Rather, it is meant to assist policymakers and generate further inquiry. Many more questions need to be explored. For example, zero tolerance may not be the answer to crime reduction. It is possible that other methods could be just as (or even more) successful. The San Diego Police Department's community policing strategy is certainly worth exploring (see, Greene, 1999).

In sum, if zero tolerance (crime control) strategies are utilized by police, then due process programs, such as CPR, should be considered by administrators as well. In this way, due process policies will help offset likely increases in police abuse of authority and misconduct associated with zero tolerance. Many police departments are currently emulating the New York City Police Department's strategy for fighting crime. The current study suggests that merely following a program of zero tolerance (i.e., crime control) without addressing the resulting problems of officer misconduct (i.e., due process) carries with it the risk of increased police abuse.

Finding the proper balance between the crime control and the due process models is a challenge to police administrators. This is what policing in a democracy is all about. It is not easy, nor is it meant to be. By design, policing in a democracy is based on a system of checks and balances. Police officers, therefore, are in a precarious position. They do not wield unlimited power, as in a police state, but are necessarily controlled by legal and other guidelines. By properly utilizing the information presented here, police administrators, trainers, and others can better understand the ramifications of zero tolerance strategies and reduce crime without, at the same time, increasing harmful police abuses of power.

Endnotes

1. This is not to suggest that other policing methods are not as good or even better than these methods (e.g., community policing as done by San Diego Police Department, see Greene, 1999).
2. The language used by some scholars and officers can be very confusing and inconsistent. For example, some use the words "community policing" as a synonym for "zero tolerance" (e.g., Kelling & Coles, 1996, pp. 168–169). In order to avoid this confusion, the definition is placed at the beginning of the chapter. Note that the definition of "zero tolerance" as used in this chapter is consistent with other research (e.g., Greene, 1999, p. 172). However, it may conflict with some notions of what these words mean (see, for example, Ryan,

1994, for an interesting discussion on difficulties with defining the term "community policing").

3. This is especially demonstrated through reductions in homicide data.
4. Data supplied by the New York City Police Department's Office of Management Analysis and Planning (OMAP).
5. Statistics indicate overall crime drop for the yearly periods.
6. Experts in policing differ as to the explanations for this decrease. Many are skeptical of the claims of police management (see, for example, Bayley, 1994).
7. Former Commissioner William Bratton describes what he believes were the policy initiatives leading to the reduction in crime in his book, *Turnaround: How America's Top Cop Reversed the Crime Epidemic* (1998). His zero tolerance policies are widely discussed in this book.
8. For example, the National Institute of Justice [NIJ] is funding research to replicate Compstat in other jurisdictions; also, representatives of other agencies often visit Compstat meetings to learn about the techniques (see, especially, Silverman, 1999, pp. 123–124).
9. This is what our system of government is all about, checks and balances. The police, as members of the executive branch should be properly checked by other branches of government (i.e., the judiciary and the legislature).
10. It has been suggested that because the NYCPD had an influx of younger officers at this time, the new officers were responsible for the large increase in civilian complaints. There may be some validity to this argument. However, the substantial increase in complaints corresponding to the decrease in crime is still stunning.
11. Total allegations were 1993 = 5,597; 1994 = 8,060; 1995 = 9,356; 1996 = 9,350; 1997 = 7,933; 1998 = 7,443.
12. There is a recognized situation in New York City where few complaints are substantiated (see, for example, Greene, 1999, p. 177). It could be a problem with CCRB, which has been modified several times over the past few years.
13. However, substantiated complaints continued to rise in 1997 to 448. In 1998, the number of substantiated complaints began to decrease (300). An explanation for the delay in the decrease of substantiated civilian complaints for one year compared to the allegations of complaints could be that the majority of officers understood the new due process programs, but a few diehards (who could be described as "very crime control-oriented") found it difficult to adjust to the new due process programs. Thus, it is possible that most officers adjusted to the new program bringing down the number of civilian complaints (and abuse complaints), but a few officers may have found it

difficult to change their crime control behaviors and were responsible for the relatively high number of substantiated complaints. Also, changes at CCRB could have contributed to this.

14. Recall that zero tolerance strategies began in 1994 under former Commissioner Bratton who left in 1996.
15. Other jurisdictions are also experiencing similar concerns. Los Angeles, for example, spent $20 million on civil suits in 1992 (Rayner, 1995). While these statistics are not conclusive, they do show indications for concern.
16. For comparison purposes, the CPR program commenced in the early summer of 1996 (i.e., June 1996).
17. Note that there were also other questions on the instrument that are not discussed in this short chapter. The questionnaire contained ambiguous legal situations, other variables in the factorial survey (the police culture, police bureaucracy, and community), officer characteristic questions, and officer attitude questions. These were used as control variables in a much more complicated and lengthy statistical analysis. Thus, the results presented here are a very brief compilation of a much larger work.
18. Reliability was demonstrated with test–retest correlations. There was about a one-month period between administrations. The correlations were significant and strong.
19. Face validity as well as concurrent validity was developed. Face validity was developed by using current literature to operationalize the concepts being measured (as suggested by Rossi & Nock, 1982, p. 35). Concurrent validity was demonstrated by showing a statistically significant and modest correlation (in the direction expected) between the answers on the survey (using a pretest) and field behavior using officers' evaluations ($r = -.19$, $p < .002$). Police officer evaluations have a measure called "apprehension/intervention." Since it captures activity other than searches, it was expected that the correlation would be attenuated (finding a similar variable to determine if your variable is properly measuring the concept being studied is a documented problem for survey research, see Bohrnstedt, 1983, pp. 97–98).
20. The control variable was measured by a question given in a different part of the questionnaire (different from the factorial survey).
21. Because the research was concerned with measuring misconduct, we utilized those activities most likely to elicit an illegal response based on previous research. Namely, situations that involve weapons and drugs were created (see, especially, Heffernan & Lovely, 1991; Nardulli, 1983). Due to this, the illegal activity measured in

this study should be considered a high estimate compared to typical activities of officers.

22. These included six attorneys from the NYCPD Legal Bureau, one from the NYCPD Personnel Bureau, and two professors who are also attorneys. Additionally, a number of social scientists, policing experts, and statisticians reviewed the instrument before distribution.
23. There were other variables and other vignettes that were asked. However, these are not pertinent to this analysis and, therefore, are not included in this work. As information, each officer answered a total of eight vignettes and the other variables included measures of police culture, the community, the police organization, officer's attitudes, and officer's characteristics.
24. The training sergeant in each precinct was given a list of 27 names and 27 alternates for that precinct (alternates were used in case of sick, retirement, transfer, or refusal to do the questionnaire). The names were chosen randomly by computer program. Sergeants were told to destroy these lists after distributing the questionnaires. Thus, the researcher had no information as to who the respondents were and, therefore, cannot link names with questionnaires.
25. Officers were given two options on the method of returning the survey. First, they could return the completed survey to the training sergeant who would, in turn, return it to the researcher. Second, if they did not feel comfortable with that method (perhaps they felt their anonymity would be compromised), they could place it in an envelope themselves and send it back to the searcher directly utilizing the Department's in-house mailing system at no cost.
26. All statistics regarding New York City police officer characteristics are as of March 1, 1998.
27. Both the Police Department figure and the sample figure for high school graduates include officers with an equivalency diploma (G.E.D). Additionally, this shows that those least likely to have reading and writing skills were responding to the survey.
28. Separate results are available from the author upon request.
29. Basically the exclusionary rule is a judicially created method of enforcing search and seizure guidelines whereby illegally obtained evidence cannot be used against a defendant.
30. The wording of this question was developed from a proven instrument utilized by Brown (1981).
31. Another cross-tab was prepared (not presented) comparing the judgments of aggressive officers in *illegal situations* versus less aggressive officers in *illegal situations*. This new table shows that we are able to explain 19% of officers' judgments in *illegal situations* merely

by knowing the category of aggressiveness. Further, this result is statistically significant ($p < .002$).

32. This difference, between aggressive officers' responses in illegal situations and less aggressive officers' responses was statistically significant (see no. 31 on other cross-tab created, not presented).
33. See any number of psychology texts regarding the use of punishment and its unpredictable results (e.g., DiCaprio, 1983). Also see Zuccotti Committee Report, *Report on the Recommendations of the Mayor's Advisory Committee on Police Management and Personnel Policy* (1987), especially page 6 regarding increased pay for police.
34. All the recommendations presented in this chapter are currently being evaluated for implementation by the NYCPD.

References

Babbie, E. (1989). *The practice of social research,* 5th ed. Belmont, CA: Wadsworth Publishing Co.

Bayley, D. H. (1994). *Police for the future.* New York: Oxford University Press.

Bohrnstedt, G. W. (1983). Measurement. In P. H. Rossi, J. D. Wright, and A. B. Anderson (Eds.), *Handbook of survey research* (pp. 70–114). 69–121. Orlando, FL: Academic Press.

Bradburn, N. M. (1983). Response effects. In P. Rossi, J. Wright, & A. Anderson (Eds.), *Handbook of survey research* (pp. 289–332). New York: Academic Press.

Bratton, W. J. (1995, November 18). Great expectations: How higher expectations for police departments can lead to a decrease in crime. Paper presented at the Annual Meeting of the American Society of Criminology, Boston.

Bratton, W. J. (1998). *Turnaround: How America's top cop reversed the crime epidemic.* New York: Random House.

Brown, M. (1981). *Working the street: Police discretion and the dilemmas of reform.* New York: Russell Sage Foundation.

DiCaprio, N. S. (1983). *Personality theories: A guide to human nature.* New York: Holt, Rinehart and Winston.

Dillman, D. A. (1983). Mail and other self-administered questionnaires. In P. Rossi, J. Wright, & A. Anderson (Eds.), *Handbook of survey research* (pp. 359–377). New York: Academic Press.

Goldstein, H. (1977). *Policing a free society.* Cambridge, MA: Balinger Publishing Co.

Greene, J. (1999). Zero tolerance: A case study of police policies and practices in New York City. *Crime and Delinquency, 45*(2), 171–187.

Heffernan, W. C., & Lovely, R. W. (1991). Evaluating the Fourth Amendment exclusionary rule: The problem of police compliance with the law. *University of Michigan Journal of Law Reform, 24,* 311–369.

Henry, V. (2000). A conversation with William J. Bratton. *Police Practice and Research: An International Journal, 1*(4), 559–580.

Hirschel, J. D. (1997). *Searching for reasonable protection of Fourth Amendment rights: The exclusionary rule and its alternates.* (Unpublished doctoral dissertation), SUNY, Albany, New York.

Kelling, G. L., & Coles, C. M. (1996). *Fixing broken windows: Restoring order and reducing crime in our communities.* New York: The Free Press.

Krauss, C. (1996, March 27). Bratton hailed as pioneer of new style of policing. *The New York Times*, p. B5.

Maple, J. (1999). *The crime righter: Putting the bad guys out of business.* New York: Doubleday.

Miller, D. C. (1991). *Handbook of research design and social measurement.* Newbury Park, CA: Sage Publications.

Nardulli, P. F. (1983). The societal cost of the exclusionary rule: An empirical assessment. *American Bar Foundation Research Journal, 3*, 585–609.

New York City Civilian Complaint Review Board Semiannual Status Report. (1997). V (2). January–December, 1997.

New York City Police Department. (1997a). *Courtesy, professionalism, and respect.* (Unpublished) New York: New York City Police Department.

New York City Police Department. (1997b). *Police student guide to the Police Academy-Police science.* (Unpublished) New York: New York City Police Department.

New York City Police Department. (1998a). *Legal bulletins.* (Unpublished) New York: New York City Police Department.

New York City Police Department. (1998b). *The Compstat process.* (Unpublished) New York: New York City Police Department.

Oaks, D. H. (1970). Studying the exclusionary rule in search and seizure. *The University of Chicago Law Review, 37*, 665–756.

Orfield, M. W., Jr. (1987). The exclusionary rule and deterrence: An empirical study of Chicago narcotics officers. *University of Chicago Law Review, 54*, 1016–1069.

Packer, H. (1966). The courts, the police, and the rest of us. *Journal of Criminal Law and Criminology, 57*, 238–240.

People v. Jackson, 79 NY 2d 907 (1992).

People v. Gokey, 469 NYS2d 618 (Ct. App. 1983).

Purdy, M. (1997, August 6). In New York, the handcuffs are one-size-fits-all. *The New York Times*, p. A1.

Rashbaum, W. K. (1996, April 23). Complaints against cops surge 135%. *New York Daily News*, p. 22.

Rayner, R. (1995, January 26). Wanted: A kinder, gentler cop. *New York Times*, magazine section, p. 22.

Rohde, D. (1998, April 9). $76 million for man shot by the police. *The New York Times*, Metro, p. B6.

Rossi, P. H., & Nock, S. L. (1982). *Measuring social judgments.* Beverly Hills, CA: Sage Publications.

Ryan, J. R. (1994). Community policing: Trends, policies, programs, and definitions. In A. R. Roberts (Ed.), *Critical issues in crime and justice* (pp. 127–144). Thousands Oaks, CA: Sage Publications.

Silverman, E. B. (1997, January 14). Why is city crime going down? Give cops most of the credit. *Daily News*, p. 27.

Silverman, E. B. (1999). *NYPD battles crime.* Boston: Northeastern University Press.

Sontag, D., & Barry, D. (1997, September 17). Police complaints settled, rarely resolved. *The New York Times,* pp. A1, B5.

Spiotto, J. E. (1973). Search and seizure: An empirical study of the exclusionary rule and its alternatives. *Journal of Legal Studies, 2,* 243–278.

Warren, E. (1959). Unanimous option that confessions obtained under duress must be excluded from criminal proceedings. In J. B. Simpson (Ed.) (1992). *Webster's II: New Riverside desk quotations.* Boston: Houghton Mifflin.

Zuccotti Committee Report. (1987, September). *Report on the recommendations of the mayor's advisory committee on police management and personnel policy.* New York: Zuccotti Committee.

Appendix

Specific Wording of Aggressiveness Measure

A good police officer is one who aggressively patrols his/her beat, stopping a number of cars, checking out people, running warrant checks on vehicles that look suspicious, and so forth.

Specific Wording of Legal Situations

Weapon Situations

Legal: . . . who fits the description of a robbery suspect. He is now sitting in a double parked vehicle along a street known for criminal activity. As you are walking your footpost, you approach the car from the passenger side (not the driver's side). No other individuals are in the car. Suddenly, you notice the outline of a gun apparently contained in a brown paper bag right next to the suspect. He seems very nervous and may well grab the gun at any moment. The passenger door is slightly open. Using all appropriate tactics, would you at this time grab the apparent gun in as cautious a manner as possible?

Illegal: . . . who double parks a vehicle along a street you are walking on. The driver then gets out and casually walks to an apartment building to ring a doorbell. You are walking your footpost and, as you approach the car, you notice the outline of a gun apparently contained in a brown paper bag on the passenger seat of the locked car. No one is in the car. Assuming you know a way to get in the car quickly and without damaging it, would you, at this time, grab the apparent gun in as cautious and tactically appropriate manner as possible?

Drug Situations

Legal: . . . who you know to be a drug dealer. He places what appears to be 100 marijuana cigarettes into an unlocked duffel bag. You immediately arrest the suspect who is holding the zippered shut duffel bag in his hand on a crowded streetcorner. You realize that the bag could easily be destroyed by throwing it into a nearby fire in a garbage can. Immediately, fearing destruction of the evidence, you take the bag from his hand. Would you without delay, at the arrest site, and in the presence of the arrestee, look inside the unlocked duffel bag?

Illegal: . . . who you have never seen before. He places what appears to be 100 marijuana cigarettes into a securely locked briefcase. You immediately arrest the suspect who now has the locked shut briefcase on the ground between his legs. You frisk the suspect with several other officers present leaving the briefcase on the ground. No key is found for the briefcase. Would you without delay, at the arrest site, and in the presence of the arrestee, force open and look inside the briefcase?

Additional Information on the Situations

Using *People v. Jackson*, the legal situation involved a hypothetical scenario that clearly amounts to the level of reasonable suspicion. The scenario contains a person who "fits the description of a robbery suspect." Furthermore, the suspect is still inside the car and is on a street known for criminal activity. The apparent gun is "right next to the suspect," obviously within reach. These criteria clearly meet the court's requirements in *Jackson* (i.e., reasonable suspicion, suspect is in the car, the gun is within reach) making it completely legal for officers to search the vehicle (see the above for wording of each of the scenarios).

An illegal scenario was also constructed. In this hypothetical situation, the individual is within walking distance of the car, but plainly far enough away so as not to be able to grab for the weapon. Since the person is not a suspect, is completely out of the vehicle, and is not even remotely able to grab the gun, it is clearly not permissible for police officers to conduct a search of the vehicle. Furthermore, the person has made no furtive movements and is "casually walking to an apartment to ring a doorbell." This vividly demonstrates that the individual represents no immediate danger and, therefore, officers cannot search the car for the weapon as per the New York State courts.

Similar situations were developed from the *Gokey* case. The legal scenario contained information that made it clear to officers that it was permissible to conduct a search. The suspect is a known drug dealer. He is immediately arrested and has the unlocked duffel bag in his hand. A nearby fire in a garage can (which is typical on cold days) is clearly a threat to the evidence. Furthermore, the search is to be done immediately and in the arrestee's presence. In the illegal scenario, however, the suspect is not a known drug dealer, the briefcase is locked shut without a key available, the case is on the ground between the suspect's legs, and is not being carried, several other officers are present, and the crime committed is very minor (i.e., possession of a small amount of marijuana). Under these circumstances, officers do not have the power to search the briefcase, but may arrest the individual, seize the briefcase, and then get a search warrant.

In Search of a Police System
From the *Quadrilheiros* to a Democratic Police System

4

LUÍS FIÃES FERNANDES

Contents

Introduction

This chapter intends to describe the evolution of the Portuguese police system, tracing its historical genesis and describing the changing of police organizational structures and of policing patterns along the institutional strengthening of the state. As we will see, the policing of the community was not always performed by the police. In fact, as we will show, the emergence of a police—understood as a specialized armed force with a legal mandate to keep the peace and enforce the law—only took place on an economically developed urban society in the 14th century.

Policing Medieval Lisbon

Portugal is one of the most ancient countries in Europe. Born of a small county in the Iberian Peninsula, its independence was forged in war (Ramos et al., 2010, pp. 40–45). The first centuries of the portucalense kingdom were marked by large-scale hunger and disease (plague) and by civil wars due to claims to the throne by the different monarchy lineages. The reconquista of the Iberian Peninsula to the Almorávida (Muslim) Empire and the intermittent warfare over territorial disputes with the kingdom of León and Castile shaped the future kingdom. The independence of the portucalense kingdom was recognized by the King Afonso VII of León and Castile by the Zamora Treaty in 1143.

By the early 13th century, the king's (Afonso II (1180–1223)) main ruling functions were the drafting of laws (e.g., the prohibition of private *vindicta*) and the administration of justice. Such ruling was aimed at the reinforcement of the king's power, which was frequently challenged by the noblemen and by the ecclesiastical local powers. Such ruling tasks were also used to strengthen the king's legitimacy while limiting the arbitrary power of the noblemen. An incipient administrative apparatus was developed along a permanent military force, making the central power present throughout the kingdom by the regulatory and supervisory action of the crown.

The Portuguese kingdom had two contrasting political and administrative realities: the feudal lands (*Senhorios*) and the municipalities (*Municipios*). In the feudal lands (economic, administrative, fiscal and judicial units under the authority of a secular nobleman or ecclesiastical entity), where the royal power was absent, the security of local communities rested on the *mesnada*, a mercenary military force that noblemen kept, and that was put at the service of the king (as part of the royal army) when the kingdom was at war.

The municipalities were one of the fundamental elements of Medieval Portugal, institutionalized by a charter granted by the king. Such charter put the local communities under the protection of the king against the noblemen arbitrariness (Araújo, 1853, pp. 49–50) and was used by the king to counterbalance the power held by the noblemen and the clergy, and as a way to strengthen the internal and external security of the kingdom (Araújo, 1864, p. 314). In these local communities, the king appointed the highest military authority in the municipality, the Alcaide-mor, who was in charge of the castle and hold the responsibility for the defense of the community (Cosme, 2006, p. 24; Ramos et al., 2010, pp. 47–77) as well as for the maintenance of public peace and the administration of justice. The Alcaide-mor commanded a militia appointed with the consent of the municipality. During the night the militia was always accompanied by a notary (Caetano, 1981, p. 497). The Alcaide and the castles were at the base of the Christian defense and protection system of the local communities as the castles were the only places that guaranteed the security of local communities against war and crime. The local communities also entrusted their protection to the *appelido*, a form of collective protection against attacks coming from the outside of the municipality. The *appelido* was based on the solidarity between all inhabitants of the municipality, as it was the duty of every single inhabitant to join a call to arms against threats to the community, and was the last resort to guarantee the freedom and security of the municipality (Araújo, 1853, p. 276).

The end of the reconquista in 1249 puts an end to the plundering of conquered Islamic cities. Wealth could no longer be achieved through war. A new economic base for the production of wealth had to be found. Such new way—based on the production of goods and exchange of commodities—introduced important changes in politics and society (Ramos et al., 2010, pp. 88–89). The king could now concentrate the state apparatus on expanding the king's authority throughout the kingdom (Ramos et al., 2010, p. 105), securing peace and administering justice.

By the middle of the 14th century, Lisbon was one of the largest cities in Europe. The Lisbon Port (midway between Northern Europe and the Mediterranean) harbored ships from various nations of Europe. The strength of the trade and economic prosperity attracted increasing numbers of inhabitants to the city, as well as criminals who sought to exploit the existing wealth in the city (Ramos et al., 2010, p. 83). Such a concentration of people attracted all sorts of crime, and the insecurity increased.

As crime mounted in Lisbon, King Fernando by Royal Charter of September 12, 1383, created the quadrilheiros (Cosme, 2006, pp. 27–28). The quadrilheiros were chosen among the men living in the municipality and appointed by judges and city council members for three years. They acted under the orders of the municipality and received no pay for their work. The quadrilheiros patrolled the streets in groups of four with the mission to guarantee the security of the territorial areas under their responsibility by keeping the public peace, preventing crimes, and watching over vagrants, foreigners, and inspecting the brothels and gambling houses (Cosme, 2006, pp. 29–31). To perform their duties, they were equipped with a wooden stick of at least nine-palmos (a *palmo* was equal to 22 centimeters (Barroca, 1992)) long (painted green with the royal arms) and a spear of 18-palmos long, purchased at their own expense. The hard conditions imposed upon the quadrilheiros led the chosen men to avoid the appointment and a new process of selection had to be implemented: the local judges and the city council members enlisted all eligible resident men, and then chose 1 man out of 20 to serve compulsorily as a quadrilheiro for three consecutive years.

By the end of 14th century, there were two distinct bodies performing security tasks: a royal body, represented by the Alcaide (appointed by the king) and his militia, in charge of the defense and security of local communities; and a municipal body, the quadrilheiros (appointed by the municipality) charged with keeping the public peace and preventing crime in the cities of Lisbon and Oporto (the quadrilheiros of Oporto were created around 1421 (Borges, 1980) or 1449 (Cosme, 2006), depending on the source). The quadrilheiros were the foundation of the Portuguese police system as for the first time a single-purpose body was created to ensure the security of the community on behalf of the king. For over 150 years the status of the quadrilheiros underwent several changes (they were exempted from taxes and military service) in order solve the chronic lack of men willing to be appointed. Still, the problem was not solved and crime found fertile ground, specially, in the city of Lisbon.

The Surveillance of Society

By the middle of the 18th century, Lisbon was one of the eight major cities on the planet, but on November 1, 1755, a brutal earthquake wiped-out more than two thirds of the buildings (Ramos et al., 2010, pp. 363–364). The need to rebuild the city from the chaos that followed created the conditions for social and institutional transformation (Ramos et al., 2010, p. 357). The state moved to the center of society by imposing its regulatory power. Such changes would affect the police system.

Five years after the earthquake, by royal decree of June 25, 1760, King José I established the General Intendancy of Police of the Court and of the Kingdom (*Intendência-Geral da Polícia da Corte e do Reino*) in Lisbon (On August 5, 1817, it was set up in Oporto (Borges, 1980)), under the tutelage of the kingdom's State Affairs Secretariat. The Intendancy hold "wide and unlimited" power over all subjects concerning the "public tranquility". Such power must be understood at the light of the 18th century European concept of police, which was understood as the good administration of the city and the civility. That was the reason why its police powers covered such tasks as public security, criminal investigation, political, fiscal, administrative, health, and foreign police, as well as the administrative licensing of certain activities, the management of education and correctional houses. Recognizing the dangers to the public health by the practice of throwing sewage and household waste out one's windows (Barreiros, 2009, p. 34) the Intendancy regulated the waste disposal and set up a public lighting system in Lisbon by December 1780 (Cardoso, 2000, pp. 500–501), as a way to prevent crime at night time.

The General Intendancy of Police was led by a General Intendant of Police and the policing system was reorganized based on the division of the city of Lisbon in neighborhoods, each consisting of 2,000 houses. In each of the neighborhoods, a police commissioner, assisted by police corporals appointed annually by the Intendant General of Police, guaranteed the security. At the same time, the First Secretary of State, Sebastião José de Carvalho e Melo (commonly known as Marquis de Pombal) used the law and the General Intendancy as instruments of population control and repression against any attempt to neutralize the royal power. The control of the population was achieved, for example, by appointing a local authority to each neighborhood, who kept a record of the people living in it, their livelihood, and professions in order to achieve a "perfect knowledge" of the unoccupied or inactive men living in his jurisdiction. All people moving to another neighborhood had to inform the officials and, upon arriving to another location, had to present themselves to the officials of the new place. The captains of the vessels entering the port of Lisbon had to declare the number of passengers on board and their quality and, before coming to shore, had to be registered and, while in the kingdom, had to carry at all times a passport or a "*carta de legitimação*" (individual credentials). The period from around 1750 to 1777 (when Pombal resigns) was characterized by censorship, arbitrary arrests, and barbaric executions (Ramos et al., 2010, p. 376).

The rise of Queen Mary (1777–1816) as regent of the kingdom in November 1776, led to a period of political appeasement (Santos, 1999, p. 56). In spite of the changes made previously to the policing system, crime continued to rage in Lisbon. On January 18, 1780, a new General Intendant was appointed. Faced by an urgent need to curb crime and violence, the General Intendant requested 13 patrols (consisting of 9 troops of cavalry and 15 of infantry) to the army to deploy to the 13 neighborhoods of Lisbon. The deployment of the army patrols did not solve the crime problems of the city due to the prevailing undisciplined among every rank (Santos, 1999, pp. 57–58). With unflagging resolved to fight the chronic criminality and insecurity in the city of Lisbon, the General Intendant set up a force made up of 100 retired army personnel. This police force was publicly presented for the first time on August 11, 1793 (Cosme, 2006, p. 42). Their effectiveness in fighting crime and keeping the public peace led to their regular establishment in the city of Lisbon in December 1801, under the name of Royal Guard of Police (Guarda Real de Polícia). In 1824, a similar force was established in Oporto.

The installation of a force of such nature and the delivery of its command to the Earl of Novion (a French exile aristocrat who fled to Portugal following the French Revolution) marked the genesis of the French influence in the Portuguese police system. Novion will use the French gendarmerie (established in 1791) as the model for the design and implementation of the Royal Guard of Police in Portugal. The Royal Guard of Police was a military force with 683 men (cavalry and infantry) with security and public order missions and its commander was under the direct orders of the General Intendant of Police. The Royal Guard of Police replaced the ineffective quadrilheiros and determined the end of this body of police (Santos, 1999, pp. 59–61).

In 1807 the invasion of Portugal by Napoleon's troops caused the regent Prince D. João VI to seek refuge in Brazil. The Intendancy "model" was taken to Brazil by the Portuguese court and by the Decree of May 10, 1808, the General Intendancy of Police was officially established in Brazil with the same scope of missions.

Due to the role of resistance played by the Royal Guard of Police to the French invaders, the French administration replaced it by the Military Guard of Police, and all ranks of the Royal Guard of Police that had not shown clear support for the invaders were compulsorily retired. The Royal Guard of Police was restored in March 1809, and the Military Guard became extinct (Cosme, 2006, p. 43).

As a sign of the times, and as a evidence of the continental European despotism, the first political police (the secret police) was established in 1808 under the supervision of General Intendant for the king's protection (Gouvêa, 1835, p. v).This "high police" (Brodeur, 2007), along the gendarmerie (the Royal Guard of Police) are clear marks of the French influence in the Portuguese police system.

Instability and Reform

The French troops left the kingdom in 1814. Meanwhile, the policy pursued by the regent prince, who was still in Brazil, aggravated the financial conditions of the kingdom, despite the repeated warnings of the Council of Regency about the growing social instability. The ruinous state of the public finances of the kingdom, the absent monarch in Brazil (while keeping a huge army, one of the largest in Europe in relation to the kingdom's population), the general discontent, and political tension led to an army uprising that ended in the 1820 liberal revolution.

The revolution took in the ideals of the French Revolution, a new Constitution came into force, and some fundamental laws were superseded. The postrevolution period was marked by intense legislative activity, in line with the European context of renewing its criminal justice institutions, but also because of the need of institutional changes. The expulsion of the queen from the kingdom for refusing to swear to the new Constitution led to a weakening of the regime and, at the same time, to its radicalization (Ramos et al., 2010, p. 469).

The era following the revolution was politically, socially, and economically complex. In such context, in March 1823, the Liberals created the National Guard mainly to defend the Constitution (and to ensure the safety and tranquility of the people). The National Guard was a force of military nature comprised of infantry and cavalry troops, without a central command and subordinate to local civil authorities. The armament and equipment of each Guard member were obtained at his own expense.

In May 1823, a coup d'état marked the first absolutist reaction and the Constitution of 1822 was suspended. The National Guard was dissolved on June 13 and on August 21, 1826, an attempt to reinstate it fails. In 1834 the liberals put an end to the ancient regime and start the rebuilding of the police system, finding inspiration in the British experience. Only at the end of the civil war in 1834, was the National Guard reinstated, and organized along the lines of a citizen militia responsible for the kingdom's internal security (Cerezales, 2011, p. 24). The short history of this force was a consequence of the civil war between liberals and absolutists during the period from April 1824 to 1834 (Cosme, 2006, p. 44). It also shows that in troubled times (the army, after its upheavals of 1820, 1823, and 1824, was divided and had descended into disorder) the police force was instrumental in supporting a given cause. The Royal Guard of Police supported the absolutist cause. However, the National Guard, with the express mission of defending the Constitution, protected the liberal regime and was used as a counterweight to the Royal Guard of Police. The Royal Guard of Police was disbanded in 1834, at the end of the civil war, by the liberals because of its support of the absolutists.

As a result of the political, social, and army upheavals, the problems of crime and insecurity were serious in Lisbon and the situation worsened with the dissolving of the office of the General Intendant of Police in November 1833. All police services were transferred to the dependency of the Prefect of the province and, later, from 1835 on, to the civilian District Governors* who had complete control over the police.

In July 1834, in order to face the extreme insecurity in Lisbon, the Municipal Guard (*Guarda Municipal*) was created in Lisbon and a year later in Porto. The Municipal Guard, with identical characteristics to the Royal Guard of Police, emerged as a local police force of a military nature, comprised of cavalry and infantry troops, commanded by army officers, and was under the orders of the police commissioners and parish magistrates. Its mission was to police the streets, ensuring the public peace, and monitoring of prisoners. The Municipal Guard became the only police force in the country (Nogueira, 1856, p. 100) before being eliminated in 1867.

The coups and civil wars between 1834 and 1851 added to the difficult financial situation and resulted in the destruction of the civil and criminal justice apparatuses and political institutions. The Old Regime, its institutions and privileges, declined, and oppression and social cleavages that characterized the period began a new, albeit, divided stage of political tensions. Governments were formed and fell at the whim of inexperienced politicians (Ramos et al., 2010). Given the fragile security situation in 1838, the Law of February 22, 1838, created the Municipal Public Security Bodies (*Corpos Municipais de Segurança Pública*) in each district.

* The district is an administrative circumscription that corresponds to the territorial jurisdiction of the civil government, a public administration body that represents the central government in the district and is nowadays subordinate to the Ministry of Internal Administration.

Finally, from 1852 on, the Portuguese society entered a new phase of freedom, major reforms, and economic development. With momentary stability and economic development, and through the Decree of July 2, 1867, King Luís created the Civic Police in the cities of Lisbon and Oporto. The text preceding the decree is, even today, true:

> Public security is an essential condition for the existence of any well-organized society.... The police must cease any disturbance in the economy of the organized and constituted society.... The police officers must be individuals who by their morality, honesty and prudence call upon them the sympathies of the public, so that the public, doing justice to their efforts, never deny them its support.*

The Civic Police was a district police dependent on the Civil Governor and headed by a General Commissioner.

By decree of December 24, 1868, the Municipal Guard was restructured through the merger of the municipal guards of Lisbon and Oporto into a single body. This new body was under a double dependency: from the Ministry of War, for promotions and discipline, and from the Ministry of the Kingdom, for the public order and security. The following year, a General Command was set in Lisbon. The Municipal Guard becomes the main force used by the monarchy to counter the Republicans.

The period from 1880 to 1910 is a time of economic crisis and high public debt. The proclamation of the republic of Brazil, the English ultimatum, and the bankruptcy of the main institution that provided credit to Portugal created conditions for increased opposition to the monarchy and for greater political relevance of the anarchists (Cosme, 2006, pp. 87–89). The growing wave of social protest associated with the increase in crime experienced in the capital coupled with the fact that police were not achieving the desired results led to a reorganization of the civic police of Lisbon in order to make it more effective in its missions. The organizational restructuring created three divisions: the public security police (*polícia de segurança pública*), with the mission of surveillance and maintenance of public order, traffic police, temples and public meetings police; the administrative inspection police (*polícia de inspecção administrative*) with the mission of monitoring the use and possession of weapons, foreigners activities, use of weights and measures, gambling houses, inns, and sanitation; and the preventive and judicial investigative police (*polícia de Investigação judicial e preventiv*) charged with criminal investigation (Cosme, 2006, p. 91).

This reform begun in 1893 and was completed in 1896. The civil nature of the police was well marked in their form of organization, uniforms, and equipment. The force was under the command of a General Commissioner, usually recruited from army officers. Initially, police officers performed their

* Translation by the author.

duties in uniform and only carried a defense weapon called the *terçado* (a short, wide sword). Only in exceptional circumstances, were the police officers allowed to carry firearms. In fact, the use of firearms, batons, and whistle only became mandatory after 1936.

In 1898, because of a new government, a further reorganization of the police was implemented. Thus, each district civil police had public security police, preventive police, administrative police, and criminal investigation police. In spite of the succeeding reorganizations that lasted until the late 19th century, the civic police kept their civil and urban nature. The worsening of the political and social situation with the intensification of antimonarchy demonstrations, led to an increase in the number of officers in some civic police bodies. The growing social unrest and antimonarchy sentiment culminated in the regicide of King Carlos and the assassination of Prince Luís Filipe in February 1908.

In Search of a Police System

In October 1910, the new political system introduced changes in the administration and police system. The Ministry of the Kingdom gave way to the Interior Ministry, which continued the control over the police. The Lisbon civic Police that was considered by the new Republican power a protector of the monarchy, under the revolutionary impulse, was dissolved on October 6 to be reinstated again on October 9.

The new Republican power needed a force of its own to ensure the consolidation of the regime. Thus, on October 12, 1910, still under the revolutionary momentum, a Republican Guard (*Guarda Republicana*) was established in the cities of Lisbon and Oporto. On May 3, 1911, it was renamed the National Republican Guard (*Guarda Nacional Republicana*). The National Republican Guard had national organization, a military nature, and public order and security missions: The first police force in Portuguese police history with nationwide jurisdiction and centralized command and control was created.

The first Republic was a very troubled period. Between January 1920 and July 1921, there were 11 governments. The National Republican Guard was converted into an army, concentrated in Lisbon, served as a *referee* in key governance combinations (Ramos et al., 2010, pp. 616–617). In 1911, the National Republican Guard absorbed the Municipal Guard.

The worsening economic situation was experienced in 1917 and gave rise to a new social reality marked by a great contestation, instability, and social conflict. In 1918, a new reform of the police services established the General Directorate of Public Security (*Direcção Geral de Segurança Pública*) under the Ministry of the Interior, responsible for the supervision of all national police services. The Directorate was organized in the following manner: the public security police, the investigation police, the administrative police, the preventive police, the immigration police, and the municipal police. The existing civic police were integrated into the public security police.

Despite the objectives of the reform—to make the police services more effective—the fact was that the political and social agitation did not end and resulted in successive reorganizations of the police system. On February 1919, the security police and the preventive police were reorganized. As of March 1919, except for the emigration police, all police forces were, again, subordinate to the civil governments.

The prevailing instability led to a further restructuring of the police services. In October 1922, a new restructuring within the General Directorate of Public Security: the civic police were restructured into four sections: administrative police, public security police, preventive police, and state security police.

In 1924, the preventive police were remodeled (the preventive police were instituted on June 23, 1824, as a descendant of the secret police) and later on the same year, the General Directorate of Public Security was abolished and replaced by the High Inspectorate of Public Security (*Inspecção Superior de Segurança Pública*).

The military coup of May 28, 1926 ended the I Republic. The establishment of the military dictatorship resulted in a further reorganization of police services. Some police civic bodies were dissolved, just to be reinstituted later on. The Police of Lisbon (*Polícia de Informações de Lisboa*) was created and, a year later, the Information Police of Oporto (Pimentel, 2007, p. 24), with the mission to prevent political crimes.

In February 1927, in Lisbon and Oporto, there was an attempted military coup with the participation of police officers. The politicization and involvement of officials and police officers in the coup attempt (Borges, 1980) led to a restructuring of the police system. In March 1927, the General Directorate of Public Security was created and the High Inspectorate of Public Security was extinct. The Public Security Police became autonomous with the civic police, which was now extinct, leaving the Public Security Police with a centralized and unified national command in Lisbon and in the direct dependency of the Interior Ministry. The investigation police were transferred to the Minister of Justice and Religious Affairs. In 1928, the General Directorate of Public Security was renamed General Intendancy of Police.

The 1930 to 1932 years were marked by political–military instability. As tension escalated, in 1931 the Police (*Polícia de Informações*) of the Ministry of Interior changed its name to Portuguese International Police (*Polícia Internacional Portuguesa*) and moved to the Ministry of Justice and Religious Affairs' (*Ministério da Justiça e Cultos*) tutelage. On July 30 of the same year, it returned to the Ministry of Interior as an autonomous division with foreign police tasks and counterespionage and Communism repression missions (Pimentel, 2007, pp. 24–25).

In 1932, the Social and Political Police (*Polícia de Defesa Política e Social*) was created under the Ministry of Interior (Pimentel, 2007, p. 25). In the same year, the government implemented a new police restructuring, the General Intendancy of Police was abandoned, and General Directorate of Public Security (*Direcção-Geral de Segurança Pública*) was created. All police bodies under the Ministry of Interior were subordinate to this "new" General Directorate, including the criminal investigation police that had left the tutelage of the Ministry of Justice and Religious Affairs. This was a clear attempt to concentrate all police services under the same Directorate. At this point, the police system showed clear signs of fragmentation (the Public Security Police and the National Republican Guard were under the tutelage of the Ministry of Interior, the Criminal Investigation Police under the Ministry of Justice). However, the policy pursued to aim at reducing the number of autonomous police forces by merging them in bodies with single and centralized command. However, the attempt failed and the General Directorate of Public Security was disbanded in 1935.

In 1933, the "Estado Novo" was established. The new regime could be characterized as authoritarian, nationalist, and corporative that did not admit political pluralism. The new regime sparked opposition, expressed through strikes (1934), conspiracies (1935 and 1936), and bombing campaigns (1937). The Surveillance and State Defense Police and the special courts dealt with these cases and, from 1931 on, the political police neutralized several coup attempts. In fact, the new regime was going to use the political police that had already proved some efficiency to fight political crimes. On August 29, 1933, the Surveillance and Defense State Police (*Polícia de Vigilância e Defesa do Estado*) was established from the merger of the International Police and of the Social and Political Defense Police with the task of preventing political and social crimes. The "new" police was organized into two sections: the social and protection section and the international section. Most of its leaders were officers of the armed forces (Pimentel, 2007, pp. 26–27). The Surveillance and Defense State Police had powers of investigation and employed physical violence to obtain confessions that could be used in court. Repression and violence also was used by other police forces in keeping public order. The political police played such an important role in protecting the regime that its Director communicated weekly with Salazar, the president of the Council (Ramos et al., 2010, pp. 650–651).

In 1945, the International and State Defense Police (*Polícia Internacional de Defesa do Estado*) replaced the Surveillance and State Defense Police. The International and State Defense Police was the political regime police of the Estado Novo, responsible for repression of political dissidence. It also had border surveillance missions and foreigners' control, as well as the repression of illegal immigration (Pimentel, 2007, p. 11). It was considered as an independent judicial body, concentrating all the functions of prevention and repression of political crimes against the internal and external security of the state (Pimentel, 2007, p. 31). The action of this political police, from 1961 onwards, focused on the fight against the African liberation movements, as part of the Portuguese colonial war effort. Yet, it is the action against the Portuguese Communist Party that shapes their action until the late 1960s (Pimentel, 2007, pp. 11–12; Ramos et al., 2010, pp. 694–695). In 1964, the International and State Defense Police was renamed the General Directorate of Security (Direcção-Geral de Segurança).

At the end of 1945, the criminal investigation police was renamed the judiciary police (*Polícia Judiciária*) and put under the tutelage of the Ministry of Justice. In June 1949, the Council of Public Security (*Conselho de Segurança Pública*) chaired by the Minister of Interior was established to coordinate the activities of the different police services. The members of the council were the General Commanders of the National Republican Guard and of Public Security Police, and the Director of the International Police for State Defense. This was an attempt to establish a coordination mechanism within the police system, although very limited as only one ministry was represented, which cut out other police services.

Policing in a Democracy

On April 25, 1974, a military revolution led to the fall of the dictatorship. The National Salvation Junta, formed by seven generals, assumed the legislative power, ousted the General Directorate of Security, and redistributed some of its missions to other police bodies. The Ministry of Interior changed its name to Ministry of Internal Administration and the National Republican Guard and the Public Security Police were kept under its tutelage. During the early years of the revolution, there were some attempts to merge the two police forces by appointing a common general commander. In 1976, with the approval of the new Constitution such a merger was ruled out.

The first years after the 1974 revolution, the economy, inflation, unemployment, and the development of basic public services were the main priorities of the government, and the police system had to wait almost 10 years before major changes. During these first years, the various police bodies went through a period of uncertainty and limited their interventions to a minimum so as not to be associated with the previous political regime where police were used as the government's main instruments of political surveillance and repression. This led many people to distrust the police and avoid any voluntary contact with its officers. Aware of such past and context, the new democratic government tried to introduce new practices and personnel statutes that would aid the democratization process of Portuguese society and, at the same time, avoided any further loss of authority by the police. A new paradigm of police action that emphasized the civic orientation over a repressive one had to be implemented.

In 1984, in the face of increasing international and domestic terrorist threat and mounting insecurity and confronted with a total absence of coordination among a multiplicity of police bodies, the Internal Security Law was approved (Law No. 20/87, of 12 June) and the Internal Security* System came to light. One of the objectives of this system was to improve coordination among the several members of the internal security system, mainly the police. The main organs of the system included:

- The High Council for Internal Security (*Conselho Superior de Segurança Interna*), an interministerial consultation organ to the Prime Minister on internal security matters. The organ was presided over by the Prime Minister and several ministers (Internal Administration, Justice, and Finance) seated in the council, as well as the top commanders and directors of the internal security players (which included not only police bodies, but also the intelligence security service and the aeronautic security authority).
- The Security Coordinator Cabinet (*Gabinete Coordenador de Segurança*), a specialized organ for the consultation and advising on the technical and operational coordination of the internal security players. This cabinet was directly by the Prime Minister (normally delegated on the Minister of the Internal Administration).

In 2007, a new internal security Law was passed (Law No. 53/2008, of August, 29). The main changes introduced by this law were the creation of the General Secretary of the Internal Security System. The General Secretary office was created to strengthen the cooperation among the several internal security players. To achieve such objective, the law granted to the General Secretary extensive powers of coordination, direction, and operational command and control of the internal security players. The current internal security players† include:

* Internal Security is the activity developed by the state to guarantee order, security, and public peace; protect the citizens and property; prevent and repress criminality; and contribute to assure the normal functioning of democratic institutions; the regular exercise of rights, liberties, and fundamental guaranties of the citizens; and the respect for the democratic legality (article 1.º, n.º 1).

† We will limit our description to the police bodies as the intelligence security service and aeronautic security authority, in this chapter. One of the police bodies, already extinct, but worth mentioning, was the Fiscal Guard. The Fiscal Guard was a special corps of troops responsible for border control and the prevention and repression of tax and customs fraud. It was under the Ministry of Finances, in peacetime, for operational policing purposes, and of the Ministry of National Defense, in case of war. The historical antecedent of the Fiscal Guard was the Customs Guard (*Guarda de Barreiras*) founded in 1885, a liberal creation that was meant to discipline the scattered and disjointed tax system of the ancient regime. In 1993, Fiscal Guard was extinct as an independent body, and its functions were integrated into the Fiscal Brigade of the National Republican Guard.

- The National Republican Guard (*Guarda Nacional Republicana*) has its historical roots in the Royal Guard of Police and in the Republican Guard. The National Republican Guard (NRG) is a Gendarmerie type of police force constituted by military personnel (it is the largest police force with strength around 25,000 militaries and 1,000 civilian staff) organized in a Special Corp of Troops. It has a double tutelage: (a) in peace time, it depends on the Ministry of Internal Administration for recruitment, administration, discipline, and for all missions related to policing matters; (b) it depends on the Ministry of the National Defense for the purpose of the military doctrine, armament, and equipment standardization. In case of war or a crisis situation, this force may be placed under the operational command of the Chief of the General Staff of the Armed Forces. The National Republican Guard is a national police force with territorial jurisdiction mainly in rural areas. Its main missions cover the activities of public order police, criminal police, environmental police, transit police, fiscal police, maritime police, and administrative police.
- The Public Security Police (*Polícia de Segurança Pública*) has its roots in the Civic Police and is currently the second largest police force in Portugal (the current strength is around 22,000 fully sworn police officers and 1,000 civilians). It is a national civilian police force under the Ministry of Internal Administration tutelage with the territorial jurisdiction over the main urban centers. Its main missions are public order, criminal investigation, VIP protection, and licensing and control of weapons and explosives, and private security, licensing, and control.
- The Judiciary Police (*Polícia Judiciária*) descended from the Civic Police and is a criminal investigation police organized hierarchically under the Minister of Justice tutelage. Its mission is to assist the judicial authorities, namely the public prosecution, in the investigation of serious and organized crimes. In 1977, the Judicial Police experienced the first major reorganization, leading to a process of territorial expansion.
- The Foreigners and Borders Service (*Serviço de Estrangeiros e Fronteiras*) is a police under the Ministry of Internal Administration's tutelage. Initially, in 1974, this police service was a branch of the Public Security Police, and only gained autonomy in 1976. Its main mission includes border control and monitoring of the activities of foreigners in Portugal as well as criminal investigation of illegal immigration. Its fundamental objective is to implement the Portuguese immigration and asylum policy. As a criminal police body, in the terms of criminal procedural law, the criminal investigations are performed under the direction of the competent judicial authority.

- The Maritime Police (*Polícia Maritíma*) is a remote descendent of the maritime police of the port of Lisbon (1818). It integrates the operational structure of the National Maritime Authority and is comprised of navy personnel and militarized agents under the Ministry of Defense's tutelage. The General Director and Deputy Director of National Maritime Authority are inherently the General Commander and the Deputy Commander of the Maritime Police. The Maritime Police have several areas of jurisdiction, namely: the policing of harbors and beaches and the inspection of ships, ensuring the compliance with laws and regulations in the area of national maritime jurisdiction, in particular, in the public spaces at sea, in inland waters, and in waters under national sovereignty.

The police system also comprises the Municipal Police, which is under the mayor (currently only the main municipalities have such a police service) and has jurisdiction within the boundaries of the municipality. The Municipal Police are municipal services that perform the tasks of administrative police, namely to enforce general municipal laws, building and environmental laws, and traffic regulations.

Increasing crime rates, mounting insecurity, shrinking public resources, and an ever-growing demand from the public for more security led the government, in the 1990s, to make crime prevention and the policing reform a priority. The democratization of the state and its increased legitimacy contributed partly to the enlargement of policing to new social sectors. The individual's security and personal feelings of insecurity became the center of the police activity. The two main police bodies (Republican National Guard and Public Security Police) implemented special community policing programs, and the official term *policiamento de proximidade* was coined (Costa, 1996). The 1990s can be characterized by the deployment of a group of special policing programs directed toward school and the elderly and victims' support programs. These programs were tailored to meet the special needs of different citizens and were implemented through a series of different actions (schools are visited by police officers who speak about crime prevention, awareness programs against violence and drugs, and elderly assistance actions aiming to raise awareness about certain types of crime). The Public Security Police (PSP), in the last quarter of 2006, launched a pilot project called Integrated Proximity Policing Program (*Programa Integrado de Policiamento de Proximidade*).* This program was borne out of the necessity to manage strategically all the special policing programs that the PSP had deployed throughout the past decade and reinforce crime prevention.

* Find the official site at http://www.psp.pt/psp/proximidade/pipp/psp.html

In 1995, another essential step in the direction of a truly democratic police system was taken with the creation of the General Inspectorate of Internal Administration (GIIA). The GIIA is an external inspection service and its main task is to guarantee the fundamental rights of the citizens before the exercise of police powers. The GIIA is under the Ministry of Internal Administration tutelage.

As a consequence of a long history of reforms and counter-reforms motivated mainly by political struggles and regime changes, the current Portuguese police system can be described as fragmented (a multiplicity of police bodies*—GNR, PSP, PJ, SEF, PM—all with national jurisdiction and under a multiplicity of tutelages), concurrent (some police organizations share the same legal jurisdictions, such as the National Republican Guard and the Public Security Police), centralized command and operational decentralization (each service has one national command/direction and have several local branches with varying levels of decentralization).

Final Remarks

In the first centuries of the Portucalense County existence the security of local communities against war and crime rested on the Alcaide-mor and its militia. The end of the reconquista, the expansion of the king's power to the entire kingdom, and the concentration of people in urban centers, made possible by the accumulation of wealth, generated the need for a police body, specially created for enforcing public peace. Such body—the quadrilheiros—was created by King Fernando by Royal Charter of September 12, 1383. Today the quadrilheiros are considered the foundation body of the Portuguese police system. Up until the middle of the 18th century the security of the local communities in the cities of Lisbon and Oporto was guaranteed by two distinct bodies: the Alcaide and his militia; and the quadrilheiros. In spite of their existence, the fact was that the insecurity—mainly in Lisbon—was chronic, and the creation of the Royal Guard of Police on the 19th century will put an end to the quadrilheiros.

The earthquake of 1755 created the conditions for social and institutional transformation. The General Intendancy of Police of the Court and of the Kingdom with its extensive powers over all sectors of society embodied the 18th century European concept of police, searching for the "perfect

* In Portugal, the current ratio police per 100,000 inhabitants is around 400. This ratio varies according to the source used. According to *The Seventh United Nations Survey on Crime Trends and the Operations of Criminal Justice Systems (1998–2000)*, the ratio is 491 (in year 2000). If we consider another source, G. Barclay and C. Tavares (2003), *International comparisons of criminal justice statistics* (No. 12/2003), United Kingdom: Home Office, the ratio is 467 (in year 2001).

knowledge" of the population. The creation of the Royal Guard of Police and of the secret police are a clear evidence of the continental European despotism influence in the Portuguese police system.

From 1800 on, the Portuguese police system was influenced first by the French policing experience and after by the ideals of the French Revolution. Instability marked the 19th century; reforms and counter-reforms succeeded at a high rhythm, most often as a consequent of political tensions and power struggles between ideologies and regimes. The liberal government, after the end of the Ancient Régime, wanted to create a modern civil police and created the Municipal Guards under the influence of the British model. The consequence of the political turmoil that marked the 19th century was, in a first moment, their militarization, and finally their integration on the army. The army, due to the lack of a police corps to enforce the law on the rural areas, took the police role, always on a supplementary role of the civilian authorities.

In the 20th century, from 1933 to 1974, the police system tended toward general stabilization around the number, nature, and jurisdiction of the police bodies. At the legislative level, an effort was made to create coordination mechanisms, although from the short life that they had one might conclude that, in practical terms, the efforts did not succeed. One particular aspect of the 1933 to 1974 period was the role played by the political police as a support pillar of the regime.

After 1974, the democratization of the state and its increased legitimacy contributed partly to the enlargement of policing to new social sectors. The police took some time to adapt to the new policing environment, where the individuals' security and personal feelings of insecurity became the center of the police activity. The deep lack of a coordination mechanism led to the creation of the internal security system.

From a chronological perspective, the political, social, and economic context varied throughout the centuries and as a result of different contexts multiple and frequent short-term reforms were implemented. These reforms affected the missions, the nature of the police organizations, and personnel status (varying between a military or civilian nature), as well as the territorial jurisdictions (varying from local to central). All of these changes affected the very structure of the police system and pushed forward the democratic policing in Portugal by the need to find new solutions to the problems of crime and insecurity and provide better police service with ever-shrinking resources.

References

Araújo, A. H. D. C. E. (1853). *Historia de Portugal*. Lisboa: Viuva Bertrand e Filhos.

Araújo, A. H. D. C. E. (1864). *Historia de Portugal*. Lisboa: Viuva Bertrand e Filhos.

Barreiros, M. H. (2009). Urban landscapes: Houses, streets and squares of 18th century Lisboa. In R. Laitinen & T. V. Cohen (Eds.), *Cultural history of early modern European streets* (pp. 11–38). Leiden, The Netherlands: Brill.

Barroca, M. J. (1992). Medidas-Padrão medievais Portuguesas. *Revista da faculdade de letras, Universidade do Porto,* II, *IX*.

Borges, A. J. (1980). *História da polícia do Porto*. Porto: Edição do Autor.

Brodeur, J. (2007). High and low policing in post-9/11 Times. *Policing, 1*(1), 25–37. doi:10.1093/police/pam002

Caetano, M. (1980). *Manual de direito administrativo,* 10th ed. (Vol. 1). Coimbra: Almedina.

Caetano, M. (1981). *História do direito Português*. Lisboa: Editorial Verbo.

Caetano, M. (1994). *Estudos de história da administração pública Portuguesa*. Coimbra: Coimbra Editora.

Cardoso, J. L. (2000). Água, iluminação e esgotos em Lisboa nos finais do século XVIII. *Análise Social, XXXV*(156), 495–509.

Cerezales, D. P. (2011). Portugal à Coronhada. Protesto Popular e Ordem Pública nos Séculos XIX e XX. Lisboa: Tinta da China.

Cosme, J. (2006). *História da polícia de segurança pública. Das origens à actualidade*. Lisboa: Edições Silabo.

Costa, A. (1996). *Para a modernização da actividade policial*. Lisboa: Ministério da Administração Interna.

Costa, F. M. D. (1989). *Do antigo regime ao liberalismo, 1750–1850*. Lisboa: Vega.

Falcone, D. N. (1998). The Illinois State Police as an archetypal model. *Police Quarterly, 1*(3), 61–83.

Ferrão, A. (1925). *A 1.ª invasão francesa*. Coimbra: Imprensa da Universidade de Coimbra.

Gouvêa, J. C. B. D. (1835). *Policia secreta dos ultimos tempos do reinado do Senhor D. João VI.: E sua continuação ate' Dezembro de 1826*. Lisboa: Imprensa de Candido Antonio da Silva Carvalho.

Mennell, S. (1992). *Norbert Elias. An introduction*. Ireland: University College Dublin Press.

Nogueira, J. F. H. (1856). *O municipio no Seculo XIX*. Lisboa: Typographia do Progresso.

Noronha, E. (1954). *A guarda real de polícia. Origens da Guarda Nacional Republicana (II parte)* (Vols. 1, 2). Lisboa: CG/GNR.

Pimentel, I. F. (2007). *A história da PIDE*. Rio de Mouros: Temas e Debates.

Ramos, R., Sousa, B. V. E., & Monteiro, N. G. (2010). *História de Portugal,* 4th ed. Lisboa: A Esfera dos Livros.

Santos, A. P. R. D. (1999). *O estado e a ordem pública. As instituições militares Portuguesas*. Lisboa: Instituto Superior de Ciências Sociais e Políticas.

Silva, L. A. R. D. (1971). *História de Portugal nos Séculos XVII e XVIII*. Lisboa: Imprensa Nacional.

Teixeira, N. S., Lourenço, N., & Piçarra, N. (2006). *Estudo para a reforma do modelo de Organização do Sistema de Segurança Interna. Relatório Preliminar*. Lisboa: Instituto Português de Relações Internacionais.

Policing, Politics and Democracy

II

Policing in Brazil at the Beginning of the 21st Century

Severe Challenges in Developing Countries

5

EMILIO E. DELLASOPPA

Private militias develop after the void of the police.

O Estado de São Paulo. Sunday, January 16, 2000. p. A1.

Contents

Introduction

In the 1980s, Brazil experienced improvements in its political processes and institutions, with democracy and civil rights re-established after almost two decades of authoritarian military rule. But, the liberal economic reforms in the 1990s also increased the inequality in the distribution of income and other social indicators, a chronic characteristic of the Brazilian social structure. The political democratization process did not include social democracy or welfare improvements for most of the Brazilian population. An inverse relationship is observed between the process of democratization experienced in Brazil and the increase in violence and crime levels in Brazilian society, as measured by crime and mortality statistics.

At the same time, Brazilian citizens' expectancies about the police have grown faster than the criminality levels, as well as the institutions' incapacity of coming up with a solution. The inefficiency and the corruption of police groups and many police officers are a well-known fact.

This chapter explores some characteristics of the public police force in the Rio de Janeiro State, Brazil. Police in Brazil are organized under a federal constitutional concept, including military and civil police for each state of the federation. Presently, as in most developing countries, public opinion sees the police as a part of the violence and insecurity problem, and not as the solution. Seven hypotheses are raised on police and their relation to specific characteristics of democracy in developing countries, on changes of the monopoly of legitimate violence by the state, on state and government's responses to public security problems, and on regulation strategies tested and implemented in Brazil. The conditions and possibilities of regulation of police forces are examined against the weaknesses of democratic regimes and the challenges that police and democratic institutions must face in their fight to change the present situation.

Crime, in Brazil, lingers. Challenges also include impunity and the fragility of the judiciary system, which uses a penal law with extremely severe punishments that most of the time are *not* enforced. In the near future, the prisons will continue to overcrowd with poor and illiterate people. Social inequalities will remain, and it will be a very difficult task for Brazilians to change their structure of social relations. Brazil is changing its economy in a profound and painful way, but crime and crime control seem to be at the end of the agenda. As a front-line social control institution, police forces face a severe challenge.

New Scenarios, Threats, and Challenges to Policing in Brazil Within the Context of Globalization

This chapter discusses policing in Brazil under the emerging security threats, emphasizing the situation of the Rio de Janeiro State and its challenges at the beginning of the 21st century. At the end of the 20th century, we witnessed a far-reaching change in the situation of the policies everywhere, compared with the situation 30 years ago. We observed diverse forms of extinction of the model of state-owned policing that Sir Robert Peel established in the 19th century, imitated and/or modified elsewhere with different degrees of success. From the point of view of social control, it was a successful regulation process of the social disorder originating in the increase of criminality and in the repression of forms of diversity that were associated with the "Great Transformation" (Polanyi, 1944) of the industrialization process experienced by Western European societies and the United States in the 19th century.

More recently, the policing models in developed countries show a diversification in the stock of policing (Braithwaite, 2000; Reiner, 2004, p. 281), and an outstanding growth (the influence of the 9/11 terrorist attack must be noted here) of cooperation among national and international police agencies. In the 1960s, the fight against the criminality still could be considered in terms of the Weberian state monopoly of the legitimate violence.* Presently, Max Weber's concept about the monopoly of physical force by the state must be qualified, as a consequence of the changes still operating on the state, originated in the worldwide profound transformations in informatics, communications, transports, and production processes organization, which also triggered changes in social, religious, and gender relations, still operating in a new scenario of international politics. Political, economic, and social theories presently debate the new state status, and the social control consequences. This is a widely open area where can be found conflicting arguments from sociology (Luhmann, 1993, 1997; Garland, 2002; Karstedt & Bussmann, 2000; Kurz, 1994; Melucci, 1982; Bauman, 1991, and Dellasoppa, 2008 for the Brazilian case), from political science and political philosophy (Bobbit, 2002; Genschel & Zangl, 2008; Heller & Fehér, 1989; Mann, 1993), and from organizations and management theory (Mayntz, 2001; Rhodes, 1997), just to cite a few authors among a vast bibliography. New concepts as "modern governance" and "market–state" emerge to explain the characteristics of present states in a fast globalizing situation. Furthermore, empirical data also weakens the validity of the Weberian concept. Since the 1970s, a steady development of private security began that would come to materialize in what today is known as the industry of the private security.† This development is

* Max Weber's classical formulation, delivered as a speech at Munich University in 1918, analyzes political claims and the ultimate justification for such claims, in the context of the prevailing Nation–state concept at that moment: "Of course, force is certainly not the normal or the only means of the state—nobody says that—but force is a means specific to the state. Today the relation between the state and violence is an especially intimate one.... Today, however, we have to say that a state is a human community that (successfully) claims the monopoly of the legitimate use of physical force within a given territory. Note that 'territory' is one of the characteristics of the state. Specifically, at the present time, the right to use physical force is ascribed to other institutions or to individuals only to the extent to which the state permits it. The state is considered the sole source of the 'right' to use violence. This corresponds essentially to ordinary usage." (Weber, 2004).

† Since 1970, a transformation has been under way. In that year, there were still more public policemen than private guards in America. The ratio of public to private was 1.4:1. Now there are three times as many private policemen as public ones; in California, four times as many. Even as early as 1978, General Motors alone had a private police force of 4,200—more than all but five American cities.... America has a larger private-security business than most western countries, but nearly everywhere there are more private policemen than public ones. (Though, admittedly, the numbers are not strictly comparable. In Britain, the number of private guards has risen from about 80,000 in 1971 to 300,000 now, roughly twice the number of public policemen. In Canada and Australia, the ratio is also about 1:2. The extreme examples are lawless places, such as Russia and South Africa, where there are at least 10 times as many private security guards. In Russia, the private security industry holds one of the country's best-attended annual meetings, with strippers performing between lectures. (Welcome to the new world of private security. From *The Economist*, print edition. April 17, 1997.)

verified today all over the world. It is associated with the increase of the rates of criminality since the 1970s, and to the disproportional increased fear of victimization (as is the case of societies in the developed countries).*

It is also related to the changes in property, such as the malls and secure condominiums, usually called "mass private property." In less than 30 years, private security established itself as an important industry.† The fundamental distinction between public and private property (and associated rights) becomes less clear with the emergency of these spaces. In the case of malls, behind the appearance of a public space there exists a private estate controlled by private security companies. In private condominiums, access is not freely available and policing is private. For the public police, these new facts questioned the private security monopoly, and raised doubts about the core tasks of the public police and which tasks can be left for the private security. These changes affect what is called *ostensive policing* in Brazil, or *police of proximity* in France. In Brazil, investigative functions of the judicial police also are affected, as some private companies offer clients investigation and intelligence services with better efficiency and secrecy. An indication of the changes of the business of private investigation and intelligence developed to adapt to the new circumstances of the states and public policies noted above is the movement of some of the biggest world firms of audit for the area of the risk management.‡

* According to the British Crime Survey, 38% of people believe that crime has risen "a lot" in the past 2 years—up from 25% for those surveyed in 2001. A further third of the population reckons crime has gone up a little, while only 4% take the optimistic (and accurate) view that it has fallen. The number of people who worry about walking the streets at night and perceive their neighborhoods to be disordered is also up. (Crime: Fear itself. From *The Economist*, print edition. July 17, 2003.)

† Private security is the primary protective resource in America in terms of spending and employment. Private security employs at least two (2) million people, and annual expenditures for security products and services are more than US$100 billion. For federal, state, and local law enforcement, the figures are about 725,000 people employed and at least US$45 billion in expenditures. A large and growing industry, private security is armed with considerable and often sophisticated resources to deter crime and prevent other losses. (*U.S. Private Security Trends*. William C. Cunningham, president, Hallcrest Systems, Inc.. *The Hallcrest Report II: Private Security Trends 1970–2000*.)

‡ "The most visible and fastest-growing parts of the private security business are in areas that were once the preserve of the public police. But, the functions of private security firms are much wider than those of policemen, so the numbers of private security guards and public policemen are not strictly comparable. The public police concentrate on arrests and investigations. The private security business is more complex and fragmented. It divides into *four* broad categories: guarding, risk management, investigation, and detection and control in the criminal justice system.... Private prisons, especially, are a booming business: between them, America, Britain, and Australia have 132 private prisons with room for 84,000 inmates. The private sector also provides new techniques of crime control, such as tagging offenders in Britain using Home Hawk Curfew, a system invented by Marconi. (Guards and gumshoes. From *The Economist*, print edition. April 17, 1997.)

In the case of Brazil, private security exists in a Californian proportion: There are four private guards for each state officer. The state has little control over these exuberant forces; three out of four private guards are illegal, working in approximately 4,500 illegal companies—which are not legally registered and therefore don't exist in the government's records—compared to 1,300 legal enterprises. The numbers for the private security industries in Brazil are impressive. In July 2000, the federal police estimated the number of the legal private guards at about 350,000, almost the contingent of the military police in Brazil at that time (approximately 369,000).

These numbers point to the definitive establishment of security as a commodity. This tendency emerged in the 1970s with a faster growth of private security forces than public forces. Hired security forces are now encouraged by what is seen to be good management. Finally, the hardware version of the business of private security, such as mass surveillance systems, also shows a steady growth, concluding the diversification of the stock of policing at the end of the 20th century.

Seven Hypotheses on Policing in Brazil

1: Policing in the countries placed at the peripheries of capitalism cannot be analyzed by simple comparisons or by "importing ideas" from developed countries. Strong differences between economical, political, social, and cultural systems must be taken seriously into account.

Here it is necessary to consider the changes in the economic and social order of capitalism. These transformations, which have led to a hegemonic global system, recognize the United States as a technological and military leader. Without exaggeration, we are watching a new Great Transformation (Polanyi, 1944) that probably will produce consequences as, or more, dramatic than the ones that occurred during the emergency of industrial capitalism in Western societies. These transformations have a completely different impact in developed countries than in developing ones, as is the case in Latin America.

These changes question the modern state and its social control agencies, particularly state police. Global conditions now include the emergency of some postmodern societies—or islands of postmodernity or informational societies—via globalization, multiculturalism, and a complex process of internationalization of law.* (For a summary of this context, see Reiner, 2004, p. 302). This picture is clearly more dramatic in the peripheries of capitalism. Here we locate the outstanding differences that separate developing countries from developed ones, and are obliged to consider *cum grano salis* (with a grain of salt) the importing of models and prescriptions of policing. In this sense, Máximo Sozzo (2004) insisted on the need of evaluating critically the warning of Stanley Cohen about what he called "exportation of crime control models" from developed countries developed for the peripheries of capitalism.†

2: Analysis of police and policing in Brazil must account for the characteristics and limitations of the "constructions of democracy" that have historically been possible.

Violence and crime in Brazil has been rising over the past 20 years. The global homicide rate for Brazil is now about 27 per 100,000 inhabitants. Urgent state action is needed to address crime control, as well as public policies or changes in the regulation of political, judicial, and social control systems including the private sector. A serious problem in Brazil that no longer exists—if it ever existed—concerns the monopoly of legitimate violence by the state, a problem of many nation-states on the fringes of capitalism (Pinheiro, 2001, p. 297). In 1985, Anthony Giddens raised similar questions for the "European nation-state" (Giddens, 2001), as did Norbert Elias

* Globalization, however, is changing all that.... Structural differentiation increasingly is spreading across borders and economic sectors, driving other changes and resulting in the increasing predominance of political and economic structures and processes that (a) are frequently (although not always) more transnational and multinational in scale (i.e., are in significant ways more inclusive) than the state, (b) potentially have a greater impact on outcomes in critical issue areas than does the state (i.e., may in effect be more "sovereign"), and (c) may permit actors to be decisionally autonomous of the state. In particular, I argue that the more the scale of goods and assets produced, exchanged, and/or used in a particular economic sector or activity diverges from the structural scale of the national state—both from above (the global scale) and from below (the local scale)—and the more that those divergences feed back into each other in complex ways, then the more that the authority, legitimacy, policymaking capacity, and policy-implementing effectiveness of states will be challenged from both without and within. A critical threshold may be crossed when the cumulative effect of globalization in strategically decisive issue areas undermines the general capacity of the state to pursue the common good or the capacity of the state to be a true civil association; even if this threshold is not crossed, however, it is arguable that the role of the state both as playing field and as a unit becomes structurally problematic. (Philip G. Cerny, Globalization and the Changing Logic of Collective Action, *International Organization* (Vol. 49, no. 4), Autumn 1995).

† Cohen proposed two different types of models for the question of the "government importing technologies and crime control": the "benign transference" and the "bad colonialism" models that "... were built from a combination of the form to think the control of the crime and of a form of think the nature of the dependent development...." in the peripheries of the capitalism. The differences look deeper when considered the specific characteristics of our democracies and of the techniques of government applied and credited as efficient. (Cohen, S. (1982) Western crime control models in the third world: benign or malignant? *Research in Law, Deviance and Social Control, 4*, 85–119.)

(Elias, 1988, 1995, 1997). Wieviorka (1997, p. 19) calls attention to the decay of the efficiency of the traditional Weberian concept of legitimate violence in developed countries. But, accepting this argument, we must think about what happens with the Weberian formula in countries where the monopoly of legitimate force was never obtained by the state. For nation–states now under the influence of the complex processes of globalization, multiculturalism marginalization, and increasing income differences, the Weberian ideal is even more remote than ever. This question is related to the complexities and problems of the democracies that emerged in the Southern Cone after the military government controls (AAVV, 2000; Debrun, 1983; Crozier, 1997; Dellasoppa, 2003, 2002a, 2002b, 2000; Méndez, O'Donnell, & Pinheiro, 2000; O'Donnell, 1994, 1997, 1999). We have here a really important point. We can raise another question: How will it be possible to develop regulation in the public security area in societies where the state never obtained the monopoly of legitimate violence within the rule of law?*

3: Changes experienced by police as a social control agency means that the monopoly of legitimate violence by the state today shows a restricted form. The state delegates noncontractual forms of coercion to private groups while at the same time, paramilitary forces are used in topical actions of level three, and sporadically the army.

The state police do not have a monopoly of legitimate violence. Police forces are presently just one of the available forms of coercion/domestic repression available to the state (Monjardet, 2003; Giddens, 2001; Reiner, 2004).

We can distinguish four levels of repression:

Level 1: Negotiation, consensus construction, without the use of force.
Level 2: Policing that includes the use of basic weapons, but without the use of military force.
Level 3: Use of military organizations, such as the National Guard (U.S.), Gendarmeria Nacional (Argentina), Força Nacional of Segurança (Brasil), and sporadic use of the army.

* Here we can quote former Minister José Dirceu (Chief of the Home Office). He admits that "Brazil has nothing to fear, nothing to conceal. . . . We cannot hide the sun with a sieve. There is torture, there are murders and there are violations of the human rights in Brazil," said Dirceu, commenting on the statements of the advisor of the UN for human rights, Asma Jahangir. That same day, the newspapers reported that a witness that had spoken with the UN advisor was shot to death in Bahia. The minister of justice, Márcio Thomaz Bastos, reluctantly recognizes that in some regions or areas in Brazil there is an intermittent form of a true "state of war." (*Sem tapar o sol com a peneira. Dirceu admite que há tortura no Brasil e que inspeção no Judiciário não fere soberania. O Globo*, October 10, 2003. p. 3.)

Level 4: Military repression in large scale (e.g., the army and Gendarmeria Nacional in Argentina for the repression of the Cordobazo (Córdoba, Argentina, in 1969)). Also used in developed nations: Little Rock (Arkansas, 1959) under President Eisenhower, the policing by the English Army of Northern Ireland, the Canadian crisis of 1970 under Prime Minister Trudeau (Monjardet, 2003, p. 37).

In Rio de Janeiro, the army was used for repression at level 3, in November 1994, at the first of the so-called "Operação Rio." The government of da Silva organized the Força Nacional of Segurança (National Security force), a task force formed of police officials from several state police forces prepared to act in case of emergencies. The governor of the Espírito Santo claims that the use of the Força Nacional against organized crime is absolutely necessary. In a former paper (Dellasoppa & St. Clair Branco, 2004), we analyzed the limitations of this proposal in terms of the political limitations that the intelligence of the army faces to fight organized crime and the restrictions that operate on regulation proposals and planning in the area of public security.

4: Global and local changes in the past 30 years determined a strongly nonideological character in state politics and regulations on social control, with strong isomorphism in the alternatives of policing.

When we analyze the answers to recent problems placed by different forms of criminality, rates increase, as well as the increase the fear of victimization in the population, we observe a strong isomorphism in the responses from the state to instrumentalize police as a social control agency (Powell & DiMaggio, 1991). Brazil shares the characteristics of a global situation that we can observe in the Scarman Report in England and in the various French reports by Peyrefitte, Belogey, Bonnemaison, Erbès, Brodry, etc. in France (Monjardet, 2003, p. 248). As a result of the contemporary reshaping of politics on public security, we observe an outstanding similarity between the approaches of the "right," the "center," and of the political "left."* Here we emphasize the disappearance of the differences of the political concepts of "right" and "left." This process began in the 1990s and continues steadily

* "Law and order a 'left-wing concept?' Yes, says an unabashed Jean-Pierre Chevènement, France's fervently left-wing interior minister, 'because in the [1789] Declaration of the Rights of Man, the basic right to security is put on a par with liberty.' Yes, adds Jospin, the Socialist prime minister, because 'a citizen whose security is not assured cannot exercise his right to liberty.' And, yes again, says Jospin, because everyone should have the right to equal protection under the law, whereas it is often the poor in the most run-down areas who suffer most from crime. It has taken France's traditionally permissive left longer than most to get round to it, but in the name of Jospin's newly adopted 'left-wing realism,' and with the far-right National Front breathing down his neck, the government now heralds law and order as its top priority after creating jobs." (France. Crime-busting. From *The Economist*, print edition. October 30, 1997.)

at present in Brazil, at least for the politically significant forces. Already at the end of the 20th century, "law and order" was a concept incorporated to the political patrimony of the left. Some differences should be noted here, as the emergence in the discourse of the right of the concepts that constitute the "punitive populism" approach (Bottoms, 1995). The left still defends, at least in the discourse, the approach that the problem of the public security mainly depends on the combination of political and social regulatory policies in the long term. Political specificities in Brazil also account for the complexity of the problem. The police forces are subordinated to political authority, and, in the case of Brazil, this authority is a state authority. Brazil has 27 states. Then the policy problem is multiplied by 27 in the case of the *polícias civis* (judiciary police) and the *polícias militares* (military police). At this point, Brazil differs markedly from France, where the police serve as an example of one of the "state institutions" (Monjardet, 2003, p. 35).

5: There are increasing demands on the state for prevention and resolution of intangible facts (e.g., crime fears). This question has no solution in terms of regulation policies from the social control agencies. Then, the state, the political forces, and the police must develop strategies of social distribution of responsibilities.

BRAZIL CONSTITUTION 1988

Title V
The Defense of the State and of the Democratic Institutions
Chapter III
Public Security

Article 144. Public security, the duty of the State and the right and responsibility of all, is exercised to preserve public order and the safety of persons and property, by means of the following agencies:

I federal police
II federal highway police
III federal railway police
IV civil polices
V military polices and military fire brigades
(...)

(See full text in Appendix at the end of the chapter.)

Article 144 of the Brazilian Constitution does not establish a definition of the concept of "security" or of "responsibility" other than that it is attributed to "all" (the citizens) in the double sense of being a right and responsibility.* This implies that the duties of the police are not more exclusive, but now shared with "all" the citizens, communities, organizations. From the point of view of the state, this concept means, in practice, the resignation of the monopoly of legitimate force and, therefore, a limitation of the duties and policies possible for the police agencies. Repressive action priorities for the police are submitted to a debate or with the participation of third parties ("all"). (Monjardet, 2003, p. 256).

If 30 years ago the efficiency of a police agency used to be measured by its clearing rates, recently this indicator is increasingly problematic.† This applies in the case of Brazil where about only 1 in 10 homicides *brought to the attention of* the police is cleared. This again seriously questions the efficiency of a public police force (Polícia Civil, the judiciary police in the case of Brazil).‡ The last decades have seen more evidence put forward to the police (as a global problem, with few exceptions): rates of crime clearly decreased or remained very low, but crime rates continue to rise (until the unexpected decline in the 1990s in some developed countries, but not in Brazil). We observe here a point of weakness of the police that is confirmed when the representatives of the "law and the order" approach adopt a regulation concept inspired in a managerial measure of efficiency indicators, as in case of the Conservative Party in England.

But, problems for the police agencies do not end there. It is well known that the statistical probability of becoming a victim and fear of becoming a victim

* "Responsibility" is a polysemic concept: The state, quality, or fact of being responsible. Something for which one is responsible; a duty, obligation, or burden. Then, responsible means:

1. Liable to be required to give account, as of one's actions or of the discharge of a duty or trust.
2. Involving personal accountability or ability to act without guidance or superior authority: *A responsible position within the firm.*
3. Being a source or cause.
4. Able to make moral or rational decisions on one's own and, therefore, answerable for one's behavior.
5. Able to be trusted or depended upon; reliable.
6. Based on or characterized by good judgment or sound thinking: *Responsible journalism.*
7. Having the means to pay debts or fulfill obligations.
8. Required to render account; answerable: *The cabinet is responsible to the parliament.*

(http://www.yourdictionary.com/ahd/r/r0182600.html (accessed August 31, 2005))

† "To some people, the growth in the private sector now has been a reaction to the failure of an 'outmoded' public police to cope with rising crime in post industrial countries. The police clear up only a fifth of the crimes reported to them in America; in Britain, a quarter; in Canada, one sixth. Rich countries have reacted by increasing public police numbers: The growth of private policing has not occurred at the expense of the public force." (Welcome to the new world of private security. From *The Economist,* print edition. April 17, 1997.)

‡ "Only about one in 10 murders is cleared up, and conviction rates for other crimes are paltry. When the big fish are caught, they often bribe their way to freedom or get their lawyers to string out the case for years." (Getting away with murder. From *The Economist,* print edition. February 20, 2003.)

are very different facts (depending on the kind of crime, and of the country/region considered, the relation between fear of becoming a victim and probability of being victimized typically oscillates between 10:1 and 5:1). Given the complex character of the "level of fear of the crime," it seems an unreasonable *indicator of performance* of the police force. *Subjective perceptions* of reality are considered at the same level as other indicators that decades ago used to be representative of *reality*. This tendency, firmly established in developed countries, can also be identified in Brazil, maybe as a tendency toward a hyperpolitization based on estimates of the subjective reactions to the crime phenomena. Even for the orthodox liberal sectors, to burden the police institution with these kinds of demands looks grossly absurd.* This is particularly true in the case of Brazil, where the police as an institution is strongly discredited and public opinion usually sees the police as a part of the problem, not the solution.†

Considering the law of diminishing returns applied to policies in the public security area, we can expect this law to be exacerbated in the case of sequential investments destined to control subjective variables. The vulnerability of the police in terms of an "institution that should show results" means police are forced to articulate a discourse where responsibilities are credited to other institutions, or at least diluted among a great number of stakeholders, including the family, the school, the judiciary, the political sys-

* "... The number of people who worry about walking the streets at night and perceive their neighborhoods to be disordered is also up. For a government that concerns itself as much with perception as with reality, this is a problem, and the government has made it a problem for the police. Fear levels are now used as 'best value performance indicators,' meaning that police forces have to keep track of them and think up ways of calming people down. In the coming year, watch for a lot of converts to the 'reassurance agenda' and the doctrine of putting more Bobbies on the beat.... Given the intangible and messy nature of crime fears, it hardly seems reasonable to expect the police to assuage them. To try to do so may even turn out to be counterproductive. After all, much the easiest way to reduce fear of crime is not to cut crime itself, but to convince people that bad things are unlikely to happen to them. At first glance, that sounds reasonable, but it risks turning the police into public relations officers and lowering people's natural defenses against crime." (Crime: Fear itself. From *The Economist*, print edition. July 17, 2003.)

† *Em relação a este ponto, pode ser observado o tratamento que a mídia da a uma pesquisa realizada pela Internet, sem apresentação sequer do número de respostas. Mas certamente pode-se inferir que está limitada às classes mais abastadas economicamente, que são as que atualmente utilizam a rede.*

Pesquisa
Você confia na polícia do Rio?
Sim, apesar de algumas exceções os policiais, em sua maioria, são honestos
13.07%
Não, a corrupção e a brutalidade são generalizadas na polícia do Rio
86.93%
Você evita a noite por causa da violência?
Sim, não há mais lugares seguros no Rio
87.16%
Não, a violência não é tão grande quanto dizem
12.84%

http://oglobo.globo.com/ (accessed August 3, 2004.)

tem, state and/or federal government, or, as usually called in Brazil, the "civil society." As we have seen above, the Brazilian Constitution offers a good juridical argument for these strategies. Thus, the strategy of "social distribution of responsibilities" enters in Brazil in the complex interplay of political alliances at all political levels, with an always growing number of stakeholders entering into the game.

6: Police as a social control agency becomes a regulation problem for the state. Police do not enjoy public trust. Also, it is probably useless to try to regulate a system when most of the systems in its boundary remain unregulated in terms of an accountable democratic system.

Trust (vertrauen) can be considered as a measure of the disorder (or deficiency of regulation) of a system or institution.* The pair—trust–distrust—regarding an institution allows it to roughly estimate its level of transparency (accountability). We can also suppose that this quality estimates the previous social experience related with an institution and its behavior according to rules (compliance) and its more or less systematic failure to comply with the rules, mainly the rule of law (Donolo, 2001). Police as an institution, as well as other fundamental institutions (judiciary, government, political parties) are closely related, but perform very badly in terms of public opinion confidence. Only 32% of the citizens trust the judiciary, 30% the police, 11% the government(s) at different levels, and, at the bottom, only 8% trust political parties. When these results are compared with the Brazilian Mail Service, an institution trusted by 93% of the population, it is clear the extent of disorder and unaccountability that pervades these institutions.

Given the constitutional character of the police forces' organization and tasks in Brazil, regulation policies on the police institutions must begin at the political system level, which is itself under the action of powerful forces and groups that are against regulation policies and institutional changes in the police institutions. Antiregulation exists in a system (economical, political) when uncertainty in the law prevails, and there exists also an opportunistic *bricollage* (random creation) of transactions and agreements, and a market of rules (what in Brazil is summarized by the expression: "[it] is giving that justifies receiving" clientelistic or physiological "commodities"). In this scenario, negative externalities are out of control and institutional trust is, as seen, extremely low.† These conditions empower illegal activities, such as organized

* *Vertrauen* is usually translated into English as "trust/trustfulness." (See Giddens, 1993, p. 39)

† "Latin Americans see their police as part of the problem, not the solution. In this year's *Latinobarómetro* poll of 18 countries, only one respondent in three expressed confidence in the police (Chile is an exception, with 60% trusting the police). With reason; police are too often abusive, corrupt, and incompetent—or even criminal." (Crime and policing in Latin America. The battle for safer streets. Mexico City and São Paulo. From *The Economist*, print edition. September 30, 2004.)

crime. As expected, the minimum level of regulation policies required by these kinds of systems is very close to the maximum (Donolo, 2001, p. 16).

7: Regulation of police and social control agencies by the state, and the operation of these social control agencies are under bounded rationality constraints and state/agencies minimum requirements satisfying criteria.

> "General, there is a lot of corruption out there, and I cannot promise you that I'm going to show up, and the kidnappings will immediately stop. Even police officers are implicated." Cerqueira reassured him: "I'm not going to demand short-term results. I only want you to contain the corruption and keep the police department under control. Afterwards, we'll see what measures we have to take" (May 1995).

> "This plan is based on the following principles: interdisciplinarity, organizational and managerial pluralism, legality, decentralization, impartiality, accountability for actions taken, community involvement, professionalism, attention to particular regions, and a strict respect for human rights. Observing these principles is a condition for success" (June 2000).

Five years separate these two statements. The first, from 1995, conveys the spirit of the task entrusted by General Nilton Cerqueira, then Secretary of Public Security for Rio de Janeiro, to Hélio Tavares Luz, at that time a candidate for Chief of the Civil Police. The second is from the presentation of the National Plan for Public Security (*Plano Nacional de Segurança Pública, PNSP*), developed by the Fernando Henrique Cardoso administration (1994–2002) and made public on June 20, 2000, a week after the hijacking of a bus 174.[*]

By way of introduction, two thoughts come to mind. The first quotation is an example of a notion of planning that is minimalistic, based on a "philosophy of satisfying," which sets deliberately suboptimal objectives and develops a fragmented and antisystemic vision of planning.[†] It is an exam-

[*] On June 12, 2000, a single assailant, Sandro do Nascimento, hijacked a bus in Rio de Janeiro in a middle-class neighborhood. The kidnapping was televised for everyone to see. The *Batalhão de Operações Especiais* (BOPE) of the Military Police were sent in, but not the *Divisão Anti-sequestro* (Anti-Hijacking Division) of the Civil Police. And, the governor would not authorize the use of an elite sharpshooter. The episode ended with the death of a teacher, Geisa Gonçalves, a bus passenger, and hostage, and of the assailant himself, who was caught by the Military Police and later strangled by three of its officers in a police vehicle. The governor, who throughout the crisis had praised the police, changed his opinion once the results were known: "[The governor] says that the conduct of the police was mediocre given the investments made and he said the policemen were criminals" (*O Globo Online*, June 14, 2000). A survey revealed the general disrepute for the police: 72% of those interviewed answered that they mistrusted the police. "A fear statistic" (*O Globo Online* June 18, 2000). One should note the connection the governor made between the investments made and the performance of the police.

[†] See James G. March and Herbert A. Simon (1958, p. 169): "The simplifications have a number of characteristic features: (a) Optimizing is replaced by satisfying—the requirement that satisfactory levels of the criterion variables are attained."

ple of "the science of muddling through," as Charles Lindblom (1980, p. 67) calls it.* In the second quotation, language in effect functions as coverage for hypothetical "strategic planning" for an area that was Objective #28 in the Justice Ministry's Strategic Guidelines for the Implementation of the 2000–2003 Multiyear Plan (*Orientação Estratégica do Ministério da Justiça para a Elaboração do Plano Plurianual 2000–2003*) (Ministry of Justice, 1999). The Multiyear Plan does not make a single reference to any process underway or about to begin in order to implement the PNSP. The implementation of the PNSP offers us a notable example of so-called "opportunistic regulation" (Donolo, 2001), and it suggests the reasons for its predictable failure.

Other quotations to support this claim could be included here, since there is abundant material and a long record. All "strategic planning" can be categorized as an attempt at regulation, but not all attempts at regulation count as "strategic planning." It is enough to recall, for example, "Operation Rio,"† launched in November 1994, which did not produce any results worthy of mention in terms of regulatory advancement despite the impact of its implementation.

Provisional Conclusions

Democracy, in its different forms, including in Latin America, implies necessarily in subordination of force and coercion to the rule of law. In democracies, a police force will act under the command of the political authority. Police forces are usually opaque in organization and operation, and usually are opposed to external political regulations and efficient at inertia. But, at the same time, police are indicators of the structure of social relations that constitute the Brazilian society. These indicators are subject to peculiar interpretations, more or less ideological. The police will be able to be seen, in an extreme case, as the entity "the elite wants." In any case, Brazilian society will support the burden to define through democratic and institutional procedures the police that it really wants, and to produce the constitutional mechanisms and policies to make real these changes.

* This expression suggests that, without a planned direction, it is still possible to arrive at (some sort of) conclusion for a given task, despite incompetence, inefficiency, and existing obstacles. In relation to problems that are difficult to solve, politicians often launch programs with objectives that are far beyond available competencies. Consequently, administrators charged with implementing them end up defining and seeking their own goals.

† On November 1, 1994, the army occupied and controlled some critical slum areas in the city of Rio de Janeiro, after a series of violent assaults and kidnappings, in what was called "Operação Rio." The practical results, as predicted by several members of federal and civil police, faded away a couple of weeks after the army evacuated. This kind of "intervention" of the army was repeated later several times, with noticeably decreasing results (see Caldeira, 1994, 1996, 1998).

All over the world, police face considerable changes. We observe the end of the myth of the British "bobbie," but also the end of the Utopia of the rational police in Germany, to pessimistic approaches in the United States ("nothing works"), and to the more balanced reports (Sherman, 1998). Nowadays, the police depend increasingly on more complex and numerous resources. The scarcity or the blockade of these resources generally will provoke the imbalance of the agencies and its incapacity to attend to political goals established by the political power, problems aggravated by the usually high inertia of the institutions.

To conclude, we must ponder the results of the public security plans that have been implemented up until now. If the null hypothesis (no observable effects) was examined in the case of the plans that have been implemented since 2000, we can affirm without any doubt that it would be fully verified. However, one cannot, as yet, definitively judge the plan that is now being implemented, even though events before Carnival 2003, which culminated with the emergency use of the army to keep order in Rio de Janeiro, suggest some signs of what it has represented. We see a case where the presumed asymmetry of authority between state and civil society has broken down, the state's monopoly on legitimate violence within the rule of law has failed, and, in some places within Rio de Janeiro state, chaos (or control by drug traffickers) has been imposed as a social rule. Under such a scenario, in crisis situations, the regulator adapts by refusing to intervene or, as in the case of Rio de Janeiro, repeating military intervention (Donolo, 2001). Even though the Justice Ministry considered it to be an "emergency measure," it clearly shows that there is no hope for short-term control by state police forces. We are again faced with muddling through, a contingent adaptation, in turn, included within the framework of limited rationales of the involved regulators, both at the federal and state levels. Only that now there is no alternative except to increase the intensity of the army's operations (or of some "task force" that will come to replace them). Once a course of action is adopted, "signals" are sent that the interested parties immediately decode as they understandably attempt to adapt to new conditions, and that implies increasing difficulties for later interventions. The states of Rio de Janeiro and Espírito Santo will constitute a field of severe trials for the security policy that President da Silva's administration is implementing.

Coda

Since November 2008 a new strategy has been tested and until now, approved, in one of the 27 states of the Federation: Rio de Janeiro. The policy now including the UPPs—Unidades de Polícia Pacificadora ("Pacifying Police Units")—began with many of the characteristics of "muddling-through" observed in previous experiences. The UPP concept was developed from an initial experience in Dona Marta slum, in the South Zone of the city of Rio de Janeiro. But this first test evolved into a strategy of success, under the command of the Secretary of Security of the State of Rio de Janeiro, José Mariano Beltrame. Presently 17 UPPs (January 21, 2010) are operational in slums previously controlled by drug-traffickers. Former president da Silva declared that the UPP project was "a successful experience that should be exported to all the states of Brazil." The present state of the project can be observed in the UPPs homepage, the UPP Repórter: http://www.upprj.com/en/ (in English). It well deserves a visit; after many years, a really new security policy is being seriously tested. Internationally, this novelty was early acknowledged. Philip Alston (Alston, 2010), Special Rapporteur of the United Nations on extrajudicial, summary or arbitrary executions, delivered a positive evaluation that clearly contrasts with previous ones:

21. Since the Special Rapporteur's mission, the Rio de Janeiro Government has introduced Unidades de Polícia Pacificadora (UPPs, "Pacifying Police Units") into a small number of favelas in the city of Rio de Janeiro. These units are a sustained police presence in each favela, and aim to re-take control from gangs, and promote security in the long term. The UPP experiment is currently under way in seven favelas.

12 The officers deployed are given special training, including human rights training, and increased salaries. The Rio de Janeiro Government planned to have some 3,500 police in 15 UPPs by the end of 2010, and intends to ultimately extend UPPs to 100 favelas, at a rate of at least 10 new favelas per year.

22. This strategy is largely to be commended. Where it has been implemented, it represents a significant departure from the "war" approach of the brief, large-scale, violent operations. The UPP approach avoids the "shoot-out" scenarios that so often result from rapid, heavily armed police incursions into the favelas. According to information provided to the Special Rapporteur, for those favelas under UPPs, the Government has made real progress in preventing gangs from re-asserting their presence. There is also strong evidence to date of community support for the UPPs.

13. Residents have reported that they feel safer, and that relationships with police have improved. In some areas, there have also been improvements to the provision of basic services."

A survey conducted in 2010 by the Instituto Brasileiro de Pesquisa Social—IBPS—pointed out that 93% of dwellers from areas with recently installed UPPs felt more secure than before. Furthermore, 70% of dwellers of other areas without UPP would like to have one. Another survey, this time from the Fundação Getúlio Vargas, asking about approval of the UPP in the slums Dona Marta and Cidade de Deus obtained 66% of positive answers.*

* "UPP: Yo quiero una también!" ("I also want an UPP!") (UPP Repórter, 23/02/2010)

Certainly the old problems will not disappear overnight: low wages, shortage and poor employ of financial resources, poor management and, above all, corruption, are expected to linger, sometimes under new forms. Like drugs-trafficking, that is quietly adapting to the new rules. The time frame of the 2014 World Cup and the 2016 Olympic Games certainly will help in Rio de Janeiro, but that may not be the case of other metropolitan areas. Other results, like the drop in the homicide rates, were operating long before the begin of the new policy (Beltrão and Dellasoppa, 2011a, 2011b). But for the first time in many years, the cariocas are reclaiming their city (Weiss, 2010).

References

AAVV. (2000, Spring). Brazil, burden of the past. Promise of the future. *Daedalus, Journal of the American Academy of Arts and Sciences, 129*(2).

Alston, P. (2010). *Report of the Special Rapporteur on extrajudicial, summary or arbitrary executions. Follow-up to country recommendations—Brazil.* United Nations. General Assembly. 2010. Human Rights Council. Fourteenth session. (May 26, 2010).

Bauman, Z. (1991). *Modernity and ambivalence.* Ithaca, NY: Cornell University Press.

Beltrão, K. I. , Dellasoppa, E. E. El designio de los hombres: años de vida perdidos en Brasil y en las grandes regiones, 1980–2005. *Estudios Demográficos y Urbanos de El Colegio de México,* v. 26, p. 299–343, 2011a.

Beltrão, K. I., Dellasoppa, E. E. Anos de vida perdidos e hiato de gênero. Brasil e Grandes Regiões: 1980–2005. *Textos para Discussão-Escola Nacional de Ciências Estatísticas,* v. 1, p. 1–77, 2011b.

Bobbitt, P. (2002). *The Shield of Achilles: War, Peace and the Course of History.* New York. Alfred A. Knopf.

Bottoms, A. (1995). The philosophy and politics of punishment and sentencing. In *The politics of sentencing reform.* Oxford, U.K.: Clarendon Press, 17–50.

Braithwaite, J. *The New Regulatory State and the Transformation of Criminology, British Journal of Criminology,* 40(2), 2000, 222–238. (Reprinted in D. Garland and R. Sparks (eds) Criminology and Social Theory, Oxford, Oxford University Press, 2000). Available in: http://www.anu.edu.au/fellows/jbraithwaite/_documents/Articles/New_Regulatory_2000.pdf (Access in January 18, 2012).

Brasil. Constituição. (1988). Constitution 1988 rev. ed. Translated and revised by Istvan Vajda, Patrícia de Queiroz Carvalho Zimbres, & Vanira Tavares de Souza. Brasília: Senado Federal, Subsecretaria de Edições Técnicas, 221.

Caldeira, C. (1996). "Operação Rio e Cidadania: las tensões entre o combate à criminalidade e la ordem jurídica." *Política e Cultura: visões do passado e perspectivas contemporâneas.* Coordinated by Elisa Reis, Maria Hermínia Tavares de Almeida, and Peter Fry. São Paulo: Hucitec–ANPOCS, pp. 50–74.

Caldeira, C. (1998). "Política de segurança pública no Rio: apresentação de um debate público." *Revista Archè,* no. 19, pp. 13–37.

Caldeira, C. (1994). "Seguridad pública e Cidadania: las instituições e suas funções no Brasil Pós-Constituinte." *Revista Archè,* nº 9, pp. 5–25.

Cardoso, F. H. (1994). *Mãos à obra.* Campanha eleitoral à presidência. PSDB.
Crozier, M. (1997, January). The transition from the bureaucratic paradigm to the public management culture. *Revista del CLAD. Reforma y Democracia, 7.* Online at http://www.clad.org.ve/rev07/0029601.pdf (accessed March 17, 2004).
Debrun, M. (1983). *La Conciliação e outras estratégias.* São Paulo: Brasiliense.
Dellasoppa, E. E. (2000). Structure of social relations and collusion processes in Brazilian society. Revista Internacional de Estudos Políticos, 2(3), 535–556. Rio de Janeiro: UERJ/Nuseg.
Dellasoppa, E. E. (2002a). Estratégias e racionalidade na polícia civil do estado do Rio de Janeiro. In R. Briceño-León (Ed.), *Violencia, sociedad y justicia en América Latina.* Buenos Aires: Consejo Latinoamericano de Ciencias Sociales–CLACSO, 201–228.
Dellasoppa, E. E. (2002b). Violencia: Planos, oportunidades e o centro radical. *Polêmica* 5 (Maio-junho) Laboratório de Estudos Contemporâneos, UERJ. http://www2.uerj.br/%7Elabore/violencia_dellasopa.htm (17 Março 2004).
Dellasoppa, E. E. (2003, February). *Corruption in post-authoritarian Brazil: An overview and many open questions.* Discussion Paper F-107. Tokyo: University of Tokyo, Institute of Social Science.
Dellasoppa, E. E. and Saint´Clair Branco, Z. (2004). *Brazil's public security plans: Rationality vs. the politics of "muddling through."* The Mexico Project. Washington, D.C.: Georgetown University.
Donolo, C. (2001). *Disordine.* Roma: Donzelli Editore.
Dellasoppa, E. E. (2012). Seguridad pública en Rio de Janeiro: un desafío de dimensiones olímpicas (Primera parte). URvio – Revista Latinoamericana de Seguridad Ciudadana. Flacso – Ecuador. No. 10. Abril 2012. (To be published)
Dellasoppa, E.E. Rex non curat de re publica. Delito y Sociedad, v. 25, p. 35-62, 2008.
Elias, N. (1988). Violence and civilization: The state monopoly of physical violence and its infringement. In J. Keane (Ed.), Civil society and the state (pp. 129–146). London: Verso.
Elias, N. (1995). O processo civilizador 2nd ed. (Vol. 1). São Paulo: Jorge Zahar Editores.
Elias, N. (1997). Os Alemães. São Paulo: Jorge Zahar Editores.
Garland, D. (2002). The Culture of Control. Chicago: The University of Chicago Press.
Genschel, P. , Zangl, B. (2008). Transformations of the State – From Monopolist to Manager of Political Authority. TranState Working Papers, 76.Bremen: Sfb 597 „Staatlichkeit im Wandel", 2008, Available at: http://econstor.eu/bitstream/10419/27908/1/600426661.PDF (Accessed January 20, 2012)
Giddens, A. (1993). *Consecuencias de la modernidad.* Madrid: Alianza Editorial.
Giddens, A. (1995). *La Constitución de la sociedad.* Buenos Aires: Amorrortu Editores.
Giddens, A. (2001). *O estado-nação e a violência.* São Paulo: Edusp.
Heller, A., Fehér, F. (1989). The Postmodern Political Condition (with), Cambridge, New York: Polity Press Columbia University Press.
Karstedt, S, e Bussmann, K. (2000). *Social Dynamics of Crime and Control.* Oxford and Portland, Oregon: Hart Publishing.
Kurz, R. (1994). Der Kollaps der Modernisierung. Vom Zusammenbruch des Kasernensozialismus zur Krise der Weltökonomie, Reclam Leipzig. 1999.
Lindblom, C. E. (1980). *The policy-making process.* Englewood Cliffs, NJ: Prentice Hall.

Lindblom, C. (1995). The science of 'muddling' through. In S. Theodoulou & M. Can (Eds.), *Public policy: The essential reading* (pp. 113–117). New York: Prentice Hall.

Luhmann, N. (1993). *Teoría Política en el Estado de Bienestar.* Madrid: Alianza Universidad.

Luhmann, N. (1997). *Observaciones de la modernidad.* Barcelona: Paidós Editores.

Mann, M. (1993). The sources of social power, (Vol. II). The rise of classes and nation states, 1760–1914. Cambridge: Cambridge University Press.

Melucci, A. (1982). L'invenzione del presente. Movimenti, identità, bisogni individuali, Bologna, Il Mulino.

March, J. G., & Simon, H. A. (1958). *Organizations.* New York: John Wiley & Sons.

Mayntz, R. (2001). The State and civil society in modern governance. Paper presented at the VI International Congress of CLAD on State and Public Administration Reform. Buenos Aires, Argentina, November 5–9, 2001.

Méndez, J., O'Donnell, G., & Pinheiro, P. S. (Eds.). (2000). Democracia, violência e injustiça. O não-estado de direito na América Latina. São Paulo: Paz e Terra.

Ministério da Justiça. (2000–2003). Orientação Estratégica do Ministério da Justicia para la Elaboração do Plan Plurianual.

Monjardet, D. (2003). *O que faz a polícia.* São Paulo: Edusp.

O'Donnell, G. (1994, January). Delegative democracy. *Journal of Democracy, 5*(1), 55–69.

O´Donnell, G. (1997). Contrapuntos. Ensayos escogidos sobre autoritarismo y democratización. Buenos Aires: Paidós.

O'Donnell, G. (1999). Horizontal accountability in new democracies. In Schedler (Eds.), *The self-restraining state* (pp. 29–62). Boulder, CO: Lynne Rienner Publishers.

Pinheiro, P. S. (2001). Transição política e não-estado de direito na República. In I. Sachs, J. Wilhem, & S. Pinheiro (Eds.), *Brasil, un século de transformações* (pp. 260–305), São Paulo: Companhia de las Letras.

Plano Nacional de Segurança Pública. Ministério da Justiça. (2000). Retrieved on: http://www.mj.gov.br/ (accessed March 8, 2003).

Polanyi, K. (1944). *The great transformation.* Boston: Beacon Press.

Powell, W. W., & DiMaggio, P. J. (1991). *The new institutionalism in organizational analysis.* Chicago: The University of Chicago Press.

Reiner, R. (2004). *A política da polícia.* São Paulo: Edusp. Secretaria Nacional de Segurança Pública—SENASP. SENASP/MJ. Retrieved on: http://www.mj.gov.br/Senasp/senasp/inst_conceitos.htm> (accessed March 3, 2003).

Rhodes, R. A. W. (1997). *Understanding governance.* Philadelphia: Open University Press, 1997.

Sherman, L. W. (1998). *Preventing crime: What works, what doesn't, what's promising.* Gaithersburg, MD: National Institute of Justice Report.

Sozzo, M. (2004). Viajes culturales y "prevención del delito" en la Argentina. Mimeo. Comunicação pessoal.

UPP Reporter. (2010). "UPP: Yo quiero una también!" ("I also want an UPP!"), February 23.

Weber, M. (1969). *Economia y sociedad.* México City: Fondo de Cultura Econômica.

Weber, M. (2004). The vocation lectures: Science as a vocation, politics as a vocation. Indianapolis, IN: Hackett Publishing Co. Also available online in http://media/pfeiffer.edu/lridner/dss/Weber/polvoc.html (accessed January 15, 2012).

Wieviorka, M. (1997). Une société fragmentée. Paris: La Découverte.Braithwaite, J. (2000). The new regulatory state and the transformation of criminology, 40(2) 222-238 (reprinted in D. Garland and R. Sparks (Eds.) Criminology and Social Theory, Oxford, UK: Oxford University Press.

Weiss, G. "Reclaiming Brazil´s cities. Interviews with the Secretary of Security of the State of Rio de Janeiro and with political scientist Emilio E. Dellasoppa". Credit Suisse GI – Global Investor October 2010. P. 27-29. Available at: http://www.raumentwicklung-tum.de/upload/aktuelles/GI2_10_englisch_web2.pdf (Accessed January 21, 2012)

Appendix

BRASIL CONSTITUTION (1988)

Title V
The Defense of the State and of the Democratic Institutions
Chapter III
Public Security

Article 144. Public security, the duty of the State and the right and responsibility of all, is exercised to preserve public order and the safety of persons and property, by means of the following agencies:

I federal police
II federal highway police
III federal railway police
IV civil polices
V military polices and military fire brigades

Paragraph 1: The federal police, instituted by law as a permanent body and structured into a career, are intended to:

I investigate criminal offenses against the political and the social order or to the detriment of property, services and interests of the Union and of its autonomous government entities and public companies, as well as other offenses with interstate or international effects and requiring uniform repression as the law shall establish;
II to prevent and repress the illegal traffic of narcotics and like drugs, as well as smuggling, without prejudice to action by the treasury authorities and other government agencies in their respective areas of competence;
III to exercise the functions of maritime, air and border police;
IV to exercise, exclusively, the functions of criminal police of the Union.

Paragraph 2: The federal highway police are a permanent body structured into a career and intended, according to the law, to patrol ostensibly the federal highways.

Paragraph 3: The federal railway police are a permanent body structured into a career and intended, according to the law, to patrol ostensibly the federal railways.

Paragraph 4: It is incumbent upon the civil police, directed by career police commissioners and except for the competence of the Union, to exercise the functions of criminal police and to investigate criminal offenses, with the exception of the military ones.

Paragraph 5: It is within the competence of the military polices the ostensive policing and the maintenance of the public order; it is incumbent upon the military fire brigades, in addition to the duties defined by law, to carry out activities of civil defense.

Paragraph 6: The military polices and military fire brigades, ancillary forces and reserve of the Army, are subject, together with the civil police, to the Governors of the states, of the Federal District and of the territories.

Paragraph 7: The law shall regulate the organization and operation of the agencies responsible for public security in such a manner as to guarantee the efficiency of their activities.

Paragraph 8: The municipalities may organize municipal guards to protect their property, services and facilities, as the law shall establish.

Adoption of Accountability and Oversight Mechanisms

6

The Case of the Indian Police

K. S. DHILLON

The rule of law in modern India, the frame upon which justice hangs, has been undermined by the rule of politics.

Prof. David H. Bayley

Contents

Introduction

One of the most important requisites of a democratic system of governance is the primacy of the rule of law. This is a dynamic concept, born out of and dependent upon constitutionalism, human rights, and social justice, and it applies equally and uniformly to the state institutions as well as the citizens, and both are required to be accountable and subject to the rule of law. A democratic polity relies on its police, as its coercive instrument, to enforce the rule of law and thereby contribute, in a major way, to the creation of a secure, vibrant, and orderly society. More than any other constituent of government, police officers, as the custodians of the rule of law on behalf of the state, are obligated to function within the four corners of law and propriety, and uphold the law of the land in all its various dimensions. Thus, it is of the utmost importance that the police, together with all its subsidiary organizations, bear absolute accountability to the rule of law on all occasions and under all circumstances. Such a theory of police accountability is a crucial ingredient of all constitutional democracies. The degree to which a failsafe system of accountability gets integrated into the functional and cultural modes of law-enforcement agencies and the extent of its efficiency and effectiveness in a given situation will determine the overall well-being of the citizen and the centrality of the norms of civilized values and human rights in that society. Whenever and wherever the state is prepared, or forced, to make compromises and allows the mechanisms that ensure such accountability to weaken and wither, democracy itself will crumble and soon become dysfunctional with good governance becoming a sure casualty.

The functional charters of Indian police departments have expanded exponentially over the past few decades. In addition to what have always been considered their traditional commitments, such as maintenance of public order, prevention, investigation and detection of crime, and prosecution of offenders, they are now called upon to assist in the implementation of a wide variety of social legislation. Then there is the vast domain of newer responsibilities in the area of guarding democratic institutions, ensuring free and fair elections not only to the houses of parliament and state legislatures, but also numerous other bodies like municipal and *panchayati raj* (village council or local court) institutions. In any event, policemen are liable to be exposed to an array of stresses and strains of many different kinds and degrees. These pressures are further compounded by lingering colonial administrative structures and practices, legal infirmities, ever-increasing diffusion of lines of command and control, and growing politicization of governmental institutions, but especially those dealing with enforcement functions, with the police being a special favorite of the political classes in this dubious business. All of these various developments, individually and collectively, have had deeply unsettling implications for police efficiency, credibility, and, most of all, accountability. It is vital that we take whatever action needs to be taken, without losing any more time and without making any compromises, to sustain, preserve, and enforce the concept of police accountability in every sense of the term, if we wish to prevent any further erosion of democratic values and community autonomy. Inarguably, the most grievous threat to the concept of police accountability, as enshrined in the existing legal framework based on the Indian Police Act of 1861, comes from rampant politicization of this vital organ of state policy. In other words, the ongoing politicization of police agencies represents the gravest danger to the concept of police accountability, severely undermining its efficacy, jeopardizing community welfare, and gravely damaging civil society institutions.

That the Indian police has been acting in a partisan manner for several decades now and getting increasingly politicized, is no longer a secret. What is even more worrisome is that all political parties, whether secularist, leftist, centrist, or rightist in orientation, freely and shamelessly indulge in politicization of governmental institutions and agencies, more particularly those charged with enforcement functions. By trivializing internal security mechanisms, the political classes have lethally dented the concepts of rule of law and equitable enforcement of public order. Many judicial pronouncements have, time and again, drawn attention to the several instances of persistent assaults on the efficiency and objectivity of the police, especially after the end of colonial rule in 1947 and recommended appropriate measures to insulate the police from the virus of politicization. All such proposals and agendas for reform in the Indian police, however, are resolutely shelved and Indian ruling classes remain impervious to all suggestions for bringing about any worthwhile change. If this state of affairs is not addressed in good time, Indian law-enforcement systems will soon reach a point of no return. The scary picture of the shape of things to come is only too manifest in the states of Bihar and Uttar Pradesh (UP), with many other parts of the country well on their way to follow suit. The deep wounds inflicted on the concepts of constitutional and democratic policing by the horrendous state-sponsored carnage against Muslim citizens of the country in the Western Indian state of Gujarat, a few years ago, will take a long time to fade from public memory. Not that the Gujarat killings were the first of their kind in independent India. Nor are they likely to be the last if issues relating to police accountability and oversight are not addressed in right earnest and with due dispatch. Similar appalling episodes have occurred in other regions, too; the worst in recent history being the Sikh killings in the national capital of Delhi in November 1984, in the wake of Indira Gandhi's assassination. If the state can periodically withdraw its protection to a section of its citizens, the rule of law and constitutional guarantees can have no meaning for the many minority segments of India's vast population. We need to take note that while the Gujarat pogroms were stage-managed by the rightist Hindu party, the Bharatiya Janata Party, those against the Sikhs were organized and led by the self-professed secularists of the Congress party. The ongoing process of rampant politicization and communalization of Indian law-enforcement agencies portends a most fearsome scenario in the region and needs to be addressed urgently and meaningfully by the Indian state before it is too late. In the words of George Bernard Shaw, "A nation's morals are like its teeth, the more decayed they are, the more it hurts to touch them."

Politicization has led to an acute degree of police malfunctioning in recent times by steadily promoting a culture of selective implementation of laws and rules, the gravest of such aberrations being wide-ranging communalization of the force all over the country, but especially in the central Hindi-speaking states and in Gujarat and Maharashtra. There is no dearth of censures and indictments of the police at the hands of judicial commissions for inaction or worse in riot situations. More recently, the police has come to serious notice for indictable malfeasance in either conniving with rioters in aggressively targeting minority populations or themselves getting actively involved in such unlawful conduct as in Meerut, Delhi, Mumbai, Ahmedabad, and several other places. Sadly, such collusive and culpable conduct of the Indian police in recent years is not confined to states, ruled by particular parties. It happens under all shades of political dispensations, the so-called secularist parties like the Congress included. A number of inquiry commissions have found the police to exhibit grossly antiminority attitudes during riot situations. The provincial armed constabulary (PAC) of Uttar Pradesh had for long enjoyed the dubious distinction of being probably the most communalized force in the country, until it recently was overtaken by the Gujarat police. However, despite frequent strictures by judicial authorities, delinquent officers are rarely brought to book. The commission of inquiry appointed to look into Meerut (UP) riots of 1987 strongly suspected officers and men of the UP PAC of having collaborated with the rioters in the killing of Muslims. There also were allegations of the force having raided a Muslim village, rounded up several villagers, taking them to the banks of a nearby canal, and shooting them in cold blood. The allegations could never be proved in a court of law because successive governments of UP, led by many different political parties, persisted in stalling the prosecutions by simply refusing to sanction prosecution. Reports of police inaction are not a new phenomenon, though active connivance with the rioters is a more recent development. The Gujarat carnage of 2002 was, undoubtedly, the most blatant illustration of total collusion between the state police and the political party in power to carry out a virtual ethnic cleansing of the principal minority in the state. This was also the clearest signal that internal control mechanisms to enforce police accountability, as provided in the Indian Police Act of 1861, the substantive law still governing the police in the country, and the rules and regulations framed thereunder, had become totally nonfunctional in the changed situation.

The British colonial power reorganized the Indian police in the mid-19th century under the Indian Police Act of 1861. Evidently, the primary purpose that this Act was meant to serve was to protect the interests and objectives of the imperial power and it was meticulously designed to accomplish precisely that purpose. The concept of democratic accountability, therefore, could hardly be expected to have featured prominently in that format. Also, there were simply no high-minded notions of human rights or fundamental freedoms in the then Indian polity. No one talked of community accountability or of civil liberties or civic oversight. These concepts remained foreign to the Indian criminal justice system as it evolved in the mid-19th and early 20th centuries. Police officers were answerable for their acts only to law courts and to their departmental superiors. The latter were empowered under the Police Act, and the rules and regulations framed under it, to discipline erring police officials. As the same Police Act continues to be in force in the country even after nearly six decades of independence, accountability mechanisms remain unchanged as far as the extant law is concerned. However, Indian political classes have sought to create many new areas of external control mechanisms through executive instructions and informal measures, but without altering the substantive law on the subject. This has led to a lot of confusion and police malfunctioning.

But, to revert to internal accountability provisions, Section 7 of the Act authorizes officers of and above the rank of district superintendents of police to dismiss, suspend, or reduce in rank any subordinate police officer they believe is unfit, remiss, or negligent in the discharge of his or her duties. Some states have their own Police Acts on the pattern of the Indian Police Act of 1861, which contain analogous provisions. The punishments that can be awarded to deviant officers include:

- dismissal;
- removal from service;
- reduction in rank or in pay;
- forfeiture of approved service,
- withholding of increments;
- fines to an amount not exceeding one month's salary;
- confinement to quarters for a term not exceeding 15 days with or without punishment drill, extra fatigue, guard, or other duties;
- deprivation of good conduct pay; and
- removal from any office of distinction or special emolument.

The first five of these punishments fall in the category of major punishments and can be awarded only by the appointing authority after conducting regular departmental inquiries. The rest are what are called minor punishments. In some of these, a show cause notice has to be issued to the concerned official and his reply considered before he may be punished; in others, an orderly room appearance is sufficient.

In the following cases of misconduct, the delinquent officers may be arraigned before a competent magistrate for punishment ranging from a fine not exceeding 3 months salary or with imprisonment for a period not exceeding 3 months or both:

- violation of any specified duty;
- willful breach or neglect of any provision of law, rule, regulation, or lawful order that such official is bound to observe or obey;
- withdrawing from duty without permission;
- engaging in any other employment without authorization;
- cowardice;
- offering unwarranted personal violence to a person in custody.

Officials guilty of criminal misconduct are liable to be prosecuted under the normal criminal law, except that they enjoy certain safeguards for acts done or purported to be done in the course of duty, in which case sanction of a competent authority is required before prosecution. This is called the doctrine of sovereign impunity, which frequently comes in handy for state bureaucracies to shield an erring, but politically useful, wrongdoer from facing the due process of law.

All these various mechanisms are internal in nature and provide no avenue for an outside oversight. It could not have been any different as they are essentially a legacy of an imperial past and reflect the imperatives and concerns of a colonialist administration. The Indian Police Act derived its primary inspiration from the need to set up a ruler-supportive colonialist police force, not a citizen-friendly institution modeled on the British police. The Indian police would, thus, evolve as an institution rooted in mid-19th century concepts and concerns, to serve as a vital instrument for the consolidation of colonial rule. And, we all know how competently the Indian police assisted the British to ruthlessly suppress the Indian struggle for freedom. The same Police Act and the same police forces that served the colonial governments so well are now being used by Indian political classes to maintain their control on the levers of power. Strangely, this state of affairs continues to persist despite the country having one of the most liberal and modernist Constitutions in the world, which guarantees a wide range of human, political, and civil rights to the citizen. Almost all of the rights included in the universal declaration of human rights are part of the fundamental rights secured by the Indian Constitution. The higher judiciary has been consistently interpreting the country's legal architecture in a way as to make it probably one of the best models of democratic governance in plural societies. However, in the absence of deep systemic reforms aimed at modernizing its structure to enable the police to measure up to the new challenges brought about by enormous changes in India's social, economic, political, and cultural spheres, the Indian police continue to falter time and again in the matter of ensuring the primacy of the rule of law. That explains the failure of the police in being accountable either to the law or to their departmental supervisors, as is amply borne out by their lawless conduct in Punjab, Gujarat, Mumbai, UP, and in many other places all over the country. The modes of ensuring police accountability through the existing internal control mechanisms have largely failed because of rampant politicization, among other things, for the simple reason that the established command and control systems have become largely dysfunctional. Since the substantive law governing the Indian police, which dates back to the colonial era, makes no provision for explicit external control mechanisms, the imperatives of full and enforceable police accountability to the community remain unaddressed. So, what can be done to remedy such a dismal state of affairs and introduce effective accountability and oversight mechanisms in the Indian police?

Blueprint for Reforming Indian Police: The National Police Commission 1977

The National Police Commission (NPC), appointed by the Indian government in late 1977 (1977–1981) to study the subject in depth and make suitable recommendations for updating the entire organization, structure, and functioning of the Indian police, came up with some eminently pertinent proposals. As the first and only national level police commission appointed after independence, the NPC labored hard to usher in the much-needed change and reform, which was aimed at making the police an appropriate vehicle to serve the free peoples of a modern democratic nation. Unfortunately, successive governments of India chose to ignore all the significant proposals of the NPC, especially those that sought to make the police more accountable and responsive to the community and uphold the rule of law. Strangely, while Indian rulers resolutely refuse to implement the NPC proposals, its neighbor, Pakistan, has replaced the Police Act of 1861 with a new law, ironically enough, based on the recommendations of the Indian NPC. Evidently, the Indian ruling classes would rather hold on to a colonial system of policing than invest it with the democratic features of a citizen-supportive and community-responsive force, which would lead to a complete depoliticization of the mechanics of law enforcement by specifying the mode of superintendence and control over the police by the state or union governments, as the case may be, within an explicit framework of parameters in order to prevent its abuse and misuse for extraneous ends. A politicized police force would forever be vulnerable to inappropriate and illegitimate pressures and be a tool in the hands of the ruling party. Assured of patronage and protection by political godfathers, it would tend to become irresponsible, irresponsive, and lawless. Just as an independent judiciary, functioning as a zealous guardian of citizens' rights and liberties, is central to democracy, so is an autonomous and apolitical police a necessary adjunct to the rule of law. An untainted judiciary that works with a diseased and deeply politicized police is like having a spotless dining hall, being served by a dirty and unhygienic kitchen. A clean and autonomous police agency is as important as an independent judiciary for the proper functioning of the criminal justice system to serve the free people of a liberal democracy.

Having identified politicization as the principal factor responsible for the failure of the existing accountability mechanisms, the NPC proposed the establishment of a statutory commission in the states and at the union level, to be called the State Security Commission (SSC), under the chairmanship of the chief ministers, or the union home minister, as the case may be. The commission would ensure external accountability and also perform an overseeing role by exercising superintendence and control over the state or central police forces. It would comprise of the following seven members:

(1) Chief minister/union home minister (Chair)
(2) An MLA (member of legislative assembly) from the ruling party (nominated by the Speaker)
(3) An opposition MLA (nominated by the Speaker)
(4–7) Persons nominated by the government from academicians, retired members of the judiciary or civil service, not involved in political activities, after approval by the legislature and for a term of 3 years.

Former police officers or bureaucrats who handled police matters, while in service, are barred from being nominated until the expiry of 3 years after their retirement. The serving Director General of Police (DGP) of the state, or the Central Police Organization (CPO) in the case of the center, would be member secretary, and would represent the department and act as the chief executive officer of the concerned SSC. The functions of the SSC shall include:

- laying down broad policy guidelines and directions for the performance of preventive tasks and service oriented functions of the police;
- evaluation of the performance of the state police every year and presentation of a report to the state legislature;
- functioning as a forum of appeal for disposing of representations from police officers of the rank of district superintendent of police and above with regard to their being subjected to illegal or irregular orders in the performance of their duties;
- functioning as a forum of appeal for disposing of representations from police officers regarding promotion to the rank of district superintendent of police and above;
- generally keeping in review the functioning of the police in the state.

With the police chief as its ex-officio member-secretary, the SSC would devise its own procedure for transaction of business. The chairman, members, and secretary of the commission will be free to bring up for its consideration any subject that falls within its charter. It shall meet at least once every month, but may meet more often if so required by its chairman, members, or the police chief, for consideration of any subject proposed by any of them. As chairman, the chief minister (CM) (or the union home minister, as the case may be) will be able to project the government's point of view during the commission's transactions. In the normal course, any policy direction or guidelines that the government desires to issue shall have to be agreed to by the SSC before being passed on to the police for implementation. However, in an emergency, the government could directly issue a policy direction or guidelines in regard to a specific situation, but such direction or guideline shall, as soon as possible, be brought before the commission for ratification and be subject to such modification as the commission might decide. Apart from the annual evaluation report on the performance of the police, the commission shall also submit to the state legislature an annual report on the working of the commission itself, highlighting noteworthy instances of corrective action taken at the instance of the commission.

The establishment of SSC will ensure that any instruction that the government may issue to the police will be open to public scrutiny and the product of an in-depth discussion in the commission. The presence of a former judge as a member will lend judicial objectivity and fairness in the formulation of views and policies in the management of police and law enforcement mechanisms. Because every act of the commission or omission by the police will be open to questioning by the SSC, which will have access to all the records and other relevant material, the police will most likely desist from taking illegal, high-handed, improper, or arbitrary action. Such an arrangement will obviously be in the best interests of the people and ensure that the police force functions within the prescribed framework of law. However, the notion that the police will no longer be under the control and superintendence of the government, if and when a statutory body like the SSC is set up, is totally misconceived, because the structural format of the SSC does not make it an outside entity, wholly delinked from the government. Its chairman is the chief minister himself, assisted by the state police as well as the state secretariat. In all its deliberations, the commission would fully reflect the views and responses of the government. It is not a new controlling institution, it is meant only to create a new mechanism of control by the chief minister, who will now enjoy the benefit of the advice and counsel of an expert body in dealing with policing policies and situations. When governmental policies and decisions are backed by the commission, public approval and support would be readily and abundantly forthcoming. Accountability to the SSC will also impart transparency, integrity, truthfulness, and efficiency to police performance from the people's point of view. Further, support from the commission will greatly help the police chief to aim at and achieve professional excellence in all police work. Police will also become citizen-friendly and would be able to secure a much higher degree of public satisfaction and cooperation than at present. It is incorrect, therefore, to claim that the proposed SSC will create difficulties for the government in discharging its constitutional mandate to maintain public peace, order, and tranquility in the state.

More than any other recommendation, it was this proposal that evoked the most determined opposition from the political classes, both in the states and at the center. Indian politicians have become so accustomed to using the police as a useful and willing collaborator in their pursuit of power that they can never think of willingly giving up their control over this coercive instrument of state power. So, they simply refuse to look at any meaningful reform in the system; the mechanics of law enforcement, thus, remain virtually unchanged since the colonial times, except that in place of one provincial governor now the police hierarchy has to dance to the tunes of scores of politicians, many of them unconcerned with public peace and welfare, irresponsible in the extreme, and, at a later stage, many of them mixed up with criminals. Policemen have now to contend with a new ruling class, consisting of self-seeking, corrupt, and, at times, criminalized politicians, who claim to be the rightful and real arbiters and decision makers in a democratic India. Police officials, even those belonging to the elite Indian Police Service (IPS), openly woo politicians for career-advancement and to corner important, and lucrative, postings. The entire political fraternity is unanimous in the rejection of the concept of an autonomous commission, which they view as a dangerous device to reduce them into toothless tigers. Being unaware of the police systems serving mature democracies in the developed world, most segments of the Indian intelligentsia, too, tend to agree with the politicians in this matter. For, how can an elected government give up its control and superintendence over as vital an organ of governance as the police, they argue? Only recently have many socially aware commentators begun to link the sharp decline in police performance with the increasing degree of its politicization.

The second important recommendation of the NPC, aimed at depoliticizing the police and other enforcement agencies, relates to providing a fixed tenure to the state police chief, once his appointment has been cleared in accordance with a prescribed procedure in which the SSC plays the key role. The presence of an opposition MLA, as well as other independent and reputed members in the commission, will make for a broad consensus in the appointment, which is bound to enhance the credibility and prestige of the appointee, unlike the existing system where the police chief is widely seen as the chief minister's creature. Public confidence in the impartiality and effectiveness of the police depends heavily on the degree of professional excellence in its various constituents. This can only be achieved by the stress laid on professionalism by the police leadership. The public image and personality of the police chief are of great importance in this connection. The removal of a police chief, before the expiry of his term, also will require the approval of the SSC, except when such removal becomes necessary due to one of the following circumstances:

- A punishment of dismissal/removal/compulsory retirement from service or reduction to a lower post, awarded under the provisions of All India Services (discipline and appeal) rules.
- Suspension orders under the above mentioned rules.
- Retirement from service on superannuating in the normal course.
- Promotion to a higher post under the state or central government, provided the officer had consented to such a promotion.

Genuine police accountability on a sustainable basis can be enforced only through a process of continuous monitoring of its performance. An important ingredient of the functional charter of the state security commissions is to constantly monitor police performance, a task entrusted to an independent evaluation cell attached to the SSC. The annual administration report prepared by the head of the police force and assessment reports of the central police committee will provide additional material to the state security commission to prepare a final report on the performance of the state police to be placed before the state legislatures. In addition, all police officials, individually and collectively, should be sensitized to the idea of accountability to the people. Sections 132 and 197 of the Criminal Procedure Code 1973 provide protection to various categories of public servants against any prosecution brought against them in relation to performance of official duties. The protection available to police officers under these sections need to be withdrawn so that private complainants are free to press their complaints against police officials for a judicial pronouncement without there being a provision to obtain prior permission of the competent authority for such prosecution.

Since the problem of politicization is itself largely the product of the Indian Police Act, which vests the superintendence of the state police in the state government, the NPC attempted to assign a precise definition to the term *superintendence* based on a few supreme court rulings. The commission proposed that "the power of superintendence of the state government over the police should be limited for the purpose of ensuring that police performance is in strict accordance with law." This was a most imaginative interpretation that would have gone a long way in checking the growing damage to police performance due to illegitimate and inappropriate demands made on the organization by outside elements. Foreign police forces have managed this problem in a highly innovative manner. It is not that foreign police departments are totally independent. Governments all over the world exercise control over their police in some way or the other. What matters is the quality of control, the purpose for and the manner in which it is exercised. What is needed is to balance two requirements: (a) to ensure that civilian political control actually leads to making the police efficient and accountable, and (b) to ensure that the organization enjoys adequate functional autonomy under a clearly defined command structure in carrying out its mandate.

Accountability

We can distinguish three distinct strands of the concept: popular accountability, legal accountability, and functional transparency. Needless to say, these three values often overlap. Whereas they may frequently tend to reinforce each other in many significant ways, at the same time they are also apt to occasionally come into conflict with one another, representing as they do different concepts and values. All acting together, they would impart and sustain the tradition of democratic policing in a police force, but taken singly none of them will be able to adequately serve the purpose.

Popular accountability entails holding the police accountable to the will of the people through electoral processes in a way that makes the police directly subordinate to elected officials and through structured engagement between the police and the community. *Legal accountability* implies that the police comply with legal constraints and procedures through judicial processes and other enforcement mechanisms. There can be no rule of law in a society where those who enforce the law are not fully subject to the law. If a police agency is allowed to flout the law with impunity, it loses legitimacy and credibility as a law-enforcement group and becomes instead a highly corrosive example of law's many inadequacies. Human rights enforcement is primarily a matter of legal accountability. The third strand in this attempted analysis of accountability is *transparency*, which means the establishment of mechanisms through which the police are required to provide, as a matter of course, information about all but the most sensitive areas of operation. Transparency and openness are, in fact, the essence of accountability. For, otherwise, how can the citizens hold the police accountable if they do not even have the elementary information with which to do so? Accountability is, thus, a cardinal principle of law enforcement in democratic societies, as opposed to authoritarian and fascist regimes wherein police organizations have to work in an environment of functional opacity, which is fundamentally inconsistent with democratic policing.

Police accountability within a set of predetermined parameters is not antithetical to functional autonomy, which is a *sine qua non* of effective and efficient policing. Nor does it mean independence from governmental control. In a democracy, government represents the people and it is the government's responsibility to provide people with an effective and efficient police service. The law must explicitly make it the responsibility of the state to provide efficient and professional policing to the people, which fulfills the state's duty to ensure safety and security, but also to function according to and within the confines of law and not to act in any way outside these limits. Any discussion of accountability must answer the questions: accountability to whom, for what, and how will it be achieved? The question of accountability *to whom* must elicit the answer that accountability in a democracy must eventually be to the citizen, i.e., to society at large. Since the citizenry has given the government it elects the guardianship to provide quality policing, accountability of the service is to the executive and to the representatives of the people, the elected legislators. Accountability will be *for* performance against mandates. This mandate must be clearly stated and widely known. The Indian police like to believe that their mandate is merely to fight crime because this is what the Police Act of 1861 prescribes as their mandate. However, with the intervention of the Constitution and the legal requirement that all laws must be read in the light of the Constitution's dictate, it is clear that the police have a duty to uphold the law and do everything to ensure that there is an environment that ensures that all citizens' rights given by law are protected and enforced. This does not mean that they have sole responsibility for ensuring that citizens realize every right, but to ensure that their work contributes to a constitutionally valid environment; that there is no lawlessness, no violation of the law; and no illegal police action or conduct. Performance must be measured against this and the needs of the service to achieve this mandate must be recognized and provided for. Indian policemen are never too happy talking about accountability and civilian oversight as they fear that such concepts and mechanisms are likely to prove too taxing for an already hard-pressed force, but, in actual fact, they will immensely benefit the department because a right mix of civilian oversight and community accountability will greatly help them in the performance of their duties by narrowing the gap between the nature of police duties and the aspirations of the people.

In terms of *how*, accountability mechanisms under current formal and informal practices range from internal accountability up the chain of command within the police hierarchy, to supervision and control by the executive and oversight by the legislature. In addition there may be external mechanisms like the human rights commissions and the judiciary to which the police must be answerable. Accountability for satisfactory performance will be to the local community as well; their satisfaction being an indicator of good performance. Each of the above vehicles for ensuring accountability have different roles to play and accountability to each will have different connotations and dimensions. Nevertheless, in all cases, control over the police itself must be such that satisfies the constitutional mandate to work within the rule of law framework. It must itself be embedded in the law, subject to checks and balances, nonarbitrary, open, objectively exercised against known criteria and in the public interest, in order to be legitimate. Presently some of the mechanisms for accountability are not as strong or effective as they need to be. Internal mechanisms lack transparency and credibility with the people; oversight by the legislature is sporadic and erratic; control by the bureaucracy is often a matter of contention and conflict, partly because its nature and parameters are not as well defined as they ought to be. Delivery of justice in the Indian judicial system is subject to frequent and inordinate delays while recommendatory bodies like the National Human Rights Commission (NHRC) suffer from structural and jurisdictional inadequacies. This means that these institutions, too, fail to ensure that the process of oversight is uniform and balanced and that, in the long term, it leads to a consistent improvement in policing standards. As for political control, the patronage and power exercised by the political executive, collectively and individually, too often assume an unhealthy and deleterious character, and, when unchecked, leads to a dangerous degree of politicization, for a long time the bane of policing in India. It is for these reasons that most advocates of deep reforms in the Indian police have consistently defended the concept of SSC that would act as a buffer between police and politicians. We have already described the constitution and functions of such commissions.

It is axiomatic that a police system serving a democracy must itself be democratic. The key principles of democratic policing include:

- policing must be subject to the rule of law and not to the rule of individuals;
- equality of all must be upheld;
- a police that is subject to the rule of law cannot be a law unto itself.

Checks and balances have to be carefully woven into the accountability processes. The circumstances in which the law enforcers can intervene in citizens' lives or exercise coercive power have to be precisely defined and adhered to. Although, these conditions have been well defined in the Indian Constitution, the penal and procedural law, police acts and manuals, as well as in numerous executive instructions, have been clarified and repeatedly emphasized by the Supreme Court and the other high courts, they are rarely strictly enforced due to a glaring dilution of chains of command and a growing culture of impunity.

Civic oversight over police is now being preferred even in advanced countries where the police have been found to be grossly racist. In the United Kingdom, following the murder in 1993 of Stephen Lawrence, a young, Black man, by White "goons," a committee appointed by the government (McPherson Committee, 1999) found that racism within the police had become institutionalized. This finding prompted across-the-board police reform dealing specifically with ways of making the police less race-biased and an independent police complaints authority was set up when surveys showed that the public had no faith in the police. Police recruitment also was reoriented to reflect the multiethnic character of the country's population. Similarly in the United States, a videotape of a Black motorist, Rodney King, being mercilessly beaten in 1991 by two or three police officers led to a change in the law that the Department of Justice will apply civil level of proof to make police liable in determining the pattern and practice of police misconduct. Civil level means that in a case of police misconduct related to racial violence and other patterns of misbehavior the complainant does not have to make his case beyond a reasonable doubt, but just up to the standard of a balance of probabilities. As a result, police authorities in these jurisdictions pay a lot of compensation to members of the public every year for illegal acts by their police. In cases where there is continuous monitoring that reveals a pattern, the government may do away with an entire department. In India, the difficulty with accountability is that while the political establishment continues to gravely undermine the existing internal accountability mechanisms by dominating its management and control systems, it stoutly refuses to supplement them by carrying out major systemic reforms. Instead of moving toward a professional corporate structure judged by its performance, the skein of patronage and pelf means that, to retain the facade of discipline, the Indian police must stay feudal. Its composition of 95% constables and 3 to 4% middle-level officers with only 1% IPS cadres requires that it stay feudal. Any program for converting the Indian police into a body of professional men and women must provide for high education levels for all ranks, no lateral induction so that every officer comes through the ranks, that specialization takes place at an early stage, and promotional avenues are governed by mid-career training and a series of in-service examinations. The current structural and functional norms in the Indian police seriously militate against the conceptual framework of multiple accountability mechanisms.

The issue of police impunity is currently engaging the attention of many Indian civil society groups. It is almost impossible for a citizen victim of police excesses to secure relief from the courts because of the law of impunity and huge pendencies,* while other oversight instruments like the legislatures and the various statutory commissions are weak and often negligent. Internal police accountability mechanisms have become defunct due to rampant politicization of law enforcement agencies.

Importance of Civic Oversight

In the absence of transparent and efficient internal accountability devices, the need for an external agency for civic oversight becomes all the more

* Pendencies refers to a large number of cases remaining pending or undecided in courts, thereby denying relief to the complainants against police for illegal, improper, or unfair action. Impunity refers to the Indian legal provision that no police official can be prosecuted for any act purported to be done in the discharge of his duties except with the prior sanction of the competent authority, which term generally means the appointing authority viz. the state or the union government as the case may be. Thus, even when sanction is available, long pendencies defeat the purpose of timely relief to the aggrieved citizen.

imperative. Police acts in most advanced countries do not talk of control and superintendence, but of responsibilities of the minister or the government to provide to the community an efficient, effective, clean, and accountable police force and lay down clearly how that responsibility has to be discharged. Thus, the secretary of state in the United Kingdom is required to exercise his powers over the police "in such manner and to such extent as it appears to him to be best calculated to promote the efficiency and effectiveness of the police." The system provides for a triangular structure—the secretary of state representing the political executive, the local chief constable representing the police, and the police authority representing the community. The act requires the secretary of state to determine the objectives of policing in different areas and this has to be done by him in consultation with the other two components of the institution, i.e., the police and the community. A statutory instrument containing the objectives as determined under this provision has to be laid before the Parliament. Police authorities are then asked to set performance targets for the police. The broad goals so determined are then made public along with expected standards of performance, which are then monitored. Political control is not compromised, but, at the same time, scope for improper or colored political interference is minimized. Performance standards are set in a manner that the political authority can monitor police performance and continue to be responsible for ensuring that the police do not fail to fulfill them. The process also ensures that both remain responsible to Parliament and the community for properly meeting the people's expectations from the police. The secretary of state also can direct the HMIC (Her Majesty's Inspectorate of Constabulary) to inspect any police force and ask the concerned police authority to take remedial action, if the inspection reveals that the force is not working efficiently or effectively. The police act of Northern Ireland introduces a new provision so far as standard setting for policing is concerned. The secretary of state is now required not merely to issue a statement of principles to guide police functioning in Northern Ireland, but also to ensure that the statement must include the principle that the policing of Northern Ireland is to be conducted in an impartial manner.

In South Africa where police reforms have been precipitated by situations of widespread conflict, the Constitution itself provides that it will be the responsibility of the cabinet minister concerned to "determine national policing policy after consulting the provincial governments and taking into account the policing needs and priorities of the provinces." The national commissioner is required to "exercise control over and manage the police service in accordance with the national policing policy." The national commissioner is required to formulate a plan before the end of each financial year, setting out the priorities and objectives of policing for the following year. In British Columbia (Canada), it is the responsibility of the cabinet minister concerned to "ensure that an adequate and effective level of policing and law enforcement is maintained throughout British Columbia." Each municipal council is required under the law to set up a police department, which is governed by a municipal police board, comprised of the mayor, one member appointed by the council, and not more than five other members to be appointed by the lieutenant governor of the province.

The mechanisms provided in the police acts of the countries mentioned above fulfill three purposes. The overall responsibility for making available an efficient and effective police force to the community rests with the political executive and yet functional autonomy remains invested with the police chief. There is a statutory public process for arriving at a careful demarcation of roles as between the politicians, the police, and the community. Goals and performances are both governed by standards set in advance and there are systems of public accountability to ensure that performance does not fall short of the predetermined goals. The preindependence Indian Police Act of 1861 and the postindependence Police Acts of some states, which have enacted new legislations in place of the 1861 Act, talk only of control and superintendence over the police, but do not explain as to how such powers are to be exercised, while the Police Acts of most Western countries make it a statutory responsibility of the government to set up an adequate, efficient, and effective police service in each area. It is this statutory obligation that makes the governments, and not the police top brass alone, accountable for failures in the field of policing and forces them to take credible steps to monitor police performance and take timely and determined action to improve such performance. The questions relating to the accountability of the police have emerged as the most difficult part of planning a course of action for early police reforms. Who should the police be answerable to for failure to provide an efficient and effective security cover to the community? Vague formulations put forward from time to time regarding its accountability to the rule of law, to the courts, to the elective representatives, or to their own superior officers, hardly serve the purpose.

In countries like the United Kingdom, United States, Japan, and South Africa, multiple mechanisms of accountability have been put in place, either by enacting separate legislation or by prescribing necessary provisions in their Police Acts. The bulk of the Indian people are not even aware of the constitutional position in this regard, nor are they overly keen to actively promote a process of reforms that might lend a measure of autonomy to police functioning in the fear that an autonomous police would surely become even more oppressive and unaccountable than what they are under the present system. One way in which police accountability can be enhanced is by creating an objective and credible organization to inquire into complaints against the police. The 1861 Police Act has little to say on the subject of public accountability of the police, as such concepts simply did not exist in the context of policing a subject nation. The NPC recommended the setting up of a judicial authority in each district to expeditiously inquire into serious complaints against the police. They also thought that the proposed SSCs would go a long way in augmenting the scope of police accountability in the discharge of their duties inasmuch as they will ensure that the police will perform and behave according to the requirements of law.

Two important functions envisaged for the SSCs proposed by the NPC are to prescribe policy guidelines and directions for the performance of preventive and service-oriented tasks of the police and to evaluate the performance of the police. Foreign police forces have different processes and models whereby they ensure adequate police accountability and responsiveness. The Police Act of South Africa, for example, provides for the establishment of an independent complaints directorate at both national and provincial levels to investigate misconduct or criminal offense allegedly committed by a police official. The directorate functions independently from the police service under a director nominated by the minister in consultation with parliamentary committees, dealing with internal security. He is required to submit an annual report to the minister in charge of the police within 3 months of the end of the financial year. The report has to be tabled in the parliament by the minister within 14 days of its receipt. In the United Kingdom, the inspectorate of constabulary and the police complaints authority perform such supervisory, monitoring, and inquiry functions as may be necessary to ensure police accountability and high levels of performance. In the United States, complaints of police brutality, particularly against the Blacks, led to the enactment of many new laws to enhance state powers to bring to book guilty policemen.

Conclusion

Unless Indian authorities move away from their traditional obsessions with control and superintendence over the police to a broader framework of functional autonomy for the police, combined with a regime of strict enforcement of accountability parameters, the Indian police will continue to prove woefully inadequate in fulfilling the demands of a democratic polity. Mere dependence on overhauling of training curricula and a profusion of executive instructions to the police departments to infuse in them the requisite degree of responsiveness and sensitivity to the democratic urges, aspirations, and rights of a free society is hardly likely to change the traditional functioning modes and attitudes of the Indian police. Not unless the basic law governing police functioning is radically altered and updated. Only a new law in conformity with the constitutional imperatives and vastly changed societal realities, buttressed with adequate and clearly defined mechanisms of civilian oversight and community accountability, can properly cope with the worsening state of law and order in the country. Indian lawmakers failed to perceive the intimate linkages between a forward-looking Constitutional framework and the vital need to restructure state instruments for the achievement of the goals enshrined in the former. In any event, while the preamble to the Constitution envisaged revolutionary changes in the pattern of governance in independent India, its makers stopped far short of providing the complete wherewithal, in the shape of state organs, to fulfill their ambitious goals. Instead of going the whole hog, they merely copied out large portions of the Government of India Act-1935, legislation dating back to the British times and designed for a totally different purpose. Democracy in postcolonial societies has to come to grips with two fundamental problems of governance. One is their inbuilt tendency to look for short-term solutions to long-standing problems. The other is the change in the nature of democracy itself since the advent and rapid spread of television, which has put a premium on the selling of politicians like the marketing of a product, thereby concealing the real worth of the political leadership. This inevitably led to a sharp qualitative decline in the credibility of the political classes and, consequently, of all state organs, among them the police, with disastrous consequences, as all know only too well. Such a decline gravely affects the quality of governance and the service that the citizen receives from the administrative structure. The resultant distortions in the modes of functioning of the state organs soon envelops the entire society in a vicious cycle of degeneration and inadequate measures to remedy it. The strange predicament in which the Indian polity and its law-enforcement agencies find themselves at the end of the first decade of the new century, is the product of over half a century of indifference and apathy in the matter of exploring innovative strategies to update and upgrade the country's legal architecture, inherited from a colonialist oligarchic administrative framework, rooted in the mid-19th century. The multiple policing challenges of a globalized world cannot be adequately addressed if the principal instruments of law enforcement and adjudication remain enmeshed in administrative concepts, legal structures, and functional charters of a bygone era.

7

Tracing the Diffusion of Policing Governance Models From the British Isles and Back Again

Some Directions for Democratic Reform in Troubled Times

MICHAEL KEMPA

Contents

Introduction

We have reached a watershed moment in policing and its governance. The public police are facing a critical "crisis of legitimacy" to the point that it has become difficult to forge the trusting police–community partnerships that are essential for effective community policing programs. The development of robust policing governance mechanisms has long been understood as the most effective institutional means to overcome these challenges. Meanwhile, it is well known that the public police have lost whatever tenuous grasp they ever held on a monopoly over the business of policing, with the resurgence in the involvement of the paid private security industry and other nonstate agencies in the process of policing over the past three decades. These trends complicate the liberal democratic riddle of who ought to direct policing and toward what ends. In this chapter, I trace the evolution of programs for policing governance as they have diffused from Britain across the once far-reaching British Empire. Through this analysis, the inadequacy of what has been our piecemeal and largely technocratic approach to resolving what I argue is the essentially political problem of policing reform more generally is revealed. Drawing upon recent fieldwork I have undertaken in Northern Ireland, the paper moves to examine the implementation and early operation of ongoing radical policing governance reforms in this territory. These initiatives are premised on a holistic and ideological rationale that rightly connects policing reform to the difficult forms of political questions that must be addressed if we are ever to achieve "democratic" policing systems in a world whose political terrain is increasingly unfamiliar and bitterly contested. The lynchpin of this program is the creation of powerful, deliberative institutions wherein groups with very different worldviews negotiate the type of policing as part of the type of polity that they agree to share.

Modern Liberal Dream: Crime Prevention Through Community Policing

In candid discussions, policing practitioners often wryly acknowledge that policing and the question of its reform is not of the same order of technical complexity as rocket science. Proof of this humbling notion is found in the fact that the huge volume of reports produced by innumerable commissions of inquiry, human rights organizations, nongovernmental policy "think tanks," and independent academic criminologists who have addressed the issue of policing reform in both established and transitional democratic contexts have tended over the past 30 or more years to produce very similar recommendations; these bodies have consistently advocated the development of the "community policing" model.

Indeed, apart from a brief period over the course of the middle decades of the 20th century wherein a "professionalized" public police service attempted to grasp the mantle of the "expert agency" that was "in charge" of fighting crime, community policing in one form or another has been the liberal democratic ideal since the time of the principal founding father of modern public policing, Sir Robert Peel. Peel and the other engineers of the modern public police agency themselves considered that the public police would only ever achieve the ideal of crime prevention through mobilizing a network of resources in the community so as to maintain an "unremitting watch" over collective goings-on (see Radzinowicz, 1968; also Critchley, 1966; Emsley, 2004; Reiner, 2000). While the established democracies of the West departed from this ideal through the aforementioned "professionalized" era of policing, which was itself largely an historical accident, we have come full circle. Very few who have subjected policing to rigorous analysis believe that the public police working on their own will ever grasp the brass ring of achieving effective crime prevention. Community policing, in which the public police work in varying degrees of partnership with the community commensurate with the degree of citizen interest and political stability that holds in a particular context, is the global reformatory order of the day.

Obstacles to the Dream: Policing Is Inherently Political

In his concluding remarks at a public conference on policing issues held in Northern Ireland in 2002, the Vice Chairman of the Policing Board for Northern Ireland, one of the primary agencies responsible for policing governance in that territory, aptly highlighted the simultaneous technical simplicity and political difficulty inherent in the issue of policing reform in contemporary times:

> We don't have to reinvent the wheel.... Ultimately policing is about making people feel safe in the houses they live in, in the streets which they walk, and the neighborhoods where they shop. And it is not a greater science than that; but in many ways it is the science that most civilizations in the third millennium face and have the greatest difficulty with (Bradley, 2002).

Bradley's allusion to the "third millennium" may seem dramatic; however, it illustrates the fact that our policing problems are the result of social, political, legal, and economic issues that extend beyond any particular shortcomings relating to the ideology, structure, and practices of the public police agency.

Indeed, fostering the trusting relationships necessary for effective community policing relationships stands as a problem as old as the modern public police service itself and amounts to the manifestation of foundational questions and tensions in liberal democratic theory and politics. Throughout the history of the development of the modern state project, liberal democratic nations have wrestled with the issue of how best to balance respect for individual liberties with the need to enforce the defined order and offer citizens assurances of security. The ingrained concern in liberal democratic culture to protect individual liberties within such a political process has translated into the constant wariness of, which has at various stages boiled over into outright opposition to, the public police organization ever since the idea for the implementation of the modern incarnation of this institution was mooted in Britain some 75 years prior to the eventual introduction of the first "bobbies" to the streets of London in 1829 (Critchley, 1966; Reiner, 2000; Williams, 2003).

These tensions have been compounded in recent times in the context of globalization. Public police institutions, as repositories of state sovereign authority, have struggled at the same time and for the same reasons that states themselves have struggled in the decades leading up to and the few years immediately following the outset of our new millennium.

Whatever "globalization" may be, it is associated with three major aspects that have shattered our ability to easily imagine the consensus of standards and opinion upon which "modern" approaches to governance wherein states take the lead in setting and enforcing rules have been premised. Firstly, in established liberal democracies, the increasing global flow of capital and, thereby people, has rendered national populations increasingly culturally (and ethnically) diverse, making it more difficult to agree on common standards that ought to form the basis of enforceable order.

Secondly, in attempting to meet the political and economic challenges associated with the competitive and unpredictable global economy, nation-states in the West have for three decades undertaken massive governmental restructuring. This has largely been according to the "neo-liberal" ideals of lean governments working "at a distance" to harness the power of the market to organize collective life (see, especially, Latour, 1987; also Burchell, 1993; Rose, 1996; Rose & Miller, 1992, p. 182). While there is a good deal of debate as to how well neo-liberal politics will work in the long term, most commentators agree that undoing the web of social security spun over the heyday of welfare liberal politics over the middle decades of the 20th century has greatly widened the gap between the wealthy and marginalized economic classes (see, e.g., Held, McGrew, Goldblatt, & Perraton, 1999; Stiglitz, 2002). As a result, we have seen protests against the ascendancy of the market and decline of the welfare liberal state take to the streets and often turn into violence in many high profile instances around the globe in recent times. Where there has been such conflict over the content of the laws and general form of the nation–state, the public police have found themselves in the middle of it.

Thirdly, globalization also has been associated with the completion of the retreat of the once great imperial empires. The economic collapse of communism in Eastern Europe and apartheid in South Africa, coupled with a surge in military adventurism in the context of a "war on terror" being spearheaded by the United States, has also seen the undoing of authoritarian systems of rule in many theatres around the planet. In these cases, the internally divided national populations (often having initially been artificially grouped together to begin with) have been left to struggle (in many cases, admirably) to achieve the internal consensus necessary for political and economic stability. The case of the Irish Nationalists/Republicans and British Unionists/Loyalists who have attempted to eke out a basis for living together within the contested territory of Northern Ireland—making much progress under the Belfast Agreement signed in April of 1998—serves as a prime example of these dynamics (see Bew, Gibbon, & Patterson, 2002; McGarry & O'Leary, 1995, 1999). Suspicion between the factions that comprise these "national" populations and the police services associated with the former imperial or authoritarian régimes remains in most cases entrenched (see, e.g., Ellison & Smyth, 2000; Los, 2002).

These trends associated with the broad umbrella concept of "globalization" have together led to the widely acknowledged resurgence in the (cyclical) "crisis in legitimacy" (Habermas, 1984, p. 361, 1987, 1996, 1998) of the public police institution at the outset of our third millennium. Caught in a broader context of political and economic turmoil, the public police have been involved in (and have been seen to be involved in) maintaining the sovereign interests of the troubled nation-state, which are often seen as overlapping with the interests of the dominant classes, whether in terms of those who control capital (see, e.g., Hall, Critcher, Jefferson, Clark, & Roberts, 1978; Scraton, 1985) or the ethnic or cultural majority (Brogden & Shearing, 1993; Ellison & Smyth, 2000; Weitzer, 1995).

The inescapable problem is that policing, as a process that directly impacts the balance of power and distribution of resources in society and that thereby plays a significant role in shaping the character of the polity, is inherently political in the macro sense (Bayley, 2001). Further, the public police represent the sovereign and cultural identity of the polity (Loader, 1997). Thus, deciding on the precise form that community policing reform initiatives must ultimately take in practice is centrally connected to the broader ideological and practical question of deciding the form that the polity ought to take in the global era—as hotly contested a political conflict as there is ever likely to be. It is a problem largely engaged in and responded to by stakeholders in both ideological (i.e., "high political") and partisan (i.e., "low political") terms. Seen in this light, our prospects for achieving the liberal democratic ideal of crime prevention through public police-led community partnerships appear dim.

A further riddle for democratic policing reform in our times (deeply related to the crisis in legitimacy of the public police) is how best to address the ongoing "quiet revolution" in nonstate security (Shearing & Stenning, 1981). It has been well documented that the paid private security sector has grown rapidly in both the established democracies (especially in the United States) and in transitional democratic contexts over the past three decades (Rigakos & Greener, 2000; Shearing & Stenning, 1981, 1983; on continental Europe, de Waard, 1999). Furthermore, the most violent forms of vigilantism have arisen in the most marginalized of communities, largely as a result of alienation from public police services.

The development of these systems of nonstate security poses many challenges to democratic values. Where the private security industry is directly hired in service of the interests of property owners, concerns arise regarding the potential for the arbitrary and excessive governance of marginalized segments of the community within large privately owned spaces where much social life takes place (see especially, Johnson, 2000; Johnston & Shearing, 2003; Shearing & Stenning, 1983). These new forms of "communal spaces" include types of "mass private property," such as shopping and entertainment complexes that dominate city landscapes in both established liberal democracies and nations in political transition around the world (Kempa, Stenning, & Wood, 2004).

As a whole, we are threatened with an emergent system of policing in which the wealthy secure themselves and their possessions within spaces that they own and police according to their own standards through private security initiatives, while less well-off communities are governed through public policing agencies that are in a poor structural and ideological position to develop robust community policing models, whatever their good intentions. Thus, we have the widely acknowledged yet tragic fact that community policing is most difficult in those communities where it is most needed; within socially disadvantaged communities where crime rates are highest and police–community relationships are poor (Jones, MacLean, & Young, 1986; Lea & Young, 1993; Leighton, 1991, p. 508). "Fire brigade" (or what is sometimes called "zero tolerance" or "confident" policing (Kelling & Wilson, 1996)) presents itself to the public police as the regrettable yet unavoidable policing alternative in such communities (Kempa et al., 2004).

In Search of Solutions: Institutionalizing Policing Governance

In contrast with the notion presented above that trends in public and private policing are deeply interrelated phenomena traceable to ideologically charged issues associated with the changing nature of the polity in the "global" era, it has been the tendency of practitioners and governments to approach the question of policing and its reform in the technical terms of a "police science," as a problem of detailed legislative and institutional design, resource allocation, and training. Practitioner attention also has been piecemeal and partial, focusing upon the "crisis of legitimacy" of the public police while glossing over the issue of how best to govern nonstate security agencies (Johnston & Shearing, 2003; Loader, 2000). Reflective of this historical focus, I will concentrate on efforts to refine the governance of public policing as a means of enhancing its legitimacy before turning to a discussion of a more synthetic approach to governing policing as a whole currently in the earliest stages of operation in Northern Ireland.

Although we have seen that the crisis in legitimacy of the public police is a rather cyclical phenomenon that, in fact, precedes the genesis of the institution, police community relations dramatically worsened in the context of the tumultuous 1960s (Hall et al., 1978; Scraton, 1985). It was in this context that the question of policing governance moved to the fore (Reiner, 2000; Walker, 2000). The foundation for our modern system of democratic policing governance, consisting of mechanisms both for handling complaints brought against police abuses of authority and for the review and shaping of policing policy and expenditure was laid down in Britain through the Police Act 1964, which was legislated in response to recommendations made by a Royal Commission into police community relationships undertaken in Britain in 1962 (Critchley, 1966).

Pursuant to this Act, complaints brought against the public police would be primarily the responsibility of the public police themselves, who would be charged with receiving and investigating complaints along with adjudicating discipline. It was only after many years of pressure (met by substantial police resistance) that an independent element for the review of the investigation and resolution of complaints was established; the Police Act 1976 created the Police Complaints Board in Britain. In the sphere of reviewing and shaping policing policy, standards, and expenditure, the Police Act 1964 established the "tripartite system" for policing governance. Within this system, these responsibilities would be divided between chief constables, the pertinent ministry within the executive branch of government, and newly minted "Police Authorities." The Police Authorities were initially comprised of a combination of locally elected councilors and magistrates, and later came to include lay members of the public. They were charged with the nebulous duty of "securing the maintenance of an adequate and efficient police force for the area" (Police Act 1964, section 4.1); a legislated responsibility that has been the source of much confusion and conflict between the three legs of the tripartite structure (see Jones & Newburn, 1997; Reiner, 2000; Walker, 2000).

This general institutional approach for dealing with complaints and shaping police policy was modeled throughout the former colonies of the once-vast British Empire; similar models were implemented in the United States, Canada (Stenning, 1996), Australia (Chan, 1999; Dupont, 2003), and the contested British statelet of Northern Ireland (Dickson, 1998; Ryder, 2004) over the course of the late 1960s through to the mid-1980s. The diffusion of the twin aspects of this model for policing governance across these contexts has been characterized by very consistent (interrelated) themes.

Firstly, while most policing reform protagonists have been in agreement as to the basic institutional form of these structures for police governance, the ideological question of where to draw the line demarcating who is responsible for precisely what functions has plagued the efficient operation of these institutions across all jurisdictions to the present day. Secondly, the perception of the weakness and inefficacy of the bodies designed to represent the public interest has rendered many of the groups that are alienated from the police reluctant to engage with such bodies. Thirdly (and consequently), these institutional arrangements for achieving police governance have been under near constant review in Britain, Canada, Australia, Northern Ireland, and various jurisdictions in the United States since their advent. There have been myriad attempts to "reinvent the wheel" as practitioners have sought the "golden fleece" of an optimal technical definition of responsibility allocation that would magically inspire confidence in the police within marginalized communities (Landau, 2000; Wood, 2000).

In the domain of contests around police complaints procedures, the critical issue has always been the degree to which there ought to be an independent civilian component at the levels of the receipt, investigation, and adjudication of complaints brought against the police. We have seen a trend toward external review in recent years (Goldsmith, 1995). Across jurisdictions in Britain, Canada, Australia, Northern Ireland, and the United States, there are in existence independent bodies responsible in most cases for receiving complaints and which are empowered in many cases to undertake investigations (though, in all but the most serious instances, the public police continue to be charged with investigating themselves under the oversight/review of these bodies), and, in some cases, are directly involved in the process of adjudicating discipline. Significantly, this general trend toward external review has not been linear (Landau, 2000).

In the second domain of policing governance, governments across each of these contexts have been very reluctant to devolve significant control over policing standards and policing budgets to local Police Authorities. Despite the oft-repeated language in governmental white papers, annual reports, and sundry public documents hailing the enhancement of democracy, deepening of local participation, and devolution of powers and responsibilities that various efforts to rebalance the tripartite system are purported to entail, the sum of governmental policy and behind-the-scenes partisan political action has amounted to a clear trend toward increasing de facto centralized control over policing policy and expenditure (on Britain, see Jones & Newburn, 1997; Reiner, 2000, p. 188–198; Australia: Chan, 1999; Dupont, 2003). This has been accomplished largely through the control of the policing purse strings at the regional and federal levels of government (Ibid.).

For their part in these matters, the public police have in many contexts been similarly reluctant to yield power to Police Authorities. Most of this has turned on the difficult concept of "operational independence," wherein police managers have asserted that the widely respected notion that nobody ought to be able to interfere in operational matters renders them accountable to the law alone. Some particularly activist members of Police Authorities across these jurisdictions, supported by the entire weight of scholarly opinion (see Lustgarten, 1986; Stenning, 1996; Walker, 2000), have countered that operational independence ought to mean that no outside body should have the ability to direct the execution of any operational matter in the instance, and that nothing in this precludes Police Authorities from having an important role in actively shaping policing policy, objectives, and expenditure in line with what they see as the overriding concerns of the communities they represent. When the police have been challenged on these points by Police Authorities, courts in Britain (Lustgarten, 1986; Walker, 2000), Canada (Hann, McGinnis, Stenning, & Farson, 1985; Stenning, 1996), and Australia (Chan, 1999; Dupont, 2003) have been sympathetic to the expansive interpretations of the operational independence construct advanced by police command, despite the fact that there exist no formal constitutional articulations of this construct.

In this context of a deep-held and vocal reluctance on the part of governments and chief constables to cede control over police policy and expenditure, the practical history of the operation of the tripartite system can only be described as woeful in Britain (Jones & Newburn, 1997), Canada (Hann et al., 1985), Australia (Dupont, 2003), and in Northern Ireland (Ryder, 2004). Timidity has characterized the action of police authorities at nearly every turn: it is a universally held view in academia that Police Authorities have never lived up to their promise as agencies that would achieve the 'democratization' of policing. As such, they are widely regarded as 'lame-duck' institutions within communities with poor trusting relationships of the public police—if such communities are aware of the existence and role of these bodies at all (Hann et al., 1985; Jones & Newburn, 1997; Ryder, 2004). Technological initiatives to recalibrate the powers of these institutions have done little to enhance the legitimacy of the public police.

We can round out this damning assessment of governmental efforts to govern policing by reiterating the notion that these technological and piecemeal approaches have accomplished next to nothing to render accountable the massive and growing paid private security industry that polices expansive tracts of mass private property. Where a citizen feels they have been treated improperly by one of these nonstate policing bodies, to whom may they turn, apart from initiating costly court proceedings? Who is making sure that the policies and practices of private security firms conform to the standards of democracy that we are so adamant that public policing agencies must meet? On these difficult questions, governments and policy makers have had very little of note to say (Joh, 2004; Sklansky, 1999; Stenning, 2000).

Recent Directions in Policing Governance: Radical Experiments in Northern Ireland

The analysis presented to this point suggests that policing reform must begin by making significant progress toward clarifying our practical objectives and normative aspirations for the polity (accepting that we will never finally resolve these issues) and then work backwards to design the policing system that will effect these ends. In the real world of fiscal constraints, the process of design must involve training a realistic eye on the resources that are already at our disposal in wondering how they might be adapted to our agreed normative ends.

This is precisely what has been done in the most recent efforts to address the question of policing reform as part of Northern Ireland's ongoing broader peace process. This territory, formed by the partition of Ireland in 1920, has been plagued by a poisoned political economy over its history of British colonization and Irish Republican resistance (in overview, see Jackson, 1999; Lydon, 1998). Policing has been at the very center of this conflict from the outset. It did not take long for alienation and hostility to develop between Northern Ireland's Nationalist and Republican communities and the Royal Ulster Constabulary, with policing militarization and local vigilantism in disaffected communities being the unfortunate results (Ellison & Smyth, 2000; Hillyard, 1993; Knox, 2002; Weitzer, 1995). Previous efforts to instill community confidence in the Royal Ulster Constabulary, which took the form of the standard piecemeal and technological initiatives outlined in the previous section, had come to naught in Nationalist and Republican communities.

It has only been in the context of massive ideological shifts reflected in the Belfast Agreement reached in April 1998 that significant (though, as yet, incomplete) progress has been made in improving relationships between the institutions for policing and the divided communities of Northern Ireland. Through the Belfast Agreement, the "constitutional question" was finally settled in terms that Northern Ireland would remain a part of the United Kingdom until such time that simultaneous majorities in both Northern Ireland and the Republic of Ireland dictated otherwise. Further, the Agreement entrenched the concept of "parity of esteem" for all political traditions in the institutions for governance in Northern Ireland, ranging from a local assembly and a public service to, as part of this, the public police (on the nature of the Agreement, see O'Leary, 2001).

In this more optimistic "transitional" (as opposed to more fully "divided") political context, an Independent Commission on Policing Reform in Northern Ireland (chaired by Chris Patten, the last governor of Hong Kong) was appointed by the British government with the view to bringing forth recommendations for policing reform that would inspire confidence across the communities of Northern Ireland. Within these broad terms of reference, the Commission addressed the issue of how best to deliver and govern policing as a whole in Northern Ireland: both state and nonstate forms. The plan that the Commission came up with was reflective of the binational character of the polity that had been agreed in the Belfast Agreement. It called for the creation of institutions for the governance of policing that were inclusive of all political traditions while rendering the ethos of policing as upholding human rights rather than representing the authority of the sovereign British state. In practical terms, this program was designed to inspire the cross-community confidence necessary to develop policing in partnership with the community.

Toward achieving these aims, Patten began with conventional reforms to the structure of the public police organization, centering on the principles of decentralization and subsidiary. It also called for a neutral name and insignia to be assigned to the public police service. More radical in the Patten Report was its treatment of the issue of policing governance. In the sphere of handling complaints brought against the public police, Patten called for the consolidation of a completely independent Police Ombudsman's Office, charged with the independent receipt and investigation of complaints brought against the police, the power of initiating investigations *ex officio* where it is in the public interest to do so, and having a direct role at the stage of adjudication in recommending disciplinary action.

More radical still were Patten's recommendations pertaining to the public oversight and shaping of policing policy and expenditure. The lynchpin of this project was the creation of powerful, deliberative institutions that would bring together representatives of all sides of the political divide in Northern Ireland, who would negotiate local plans for policing in line with the type of society that they themselves considered they were working toward. One of the key features of these forums was the degree to which they would be unconstrained in their internal operation by central government. Apart from setting broad limits on what these bodies could not do, Patten included no specific program specifying how these bodies should go about their day-to-day business; there were to be the minimum possible number of centrally defined rules for deliberation.

At the national level, Patten called for the replacement of the old Police Authority with a "Policing Board" whose powers would radically tilt the balance of power within the tripartite system away from central government in favor of local community representatives and, additionally, broaden the scope of the agency beyond governing the public police to address policing as a whole. A number of powers and mechanisms were to be granted to the Board toward meeting this novel role. With respect to becoming the dominant institution for governing the public police, the Board was to be given extensive powers to request reports of the chief constable into any aspect of police operations. These were only to be limited in the instance that it was in the public rather than the police interest to hold back such information. Where unsatisfied with such reports, the Board would be empowered to initiate inquiries into the same matter. The same, very limited caveats would apply. Thus, Patten had attempted to cut through the "Gordian knot" of the operational independence construct, through substituting the conception of "operational responsibility" wherein the public police would be charged with independently undertaking operational matters, but would clearly be responsible for accounting for all operational decisions after the fact. Furthermore, Patten was unambiguous that the Board be empowered to set mid- and long-range policing priorities (and the measures for assessing whether these priorities were being met) for the chief constable. With respect to more immediate matters, the Board and chief constable would agree on annual plans in collaboration.

Toward the regulation of policing as a whole, the Board was to be charged with the administration of a broader policing budget. All agencies involved in policing as an aspect of the "common good"—including the public police, private security, and voluntary community organizations—would be required to submit costed plans to the Board for its approval. Thus, in addition to traditional levers of accountability over the public police and other policing agencies held by Police Authorities in Britain and farther afield, Patten was explicit that the local Policing Board ought to be empowered to control the budget for "public interest" policing. It would not be expected that the Board would simply hand over all of the budget to the public police.

At the local level, Patten also called for the establishment of District Policing Partnership Boards, comprised of local councilors and lay members of the public who would be charged with the development of local safety plans in collaboration with their local public police detachment. Significantly, these bodies would also have the power to generate small amounts of local tax revenues that they could spend on community safety initiatives that could involve any agencies capable of making a contribution to public safety.

If the Patten program is the future of policing and its governance, it is instructive to look at the recent implementation and early operation of this radical system in Northern Ireland (Ellison & Smyth, 2000, p. 189). The reaction of governmental programmers and stakeholders in policing reform concretizes the argument presented above that policing reform is a difficult political issue that will best be settled by those citizens directly affected by how policing is undertaken through ongoing processes of negotiation in innovative deliberative structures.

The Implementation and Early Operation of the Patten Program

The responses to the Patten program of the British government and the range of stakeholders in policing reform in Northern Ireland are entirely predictable in terms of the long-term trends in the diffusion of policing governance initiatives presented above. On the one hand, the radical stream of the Patten program was "gutted" as the report was translated by the British government into the Police (Northern Ireland) Act 2000 (Hillyard & Tomlinson, 2000; Shearing, 2000). On the other hand, stakeholders initially received, interpreted, and contested Patten and the legislation, which resulted from it in nearly entirely symbolic terms related to their aspirations for the nature and identity of the contested polity.

Thus, the British government turned the ethos of the legislation from a Policing Act to a Police Act. The Policing Board was to be involved in the circumspect task of overseeing and shaping police rather than polic*ing* practice, policy, and expenditure, and, moreover, the powers awarded to them in this more circumspect domain did not reflect the radical realignment of the tripartite structure envisaged in the Patten Report. The power of the Board to hold the chief constable operationally responsible was diminished, with the secretary of state being rendered the ultimate "guarantor" of the democratic standard of policing. First, expansive clauses enabling the secretary of state to limit the Board's power to request reports and further initiate inquiries into police practice and policy were added to the legislation. Second, the broader "policing" budget was redefined as a police budget, and would not be placed directly under the control of the Policing Board in the fashion that Patten had intended. Timidity in budgeting matters was repeated at the level of the District Policing Partnership Boards, whereas the power of these bodies to raise local revenues to spend on broader policing initiatives advocated in Patten was rejected by the British government.

Two aspects of the worldview of the British government render these legislative shifts intelligible. First, the British government considered that the Patten recommendations were radical compared with any other policing initiatives in existence in the balance of the United Kingdom and, indeed, throughout the world. Second, the "administrative anthropological" (O'Malley, 1996) assessment of the "readiness" of the people of Northern Ireland to implement such a radical model was poor. The British government considered that it was pursuing a strategy of implementing Patten in full through a process of "gradations" in keeping with developments in the Northern Irish peace process (Northern Ireland Office, 2000, p. 10). As such, trimming back the radical stream of the Patten project can be understood as an effort made by the British government to maintain a firm hand on the rudder steering political progress in Northern Ireland.

If indeed these were the true underlying motivations of the British government, to understand the fallout of these initiatives, it is critical to realize that none of the stakeholder organizations in Northern Ireland interpreted or understood the actions of the British government in these benign terms. Unionist and Loyalist politicians interpreted the efforts of the British government to install themselves as the ultimate guarantors of policing as part of a disingenuous effort to leave the door open to further concessions for Irish Republicanism beyond what had been negotiated through the Belfast Agreement in time. Conversely, departure from Patten was interpreted by Nationalists and Republicans as an insulting appraisal of the readiness of the people of Northern Ireland to govern themselves. Such resentment across the divide in Northern Ireland was the result of a deeply held suspicion of the intentions of the British government, coupled with a refusal to engage the novel policing institutions emergent from the new legislation until such time that the British government went farther in implementing Patten.

Nearly two years of such boycott and ongoing negotiations in a broader context of allegations of ongoing paramilitary operations and consequent pressure on the Provisional Irish Republican Army to accelerate its pace of disarmament saw the British government promise to render policing legislation further in line with the Patten program. The most important of these promises, from the perspective of all of the stakeholders in the reform process, centered on broadening the powers of the Policing Board in line with what had initially been recommended in the report in the event of further political progress in the province (Northern Ireland Office, 2001). These plans proved sufficient for Unionists and Loyalists along with constitutional Nationalists to take up their positions on the new Policing Board and endorse the reformed Police Service of Northern Ireland. It was, however, insufficient for representatives of mainstream Irish Republicanism to follow suit.

The early operation of these bodies—absent Republican representation—has yielded very positive results, all the more incredible given poor progress made on the broader political front in Northern Ireland. In the domain of handling complaints brought against the public police, tremendous public confidence across the political divide in Northern Ireland has been witnessed in the office of the police ombudsman.

The operation of the new deliberative Policing Board has likewise been extraordinary. Contrary to the bleak assessment of the readiness of the people of Northern Ireland to handle issues as serious as policing, groups that have for decades been bitterly divided over policing in largely emotional and symbolic terms have come together within the deliberative structure of the Board to agree on a common strategy for the future direction of policing in Northern Ireland as a whole. This program involves the development of the

District Policing Partnership structures. Critically, Board members understand the role of these bodies as "reintroducing the police to the community," which they understand to be in service of both immediate and broader purposes. In an immediate sense, the Board hopes that this program will improve police and community perceptions of one another through exposure and cooperation. In a broader sense, the Board considers that getting policing working on the ground in this fashion will naturally force or enable militant Republicans to sign up to policing and abandon their armed campaign through undermining remnants of popular support for paramilitary activity through providing a workable structured alternative. It is critical to note that the Board regards itself as prepared to stand up to any political opposition in achieving its aims.

The early successes of the Board are intriguing in what they suggest about how best we can achieve democratic policing in a global future likely to be characterized by increasing diversity and political conflict. Each member of the Board I interviewed indicated a high degree of motivation to create the conditions that would encourage the British government to devolve further policing powers to Northern Ireland in time. They considered that progress on the policing front was a vital part of improving the economic, social, and political future of Northern Ireland. This unity of purpose is intelligible in terms of Board members' common perception that the body was sufficiently empowered to achieve these "high political" aims. Significantly, most read this authority not in terms of any particular "technical" powers contained in legislation, but rather in terms that the contentious strictures placed over its internal business by the secretary of state in the Police (Northern Ireland) Act 2000 were to be removed in promised legislation (which ultimately came to pass in the Police (Northern Ireland) Act 2003).

Unencumbered by such contentious strictures, the Board engaged a process of deliberative negotiation wherein they reached compromise on policing approaches, not in terms of political horse trading on symbolic issues, but rather through a process of mutual persuasion and contestation as to the best synthetic programs for policing in the interests of the common good of all persons residing within Northern Ireland. As such, recent developments in policing governance in Northern Ireland would indicate that stakeholders in the policing process will seek out and avail themselves of opportunities to take control over the process of policing and, subsequently, behave responsibly owing to the importance of the task.

In this context of activist, civilian governance bodies widely perceived to be empowered to hold the public police to the standards of operational responsibility, Northern Ireland has seen some significant improvement in police–community relations. While the process of transformation is far from complete, and the data regarding shifts in levels of public acceptance for the police are more suggestive than conclusive, the trends are very positive. The most encouraging numbers concern public awareness and confidence in the new institutions for policing governance, which correspond with higher numbers of Catholic recruits joining the public police service than at any other point in Northern Ireland's history (Staff Reporter, 2003).

Concluding Comments

The review of the diffusion of systems for policing governance from Britain and across its onetime colonies bears important lessons for the development of democratic policing systems in our contested global times. It is clear that efforts to approach the problem of policing governance in terms of piecemeal issues that are amenable to technical solutions have proven counterproductive to deal with the changing policing and political landscape. The fact that decades of reviewing and realigning the technical distribution of responsibilities between civilian complaints bodies enjoying varying degrees of independence along with the three traditional legs of the tripartite structure has failed to produce any significant improvement in police–community relationships toward achieving the "modern liberal dream," of crime prevention through policing in partnership with the community can lead to no other conclusion. The particular case of Northern Ireland highlights that the tendency of political practitioners to want to retain centralized control over the process of policing reform can bring with it many unintended consequences. Stakeholders in the policing reform process, as the case of Northern Ireland indicates, may often interpret such actions on the part of governmental programmers in the most unflattering light, whatever the stated good intentions of governmental programmers themselves. In Northern Ireland, this process led to the refusal of stakeholders in the policing reform process to take up their positions within the novel institutions resultant of the Patten recommendations.

The experience of the Policing Board in Northern Ireland suggests that divergent political groups will likely approach the policing issue on responsible terms on the basis of their perceived importance of this issue for social justice, especially where they see a legitimate opportunity to shape the future. Against all expectations, the Board managed to achieve unity on the most divisive of issues, despite the initial efforts of the government to constrain it through legislative safeguards. While we cannot be certain that such approaches to deliberative governance will work in all instances, we can at least be certain—on the weight of the evidence presented in this chapter—that such approaches to reforming policing in our diverse and contested global times at least have the potential to work. As part of our strategy forward, we should reject those institutions and legislative approaches that we recognize on the balance of years of evidence to be obsolescent for addressing our present needs, not through simply condemning them, but through attempting to call attention to, build, refine, and participate in viable alternatives that at least offer the hope of policing and political reinvention.

References

Bayley, D. (2001). Democratizing the police abroad: What to do and how to do it. Washington, D.C.: U.S. Department of Justice.

Bew, P., Gibbon, P., & Patterson, H. (2002). Northern Ireland 1921–2001: Political forces and social classes. London: Serif.

Bradley, D. (2002). Closing comments. Paper presented at the Public Conference on Policing, the Policing Board for Northern Ireland, Belfast, June 5.

Brogden, M., & Shearing, C. (1993). Policing for new South Africa. London: Routledge.

Burchell, G. (1993). Liberal government and techniques of the self. Economy and Society, 22, 267–282.

Chan, J. (1999). Governing police practice: Limits of the new accountability. British Journal of Sociology, 50, 251–270.

Critchley, T. A. (1966). A history of police in England and Wales. London: Constable & Co.

De Waard, J. (1999). The private security industry in international perspective. European Journal on Criminal Policy and Research, 7, 143–174.

Dickson, B. (1998). The Police Authority for Northern Ireland: Comments and notes. Northern Ireland Legal Quarterly, 39, 277–283.

Dupont, B. (2003). The new governance of Australian police services. Journal of Australian Studies, 78, 15–24.

Ellison, G., & Smyth, J. (2000). The crowned harp: Policing Northern Ireland. London: Pluto Press.

Emsley, C. (2004). The birth and development of the police. In T. Newburn (Ed.), Handbook of policing (pp. 66–83). Cullompton, Devon, and Portland, OR: Willan Publishing.

Goldsmith, A. (1995). Necessary but not sufficient: the role of public complaints procedures in police accountability. In P. Stenning (Ed.), Accountability for criminal justice: Selected essays (pp. 110–134). Toronto: University of Toronto Press.

Habermas, J. (1984). The theory of communicative action: Reason and the rationalization of society (Vol. 1). Boston: Beacon Press.

Habermas, J. (1987). The theory of communicative action: Lifeworld and system: A critique of functionalist reason (Vol. 2). Cambridge, U.K.: Polity.

Habermas, J. (1996). Between facts and norms: Contributions to a discourse theory of law and democracy. Cambridge, MA: MIT Press.

Habermas, J. (1998). The inclusion of the other: Studies in political theory. In C. Cronin & P. de Greif (Eds.). Cambridge, MA: MIT Press.

Hall, S., Critcher, C., Jefferson, T., Clark, J., & Roberts, B. (1978). Policing the crisis: Mugging, the state, and law and order. New York: Holmes and Meier.

Hann, R., McGinnis, J., Stenning, P., & Farson, S. (1985). Municipal police governance and accountability in Canada: An empirical study. Canadian Police College Journal, 9, 1–85.

Held, D., McGrew, A., Goldblatt, D., & Parraton, J. (1999). Global transformations: Politics, economics and culture. Cambridge, U.K.: Polity.

Hillyard, P. (1993). Paramilitary policing and popular justice in Northern Ireland. In M. Findlay & U. Zvekic (Eds.), Alternative policing styles: Cross cultural perspectives (pp. 139–156). Deventer/Boston: Kluwer Law and Taxation Publishers.

Hillyard, P., & Tomlinson, M. (2000). Patterns of policing and policing Patten. Journal of Law and Society, 27, 394–415.

Jackson, A. (1999). Ireland: 1798–1998. Oxford: Blackwell Publishers.

Joh, E. (2004). The paradox of private policing. The Journal of Criminal Law and Criminology, 95, 49–131.

Johnson, L. (2000). Policing Britain: Risk, security and governance. London: Harlow Longman.

Johnston, L., & Shearing, C. (2003). Governing security: Explorations in policing and justice. London, New York: Routledge.

Jones, T., MacLean, B., & Young, J. (1986). The Islington crime survey: Crime, victimization and policing in inner-city London. Brookfield, VT: Gower.

Jones, T., & Newburn, T. (1997). Policing after the Act: Police governance after The Police and Magistrates' Courts Act 1994. London: Policy Studies Institute.

Kelling, G., & Wilson, C. (1996). Fixing broken windows. New York: The Free Press.

Kempa, M., Stenning, P., & Wood, J. (2004). Policing communal spaces: A reconfiguration of the 'mass private property' hypothesis. British Journal of Criminology, 44, 562–581.

Knox, C. (2002). 'See no evil, hear no evil': Insidious paramilitary violence in Northern Ireland. British Journal of Criminology, 42, 164–185.

Landau, T. (2000). Back to the future: The death of civilian review of public complaints against the police in Ontario, Canada. In A. Goldsmith & C. Lewis (Eds.), Civilian oversight of policing: Governance, democracy and human rights (pp. 63–79). Oxford: Hart Publishing.

Latour, B. (1987). Science in action: How to follow scientists and engineers through society. Cambridge, MA: Harvard University Press.

Lea, J., & Young, J. (1993). What is to be done about law and order? Crisis in the Nineties, 2nd ed. London: Pluto Press.

Leighton, B. (1991, July–October). Visions of community policing: rhetoric and reality in Canada. Canadian Journal of Criminology, 485–522.

Loader, I. (1997). Policing and the social: Questions of symbolic power. British Journal of Sociology, 48, 1–18.

Loader, I. (2000). Plural policing and democratic governance. Social and Legal Studies, 93, 323–345.

Los, M. (2002). Post-Communist fear of crime and the commercialization of security. Theoretical Criminology, 6, 165–188.

Lustgarten, L. (1986). The governance of police. London: Sweet and Maxwell.

Lydon, J. (1998). The making of Ireland: From ancient times to the present. London, New York: Routledge.

McGarry, J., & O'Leary, B. (1995). Explaining Northern Ireland: Broken images. Oxford, U.K., Cambridge, MA: Blackwell.

McGarry, J., & O'Leary, B. (1999). Policing Northern Ireland: Proposals for a new start. Belfast: Blackstaff Press.

Northern Ireland Office. (2000). The Patten Report: Secretary of State's implementation plan. Belfast: Northern Ireland Office.
Northern Ireland Office. (2001). The Patten Report: Revised implementation plan. Belfast: Northern Ireland Office.
O'Leary, B. (2001). The character of the 1998 Agreement: Results and prospects. In R. Wilford (Ed.), Aspects of the Belfast Agreement (pp. 49–83). Oxford, New York: Oxford University Press.
O'Malley, P. (1996). Indigenous governance. Economy and Society, 25, 310–326.
Radzinowicz, L. (1968). A history of English criminal law, Vol. 4: Grappling for control. London: Stevens and Sons.
Reiner, R. (2000). The politics of the police, 3rd ed. Oxford: Oxford University Press.
Rigakos, G., & Greener, D. (2000). Bubbles of governance: Private policing and the law in Canada. Canadian Journal of Law and Society, 15, 145–184.
Rose, N. (1996). The death of the social? Refiguring the territory of government. Economy and Society, 25, 327–356.
Rose, N., & Miller, P. (1992). Political power beyond the state: Problematics of government. British Journal of Sociology, 43, 173–205.
Ryder, C. (2004). The fateful split: Catholics and the Royal Ulster Constabulary. London: Methuen.
Scraton, P. (1985). The state of the police. London: Pluto Press.
Shearing, C. (2000, November 14). Patten has been gutted. The Guardian.
Shearing, C., & Stenning, P. (1981). Modern private security: Its growth and implications. In M. Tonry & N. Morris (Eds.), Crime and justice: An annual review of the research (Vol. 3) (pp. 193–245). Chicago: University of Chicago Press.
Shearing, C., & Stenning, P. (1983). Private security: Implications for social control. Social Problems, 30, 493–506.
Sklansky, D. (1999). The private police. UCLA Law Review, 46, 1165–1287.
Staff Reporter. (2003, May 14). One third of PSNI applicants are Catholics. Belfast Telegraph.
Stenning, P. (1996). Police governance in First Nations in Ontario. Toronto: Centre of Criminology.
Stenning, P. (2000). The powers and accountability of the private police. European Journal on Criminal Policy and Research, 8, 325–352.
Stiglitz, J. (2002). Globalisation and its discontents. London: Penguin.
Walker, N. (2000). Policing in a changing constitutional order. London: Sweet and Maxwell.
Weitzer, R. (1995). Policing under fire: Ethnic conflict and police-community relations in Northern Ireland. New York: State University of New York Press.
Williams, R. (2003). A state of permanent exception: The birth of modern policing and colonial capitalism. Interventions, 5, 322–344.
Wood, J. (2000). Reinventing governance: A study of transformations in the Ontario Provincial Police. (Unpublished doctoral dissertation). University of Toronto, Toronto, Canada.

III

Policing

Global Challenges

Policing Cybercrimes
Situating the Public Police in Networks of Security Within Cyberspace

8

DAVID S. WALL

Contents

Introduction

The Internet and the criminal and deviant behavior it transforms pose considerable challenges for order maintenance and law enforcement. In many ways, the relationship between the public police and technology is not new and spans the history of the police. Throughout this article the term *the police* refers to public police forces and their officers, and *policing* refers to the broader function of regulating behavior to enforce law and maintain order. Traditionally, a responsive organization designed to counter the dangers created by urban migration caused by 18th-century industrial technology, the police had, by the second half of the 19th century, situated themselves as an all-purpose emergency service. It is a heritage that gave them consensual public support and a high degree of local police force independence. As a consequence, it has left ingrained within the organizational and occupational cultures of the police the instinct to protect the public and claim ownership over policing. Although the police and their constitutional position has changed considerably since their formation, many of the original Peelian police principles survive, though adapted to modernity—a bureaucratically organized, responsive local police that maintain order and enforces law; officers who are identifiable from the rest of the public, professional in conduct, accountable to law, and the community for their actions. However, the increasing pervasiveness of the Internet and the cyberspace it creates, along with its global, transformative impacts create a range of entirely new challenges for public police that question their traditional local dominance over the security domain and could, in fact, marginalize them completely. Not only does the concept of cybercrime produce problems for the police because Internet-related offending takes place within a global context whereas crime tends to be nationally defined, but policing the Internet is also a complex affair by the very nature of policing and security being networked and nodal (Johnston & Shearing, 2003). While the application of concepts of networked and nodal security may be challenged in the "terrestrial world" (Crawford & Lister, 2004, p. 426), nowhere is it more networked and nodal than in cyberspace.

This chapter examines the challenge that cybercrime poses for the public police in order to explore how they are situated in the networks of security that contribute to policing harmful behavior in cyberspace. The first part will question our understanding of cybercrime to identify the tensions arising between the globalization of harmful behavior and specific jurisdictional definitions of crime. The second part will probe the networked and nodal architecture of Internet policing to locate, and then situate, the role of the police. It will be argued that the future of the public police role in policing the Internet is more than simply acquiring new knowledge and capacity. For the police to have a role in the policing of cyberspace, they will need to forge new relationships with the other nodes that constitute the networks of Internet security. These relationships will require a range of transformations to take place in order to enhance the effectiveness and legitimacy of the nodal architecture. The third part of this chapter will identify the challenges that face the police if they are to maintain their role in networked policing. Finally, the fourth part will look at those responses to argue that some of the contradictions faced by "the police" have been reconciled by the reconstitution of a neo-Peelian paradigm across a global span. Whilst this may (re) situate the police, it nevertheless causes a range of fresh instrumental and normative challenges.

Cybercrime as the Focus of Policing Cyberspace

Although a topical and newsworthy subject, little is known about "cybercrime" other than that drawn from press and television reporting. Upon reflection, the term *cyberspace crime* would have been more meaningful because it more clearly signifies the space in which the harmful behavior takes place. However, because the term is principally a media construct, it has subsequently obtained its own linguistic agency and it has entered the public parlance and we are stuck with it (Wall, 2005a, p. 79). Cyberterrorism, information warfare, phishing (an email purporting to be from a legitimate bank requesting confirmation of personal details (Toyne, 2003)), spams, denial of service attacks, hacktivism, hate crime, identity thefts, online gambling, plus the criminal exploitation of a new generation of pornographic peccadilloes, conspire, it is alleged, to threaten public safety and temper governmental and commercial ambitions for the growth of an information society. Although there is fairly widespread consensus that cybercrimes exist, there is much confusion as to what they actually are and what risks they pose (Wall, 2005a, p. 77; see Brenner, 2001; Walden, 2003).

The confusion about what constitutes a cybercrime creates a "reassurance gap" between crimes experienced and those felt (Innes, 2004, p. 151), and leads to public concern about cybercrime, which subsequently shapes the demands made of the police (for reassurance). Therefore, it is important to look first at what is being understood as cybercrime because it contributes to setting the policing agenda. Furthermore, without reliable sources of knowledge, misinformation cannot be countered and misunderstandings are perpetuated and there is no firm platform to establish a responsive criminal justice policy. Particularly confusing is the common tendency to call any offense involving a computer a cybercrime. Equally confusing is the general tendency to talk in global terms about offending and deviant behaviors when in fact their definitions and solutions are usually found locally.

Since cybercrimes are the product of networked computers, they must be defined in terms of the informational, networked, and globalized transformation of deviant or criminal behavior by networked technologies. These transformations give Internet users a global reach, new capacities for distributed peer-to-peer networking, a panoptic gaze that creates an asymmetric capacity to enable one person to simultaneously reach many. These characteristics also contribute to the reorganization of the division of criminal labor, on the one hand automating and deskilling it (Braverman, 1976), while on the other hand "reskilling" and empowering the "single agent" who can single-handedly control a complete and complex criminal activity (Wall, 2005a, p. 80; Pease, 2001, p. 24; Savona & Mignone, 2004, p. 4). The implications of this are profound because the overall setup and running costs are low, and, because so few individuals are involved in each incidence of offending, intelligence about the perpetrator is unlikely to leak out.

If Internet transformations are the key to understanding cybercrime, then in order to understand their impact it is necessary to consider what happens if the Internet is removed from the equation. By applying a simple "transformation test," three different groups of cyber-criminal opportunity can be identified as points on a spectrum (Wall, 2007). At the near end lie behaviors that are commonly referred to as cybercrimes, but are, in fact, first generation "traditional" crimes in which computers have been used for information gathering or communication to assist with the organization of a crime. Remove the computer and the criminal behavior persists because the offenders will revert to using other information sources or types of communication. Toward the middle of the spectrum lie the second generation *hybrid* cybercrimes. These are traditional crimes for which entirely new global opportunities have emerged (e.g., globalized frauds and deceptions, also the global trade in pornographic materials including child pornography). Take away the Internet and the behavior will continue by other means, but not by the same great volume or across such a wide span.

At the far end of the spectrum, however, are the third generation "true" cybercrimes that are solely the product of opportunities created by the Internet and which can only be perpetrated within cyberspace (online intellectual property thefts, spams). These are the spawn of the Internet and, therefore, embody all of its transformative characteristics. Spamming is a good example of a true cybercrime. It is an illegal behavior in its own right in the laws of the United States, the European Union (EU), and many other jurisdictions, but it also facilitates secondary offending by enabling engagement with potential victims (Wall, 2005b). Many of the offenses that result are small-impact bulk victimizations—*de minimis* offenses. Take away the Internet and spamming and true cybercrimes vanish. These distinctions are important because the first two types tend to be subject to existing laws and existing professional experience can be applied to law enforcement regarding these offenses. Any legal problems arising tend to relate more to legal procedures than substantive law. The final group, however, are solely the product of the Internet and pose the greater regulatory challenges.

It is also important, of course, to look for any common features in the substantive behaviors. In this way they can be linked to existing substantive bodies of law and associated experience within the criminal justice processes.

"Computer integrity" crimes are offending behaviors that assault the integrity of network access mechanisms. They include hacking and cracking, vandalism, spying, denial of service, and the planting and use of viruses and Trojans. Many jurisdictions now have legislation, such as the Computer Misuse Act 1990 (U.K.), the Computer Fraud and Abuse Act 1986 (U.S.) (18 U.S.C. 1030), internationally harmonized by conventions, such as the

Council of Europe's Convention on Cybercrime (ETS No. 185), to protect against unauthorized access to computer material; unauthorized access with intent to commit further offenses; and unauthorized modification of computer material. Computer integrity cybercrimes also pave the way for further offending. For example, unauthorized access also can be the precursor to more serious crimes. Identity theft from computers becomes serious when the information is subsequently used against the owner in a theft. Similarly, crackers may use Trojan viruses to install "back doors" that are later used to facilitate other crimes, possibly by spammers who have bought lists of IP (Internet protocol) addresses of infected computers (BBC, 2003).

Computer-related crimes are committed using networked computers to engage with victims in order to dishonestly acquire cash, goods, or services. In addition, there are socially engineered variants, such as "phishing" and advanced fee frauds and the manipulation of new online sales environments, particularly auction sites. Most jurisdictions have legislation concerning thefts and provide legal measures for the recovery of lost assets as well as intellectual property laws to protect against the unauthorized exploitation of intellectual property.

"Computer content" crimes relate to the content of computers—materials held on networked computer systems. They include the trade and distribution of pornographic materials, the dissemination of hate crime materials, and, more recently, the publication of video nasties of the murders of kidnapped foreign nationals. Most jurisdictions have variants of the obscenity laws and laws that prohibit incitement, although their legislative strength can vary where Internet content is also protected by laws of free speech. In common with the other two crime groups, legislation does nevertheless vary across jurisdictions in terms of judicial seriousness (see Jurisdictional Disparities).

This mental map or "matrix" (see Wall 2002a, p. 192) illustrates that true cybercrimes are criminal behaviors transformed or mediated by the Internet and distinguishes them from more traditional forms of criminal behavior. They are, to all intents and purposes, new wines in no bottles! Of the wide range of deviant and criminal behaviors that fall under the rubric of cybercrime, many—both traditional and hybrid—are already covered by existing areas of law. However, while they can be found in the police crime diet, they are not a particularly large part of it and tend to fall within the scope of specialist, rather than everyday, police work while other behaviors, those referred to as true cybercrimes, are entirely alien to the police. This raises questions not only about whether it is the police who should deal with these crimes, but also, in the light of the disparity between the high levels of incidence reported by some statistical sources, and very low levels of computer misuse prosecutions, who should be policing cyberspace if the police are not? In the United Kingdom, for example, during the first decade following the introduction of the Computer Misuse Act 1990, there were only about 100 or so prosecutions against hackers and even fewer convictions (Hansard, 26/3/02, Col. WA35), and this disparity is also found outside the United Kingdom (see Smith, Grabosky, & Urbas, 2004).

The Panoptic and Synoptic Gaze

The "digital" realism of network technology is that the same characteristics that create new opportunities for crime also create powerful new tools for policing the Internet. As a rule of thumb, the more "transformed" by the Internet a behavior is, the greater is the potential for that same technology to be used to police the same behavior. The globally surveillant and "dataveillant" (Clarke, 1994) panoptic qualities of Internet technology that enable offenders to engage with many victims also facilitate synopticism, thus reversing the direction of the gaze (Mathieson, 1997, p. 215). This asymmetric two-way flow of information provides powerful new tools for policing the Internet: tools that not only enable investigation, but also aid with the collection of new sources of evidence that can be utilized to secure prosecutions and convictions and facilitate cybercrime control and prevention.

The root of the "disciplinary" potential of networked technology lies in the routine collection and retention of Internet traffic data that records and traces virtually every Internet transaction and which can subsequently be data mined (Gandy, 2003, p. 26). These "... fine-grained distributed systems; through computer chips linked by the Net to every part of social life..." (Lessig, 1999, p. 1) establish the potential for online monitoring and also for the mining of the various databases of Internet traffic. One of the great public misperceptions about the Internet is the myth of anonymity; in fact, networked technology leans in the opposite direction, to the point that we are now in danger of experiencing what has been described as "the disappearance of disappearance" (Haggerty & Ericson, 2000, p. 605). This adds further weight to Ericson and Haggerty's (1997) arguments that policing of "the risk society" is increasingly information-driven, and that relations between policing bodies are becoming largely concerned with negotiating the exchange of information (Ericson & Haggerty, 1997; Crawford & Lister, 2004, p. 425). In this case, the exchange of information relates to Internet traffic data that can be used more broadly to gather intelligence about deviant (including terrorist) networks or in relevant cases to establish conclusive evidence of wrongdoing (Walker & Akdeniz, 2003) leading to the emergence of formal and informal relationships that underpin the networks of security.

Thus, crime opportunities can be actively designed out of new software products and technologies, and security inserted by the modification of "code." Katyal (2003) states that cyberspace solutions to cybercrime must try to capture the root benefits of the potential for natural surveillance, territoriality (stewardship of a virtual area), and capacity for building online communities and protecting targets, without damaging the Internet's principal design innovation—its openness (Katyal 2003, p. 2268). They also can be used to generate a range of automated active policing tools, such as the "honeynets;" fake websites that possess "key words" that offenders search for and have the outward appearance of the "real thing" (The Honeynet Project, 2002). Users who access sites containing illegal images willfully pass through various levels, agreeing at each stage that they are aware of the content and indicating their intent. They eventually find themselves facing a law enforcement message—a "gotcha"—and a notice that their details will be recorded, or, in cases where intent is clear, subsequently becomes the subject of investigation. Currently, cyberspace solutions are used to exploit the discipline of the panopticon (everything visible in one view) (Foucault, 1983, p. 206), and create a "chilling effect" on consumers of child pornography, spammers (Sophos, 2004), hackers (The Honeynet Project, 2002), and many other forms of undesirable behavior online. This "electronic panopticon" (Lyon, 1994, p. 69; Gordon, 1987, p. 483) or "Super panopticon" (Poster, 2000) also has even broader applications (see The Honeynet Project, 2002).

However, these observations take us even farther away from understanding the low prosecution figures illustrated above. Indeed, they can take us in the opposite direction, to the very edge of what one of the original architects of the Internet has described as "ubiquitous law enforcement" (Vinge, 2000).

Situating the Public Police in the Networks and Nodes of Security in Cyberspace

The public police role has to be understood within the broader and largely informal architecture of Internet policing, which not only enforces norms and laws, but also maintains order in very different ways. Understanding this position enables more realistic expectations and understanding of the police role. It also helps to identify a broader range of cross-jurisdictional and cross-sectoral issues that the police have to attend to in order to participate fully in policing the Internet, by fully embracing both the concept of networking and the subsequent network technology. This growing networking of sources of security during recent decades (Johnston & Shearing, 2003; Dupont, 2004) has arisen as one part of the shift toward the networked society (Castells, 2000).

Below are outlined the principal interest groups that constitute the nodes of networked Internet governance and, without making any specific empirical claims, a brief distinction is made between the "auspices" (entities that authorize governance) and the providers of governance (Shearing,

2004, p. 6), thus encompassing the strategies that shape Internet behavior (for further information, see Wall, 2005a, 2007).

Internet users and user groups exert a very potent influence upon online behavior through censure, usually after the occurrence of "signal events," which are behaviors that may not necessarily constitute a major infraction of criminal law, but "nonetheless disrupt the sense of social order" (Innes, 2004, p. 151). Cases of more extreme behavior also may be reported to relevant authorities, such as the Internet Watch Foundation, Trading Standards, or directly to the police, either in person or through one of the many crime reporting websites. In addition, individual Internet users can employ a range of software solutions to prevent themselves becoming victims of cybercrime. Solutions available include the use of firewalls and encryption in order to protect personal space, and the application of spam filters and virus checkers. Working on a self-appointed mandate, the Internet users are both auspices and providers of governance.

As virtual environments become more established and heavily populated, so does the need to maintain order on them. To this end, most virtual environments now appoint moderators, usually lay volunteers, to police the behavior of the online community according to the particular norms of that community. These online virtual environment security managers are collectively emerging as a new strata of behavior governance. "Habbo Hotel," for example, "a virtual hotel, where teenagers can hang out and chat," is constantly monitored by trained and police-vetted moderators and "hotel guides" drawn from within the community. The (auspices) values and norms that moderators maintain, as in other environments, combine the interests of the particular online community with the legal and corporate responsibilities that the virtual environment "owner" has to the host ISP (Internet service provider) to comply with law and also maintain the stated functions of the forum. The sanctions that moderators can invoke when community norms or rules are broken include the temporary removal of access rights if the offending is minor, or permanent exclusion from the environment if it is serious.

Another principal interest group consists of network infrastructure providers. ISPs exert governance by influencing online behavior through "contractual governance" (Crawford, 2003; Vincent-Jones, 2000) that is effected through the terms and conditions (auspices) of their contracts with individual clients—the Internet users. Terms and conditions are largely determined by the market, the law, and also the interests of the ISPs. The ISPs themselves also are subject to contractual governance through the terms and conditions laid down in their contracts with the telecommunications providers who host their Internet services. In addition, Internet service providers can, because of their strategic position in the communications networks, also employ a range of software solutions to reduce offending online. Most typical of these are robust security systems accompanied by sophisticated professional spam filters.

Corporate security organizations also exercise contractual governance over members of their organization (employees and clients), as well as outsiders, to protect their corporate interests through contractual terms and conditions (auspices) that threaten the removal of privileges, or private or criminal prosecution in the case of more serious transgressions. In addition, corporate security organizations will employ a range of software solutions, not just to protect themselves, but also to identify and investigate abnormal patterns of behavior in their systems and, also, in some cases, their clients.

Nongovernmental, nonpolice organizations are another influential interest group. Internet Watch Foundation (IWF), for example, provides governance under the auspices of a mandate from the U.K. ISPs and the U.K. government. It works with the police service by receiving and processing reports of content-related offending (usually child pornography and racist) material through its online facility (Hotline). If deemed actionable following a judgment by a trained operative, the IWF takes appropriate action either by informing the "offender's" Internet services provider, or by alerting comparable hotlines in the "offender's" jurisdictions. It may alternatively pass on details of an Internet site directly to the police. The IWF also contributes more generally toward (cyber)crime prevention and public awareness.

Governmental nonpolice organizations provide governance under the auspices of rules, law, charges, fines, and the threat of prosecution. Not normally perceived as "police," they include agencies such as Customs, the Postal Service, and Trading Standards organizations.

Public police organizations, as stated earlier, play a comparatively small, though nevertheless significant, role in enforcing state criminal sanctions upon wrongdoers. Whilst located within nation–states, which impose criminal definitions through the law of the jurisdiction, the public police are nevertheless networked by transnational policing organizations, such as Europol and Interpol. Police organizations may employ a range of software solutions to protect themselves, investigate wrongdoers, and collect evidence, and also may use software to proactively police some priority concerns (Sommer, 2004).

The answer to the earlier questions posed about the effectiveness of the role of the public police in cyberspace in the light of low levels of police performance indicators against high levels of policing technology is quite simple: The police actually only play a very small part in governing the Internet and even then it tends to be jurisdictionally based. This is not, however, to say that cyberspace goes unpoliced; as Reiner has observed more generally with regard to the terrestrial world: "... not all policing lies in the police" (Reiner, 2000). This is even more poignant with regard to cyberspace.

The broader governance of the Internet is, then, characterized by a sense of order resulting from a complex "assemblage" of networked nodes of security that continually shape virtual behavior (Wall, 1997; 2001, p. 171; 2002a, p. 192; Walker & Akdeniz, 1998, p. 8), transcend the "state/nonstate binary"

(Dupont, 2004, p. 76) and also state sovereignty (Shearing, 2004, p. 6). The term *assemblage* is particularly useful in this context when considering the relationships between nodes and also within them. Without attributing causality, assemblage describes the relationship between heterogeneous contributors to governance that work together as a networked and functional entity, but do not necessarily have any other unity (see Miller & Rose, 1990; Haggerty & Ericson, 2000, p. 605). In some of these networked relationships there may be a consensus of interest in approach, while in others the consensus may be in the outcomes or goals achieved. Consequently, a replication is found in the bifurcation of broader functions in terrestrial policing between the maintenance of order through the assemblage and the enforcement of law on the other to deal with the more serious offending behavior. By separating the two, some sense can be made of the rather conflicting messages that are emerging in debates over policing the Internet. Networked security, for example, exploits the "natural surveillance" (see earlier) that networked technologies enable and allows both primary and secondary social control functions to operate. Furthermore it also tends to mediate, to some extent, global disparities arising from national or jurisdictional legal differences in definition.

The observation made earlier that many cybercrimes fall outside the traditional police agenda would seem to render them unproblematic from a police resourcing point of view; they simply do not get resourced. On the other hand, the public police not only tend to lay claim culturally (organizational and occupational) to a greater ownership of policing the Internet than "they actually own," but, more importantly, they also are expected to do so by the public because of their traditional consensual relationship with the state and citizens and their traditional symbolic duty to protect the public from danger.

We see here in the debates over the policing of the Internet a replication of the reassurance policing debate (Crawford & Lister, 2004), though with a slight twist. The reassurance policing debate is borne out of the "increasing recognition that the police alone cannot win the fight against crime and disorder nor meet the public's seemingly insatiable demand for a visible policing presence" (Crawford & Lister, 2004, p. 413). The debate, when shifted to cyberspace, takes for granted that the police alone cannot win the fight against crime, but nevertheless demands a more visible policing presence. This begs two questions: What challenges do cybercrimes pose for the public police? And, how do the police deal with these challenges?

The Challenge of Cybercrime for the Public Police

The relationship between the police and technology is long-standing and complex, and a brief reflection explains much about the situation of the public police today. On the one hand, the police were created to deal with the social disorder caused by the technologies of the industrial revolution. On the other hand, their responsive and localized nature always meant that they fell behind in their access to, and use of, technology. A long-standing complaint made by members of police and law enforcement agencies is that they do not have the facilities to keep up with criminals, especially with regard to offenses that require, what Brodeur has termed, a "high policing" response (Brodeur, 1983; Sheptycki, 2000, p. 11). Indeed, for over a century readers of the *Police Review* and other contemporary police journals were regularly told by police officers that they lacked the resources to obtain the latest technologies that would help them to respond to criminals. In the early years of the 20th century, the letters page of *Police Review* contained much correspondence on the subject. More recently, the complaints have focused upon obtaining modern IT (information technology) equipment and high specification broadband links. Of course, such complaints inevitably backfire because they result in (often unfounded) allegations about police ineffectiveness, which ultimately reinforce the police-originated myth that criminals are ahead of the game. However, while historical themes can be drawn out, what distinguishes the modern debates from their predecessors is not just access to latest technology and skill sets, but access to technology to facilitate networking and networked policing, including access to relevant networks of security.

But, it is one thing to possess the technological capabilities and another to be able to utilize them, and there are a number of institutional obstacles to this task. The public police, like the other criminal justice agencies are deeply conservative institutions that have been molded by time-honored traditions, and, therefore, do not respond readily to rapid change. Furthermore, much of this innate conservatism originates in the police also being symbolic expressions of state sovereignty. Therefore, one way that the police forces generally respond to new issues, whilst preserving their symbolic and organizational conservatism, is through the origination of specialist units into which officers with appropriate specialisms are absorbed. While this tactic constitutes an actual and visible response, it nevertheless tends to marginalize the problem it sets out to solve, and runs the risk of preventing the broader accumulation of organizational and professional experience across the force in dealing with the issue at hand. Ultimately, it is the presence of a relevant body of specialist knowledge and expertise within a police force (and whether the other officers know about it) that can determine whether or not the organizational and occupational response of the police to a new public concern is effective or not.

Nevertheless, the global and interjurisdictional reach and new forms of technological crime organization, such as cybercrimes, are markedly different to the daily public police crime portfolio. The public police were originally introduced to "keep the dangerous classes off the streets" by maintaining local order and enforcing law (mostly the former) (Critchley, 1978; Manning, 1998; Reiner, 2000, Ch 2; Wall, 1998, p. 23) and modern police agencies remain largely responsive to public complaints. They tend to deal with routine matters and are subject to tight budgetary constraints that restrict the immediate allocation of major resources to emerging matters and, therefore, their responsive capability.

The limitations of the Peelian paradigm have long been understood and there have been employed a number of strategies to resolve the contradictions. At a procedural level, there has been the establishment of international harmonization and police coordination treaties, such as the Council of Europe's *Convention on Cybercrime.* A range of national/federal and even international police organizations (e.g., Interpol, Europol) have been introduced to complement locally organized police in their investigation of crimes occurring across police jurisdictions. However, despite these procedural and organizational responses, cybercrimes still pose a range of challenges to the police, which are outlined below.

De Minimism

The first challenge is the *de minimis* trap—the "law does not deal with trifles" *(de minimis non-curat lex).* Characteristic of many cybercrimes is that they are small-impact, bulk victimizations with a large aggregated loss, but spread out globally across a range of jurisdictions. Since local policing strategies are often reduced to decisions that are made at a very local level over the most efficient expenditure of finite resources (Goodman, 1997, p. 686), the public interest, a key criteria in releasing police resources for an investigation, is often hard to justify in individual cases of cybercrime victimization.

Nullum Crimen Disparities

The second challenge is the problem of *nullum crimen* legal disparities in inter-jurisdictional cases (*nullum crimen sine lege:* no crime without law). Recent protocols, including the cybercrime convention and the establishment of multiagency partnerships and fora (see later), assist in facilitating interforce cooperation, but they rely upon the offense in question to have similar priority in each jurisdiction. If, for example, a case is clearly a criminal offense for which the investigation carries a strong mandate from the public, such as the investigation of child pornography, then resourcing its investigation is usually fairly unproblematic from a police point of view. However, where there is not such a mandate, resourcing becomes all the more problematic, especially if the deviant behavior in question is an offense in one jurisdiction and not in another. Of course, there also may be cultural differences in seriousness attached to specific forms of offending. Some offenses may fall under civil laws in one jurisdiction and criminal law in another, such as in the case of the theft of trade secrets, which is a criminal offense in the United States, but civil in the United Kingdom (see Law Commission, 1997).

Jurisdictional Disparities

Faced with a jurisdictional or evidential disparity, police or prosecutors use their resourcefulness to forum shop (Braithwaite & Drahos, 2000) to increase the prospect of obtaining a conviction (Wall, 2002b). This process was very evident in *United States of America v. Robert A. Thomas and Carleen Thomas* (1996) where the prosecutors chose Tennessee because they felt a conviction would best be secured. In *R v. Arnold* and *R v. Fellows* (1997) the U.S. investigation was passed to the U.K. police because they were more likely to secure a conviction. However, these were successful examples of cooperation because they were relatively unproblematic in that they concerned extreme pornography. Interjurisdictional cooperation is less likely to be successful with the more contentious types of nonroutine offending.

Nonroutine Activity and Police Culture

The fourth challenge is the *solitus* or routinization issue that affects the ability of the police to respond to nonroutine criminal activity in terms of their possession of relevant skill sets and experience. Because most public policing tends to be based upon local and routinized practices that define occupational cultures and working patterns, and ultimately professional policing, investigative difficulties can arise when nonroutine events occur (Reiner, 2000; Wall, 1997, p. 223). In this case, nonroutine events include those created by the Internet, such as cross-border investigations, or types of deviant behavior not normally regarded as criminal by police officers.

Routine events are important to the construction of police occupational culture because they generate stories that are told to others, which, through "figurative action," can eventually structure the way that police officers interpret events (Shearing & Ericson, 1991, p. 481). Police occupational culture is the accumulation of collective "routine" experience of police officers and it is an important component of police work because, with appropriate safeguards in place to prevent corruption and unfairness in the application of law, it enables officers to make sense of the world they have to police and enables them to apply the law (McBarnet, 1979). Since cybercrimes are rather unique events for most officers, the culture does not assist them. In fact, it can lead to the opposite. Police officers, as a number of research findings show, tend to draw upon the "cynical" application of conventional wisdoms (Reiner, 2000); recall the earlier vignette about the recurring century-old call for more technological resources to fight crime. So, it is understandable that street police officers are unlikely to see the Internet in terms of its potential for the democratization of knowledge and growth in active citizenship (Walker & Akdeniz, 1998) or the leveling of ethnic, social, or cultural boundaries. Rather, they are more likely to see it as a site characterized by risk (Shearing & Ericson, 1991, p. 500), as a place where criminals, notably pedophiles, Russian gangsters, fraudsters, and other wrongdoers ply their trade. Although great advances in police officer awareness of technology have taken place over the past decade, a cultural dissonance between traditional occupational police culture and the demands created by the Internet pervades, which allows the view to persist amongst many officers that "cyberspace is like a neighborhood without a police department" (Sussman, 1995, p. 59).

Underreporting

A fifth, and most revealing challenge is the underreporting of cybercrimes to the police. The (assumed) problem of underreporting to the police has long been argued and the small amount of research into reporting practices, police recording procedures, and prosecutions reveals some startling information shortfalls. The various cybercrime surveys published by Experian®, (U.S.) CSI (Computer Security Institute)/FBI (Federal Bureau of Investigation), the (U.K.) DTI (Department of Trade and Industry), and many others all indicate a large volume of victimizations numbering tens of thousands each year. This contrasts sharply with the findings of empirical research conducted for the U.K. Home Office in 2002, which found that relatively few Internet-related offenses were reported to the police (Wall, 2002b; 2007). A detailed study of various police databases in one police force, followed up by interviews with reporting center staff, revealed that only about 120 to 150 Internet-related offenses per 1 million recorded crimes had been reported to the police during 1 year and most of these were reasonably minor frauds over which no further action was taken. When extrapolated to the national figures (taking into account relative police force sizes), a statistic was obtained of about 2,000 Internet-related offenses per year throughout England and Wales being reported by the public to the police (Wall, 2002b, p. 132). Even if these figures were five- or tenfold, there would still be an apparent shortfall in reporting.

This apparent underreporting could be interpreted as evidence of low public expectations of the ability of the police to resolve Internet-related crimes. Furthermore, in recent years, catalyzed by, though not wholly attributable to, the hardened security following the events of 9/11 (Levi & Wall, 2004, p. 196) there now exist a range of national and international police organizations that address cybercrimes. There are also national intelligence models, for example, in the United Kingdom, the National Intelligence Model (NIM) (NCIS, 2000, p. 8) that structures the collection of intelligence about all crimes, including low-level losses, in order to construct a national or international picture of criminal activity. Whether or not they would pick up the very minor *de minimis* cybercrimes is debatable, but a criminal intelligence model now exists in the United Kingdom to link the local with the national and international, whereas 5 years ago none existed. In addition, many of the larger local police forces/services have for some time possessed a capability to respond to Internet-related complaints from the public and also have local facilities to investigate computer crimes and conduct the forensic examination of computers. The latter also have been introduced because in an increasing number of traditional criminal code offenses now seeking electronic evidence to establish offenders' motives or whereabouts, much of this information is located in computers, Internet traffic data, and also mobile phone records. Finally, there is a growing number of online public portals in both the United Kingdom and United States through which to report victimizations.* In the United Kingdom, the Police Information Technology Organization (PITO) provides a range of online services through which nonemergency minor crimes can be notified to U.K. police forces. This site also has links to the U.S. Internet Fraud Complaint Center, which is operated by the FBI and National White Collar Crime Center, and also RECOL.CA, a Canadian facility for reporting economic crime online.

One could argue that many of the above reporting facilities are fairly recent interventions and it will take some time for the public to become aware of them and to use them. While there may be some truth to this observation, there currently exist many systematic disincentives to reporting cybercrime arising from the challenges mentioned earlier, especially *de minimis* crimes or where an offense is not regarded as a crime. Many victims of cybercrime, be they primary or secondary victims, individuals, or organizations, may be unwilling to acknowledge that they have been victimized, or, at least, it may take some time for them to realize it. At a personal level, reluctance to report offenses could arise because of embarrassment, ignorance of what to do, or just simply by "putting it down to experience." Alternatively, where victimization has been imputed by a third party upon the basis of an ideological, political, moral, or commercial assessment of risk, the victim or victim group may simply be unaware that they have been victimized or may even believe that they have not been victimized, as is the case in some debates over pornography on the Internet. In the commercial sector, fear of the negative impact of adverse publicity greatly reduces their willingness to report their victimization to the police, preferring to pursue a private rather than public model of justice, which furthers the corporate, rather than the public, interest. One way that law enforcement agencies have addressed the issue of underreporting by businesses has been through the introduction of

* A search using the key words *reporting crimes to the police online* reveals many police-driven Internet sites.

confidentiality charters, for example, as run by the U.K. National Hi-Tech Crime Unit between 2002 and April 2006, when it was absorbed into the Serious Organized Crime Agency (SOCA). The charter assured businesses that communications would be kept confidential. The story with regard to individuals is somewhat different. The 2002 study (Wall, 2005a) found that although relatively few Internet offenses were reported directly to the police as primary responder, the bulk of those were related to credit cards. As a matter of policy, complainants were usually referred back to their banks, which were regarded as the actual victims. The banks then tended to "charge back" the loss to the merchants and retailers.

What we have here is a combination of different factors at play that can explain underreporting, most of which are clear evidence of the influence of the Peelian paradigm driving public expectations of the police and suggest that cybercrimes simply do not fit into the broader public perception of what the police do. This contrast in perceptions is exacerbated by the reassurance gap between what the police and the media perceive as the problem and the "signal events" (mentioned earlier) (Innes, 2004, p. 151) that actually shape public perceptions and increase levels of fear of cybercrime. These signal events are often spam-driven, small-impact bulk-victimizations, or attempts to victimize, which users commonly experience, and which add personal experience to the much less prevalent forms of offending to increase perceptions of levels of cybercrime and the dangerousness of the Internet.

The police gaze, therefore, tends to focus on crimes committed online where offenders are "dangerous," such is the example of pedophiles and also the more notorious hackers. The dangerousness of the former is undisputed; however, it is more contestable with regard to the latter. Indeed there exists some anecdotal evidence of the deliberate demonization of hackers as a "dangerous other" to play up public fears in order to obtain public funding. Former hacker Bevan (aka Kuji) argues that it is no coincidence "that requests for increased funding [for an Information Warfare program] coincide with news headlines of 'dangerous hackers' or computer viruses" (Bevan, 2001). Bevan himself was once described in overly dramatic terms by a Pentagon official as "possibly the single biggest threat to world peace since Adolf Hitler" (Wall, 2001, p. 9; Bevan, 2001; Power, 2000, Chapter 6; Campbell, 1997).

It is increasingly apparent that the underreporting of cybercrimes to the police is a reflection of the diverse nature of the provenance of the individual acts of cybercrime as described earlier. Simply put, relatively few Internet-related crimes are reported to the police because most are dealt with and resolved elsewhere by the individual victims or by the panoply of other types of organizations and social groups involved in the regulation of behavior in cyberspace.

The Neo-Peelian Agenda: Renegotiating the Police Role

The above discussion situates the police as a relatively minor player in the broader network of security that constitutes the policing of cyberspace. By outlining the various challenges faced by local police when policing globalized and transformed offending, the preceding analysis suggests that the police, in fact, are ill-equipped organizationally, occupationally, and culturally. However, that is only part of the story.

As Crawford and Lister (2004) observe, during the past decade or so, we have witnessed the increasing pluralization of policing. The "public police are becoming part of a more varied and complex assortment of organizations and agencies with different policing functions together with a more diffuse array of processes of control and regulation" (Crawford & Lister, 2004, p. 414). Crawford and Lister show that while "much policing is now taking place beyond the auspices" of the public police (2004, p. 426), it would be premature to view the partnerships that form plural policing as facilitating a form of "networked governance" in the British context: "[t]he reality, at the moment at least, is that crime and disorder partnership remain state-dominated institutions" (Ibid.). However, these observations can inform our understanding of the police role in cyberspace because of its networked and nodal architecture. The earlier discussion about situating the police demonstrated a considerable pluralism in the policing of cyberspace that was beyond the auspices of the public police. However, the twist here is that the increasing role of the police as information brokers (Ericson & Haggerty, 1997) has led to the emergence during the past decade of a new role for the public police in which the original Peelian principles outlined earlier are promoted within the networks and nodes of multiagency cross-sector partnerships, fora, and coalitions.

Traditionally, the tensions between the commercial and public sectors arise because the primary function of the former is to police their own private interests. In so doing, they pursue a private model of justice that does not expose publicly their organization's weaknesses and thereby maintains the confidence of the market. The public criminal justice model, on the other hand, is public and the prosecution of offenders is carried out in the public interest and in the public gaze—not a model of criminal justice that many corporate entities want (Wall, 2001, p. 174). Within the public sector are found equally destructive differences between different policing agencies. Not only do turf wars take place between national and local police forces for ownership of cases, but there are also distinct contrasts between the organizational and occupational ethos of law enforcement and police agencies that can damage the collective effort. In an analysis of governmental responses to the September 11 terrorist attacks, Gorman (2003) argues that the "FBI [are] from Mars, and the CIA from Venus.... it's not that [FBI agents and CIA officers] don't like each other... they're really different people... they have a hard time communicating."

The purpose of the multiagency, cross-sector partnerships is, therefore, to build up networked trust relationships through what is effectively a form of "peacebuilding" (Wood, 2004, p. 41) in order to engender a willingness to share information. Although these partnerships tend to be driven by Internet security and law enforcement initiatives, it would be wrong simply to assume they are the product of formal policy and also that they are necessarily dominated by state law enforcement imperatives. The following three North American examples (of many similar enterprises) illustrate how the partnerships, fora, and coalitions of interest can vary in terms of their being multiagency or cross sector (or both) and also the boundaries between them can overlap. POLCYB (The Society for the Policing of Cyberspace) is both multiagency and cross sectoral, and exists to share information across micronetworks of trusted individuals and agencies to promote cooperation between sectors, while actively inviting international involvement from law enforcement, corporate entities, and interest groups. The High Tech Crime Consortium (HTCC), on the other hand, is more multiagency than cross sectoral. Largely Internet-based, it provides a closed forum for law enforcement and security officers—mostly, but not exclusively, from North America—to discuss matters within a secure environment. Whereas POLCYB tends to discuss policy-end issues face to face, HTCC is more about sharing information about problem solving, providing solutions, and identifying emerging problems, mostly on a day-to-day basis. Other fora are much looser coalitions or friendship associations of law enforcement and security experts. The AGORA, for example, encourages cross-sector relationships and provides a face-to-face environment for information exchange between members/associates about Internet-related security matters. In a similar manner to POLCYB, the discussion about information-sharing in AGORA tends to take place at a policy level rather than specifically sharing substantive intelligence data. An example is developing ideas about security issues and good practice, while also identifying, and even agreeing (prepolicy) upon possible acceptable limits for data storage concerning economic transactions and Internet traffic flows. However, the networked trust relationships established within the fora also facilitate the subsequent sharing of intelligence, even criminal intelligence accrued in protecting commercial interests, which includes the reporting of commercial victimizations. Importantly, the personal and occupational interests of the members indicate a substantial crossover of membership between the three organizations.

Alternatively, the partnerships may be driven by specific national policies, or legislation, and be primarily multiagency in emphasis, drawing together relevant aspects of (governmental and nongovernmental) agencies under the auspices of a coordinating body. Appel (2003) provides a very detailed and useful list of the many private–public multisector partnerships that operate in the United States with regard to different types of cybercrime that are associated with the Department of Justice and the Department of Homeland Security. The United Kingdom equivalent would be the National Infrastructure Security Coordination Centre, NISCC, which coordinates key agencies. Within the U.S. context, Appel (2003) argues that public–private collaborations are currently working in many states, counties, regions, and cities and cites many examples of effective solutions with many different approaches that involve law enforcement, business, private security, government, and academia.

It is difficult to assess how effective these partnerships and fora are in achieving their respective tasks because there are few applicable performance indicators and multiple information flows arising from the networking of nodes of security that evade capture at a single portal, such as the police. However, by creating environments of openness through the establishment of trust, the networks created by the partnerships, fora, and coalitions facilitate the flow of essential information to the nodes. At the center of the establishment of trust appears the "police" bond (this is a hypothesis based upon observations and requires further research). A brief examination of the composition of management boards indicates a mix of law enforcement and other organizations. What comes across very strongly, from a cursory examination of their activities, is that the police clearly play an important, though not always a leading, role in these multiagency and cross-sector partnership fora. Despite this, there remain a number of unanswered questions about the nature of their role because the actual working of the partnership operation tends to lack oversight and transparency; discretion, of course, is one of the main reasons why the partnerships work. Also, relatively unknown is the extent to which the nonpolice contacts in these networks of trust are themselves former police officers. Again, a brief look at the composition of the boards of these agencies and their working parties suggests that the number is fairly high. At the heart of the trust-building dynamics appears to be a meeting of minds that possess a similar *weltanschaung* (a particular philosophy or view of life), which is probably the main reason why the networks actually work (this is another research project). Indeed, the shared occupational values may sustain and culturally reproduce the Peelian paradigm so that while the milieu of policing cybercrimes may be different, the public mandate remains much the same.

The Challenge of Cybercrime for the Police–Public Mandate

The future of the public police role in policing the Internet is about more than simply acquiring new expert knowledge and capacity. As is increasingly the case with "terrestrial policing," it is about forging new types of working relationships with other nodes within the networks of Internet security. Relationships that require a range of new transformations to take place in order to enhance the effectiveness and legitimacy of the nodal architecture: a flattening of policing structures, parity of legal definitions across boundaries, broadly accepted frameworks of accountability to the public, shared values, multiagency and cross-sectoral dialogues, and more. Without these transformations, there will always be the danger of a drift towards ubiquitous law enforcement and also ubiquitous crime prevention. However, this adverse potential, for the time being, is tempered by the intervention of law, the human condition (through inaccurate data entry), and some theory failure in crime prevention caused by an inadequate conceptualization and understanding of cybercrime and its associated risks. This will not last indefinitely, however.

Some of the contradictions faced by the police have been reconciled by the reconstitution of the Peelian principles of policing and the emergence of a neo-Peelian agenda across a global span. While this resituates the police as an authority within the networks of security, it nevertheless creates a range of instrumental and normative challenges for them. While one of those challenges is tempering the drift toward ubiquity, there is also optimism in the potential for those same technologies also to provide important opportunities for police reform (Chan, Brereton, Legosz, & Doran, 2001). The surveillant characteristics that make technology a powerful policing tool also make it a natural tool for overseeing police practice, and for creating broader organizational and public accountability (see debate in Newburn & Hayman, 2001).

The prognosis is fairly good in one respect, we are gradually learning more about the impact of networked technologies upon criminal behavior, and, therefore, learning more effective, and acceptable, ways of dealing with them. More research about Internet victimization is being commissioned by funding bodies and the recent inclusion of relevant questions in the Bureau of Justice Statistics' National Crime Victimization Survey (NCVS) and the British Crime Survey (from 2003) will yield useful empirical data about victimization that will counter some of the misinformation that has accrued during the past decade. Within the police, the maturation of the U.K.'s National Hi-Tech Crime Unit (absorbed into SOCA in April 2006) and the various regional police units are establishing a corpus of policing experience in the field, as is also the case in other jurisdictions. And, the laws are still being revised. In the United Kingdom, the Computer Misuse Act 1990 has been expanded by sections 35–38 of the Police and Justice Act 2006 to make DDOS (distributed denial-of-service) attacks and the distribution of hacking tools illegal. In the common law jurisdictions, the laws, of course, are being clarified by case law as well.

Another plus is that the actions of police officers are currently framed by legislation and codes of practice; however, it is of concern that many of the other partners in policing the Internet are not, other than within the broader confines of law. Particularly worrying is the lack of checks and balances on the noticeable shift toward the technological determinism of automated policing initiatives, driven largely by the influence of the cybersecurity industry in the application of software solutions to cybercrime. There are, for example, a broad range of moral, ethical, and legal concerns about the implications of the high degree of entrapment when employing "honeypots" and "honeynets," not least in the validity and strength of evidence presented to the court, that is, if this form of policing, in fact, is designed to capture offenders or simply deter offending through the technological imposition of panoptic "discipline" and its chilling effect. Take for example, something as seemingly innocuous as spamming, which is a true cybercrime in more ways than one (Wall, 2005b). Many Internet Service Providers (ISPs) are in the process of introducing antispam software into the delivery process and, in so doing, contravene the long-standing end-to-end principle of the Internet, which is freedom of movement across the network to its nodes while leaving choice and mode of receipt to the end users. No one wants spam, and few would be unhappy to see it disappear, yet there has been, to date, little critical discussion about the application of spam filters into the delivery mechanisms. The point here is that true cybercrime is increasingly regarded as a "technical problem" and, as a consequence, important decisions are being made largely on scientific grounds, simply because a filter can be made possible. In the case of spam, there is understandably little objection, but since the technological solutions, why not also apply similar filtering to hash-set analyses of images or to certain words or combinations of words and filter out everything that is deemed undesirable? The main concern here is that while the offending behaviors may be the provenance of comparatively few individuals (compared with all Internet users), all users are affected by what effectively become the application of an "antisocial criminology of everyday life" (Hughes, McLaughlin, & Muncie, 2001). In this matter, we may do well here to take heed of the concerns expressed by the Frankfurt School—Horkheimer and Adorno in the *Dialectic of Enlightenment* (Verso Classics, 1997)—about using technology to solve problems, because without balances and checks, the technology becomes "aware of everything but itself and its own blind spots and biases" (Agger, 2004, p. 147).

Conclusions

This article has explored the challenges that cybercrimes pose for the police and their mandate from the public. It has mapped out the nature of the cybercrime issue, highlighted some of the public misunderstandings about it, before examining the role played by the public police in policing the Internet within the broader architecture of Internet governance. It has illustrated how the Internet and the criminal behavior it transforms challenge the processes of order maintenance and law enforcement. Not only does Internet-related offending take place within a global context while crime tends to be nationally defined, but the police's public mandate prioritizes some offending over others, particularly where there is a perceived dangerous "other," as in the production of child pornographic images. Furthermore, policing the Internet is a very complex affair by the very nature of policing and security being networked and nodal. It is also complex because within this framework the public police play only a small part in the overall policing process. Yet the Peelian heritage of the police that has long defined their relationship with the state and the public has caused the police to instinctively assert ownership over the policing function. Cyberspace generates many questions about whether their cultural heritage and traditional constitutional position actually fits them organizationally for a role in policing cyberspace.

In formulating responsive strategies to cybercrime, we need realistic expectations of what the police can and cannot do and what are the capacities of the other nodes in the security networks. Accordingly, Internet governance should be configured to assist and strengthen the Internet's natural inclinations to police itself, keeping levels of intervention apposite while installing appropriate structures of accountability. Remember that the same networked technologies that empower criminals also provide a range of highly effective policing tools that are made all the more powerful by the capture of data trails following each Internet transaction and which enable policing to transcend time, place, and space. Indeed, much of the debate in past years about equipping a beleaguered and underequipped police to cope with technology is rapidly being replaced by increased concerns about over-surveillance through the gradual "hard-wiring of society" (Levi & Wall, 2004, p. 205). A delicate balance has to be drawn between the need to maintain order and the enforcement of laws in order to provide a balance between the desires of law and the desires of law enforcement. Without such balance, every infringement of law will be automatically identified technologically and we will descend into a world of de facto strict liability and, very quickly, the entire population will be identified as criminals.

References

Agger, B. (2004). The virtual self: A contemporary sociology. Oxford: Blackwell.

APIG. (2004, June). Revision of the Computer Misuse Act: Report of an inquiry by the all party Internet group. Retrieved November 5, 2004, from http://www.apig.org.uk/CMAReportFinalVersion1.pdf

Appel, E. (2003, September 23). U.S. cybercrime: Model solutions. Paper presented to the Technologies for Public Safety In Critical Incident Response. National Institute of Justice, Office of Science & Technology. Retrieved November 5, 2004, from http://www.nlectc.org/training/nij2003/Appel.pdf

BBC. (2003, April 30). Spammers and virus writers unite. BBC News Online. Retrieved November 5, 2004, from http://news.bbc.co.uk/1/hi/technology/2988209.stm

Bevan, M. (2001). 4.2.6. Mathew Bevan, infamous hackers and phreaks. Retrieved November 5, 2004, from http://alt.ph.uk.com/node20.html

Braithwaite, J., & Drahos, P. (2000). Global business regulation. Cambridge, U.K.: Cambridge University Press.

Braverman, H. (1976). Labor and monopoly capital. New York: Monthly Review Press.

Brenner, S. (2001). Is there such a thing as virtual Crime? California Criminal Law Review, 4(1), 11.

Brodeur, J.-P. (1983). High policing and low policing: Remarks about the policing of political activities. Social Problems, 30(5), 507–520.

Campbell, D. (1997, November 27). More naked gun than top gun. The Guardian, http://duncan.gn.apc.org/880564579-fumble.html.

Castells, M. (2000). Materials for an explanatory theory of the network society. British Journal of Sociology, 51, 5–24.

Chan, J., Brereton, D., Legosz, M., & Doran, S. (2001). E-policing: The impact of information technology on police practices. Brisbane: Queensland Criminal Justice Commission.

Clarke, R. (1994). Dataveillance: Delivering 1984. In L. Green & R. Guinery (Eds.), Framing technology: Society, choice and change (pp. 117–130). Sydney: Allen & Unwin.

Crawford, A. (2003). Contractual governance of deviant behaviour. Journal of Law and Society, 30(4), 479–505.

Crawford, A., & Lister, S. (2004). The patchwork future of reassurance policing in England & Wales: Integrated local security quilts or frayed, fragmented and fragile tangled webs? Policing: An International Journal of Police Strategies & Management, 27(3), 413–430.

Critchley, T. A. (1978). A history of the police in England and Wales. London: Constable.

Dupont, B. (2004). Security in the age of networks. Policing and Society, 14(1), 76–91.

Ericson, R., & Haggerty, K. (1997). Policing the risk society. Oxford: Oxford University Press.

Foucault, M. (1983). Afterword: The subject and power. In H. Dreyfus & P. Rainbow (Eds.), Michel Foucault: Beyond structuralism and hermeneutics, 2nd ed. (pp. 208–226). Chicago: University of Chicago Press.

Gandy, O. (2003). Data mining and surveillance in the post-9/11 environment. In K. Ball & F. Webster (Eds.), The intensification of surveillance: Crime terrorism and warfare in the information age (pp. 26–41). London: Pluto Press.

Goodman, M. (1997). Why the police don't care about computer crime. Harvard Journal of Law and Technology, 10, 645–694.

Gordon, D. (1987). The electronic panopticon: A case-study of the development of the National Criminal Records System. Politics and Society, 15, 483–511.

Gorman, S. (2003, August 1). FBI, CIA remain worlds apart. The National Journal. Retrieved November 5, 2004, from http://198.65.138.161/org/news/2003/030801-fbi-cia01.htm

Haggerty, K., & Ericson, R. (2000). The surveillant assemblage. British Journal of Sociology, 51(4), 605–622.

Honeynet Project. (2002). Know your enemy: Revealing the security tools, tactics, and motives of the Blackhat Community. Essex, U.K.: Addison Wesley.

Hughes, G., McLaughlin, E., & Muncie, J. (2001). Teetering on the edge: The futures of crime control and community safety. In G. Hughes, E. McLaughlin, & J. Muncie (Eds.), Crime prevention and community safety: Future directions. London: Sage.

Innes, M. (2004). Reinventing tradition? Reassurance, neighbourhood security and policing. Criminal Justice, 4(2), 151–171.

Johnston, L., & Shearing, C. (2003). Governing security. Explorations in policing and justice. London: Routledge.

Katyal, N. K. (2003). Digital architecture as crime control. Yale Law Journal, 112, 2261–2289.

Law Commission. (1997). Legislating the criminal code: Misuse of trade secrets. Consultation (Paper 150). Retrieved November 5, 2004, from http://www.lawcom.gov.uk/library/lccp150/summary.htm.

Lessig, L. (1999). Code and other laws of cyberspace. New York: Basic Books.

Levi, M., & Wall, D. S. (2004). Technologies, security and privacy in the post-9/11 European Information Society. Journal of Law and Society, 312, 194–220.

Lyon, D. (1994). The electronic eye: The rise of surveillance society. Minneapolis: University of Minnesota Press.

Manning, P. K. (1998). The police: Mandate, strategies, and appearances. In P. Manning & J. Van Maanen (Eds.), Policing: A view from the street (pp. 7–32). New York: Random House.

Mathieson, T. (1997). The viewer society: Foucault's panopticon revisited. Theoretical Criminology, 1, 215–234.

McBarnet, D. (1979). Arrest: The legal context of policing. In S. Holdaway (Ed.), The British police. London: Arnold.

Miller, P., & Rose, N. (1990). Governing economic life. Economy and Society, 19, 1–31.

NCIS. (2000). The national intelligence model. London: NCIS.

Newburn, T., & Hayman, S. (2001). Policing, CCTV and social control: Police surveillance of suspects in custody. Cullompton, U.K.: Willan.

Pease, K. (2001). Crime futures and foresight. In D. S. Wall (Ed.), Crime and the Internet (pp. 18–28). London: Routledge.

Poster, M. (2000). Second media age. Cambridge: Polity Press.

Power, R. (2000). Tangled web: Tales of digital crime from the shadows of cyberspace. Indianapolis: Que Publishing.

R v. Fellows; R v. Arnold, 2 All ER 548 (1997).

Reiner, R. (2000). The politics of the police. 3rd ed. Oxford: Oxford University Press.

Savona, E., & Mignone, M. (2004). The fox and the hunters: How IC technologies change the crime race. European Journal on Criminal Policy and Research, 10(1), 3–26.

Shearing, C. (2004). Thoughts on sovereignty. Policing and Society, 14(1), 5–12.

Shearing, C., & Ericson, R. (1991). Culture as figurative action. British Journal of Sociology, 42(4), 481–506.

Sheptycki, J. E. (Ed.) (2000). Introduction. In Issues in transnational policing (pp. 1–20). London: Routledge.

Smith, R. G., Grabosky, P. N., & Urbas, G. (2004). Cyber criminals on trial. Cambridge: Cambridge University Press.
Sommer, P. (2004). The future for the policing of cybercrime. Computer Fraud & Security, 1, 8–12.
Sophos. (2004). The threat of the spam economy. SysAdmin Magazine (Spam Supplement). Retrieved November 5, 2004, from http://www.sysadminmag.com/articles/2004/0413/
Sussman, V. (1995, January 23). Policing cyberspace. U.S. News & World Report, 54–61.
Toyne, S. (2003, October 24). Scam targets NatWest customers. BBC News Online. Retrieved November 5, 2004, from http://news.bbc.co.uk/1/hi/business/3211635.stm
United States of America v. Robert A. Thomas and Carleen Thomas, 74 F.3d 701 (6th Cir. 1996).
Vincent-Jones, P. (2000). Contractual governance: Institutional and organisational Analysis. Oxford Journal of Legal Studies, 20, 317–351.
Vinge, V. (2000). The digital gaia: As computing power accelerates, the network knows all—and it's everywhere. Wired, 8(1). Retrieved November 5, 2004, from http://www.wired.com/wired/archive/8.01/forward.html
Walden, I. (2003). Computer crime. In C. Reed & J. Angel (Eds.), Computer Law (pp. 295–329). Oxford: Oxford University Press.
Walker, C., & Akdeniz, Y. (1998). The governance of the Internet in Europe with special reference to illegal and harmful content. Criminal Law Review, (Spec. issue on crime, criminal justice and the Internet), 5–18.
Walker, C., & Akdeniz, Y. (2003). Anti-terrorism laws and data retention: War is over? Northern Ireland Legal Quarterly, 50(2), 159–182.
Wall, D. S. (1997). Policing the virtual community: The Internet, cyber-crimes and the policing of cyberspace. In P. Francis, P. Davies, & V. Jupp (Eds.), Policing Futures (pp. 208–236). London: Macmillan.
Wall, D. S. (1998). The chief constables of England and Wales: The socio-legal history of a criminal justice elite. Aldershot: Dartmouth.
Wall, D. S. (Ed.) (2001). Maintaining order and law on the Internet. In Crime and the Internet (pp. 167–183). London: Routledge.
Wall, D. S. (2002a). Insecurity and the policing of cyberspace. In A. Crawford (Ed.), Crime and insecurity (pp. 186–209). Cullompton, U.K.: Willan.
Wall, D. S. (2002b, March). DOT.CONS: Internet-related frauds and deceptions upon individuals within the UK. Final Report to the Home Office.
Wall, D. S. (2005a). The Internet as a conduit for criminals. In A. Pattavina (Ed.), Information technology and the criminal justice system (pp. 77–98). Thousand Oaks, CA: Sage.
Wall, D. S. (2005b). Digital realism and the governance of spam as cybercrime. European Journal on Criminal Policy and Research, 10(4), 309–335.
Wall, D. S. (2007). Cybercrime: The transformation of crime in the information age. Cambridge: Polity.
Wood, J. (2004). Cultural change in the governance of security. Policing and Society, 14(1), 31–48.

Internet Sources

High Tech Crime Consortium: http://www.hightechcrimecops.org/
Internet Fraud Complaint Centre: http://www.ifccfbi.gov/index.asp
NISCC: http://www.niscc.gov.uk/
National Crime Victimization Survey: http://www.ojp.usdoj.gov/bjs/cvict.htm
Police Information Technology Organization: http://www.pito.org.uk/
Police U.K. Online Services: http://www.police.uk/services/default.asp
RECOL.CA: http://www.recol.ca/
Society for the Policing of Cyberspace: http://www.polcyb.org/index.htm
The (U.K.) National Reassurance Policing Programme: http://www.reassurancepolicing.co.uk/theperspective.asp
The Internet Watch Foundation: http://www.iwf.org.uk/index.html
U.K. Press Complaints Commission: http://www.pcc.org.uk/index2.html

9 Police Memory as a Global Policing Movement

DARREN PALMER

Contents

Introduction

Research into public memorials critically informs public deliberation on national and individual identity, cultural meaning, and citizenship. In the sphere of civil society, the police occupy an important place for the expression of collective values concerning morality, orderliness, and security. The public police are the visible embodiment of the power of the state and a key institutional means to the public good of security (Loader & Walker, 2001). So, what we celebrate through the processes of memorialization of police are suggestive of deeper insights into contemporary cultural attitudes to the police specifically, and public security generally. However, research into memorials and memorialization has been dominated by war: either in terms of the study of war memorials and their relationship to individual and collective memory, or in terms of the consequences of war, most noticeably, though not exclusively, the holocaust. In their detailed study of "the politics of memory," Ashplant, Dawson, and Roper (2000, p. 3) argue that war commemoration has been fueled in recent years by cultural and political elements that have been facilitating the memory and commemoration of war as well as the "proliferation of academic research and critical enquiry—particularly by historians—which has accompanied these developments, reflected upon them, and itself contributed to the widening public interest in the phenomena. . . ." (cf. Moriarty, 1999).

Perhaps it is no surprise that the same cannot be said generally of the study of memorialization of policing, because, after all, we are not talking about the defense of the nation or of an empire, but rather the everyday and mundane practice of internal ordering where sometimes a police officer loses his life. It can be said with confidence that the research literature is almost nonexistent on this topic. Yet, when one looks more closely at the practice of memorializing police deaths, there can be no doubt that the cultural and political elements that pertain to the commemoration of war have of recent years been quite intense in the field of policing.

This chapter is exploratory in nature and derives from the questions and themes developed to guide a larger study into the rise of the police memorial.* The desire is to locate the development of police memorials within a broader "politics of police" (Reiner, 2000) and set out the parameters for the development of systematic studies in policing memorialization. Such themes are then applied to examples drawn across various countries. The approach taken differs significantly from much of the recent research into police legitimacy focused on procedural justice. However, there is much greater literature that has set this issue (legitimacy) as a centerpiece for understanding policing (for a good example of earlier detailed research, see Manning, 1977; for a more general account of the influence of Weber's account of the legitimacy of police authority, see Reiner, 1985). Second, the procedural justice approach seeks to understand legitimacy through large-scale surveys and quantitative analyses of how procedural factors—police adherence to fair procedures—shape the perceptions of the legitimacy of police, which, in turn, is seen to enhance compliance with policing. While this is an interesting pathway to understanding factors shaping police legitimacy, procedural justice is but one means for understanding this. As Herbert comments, "This approach neglects the significance of other paths to police legitimacy" (2006, p. 498). Furthermore, survey-based research is but one means of assessing police legitimacy. Others are equally viable, for instance, Manning's earlier work (1977) tied legitimacy of policing in part to the symbolic displays of their moralized authority.

* This chapter is based on a collaborative research grant with Professor Joan Beaumont, previously Dean of Arts at Deakin University and currently Dean of Education at the Australian National University.

Memory and Culture

Is it the case that police memorials have become organized sites that enable police and the broader community to address something that cannot be experienced without ritual? Police memorials, thus, become the sites at which rituals concerning police sacrifices and their importance to the local, regional, and national physical sovereign state, as well as attendant cultural meanings and reproductions related to that territory, are played out. Yet, at the same time, we also need to take account of the specificities on context, for while, as it will be argued below, police memorialization has a certain global element, there does remain important differences that the broad brush of globalization cannot accommodate. In addition, even within one sovereign territory the variation in forms of memorials and related rituals and practices of collective memory vary considerably.

Police, Memory, and Memorialization

As Peter Manning has argued in his analysis of police funerals, memorialization is part of the dramatization of police work, communicating the danger and sacrifices made in police work (Manning, 1997, p. 22); emphasizing bravery and commitment of police for the public good and garnering the public support of the silent majority in the face of scandals and misdeeds that foster critique and demands for greater accountability (Mulcahy, 2000, p. 75). Memorialization embodies and shapes the "meanings attached to the idea of policing within [cultural] memory and sensibility [and] the ways in which policing has intersected with forms of social and political change" (Loader & Mulcahy, 2003, p. vii). Our analysis positions these practices in the "politics of memory" within broader "presentational strategies" (Manning, 2006) on the part of police to improve their professional status and distinctiveness, to reinstate a positive image of community policing, and, through invoking the discourse of war and memory, to negotiate a high status position within constructions of national identity.

It is now axiomatic in the extensive international literature on war and memory, which largely defines the research field of memorial studies, that memory operates at a number of levels: ranging from the individual to the collective, be that collective at the level of the local organization or national politics (Ashplant, Dawson, & Roper, 2000). It also is clear that the development of commemorative practices therefore is deeply politicized and inherently contested.

Memories of the past only gain a subjective hold within a community if they engage with wider cultural practices of cultural representation in civil society and the state. How have police, who are developing memorialization practices, achieved this engagement? Has this process been conscious and deliberate? How does memorialization shape the memories and sensibilities of the wider community toward policing (Loader & Mulcahy, 2003, p. viii)? Policing, it is now widely accepted (Finnane, 1994, p. 6), is a function of social relations and historical conjuncture characterizing those who are being policed. Commemoration of police, it will be argued, has changed considerably in recent years, shaped by and shaping the images and imagination of the "idea of police" (Klockars, 1985).

The larger research program investigates the memorialization of police forces in the United States, Canada, Northern Ireland, Scotland, England, and Australia during the past two decades. This phenomenon is part of a wider global explosion of memory, particularly memory of war and its victims. How, why, and to what effect police forces have appropriated the ritual and commemorative practice of war memory is the central issue to be explored in this chapter.

In general, police memorialization has met with a positive reception in the countries under analysis. The development of police memorials can only be understood as part of, firstly, the global phenomenon of "memory politics" that has occurred over the past two decades; secondly, the manner in which policing had converged, nationally and internationally, in the minds of the public and in public rhetoric with more traditional forms of security; and, finally, changing conceptions in the secular state about death, loss, and the mutual obligations between the citizen and the state.

Police memorialization has been successfully positioned within this wider agenda of war commemoration, though whether this has been a conscious process or not is a matter that will be one of the objects of ongoing research. Police forces have a natural advantage in seeking to appropriate an agenda of war commemoration because militarization has been a feature of police culture and organization since the creation of state-sponsored police forces in the early to mid-19th century. Not only was the introduction of uniforms a critical feature of the creation of police forces in Britain, Northern Ireland, the United States, Canada, and Australia (Monkkonen, 1981), but police organization has traditionally been strongly hierarchical with command structures reflecting those of the military (Finnane, 1994), including the appointment of "military men" as police commissioners up to the mid-20th century. In Australia, particularly, given the convict origins of a number of colonies and its derivation from the Royal Irish Constabulary, policing has had a strongly military character. Police also share with the defense forces a monopoly over the state-sanctioned use of force (though whether they should be constructed as agents of the state, or, in their initial decades, an instrument of its dominant (capitalist) elite is a matter that has engaged police historians) (see Reiner, 2000; Palmer, 1988).

In the literature of war memory, there is an ongoing debate about the degree to which recent commemorative practices have been created "top down" through the agency of the state or military hierarchies or rather have been the manifestations of individual grief. In almost all cases, it would appear that those commemorative practices that acquire public acceptability, and in which the inevitable contestation about memory is minimal, are those that resonate with individual grief, through the listing of the names of the individual dead. Initial examination of police memorials indicates that the practice of lists of individuals is now well entrenched.

Such developments are not limited to Western democracies. For instance, China has developed a national police memorial seeking to locate policing "sacrifices" within the broader cultural and economic rebuilding [*I am indebted to Professor Mark Finnane for this point*].

Finally, we should not ignore the politics of memory. No better case study for this can be found than the intense political contestation over the nature of commemorialization at the World Trade Center site. The planned International Freedom Center (2005), now abandoned, was described in the *Wall Street Journal* as "The Great Ground Zero Heist" (Burlingame, 2005) in reference to the proposed "multimedia tutorial about man's inhumanity to man . . . a history all should know and learn, but dispensing it over the ashes of Ground Zero is like creating a Museum of Tolerance over the sunken graves of the USS Arizona" (in reference to a U.S. Navy ship bombed by the Japanese in Pearl Harbor on December 7, 1941). The Internet activities of groups such as *9/11 Families for Safe & Strong America* (http://www.911familiesforamerica.org/) and *Take Back the Memorial* (http://takebackthememorial.org/) helped shape a discourse in opposition to "a Who's Who of the human rights, Guantanamo-obsessed world" (Burlingame, 2005).

Memorial Locations

The location of police memorials raises questions of the relation between police and other institutions of the state. National memorials to police officers have been erected in the United States (1991), Canada (initially in 1978 and then expanded significantly in 1994 and after the introduction of the National Memorial Day in 1998), the RCMP National Memorial at Fort Calgary in September 2005, Northern Ireland (2003), Scotland (2004), and England (2005). The U.S. police memorial is located in Judiciary Square, in Washington D.C., "The seat of our nation's judicial branch of government" (http://www.nleomf.com). The Canadian national police memorial is located "along the perimeter wall on Parliament Hill overlooking the Ottawa River and the Supreme Court of Canada." (http://www.cacp.ca/english/memoriam/english/default.htm). On the other hand, the the U.K. National Police

Memorial is in London on the corner of The Mall and Horse Guards (http://www.policememorial.org.uk/Police_Memorial_Trust/NPM.htm).

There is also a proposal in United Kingdom for the National Memorial Aboretum to "erect a single memorial where the names of *all* fallen members of the British Police Forces police" are located, a campaign organized by the Care of Police Survivors (emphasis original, www.ukcops.org). Similarly, there are also proposals for a new memorial in New Zealand and a "national" garden memorial. Memorials to police also have proliferated at the local level: in at least 34 states of the United States and nearly 30 locations in the United Kingdom. Other memorials have emerged or are being planned outside the Western developed countries (e.g., in New Delhi and Beijing), indicating more the "global" than merely "western" spread of national police memorials. In this chapter, we limit the analysis to the national memorials in the six Western countries identified.

Memorials to police who died while on duty have proliferated in Australia in recent years. In 1999, New South Wales established a police Wall of Remembrance in the Domain, Sydney, and it has become a key site for commemorative activities on the Australian National Police Remembrance Day. Victoria followed in August 2003 with a more substantial police memorial on St. Kilda Road (possibly not coincidentally) in the vicinity of the major war memorial, the Shrine of Remembrance. Western Australia and Tasmania followed suit with memorial gardens in 2004 and 2005, respectively: the former on the grounds of the new Police Academy and adjoining the Wall of Remembrance in the police chapel; in the case of the latter (Tasmania), a "new remembrance memorial was commissioned" in 2005 and located "on permanent display in the foyer at the Tasmania Police Academy" (http://www.police.tas.gov.au/about-us/remembrance). Commemoration moved to the national level in 2006 when an Australian National Police Memorial Opening Ceremony was conducted. These memorials were preceded by the introduction in 1989 of the Australian National Police Remembrance Day on September 29, the Feast of Archangel St. Michael, who was always fighting evil (http://www.police.qld.gov.au/). The Australian National day has since spread beyond Australia to the South Pacific Regional Annual Police Remembrance Day Service also held on September 29.

In each instance, police memorials are located in sites that connect either the security of sovereign authority and security of the state and/or "lawmaking"—courts, parliaments—and law enforcement (police). In 2005, the New Zealand Police held the Australasian and South Pacific Regional Annual Police Remembrance Day Service on September 29, with the cover of the formal brochure consisting of a full-page reproduction of Pietro Perugina's (1469–1523) painting *The Archangel Michael*, referred to as the Patron Saint of Police Officers.

How do we explain this phenomenon and how do we account for this rapid globalization of national police memorials? In order to explore the three central hypotheses outlined above—(a) the impact of the global phenomenon of "memory politics," (b) the effort within police forces to enhance their professional status and legitimacy in the face of sustained critique, and (c) the effects of the convergence of policing with national security—we pose four broad questions and tentative responses.

Question 1

Why have police memorials and commemorative practices emerged at this historical moment in each of the national settings under analysis?

The causes for what might now be called an explosion of interest in memory and memorialization are complex and the subject of considerable debate within the burgeoning international literature. In increasingly pluralized and fragmented societies, the mobilization of collective memories is used to shape founding myths, assert new minority identities, provide social cohesion, and reinvigorate, to adapt Beck's (2002, p. 203) phrase, "zombie institutions"—institutions having ongoing political and cultural force, but whose original purposes are all but dead. The "war memory boom" was also encouraged globally by a *fin de siècle* (end of a century, especially the 19th) mood: a need, as not only the 20th century, but also the millennium closed, to make sense of that immensely violent century. In Australia, this mood coincided with two major national celebrations—the bicentennial of white settlement in 1988 and the centenary of federation in 2001—which governments of both political parties capitalized upon to enhance their constructions of nationalism and national identity. The 1980s and 1990s were a period of war memorial building, in Australia and on foreign battlefields, unrivalled since the 1920s. In 1983, there were two memorials on Anzac Parade, Canberra, the heart of national memorials; in 2006, there were 11.

Police memorialization in Australia has been positioned within this wider agenda of war commemoration, though whether this has been a conscious process or not is a matter that will be one of the foci of our research. Preliminary research of the Australian police memorials reveals appropriation of the use language of Anzac (members of armed services in Australia and New Zealand) in police commemoration, even when officers have died in traffic accidents. How has war commemorative practice informed the development of police memorials in North America and the United Kingdom?

Police memorials also must be positioned within the changing sensitivities to death within postmodern Western society. The concurrent birth of roadside memorials to traffic accident victims (often called "shrines") is indicative of a need to celebrate traumatic death and to give private grief a visible and enduring public expression. More specific to policing, we seek to interrogate the relationship between police deaths and memorialization. Preliminary analysis indicates a complex relationship between police deaths and memorials. For instance, in the United States, the historical peak in police deaths occurred in the 1970s, though did increase again in the late 1980s prior to the introduction of the memorial. Information obtained on Australia is instructive in suggesting that it is "signal events" in police deaths that might be connected to memorialization. Two incidences led to the Victorian lobbying for a national memorial day: the "Walsh street" shooting murders of two police officers (October 12, 1998) and the death of police constable Angela Taylor when the police headquarters on Russell Street was bombed (March 27, 1986). Victorian Police proposed to the Commissioners Conference that the national memorial day to be held on the anniversary of the Russell Street bombing.

Police memorialization can be explored as well as a response to the challenges of legitimacy facing police forces in late 20th and early 21st centuries. Firstly, policing is increasingly under pressure from diverse and competing social groups. These make police claims that they are responsive to some homogeneous "public" difficult to sustain and increasing the possibilities for conflict toward, and "delegitimation" of the police. The police find it difficult to "stand as the embodiment of a common moral and political community" (Loader & Mulcahy, 2003, p. 16). As Mulcahy argues, in the case of Royal Ulster Constabulary in Northern Ireland, the dramatization of deaths through memorials has been used as "moral appeals emphasizing issues of sacrifice, bravery, and commitment" (2000, p. 75); a strategy intended internally to shape the solidarity and commitment of police, and externally as part of a "strategy of legitimation" (p. 69). Is this valid for the other countries under study?

Secondly, the monopolistic claim of national and state police forces to be the protector of domestic social order has become an increasingly contested field. The "rebirth of private policing" (Johnston, 1992); the "multilateralization" or even "Balkanization" of policing providers (Bayley & Shearing, 2001; Zedner, 2006); and the mix of military and paramilitary policing in the war on terror has decentered state police. It has reduced them from being the dominant form of "primary definers" (Hall, Critcher, Jefferson, Clarke, & Roberts, 1978) to but one (albeit still significant) voice amongst many in the discourses on law and order, security, and, indeed, the condition of the nation and world. For instance, London Metropolitan Police Commissioner Ian Blair commented during his 2005 BBC Dimbleby Lecture that, in recent times, police have become an agency of "social cohesion" and "healing" while recognizing that "policing is becoming not only central to our understanding of citizenship, it is becoming a contestable political issue as never before" (Blair, 2005). In another example of but one of his many commentaries on the state of the nation, Australian Federal Police Commissioner Mick Keelty recently stated, "The balance between security and freedoms is a delicate one... This involves weighing up the developments, imperatives, and dangers that confront our society, against the added safeguards that have come with greater public scrutiny and accountability requirements [of police]" (Keelty, 2004).

At the same time, police forces have, in the case of Australia notably, become projected onto the global security environment, being deployed in peacekeeping operations and in "failed states." This further erodes the boundaries between policing and more traditional military security at a time when terrorism has brought war into the domestic national realm, making trains, airports, and civilians explicitly the object of attack, more so than other wars on crime. The military rhetoric deployed in these earlier wars also had material effects on policing. In these earlier wars, police agencies increasingly resorted to, or more accurately, returned to paramilitary policing, again led by the U.S. introduction of SWAT teams across the country from the 1970s and Special Operations units in Australia and the United Kingdom during the 1980s (of course, the RUC (Royal Ulster Constabulary) was seen to be a fundamentally paramilitary policing agency). The RCMP (Royal Canadian Mounted Police) in Canada similarly increased the use of paramilitary policing in this period, albeit checked by the MacDonald Commission and subsequent loss of its security function to a new agency (Beare, 2004).

Memorialization therefore can be seen as an important means of negotiating these changing social and political conditions through the recasting of the individual loss of police into public loss, dramatizing police bravery and sacrifice (Mulcahy, 2000), and thereby enhancing the power and authority of the police and its unique status as the "thin blue line" between social order and a Hobbesian dystopia. Just how much this is so in the case of the memorial sites under study can only be established through the detailed analysis proposed in this chapter.

Question 2

How are police memorials developed and through what particular "agents of memory?"

The history of policing suggests cultural linkages between military commemoration and police commemorative practices. We seek to analyze police commemorative practices through the introduction of memorials that dramatize the sacrifices of individual police (Manning, 1997) by researching the question of agency. As Otwin Marenin (2005, pp. 102–103) states, "Symbolism matters to policing because policing is a form of social ordering that seeks to promote, objectively, conditions of safety, and, subjectively, perceptions that justice is being done." Who organizes the memorials? What motivates these "agents of memory?" Who contributes to the planning of the memorialization of state police? How are these practices financed? What physical forms, and cultural associations, are invoked in memorials to police deaths? What is the interface in these processes between individual police memory, their local force, and state agencies?

From prior research, we can identify that Australian State Police memorials have emerged at a time when police agencies were under considerable strain, criticized variously for the level of force used by police (police shootings in Victoria) and police corruption (all jurisdictions, but particularly New South Wales and Western Australia). In broader terms, the memorials are part of an organized response to the "desacralization" of state police; the loss of faith in the competence of the police over the past three decades (Loader & Mulcahey, 2003, p. 3) as various incidences and inquiries have contributed to a public sense of the "loss of innocence" through police malpractice and corruption. Our preliminary analysis is suggestive of a temporal link between memorialization and substantive critique of policing. For instance, the Fitzgerald Inquiry (1987–1989) in Queensland identifying systemic corruption in that state (though having a national impact) overlaps with the introduction of the Australian national Memorial Day in 1989. In the United States, the national memorial was introduced soon after the internationally reported beating of Rodney King in March 1991. In England, the police memorial followed severe criticism of police culture in the Macpherson report (1999), a report that further undermined British policing following a series of miscarriages of justice findings. Macpherson was also followed by a number of Home Office publications heavily critical of police (Miller, 2003), which immediately predated the 2005 memorial. In Canada, the McDonald Commission (1977–1981) investigated and reported on a series of RCMP crimes (thefts, arson, and break and enter, for instance) and a general culture of breaking the law, which it labeled *institutionalized wrongdoings*. This report overlapped with the introduction of the first minimal memorial. In 1994, the memorial was made significantly more substantial. In the leadup to the new memorial, the Oppal inquiry into problems of policing in British Columbia (1992–1994) was being concluded. This inquiry had national consequences as the RCMP provided BC provincial policing services. This was a period that Paul Palango (1994) describes as the RCMP being "Above the Law" and a "Crisis in the RCMP . . . and in Canada" (1998). National Memorial Day was introduced in 1998, just a few years after the new national memorial and the Oppal inquiry presented competing narratives of Canadian policing.

But to what degree have those initiating the building of police memorials consciously responded to these issues? The associations establishing the memorials, though often drawn from key police or e-police personnel, can vary in membership, indicating that we need to ask whether there has been a broader community sensibility, beyond police representatives, which is concerned with a general malaise in public attitudes to the sacrifices of police work. In the case of two memorials in the United States (1991) and Canada (1994), the memorial organizing group included stakeholders beyond the police themselves. In part, this has been due to both memorials covering more than state police—"law enforcement officers" in the United States, and "peace officers in Canada.

However, in terms of the introduction of the memorials, we can identify that the development of various forms of police executive officer groups formalized into lobbying agencies has had an important role in shaping the memorialization of police. In Australia, the Australasian Commissioners of Police Conference developed into a significant lobby group in the late 1980s, seeking to shape the national agenda on policing reform. This group worked through the Australasian Police Ministers' Council (1980) to establish the police memorial with significant additional impetus by the introduction of the Police Federation of Australia (formed in 1998, but moved to establishing itself as a Canberra-based lobby group in 2003). In the United Kingdom, the Association of Chiefs of Police forum (England and Wales are in one ACPO (Association of Chief Police Officers) grouping, Scotland is on its own) developed significant political power during the 1990s. The Canadian Association of Chiefs of Police has been instrumental in the development of the police memorial. In the United States, there are several executive organizations that have been involved in shaping the development of the national memorial, including influential research organizations, such as the Police Foundation, the Police Executive Research Foundation, various forms of police industrial associations, and the International Association of Chiefs of Police. Indeed, this latter organization points to an additional dimension to the development of police memorials—the possibility that in increasingly transnational policing networks, police memorials are a new form of "policy transfer" overlooked in the standard accounts of criminal justice policy transfer (see Newburn, 2005).

Through interviews and the review of contemporary documentation, this chapter will identify how organizing committees for each of the memorials under study were established and the insights that can be gained from committee composition into the processes and control of "memory formation"? How did these agents of memory construct their memorializing activities? Did they, for example, articulate and position their activities within contexts, such as desacralization and legitimation? How deliberately responsive were they to the political, cultural, and social contexts within which they were situated?

Northern Ireland is instructive as a memorial garden was introduced in 2003, after the RUC was disbanded and replaced by the Police Service of Northern Ireland in November 2001. Is this then an attempt to rewrite history? Scotland is equally intriguing as memorialization of Scottish police coincides with a period of resurgent Scottish nationalism, wherein greater devolution of authority from London and Scottish political and cultural autonomy is sought. In Australia, the national police memorial has been significantly influenced by the introduction of the Police Federation of Australia (January 1, 1998). This builds upon earlier efforts seeking national recognition of police sacrifice though gaining political support for a national memorial precisely at a time when "national policing" was increasing dramatically post September 11, 2005, through the Australian Federal Police operations at national and transnational levels.

Finally, there is the question of the interface between the memory of organizations and those of individuals. War memorials, historically, have often had their origins in the grief of bereaved families. It was their need to give public expression to private mourning that initiated fundraising and memorial building, even if this might have been ultimately taken over by government agencies. Very commonly, this interface between private and public grief was accompanied by conflict and contest over the purpose and form of the commemoration process. Is a similar process evident in police memorials?

Question 3

How and to what extent have police memorials managed to develop a subjective hold on police, political, and popular consciousness?

Preliminary analysis indicates that police memorialization has met with a positive reception in the countries under analysis. However, more research is necessary given that, in some instances, police memorials initially struggled to generate the necessary support (political, popular, and administrative). The time between proposal and implementation of the memorial was over 15 years in the case of the Australian memorial (1989–2006). In the United States, the key agency behind the U.S. National Police Memorial (the National Law Enforcement Officers Memorial Fund) had to lobby and raise funds over 7 years. Moreover, the memorial was built some 30 years after President John F. Kennedy designated May 15 as National Peace Officers Memorial Day in 1962. In Canada, there was a considerable gap between the introduction of a specific memorial service in 1978 and the larger memorial pavilion built in 1994 (this was further expanded in 1998). In England, the gap was also considerable, either 21 years or 13 years depending on which account is accepted; the former is the formation of the Police Memorial Trust with a general interest in a memorial, the latter is when the Trust began to campaign for the national memorial. In the case of the other two memorials, the gap between establishing a planning committee and the dedication of the memorial was considerably shorter: in Scotland 18 months, in Northern Ireland 2 years. We seek to understand the process involved in gaining political and financial support for these memorials, and how these are illustrative of the "subjective hold" of police memorialization on governments and popular consciousness. Has this changed in recent years as memorials increasingly become a standard accoutrement to both Western policing and Western democracies?

The cultural form that police memorials take, and the discourse invoked in police commemoration, provides another entré into the difficult question of "subjective hold." In Australia, our research has revealed that the language employed on police memorials is unequivocally the hegemonic discourse of long established war commemoration. This is manifest not only in the use of "high diction" (to use the term of Paul Fussell (1975) so common in war commemorations throughout the Anglo-Saxon world, but also in the invocation of nationalistic rhetoric). Police officers are described as having died "in the line of duty." They are routinely referred to as being "slain" or "fallen" even when their deaths have not resulted from deliberate acts of violence. Deceased officers are portrayed as having made the "ultimate sacrifice." Anzac is now so hegemonic a discourse that it provides the natural language of public commemoration. Police are construed as being protectors of basic freedoms and the embodiment of national identity. A Victorian police officer, Anthony Hogarth-Clarke, who was recently shot after a routine traffic stop was described as an Anzac by the presiding police chaplain: "Policing is one of the ways our hard won freedoms are protected. Officers who sacrifice their lives do so in the spirit of Anzac, protecting what was fought for and won by others. It is about being Australian," (*Victoria Police Association News,* 2005). Paul Gilroy (1987, p. 74) remarked that police appear to have the "capacity to show a nation to itself."

Is the invoking of this language a conscious attempt on the part of police forces to present themselves as warriors through mobilizing the tested and proven war commemoration practices? Or, is it the case (as state police are continually found by public inquiries to be wanting as exemplars and arbiters of the moral authority of the state) that considerably more symbolic work is needed to reaffirm the "traditional values of patriotism, honor, duty, and commitment" (Manning, 1997, p. 20) both within the police and beyond?

Our initial research into the international experience suggests that the appropriation of war ritual by police is a wider phenomenon than just in Australia. For instance, in his Patrons message for the opening of the RUC memorial, HRH Prince Charles commented on the "remarkable heroism [of] those who have given their lives in the line of duty," that we should "acknowledge their sacrifice" and that the "commemoration is a way for the nation to recognize the best of all human qualities—selfless and devoted courage." In addition, the Queen posthumously awarded the RUC a collective George Cross in recognition of the sacrifice and bravery of its members (*The Daily Telegraph*, 2003). The Arkansas (U.S.) police memorial invokes the classic text from the gospel of Luke that is central to the Anglo-Saxon tradition of war commemoration, "Greater Love hath no man . . .". The U.S. National Law Enforcement Officers Memorial has the central engraving: "In valor there is hope." The Canadian Police and Peace Officers Memorial website opens with the statement: "They are our heroes. We shall not forget them." Again a phrase that resonates strongly with the war ritual: At the going down of the sun and in the morning, we will remember them and lest we forget... (http://www.cacp.ca/english/memoriam/). The Rudyard Kipling war commemoration admonition "lest we forget" is commonly used across police memorials.

This chapter examines the processes whereby this appropriation of war diction by police forces has occurred. Is it an affirmation of Jay Winter's thesis (1995) that communities seek solace through positioning their own grief within a traditional rather than a modernist frame of reference? Are they intended to align police with hegemonic constructions of national identity and/or to acquire the stronger professional status that the military traditionally have possessed? Are these processes organic or orchestrated? If the latter, by whom? Detailed analysis through interviews and planning documentation will allow us to understand how planners sought to develop a subjective hold on police, political, and popular consciousness.

Question 4

How are memorial sites used?

As the international literature on war memorials reveals, the mere construction of a memorial does not ensure it becomes an active "site of memory" (to use Pierre Nora's 1989 now classic term). For this often unpredictable translation to occur, memorials need to generate an interplay between private and official memories that allows both "an individuated memory of war" (Ann Hass, 2000, p. 15) and wider communal engagement with a memorial. Location is often important, as are the rituals that develop around the memorial site. A key element of the recent memorialization of police deaths has been the moving of the site of commemoration from the private (in the organizational sense) terrain of the police chapel or academy to more public spheres, and moreover, spheres that are associated with the state. As indicated above, the U.S. police memorial is located in Judiciary Square, in Washington, D.C., the seat of the nation's judicial branch of government, while the Canadian national memorial is located alongside Parliament overlooking the Supreme Court of Canada and chosen to remind parliament of the centrality of police to good order for all and the sacrifices made by police. The Australian Police memorial is in Kings Park, Canberra, within the official realm of the High Court and national Parliament.

Police memorials are thereby connected visibly to the agencies of the state that provide and affirm their legitimacy and core role in law enforcement. How much was this juxtaposition a deliberate strategy? The memorial sites in the United Kingdom are quite distinct in not being in locations of both high public and symbolic profile. The Scottish and RUC memorials are removed from the public, the former being within the Police College, the latter located in a secluded garden at police headquarters in east Belfast. This latter case represents the specific context of "the Troubles," whereas Jane Leonard (1997) documents that locating memorials in public places and, particularly, police memorials, leads to their desecration. On the other hand, the London memorial is in a high profile location on the corner of Mall and Horse Guard, connected symbolically to the powers of state and the monarchy, a site actively sought by the Memorial Trust founder as a "significant place in our cultural capital," commenting that "memorials to soldiers, sailors, and airmen were common place. But the police fight a war with no beginning and no end."

We seek to analyze what factors have shaped the selection of the sites for the police memorials, how site location is informed by different concepts of memorial audience and usage, and finally how the location actually shapes the manner of usage.

It is quite clear that national police memorials are not the first attempt to dramatize police work in the public sphere. Individual police funerals have long been conducted in the public sphere on an ad hoc basis. Similarly, local sites of memory have been used over a long period of time to mark the spot where the ultimate sacrifice was made. However, with the creation of permanent national police memorials, new questions arise concerning how these public memorials are used by police and public alike. Do the memorials operate as a physical space that reconnects the police officer to the public? Alternatively, in the increasingly pluralized and consumer-based cultures under study, how are the memorial sites consumed? For instance, in the United States, it is estimated that more than 200,000 people visit the national memorial each year and in excess of 20,000 attend the annual candlelight vigil held during memorial week. No data is available for the Canadian memorial, though Internet sources indicate relatively far less associated consumerism occurs in the United States. In Australia, approximately 5,000 people attended the dedication of the new national memorial in 2006. For the London, Scottish, and RUC memorial, there is little information available on site usage, the latter two partly explained by their location on police grounds, and from personal experience, locations where ad hoc public access requests (i.e., not part of a memorial event) meet considerable surprise and questioning. We seek to complete the empirical data on site usage and examine what explains the differences in site usage across different countries.

Conclusion

The Australian National Police Memorial was finally opened on September 29, 2006, in Kings Park, Canberra, as part of the Parliament House Vista and within view of the High Court and national Parliament. The planning for the memorial had begun in 1989 when the possibilities of developing a memorial were discussed amongst chief police officers. Following this, the Commissioners and Police Ministers placed the memorial on the agenda of the Australasian Police Ministers Council and, in 2005, an Australian national design competition was launched for a national police memorial to be situated at the heart of the national capital, Canberra.

In a rather strange twist of fate, the opening also included condolences to the family of a police officer who died the previous evening during rehearsal for the opening dedication. The dedication itself was a highly ritualized event, with police executives (Commissioners) and union leaders (including the top representative body the Police Federation of Australia, which also acts as the secretariat for the memorial) from across the country in attendance as well as senior politicians from the Prime Minister down. In a symbolic move, the Prime Minister arrived via boat, sailing across Lake Burley Griffin from the High Court and old and new national Parliament buildings and mooring close to the memorial site. Upon disembarking, the event was rich with the symbols of state, tapping into not only the image of the first settlers arriving by boat to colonize the country, but also one of legitimate state authority meeting the loss and sorrow of grieving relatives of the fallen. It was a moment, despite the tragic loss of life in its preparation and indeed gestation, in which the powerful symbols of state *and* law enforcement authority were entwined. It was a truly moving moment, yet one also redolent of so many questions regarding its meaning, not the least of which is the extent that memorialization is, more or less, a strategic response to the critique of policing. It was an attempt to recapture police legitimacy in a time of loss, a loss that fuses the loss of legitimacy with the loss of life. And, this is the exact nature of the larger research program we are undertaking.

References

Ann Hass, K. (2000). Carried to the wall: American memory and the Vietnam Veterans Memorial. In T. G. Ashplant, G. Dawson, & M. Roper (Eds.), *The politics of memory: Commemorating war.* London: Routledge.

Ashplant, T. G., Dawson, G., & Roper, M., (Eds.). (2000). *The politics of memory: Commemorating war.* London: Routledge.

Australian Government. (2005). National Police Memorial Design Competition.

Bayley, D., & Shearing, C. (2001). *The new structure of policing: Description, conceptualization, and research agenda.* Washington, D.C.: National Institute of Justice, U.S. Department of Justice.

Beare, M. (2004). The history and the future of the politics of policing, Research Paper commissioned by The Ipperwash Inquiry (Hon. S. B. Lindon, Commissioner), http://crpr.icaap.org/index.php/crpr/article/view/30/27

Beck, U. (2002). Zombie categories: Interview with Ulrich Beck. In U. Beck and E. Beck-Gernsheim (Eds.)., *Individualization*. London: Sage.

Blair, I. (2005). Dimbleby lecture. Available at http://news.bbc.co.uk/2/hi/uk_news/4443386.stm

Burlingame, D. (2005). The Great Ground Zero Heist. *The Wall Street Journal*, June 7.

Canadian Police and Peace Officers Memorial. Online at: http://www.cacp.ca/english/memoriam/ (accessed December 20, 2005).

Finnane, M. (1994). *Police and government: Histories of policing in Australia*. Melbourne, Australia: Oxford University Press.

Fussell, P. (1975). *The great war and modern memory*. Oxford, U.K.: Oxford University Press.

Gilroy, P. (1987). *There an't no black in the Union Jack*. London: Hutchinson.

Hall, S., Critcher, C., Jefferson, T., Clarke, J. & Roberts, B. (1978). *Policing the crisis: Mugging, the state, and law and order*. London: Macmillan.

Herbert, S. (2006). Tangled up in blue: Conflicting paths to police legitimacy. *Theoretical Criminology, 10*(4), 481–504.

International Freedom Center. (2005). *Content and governance report*. New York: Lower Manhattan Development Corporation.

Johnston, L. (1992). *The re-birth of private policing*. London: Routledge.

Keelty, M. (2005). John Barry Memorial Lecture, University of Melbourne. December 6. http://www.afp.gov.au/media-centre/speeches/2004/john-barry-memorial-lecture-2004.aspx

Klockars, K. (1985). *The idea of police*. Beverly Hills: Sage.

Leonard, J. (1997). *Memorials to the casualties of conflict: Northern Ireland 1969 to 1997*. A report commissioned by the Northern Ireland Community Relations Council and the Arts Council of Northern Ireland. November.

Loader, I., & Mulcahy, A. (2003). *Policing and the condition of England*. Oxford, U.K.: Oxford University Press.

Loader, I., & Walker, N. (2001). Policing as a public good: Reconstituting the connections between policing and the state. *Theoretical Criminology*, 5(1): 9–35.

MacPherson, W. (1999). *The Stephen Lawrence inquiry*. London: Stationary Office Ltd.

Manning, P. (1997). *Police work: The social organization of policing*. Cambridge, MA: MIT Press.

Manning, P. (2006). Case studies of American anti-terrorism. In J. Wood & B. Dupont (Eds.), *Democracy, society and the governance of security* (pp. 52–85), Cambridge, UK: Cambridge University Press.

Marenin, O. (2005). Building a global police studies community. *Police Quarterly*, 8(1), 99–136.

Miller, J. (2003). *Police corruption in England and Wales: An assessment of current evidence*. London: Home Office. Online Report, 11/03.

Moriarty, C. (1999). The material culture of Great War remembrance: review article. *Journal of Contemporary History, 34*(4), 655.

Monkkonen, E. (1981). *Police in urban America, 1860–1920*. New York: Cambridge University Press.

Mulcahy, A. (2000). Police history: The official discourse and organizational memory of the Royal Ulster Constabulary. *British Journal of Criminology, 40*, 68–87.

National Law Enforcement Officers Memorial Fund. Online at: http://www.nleomf.com (accessed June 22, 2006).

Newburn, T. (2005). Comparative criminal justice policy-making in the United States and the United Kingdom. *British Journal of Criminology, 45*(1), 58–80.

Nora, P. (1989). Between memory and history: Les lieux de mémoire. *Representations, 26*, 7–25.

Palango, P. (1994). *Above the law: The crooks, the politicians, the Mounties, and Rod Stamler.* Toronto: McClelland & Stewart.

Palmer, S. (1988). *Police and protest in England and Ireland 1750–1850.* Cambridge: Cambridge University Press.

Reiner, R. (2000). *The politics of the police*, 3rd ed. Oxford, U.K.: Oxford University Press.

Victoria Police Association News. (2005, June). Vale Anthony Hogarth-Clarke. 10–11.

Winter, J. (1995). *Sites of memory, sites of mourning: The Great War in European cultural history.* Cambridge: Cambridge University Press.

Zedner, L. (2006). Policing before and after the police. *British Journal of Criminology, 46*, 78–96.

Further Readings

Beaumont, J. (2004). Australian memory and the U.S. wartime alliance: The Australian-American Memorial and the Battle of the Coral Sea. *War & Society, 22*(1), 69–87.

de Brito, A. B. (2001). *The politics of memory: Transitional justice in democratizing societies.* Oxford, U.K.: Oxford University Press.

Finnane, M. (2001). Introduction. In M. Enders & B. DuPont (Eds.), *Policing the lucky country.* Annandale, NSW: Hawkins Press.

Ingliss, K. S. (2005). *Sacred places: War memorials in the Australian landscape.* Carlton: Melbourne University Publishing.

Jupp, V. (1989). *Methods of criminological research.* London: Unwin Hymin.

Jupp, V., Davies, P., & Francis, P. (2000). *Doing criminological research.* London: Sage.

Kidd, W., & Murdoch, B. (2004). *Memory and memorials: The commemorative century.* London: Ashgate.

Manning, P. (2003). *Policing contingencies.* Chicago: University of Chicago Press.

Mayo, J. (1989). *War memorials as political landscape.* New York: Praeger.

Queensland Police Service. Online at: http://www.police.qld.gov.au/ (accessed November 18, 2005).

Stier, O. B. (2003). *Committed to memory: Cultural mediations of the Holocaust.* Amherst, Boston: University of Massachusetts Press.

Walden, K. (1982). *Visions of order: The Canadian Mounties in symbol and myth.* Toronto: Butterworths.

Weitzer, R. (2002). Incidents of police misconduct and public opinion. *Journal of Criminal Justice, 30*, 397–405.

Creating Institutions
Linking the 'Local' and the 'Global' in the Travel of Crime Policies

10

SUSANNE KARSTEDT

Contents

Introduction

Recently, people from indigenous communities at the shores of the Amazon River got in touch with the Metropolitan Police of London via the Internet. They wanted advice on the most successful crime prevention policies and policing strategies for deployment in their remote communities. What advice they got, and if they could put it to good use, is not known. What vexed the small audience of criminologists, most of whom were stunned by this story, were two questions: Why did they think that strategies of metropolitan policing in the United Kingdom had something to offer for their crime problems, and, secondly, was there any chance that the most recent inventions of community policing could be useful advice for their small and, presumably, closely knit communities?

At the beginning of the 1980s, Cohen (1982) had fervently warned against the (then) uncritical transport of Western and First World crime policies to Third World countries. He pointed out the "iatrogenic" effects of such transport from the center to the periphery, i.e., that what should heal and solve the problems actually exacerbated them or, in the worst case, produced new and unintended ones. Moreover, while countries in the Third World were in the course of abandoning traditional forms of social control and criminal justice that had been firmly embedded in their communities for centuries, under the pressure of introducing modernized forms of criminal justice, the very countries from which they were going to import these models were reverting to "community crime prevention," and rediscovering the potential of neighborhoods and communities for more parochial forms of crime control.

Presently, the global travel of crime policies and policing strategies takes many roads and has many faces. First, the routes of travel are neither one-way routes from the center to the periphery, or back, but can be best described as crisscrossing the globe. The Zwelethemba model of Community Peace Committees in South Africa (Johnston & Shearing, 2003) has been transported to Argentina on a "South-to-South" route, and exchanges are taking place within Asia and Africa. Second, the types of criminal justice policies that travel are increasingly varied. Restorative justice in many forms has become one of the most successful traveling models; the agenda of "what works" in crime prevention and criminal justice has provided models for community policing, offender treatment, and crime prevention that promise universal applicability independent of the circumstances and environment where they are implanted (Worrall, 2004). Finally, the argument has been made that, in the wake of (neo-liberal) economic policies, the United States is presently the source of the greatest number of exported ideas and practices, having spread its ideas to Western Europe (Jones & Newburn, 2003); to the transitional countries of East and Central Europe, to South Africa (Dixon, 2004); and to Latin America (Wacquant, 2003).

Two other aspects of this global travel need to be mentioned here: (a) the import and export of the most advanced information technologies, and (b) the exchange of knowledge as a most important resource in this process. The pool of knowledge on crime prevention is becoming international and transnational. As a result, the problems, underlying theoretical assumptions, and shortfalls of crime prevention measures and criminal justice programs in one system are being transported with equal speed into other systems and tend to multiply, often in the form of unintended consequences and failures (see Cohen, 1982; Karstedt, 2001).

This crime policy transfer raises a number of questions (Newburn & Sparks, 2003, p. 4). Specifically, which particular policies, practices, or ideas are transferred? Who is involved in such transfers? What is transferred? Are these programs, instruments, information technologies, and their innovative use institutions or just ideas? From where do the policies originate? And, finally, what are the results of the global spread of policies? Do they work everywhere or is it the case that "successful interventions do not travel well" (Pitts, 1992, p. 144), and if so, what are the causes of their failure?

The analysis of the development of crime prevention and criminal justice policies in South Africa by van Zyl Smit and van der Spuy (2003) demonstrates how these questions are intricately interrelated. South Africa can be regarded as a showcase of a transitional country, and may harbor lessons for the crime policy transfers of a number of other countries. These authors found that while juvenile justice and prisons made some considerable inroads into change and improvement, these went largely unnoticed. The thrust of policy transfers—extensively driven by international donors and powerful national interest groups—concerned security and policing. This process started with an agenda that focused on community models of crime prevention that had emerged during apartheid, but under internal pressures and external offers of policy models, it soon transformed into the rhetoric and strategies of a "war on crime." Realizing that the latter was not very successful, policy makers and the police have taken up the former community model again (see Dixon, 2004). South Africa is a perfect demonstration that, presently, models and policies of policing and provision of security are the foremost global travelers.

It has been argued that policy transfers are mainly shaped and influenced by the complexity and feasibility of the policy (or instruments, practices, and programs) in question. I will argue in contrast (as I have done elsewhere; see Karstedt, 2001; 2003) that the cultural, sociopolitical, and, in particular, institutional context at the receiving end is decisive for the success and impact of such transfers. If successful interventions neither travel nor settle down well, their failure in cultures and environments different from those where they have been invented and proved a success, seems to be much less the result of specific features, traits, and deficiencies of the intervention, than of cultural, structural, and institutional "misfits." Consequently, the focus of this chapter is on the "local" and "particular," in contrast to the global and universal. While a certain level of convergence between crime policies and a certain measure of universality in the causes of cannot be denied, I will focus on local institutions and the key role they play in the traveling of crime policies.

Institutions, in particular criminal justice institutions, are thoroughly local and parochial. The imaginative faculties of collectives, such as groups, communities, and nations, are most visible in the creation of their institutions. Institutions can be termed *technologies of the social*, and the invention of institutions is the field where the social creativity of humankind most visibly thrives. Criminal justice institutions—from penal codes, policing, or security provision to prisons, offender treatment, or restorative justice—are most apt to demonstrate this institutional inventiveness by their sheer diversity across history as well as the globe. Criminal justice institutions (besides family law) may be the most traditional, parochial, and local set of institutions to be found in our age of global exchange. Consequently, the change of institutions is overwhelmingly incremental and path dependent. That is, yesterday's practices and choices are the initial starting point for today's practices and choices, and, thus, shape future ones to a considerable degree. Or, in other words, the process of learning by which we arrived at today's institutions constrains future choices. This is exactly the reason why the institutional framework of criminal justice is of utmost importance in the transfer of crime policies, and why this framework is decisively local.

Consequently, criminal justice institutions and policies differ widely even between countries that are generally seen as very similar, like Western democracies, and crime policies do not travel easily even between these. Thus, the United Kingdom did not adopt Megan's Law from the United States, a law which requires convicted sex offenders to reveal themselves to the community before settling down (Jones & Newburn, 2003). Australia implemented a "harm reduction" strategy for drug users instead of waging a "war on drugs" (O'Malley, 2003; 2004), and most Western European countries do not follow the model of the United Kingdom by clearly restricting or outright rejecting the use of CCTV (closed-circuit television) cameras.

Further, the institutional framework is the place of relevant local and particularistic knowledge for solving crime problems and designing preventive policies. In contrast, when crime policies travel, they do so on the assumption that they are founded on universal knowledge and theories that apply mostly independent of specific contexts, or can be adapted to a small number of contextual factors (see Karstedt, 2001). Cognitive behavioral treatment programs for offenders are based on this assumption (Worrall, 2004), as are programs targeting early intervention for children at risk. In a similar vein, situational crime prevention programs, such as target hardening or other strategies that change the physical environment, are assumed to work everywhere. Notably, both early risk intervention and situational (designing out crime) prevention figured prominently in the planning of crime prevention policies in postapartheid South Africa (Dixon, 2004, p. 170).

This assumption of "universal foundations" and a small number of universal criminogenic factors was criticized by Cohen (1982) on the grounds that formal criminal justice procedures as well as crime prevention programs could (like health policies) engender unintended consequences when implanted in different cultural, sociopolitical, and institutional environments. Cohen, at that time, observed that crime prevention programs were often suggested on purely theoretical reasoning, and nearly all of those transported from the United States or Western European countries had not, even there, been properly evaluated, and any effect remained highly contested. This situation basically has not changed. The Broken Windows theory on which zero tolerance policing was based theoretically (besides its managerial and information technology foundation) has been severely challenged in recent research (Eck & Maguire, 2000; Harcourt, 2001; Taylor, 2001). Cognitive behavioral programs for offenders have meanwhile been found to have little or even counterproductive impact in the United Kingdom, presumably for very similar reasons why they failed to help aboriginal offenders in Australia. According to Worrall (2004), in an environment of 300 different aboriginal languages, many aboriginal offenders can barely speak English. Similarly, one of the reasons for the failure of the program as per the evaluation report was the lack of literacy skills among United Kingdom offenders (ibid.). Many "importing" countries cannot afford expensive evaluation programs in order to find out how these programs work in their environment (for South Africa see Dixon, 2004, p. 171). This does not imply that universal knowledge does not exist in the field of crime prevention and criminal justice; the problem seems to be that like all new technologies, the technologies of the social have to be adapted to different environments.

Not incidentally, most critics of traveling crime prevention programs identify the lack of a functioning framework of criminal justice institutions (Wacquant for Brazil, 2003) and of vertical links between the state and its overarching institutions and crime prevention programs "on the ground" in communities (Dixon, 2004) as decisive reasons not only for failure, but for far-reaching and detrimental consequences. Wacquant predicts for Brazil that the dramatic increase in police repression in the wake of the introduction of zero tolerance policing has dire "consequences on the social fabric as well as on state–society relationships" (Wacquant, 2004, p. 198). He identifies three causes, two of which are directly related to criminal justice policies. First, criminal justice interventions are themselves extremely violent, and firmly embedded in a violent police culture. Second, color discrimination is endemic to the Brazilian police and judicial bureaucracies, both systematically disadvantaging the poor. Consequently, zero tolerance policies—far beyond offering managerial security solutions—exacerbate the built-in failings of criminal justice institutions. For South Africa, Dixon (2004, p. 170) identifies the lack of established links that vertically connect local communities to resources (of power and participation) as well as authority in civil society as reasons behind the failure of these polices (see also van Zyl Smit & van der Spuy, 2003). However, crime prevention policies might generate similar problems in the exporting countries, and, in fact, more convergence in failure and problems than originally assumed seems to exist. As Hope and Karstedt (2003) point out for the United Kingdom, the reliance on formal social control or CCTV depletes the "natural social controls" in communities, and community crime prevention schemes actually are taken up by, and provide security to, the better off (and those who live in higher security environments) instead to those who are most affected by crime in their neighborhoods. The following sections will address two questions that arise from these various problems and failures. First, what is the role of institutions in the travel of crime policies? Second, how can we tap into and make proper use of local knowledge in crime prevention and criminal justice?

Forging the Links: The Role of Institutions

We find all types of practices, strategies, and technologies of crime prevention traveling around the globe. CCTV is a technology that is spreading rapidly. Private policing has risen to or even overtaken the number of public police nearly everywhere (Braithwaite, 2000; Johnston & Shearing, 2003). A combined package of managerial approaches, new technologies, and theories like zero tolerance travels swiftly with doubtful impact. Private prisons or electronic monitoring obviously travel at a much slower pace, even to countries that can provide the necessary infrastructure and cover their costs. Neighborhood Watch schemes have travelled from Britain to South Africa, linking up there with community and popular justice, while they never became popular in most of the other West European countries. Even if practices, technologies, or packaged programs seem to travel more or less on their own, they need an institutional link to be "plugged in." South Africa offered established institutions of community justice that could be dated back to preapartheid and were not abolished during this period, for community crime prevention schemes to be plugged in. Germans, for reasons also dating back to their history of authoritarian regimes are extremely reluctant to subscribe to Neighborhood Watch schemes.

I will try to explore the role of the institutional/organizational structure in the traveling of crime prevention and justice programs by analyzing cases of success and failure. They will inform us about mechanisms that institutions contribute in the framework of criminal justice: links between people of difference, links between people and institutions, and trust in institutions. I will start by briefly sketching the specific institutional/organizational structure within the field of criminal justice.

Institutions—at the most general level—provide the formal structure that humans impose on human interactions in order to reduce insecurity. As such, institutions are the rule of the game, both formal rules and informal constraints; these are laws, conventions, norms of behavior, self-imposed codes of conduct as well as the ways in which these are enforced. As such, institutions include our moral codes as well as our formal laws (North, 1996). Institutions create special situations (like trials in court, arrests by police officers, searches, or training of offenders in prison) with a special system of authority, accountability, and responsibility (Stinchcombe, 2003). Organizations are the players in this game by combining the efforts of a group of people under a common objective and regulating their day-to-day operations (North, 1996). Institutions and organizations thus interact in their respective field.

The system of criminal justice and the provision of security can be singled out as a special institutional field or "matrix" (North, 1996), where organizations are tasked to enforce the rules. "Legal pluralism" characterizes this field, indicating that enforcement of rules is taking very different shapes, and takes place within highly diverse settings—from courts to informal or popular justice. The institutional matrix of criminal justice and the provision of security further occupies a unique position in the societal framework of institutions. It is intricately linked to the political institutions while firmly embedded in the general belief systems of society, and embodied in communities. Thus, criminal justice can be easily "captured" by political institutions, but it also mirrors and supports social institutions and deeply rooted belief systems of a wide range. Unlike the market and market institutions, the institutional framework of criminal justice is much less a driving force of social change than reactive toward changes. Markets easily globalize; however, political institutions and belief systems build a set of strong constraints against change into criminal justice, and thus make it a unique institutional environment for the import of practices, programs, and technologies of crime prevention, security, and justice delivery. Conceptualizing the institutional/organizational framework of the criminal justice field in this more narrow way (as attempted here), however, draws attention to imports from other institutional fields within society. Most important in this respect are regulatory institutions that have evolved in the economy (see Braithwaite, 2003; Braithwaite & Drahos, 2002).

Success and the Role of Principles

According to van Zyl Smit and van der Spuy (2003), both prison reforms and reforms of the juvenile justice system in South Africa were partially and moderately successful in introducing profound legal changes, which were the result of modeling legislation from other countries (see Braithwaite & Drahos, 2000; Karstedt, 2003), and of changes driven by the new constitution and the constitutional court. In other words, these were simultaneously exogenous and endogenous changes, which interacted in the process. In particular, the endogenous changes encouraged by the new constitution and constitutional court transformed the larger institutional environment. These changes were principled and less driven by outcome considerations in the form of crime reduction, though, constantly in danger of being subjected to tough law and order policies. It is interesting that these were institutional changes that were linked to human rights, international charters and legislation, and sought to establish an institutional framework that was compatible with democratic institutions. However, these, in turn, led to substantial reforms of prisons and children's justice, which can at least be regarded as a moderate and partial success.

The significance of imports that are driven by principle and not by outcome is pertinently illustrated by a particular "negative policy transfer," that is, by the nonadoption of a particular policy (Newburn & Sparks, 2003, p. 5). Western European countries would not import practices of corporal punishment from Singapore, despite the low crime rate in this city. Such an import would not be compatible with their institutional framework in the field of criminal justice, and further, would be in stark contrast to the belief systems on which criminal justice institutions are rested in these countries.

It is the change of the formal rules of the institutional "game," which made the difference in South Africa. While not ensuring substantial justice, they provide a type of inclusionary links that can ensure formal justice. The rule of law, human rights, and constitutional principles give individuals the opportunity to solve conflicts on an equal basis, provide the prospect that their complaints are heard (even as prisoners), and ensure that their rights are respected. Institutions provide these types of formal links between individuals and groups; they transform the actions and interactions between parties and individuals. Highly developed institutions, therefore, significantly mitigate the negative effects of social inequality and ethnic diversity (Easterlin, 2001). Imports from countries where these institutional rules are not only well developed and enforced, but also act as safeguards in a number of ways, can easily fail in an environment with less developed institutions in the field of criminal justice. They might not build formal links between social groups, but widen the gaps and exacerbate conflicts between them, thus impeding the proper functioning of criminal justice institutions.

As Comaroff and Comaroff (2000; 2003) show for South Africa, these formal institutions provide a neutral medium for people to deal with conflicts and to make claims on each other and the polity where otherwise irreducible differences exist. It is a paradox—and exactly reversed from what Cohen (1982) observed two decades earlier on the travel of crime policies to postcolonial environments—that much of the export from the First World is now in crime prevention projects that are based on the assumption of closely knit communities and that promote traditionally parochial forms of social control, neglecting the formal and more universal institutions in criminal justice that provide vital linking functions between different people and different communities. These institutional links will be explored in the next section, which focuses on failure.

Failure: Missing Links

In his detailed narrative of the recent history of crime prevention in South Africa, Dixon (2004) identifies the neglect and absence of the "vertical dimension" in community crime prevention programs as a major failure. Linking communities vertically to resources, power, and authority in the institutional field is vital for their ability to reduce crime (Hope, 2001). The institutional dimension in parochial social control in neighborhoods is an essential part of what Sampson, Raudenbusch, and Earls (1997) have termed the *collective efficacy* of communities to establish social order and prevent crime. Collective efficacy comprises, on the one hand, the social control of children and young people, and, on the other hand, the links that individuals (and collectively in the neighborhood) have established with the local institutions of order and control: police, social services, the authorities, and the polity. These are links of confidence, through which rights are voiced, and requests forwarded, and which provide a minimum of commonweal, recognition, and belonging where irreducible differences prevail. The capacities of institutions in dealing with differences and providing (formal) routes for individuals and groups to relate to each other beyond differences are vital in producing and nourishing links of confidence. In this capacity, institutions are decisively nonparochial, and nonlocal, but transcend the conflicts of the local (Karstedt, 2004).

Wacquant's (2003, p. 199) description of the potential impact of zero tolerance policing on Brazilian society and its poor provides the lens of failure that allows for focusing on institutional mechanisms of linking. The point is not so much that zero tolerance policing might increase an already incredibly high level of lethal violence inflicted by the police, but that police and the courts are discriminating along racial lines, and that their incapacity and disinterest to enforce the law has led to general distrust among the population. Zero tolerance policing, it can be concluded, will further decrease confidence in criminal justice institutions, and increase legal cynicism equally among the poor and the rich. Both societal groups will be further alienated from the system of criminal justice, and their support for it will dwindle. Private solutions to crime and security problems will prevail, which mostly disadvantage the poor (Hope, 2000). Ultimately, zero tolerance will exacerbate the crime problems it was designed to solve.

It is doubtful if community crime prevention practices that focus on highly parochial forms of social control will provide a solution to the soaring crime problems in Latin American cities (Loader & Walker, 2004, p. 227). If anything, they will hardly build institutional links and instill confidence in criminal justice institutions. However, it is exactly the institutional aspect of the zero tolerance package that has been left behind in traveling to Brazil. Zero tolerance was to a not insignificant extent a thorough reform of internal police management, including a crackdown on police corruption (Braithwaite, 2003, p. 21). This managerial package with closer monitoring of police might have made inroads into the use of force by the police, and through this route actually instilled more confidence in the institutions of criminal justice.

Role of the Local and the Production of Criminological Knowledge

Crime prevention and criminal justice institutions represent an increasingly important arena where criminological knowledge is produced. Projects and programs are the sites where the expertise of different practitioners in the field, government experts, criminologists, nongovernment organizations (NGOs), and, ultimately, citizens, are brought together to provide solutions to crime problems in neighborhoods, communities, and on the national level. National and international networks for exchange have emerged and, presently, the pool of knowledge on crime prevention is becoming inter- and transnational. Local knowledge is linked and can contribute to the production of universal criminological knowledge. However, it needs to be tapped, stored, and integrated into the common knowledge base (see Karstedt, 2001). Local knowledge is neither superior to nor does it differ in principle from universal knowledge, but it adds particular types of knowledge, such as particular historical trajectories, institutional traditions, and cultural practices that help to contextualize universal criminological knowledge, and to identify conditional and qualifying factors, and ultimately make full use of its potential.

The goal of crime prevention measures and criminal justice policies can be defined as responsible decision making for the public good (whatever is defined as such). Such decision making has to take inherent scientific uncertainties into account (see Hope, 2001). The decisions about which of the programs and projects that circulate the globe should be implemented in a specific criminal justice environment, institutional framework, or community, and, thus, be made local, can neither fully rely on evidence from abroad or on local evaluations. The introduction of mandatory sentencing including a "third strike" policy in Australian states demonstrates the role of the public good (Worrall, 2004). The decision in the Northern Territory (Australia) to withdraw mandatory sentencing was informed by considerations of the impact on aboriginal communities, and not by a "what works" agenda, which at this time was neither available on the exporting side nor, of course, the importing one. Responsible decision making for the public good in each local site needs to be properly assessed and tapped into the local knowledge in order to implement the universal program, and finally to blend the local with the imported knowledge. The withdrawal of mandatory sentencing programs in Australia was clearly informed by local knowledge on and from aboriginal communities, which suffered most from these sentencing principles.

It also is highly doubtful to what extent crime prevention programs and criminal justice policies are based on genuinely universal knowledge, even if they are traveling as certificated programs. Community crime prevention might be shaped by the particular institutional, cultural, and political environments, and, thus, are profoundly "local" in many respects. On the other hand, Community Peace Committees, other types of community, or "popular justice" in South Africa, or Women's Night Patrols in aboriginal communities in the Australian North seem to be genuinely "local," but, might have a not-so-visible core of universal knowledge. The boundaries between the local and the universal are blurred in the field of crime prevention and criminal justice. To identify local knowledge and institutions with the traditional or with culture is as wrong as identifying universal knowledge as independent of traditions and cultural environments. Neither particularistic or local knowledge, nor universalistic knowledge as such travels well, and it is doubtful if one has a competitive edge over the other in the global exchange of crime policies. It might be more useful to think of criminological knowledge in crime prevention, sentencing, and offender treatment programs as multisite local in principle. The international trade in penal ideas and practices needs a strong foundation in both local and universal knowledge unless they degenerate into mere politics, and little more than symbols are traded.

Responsible, public decision making on the ground, with its inherent uncertainties in the field of crime prevention, is not inimical as such to the production of criminological knowledge. "Responsible" here implies that the scientific enterprise related to decision making is organized as a program of a rationally planned and executed collection of experience and data, thus, allowing for reliable, well-founded, justified, and/or proven statements and propositions (Bauman & May, 2001, p. 8). Evidence and theories that are derived in such a responsible way can be agreed upon in scientific discourse and can include experts, practitioners, politicians, and the public. However, these are theories and propositions that are informed by knowledge of the local. How can, in the process of the export and import of criminal justice and crime prevention programs, the local knowledge that is produced be preserved and contribute to the local as well as to the global stock of criminological knowledge?

Notwithstanding the current effort and amount of evaluation of crime prevention, the production of local knowledge seems to contribute much less to the stock of criminological knowledge than it could. There are a number of reasons to explain this. Politicians and government officials need short-term evaluation and positive outcomes in order to legitimate their policies and efforts, and the process of collecting evidence is much less driven and controlled by the responsible methodologies of science than it is by the demands of governmental decision making or other vested interests. Consequently, evaluation research focuses on the administration of projects and less on the processes that actually produce their results. That being said, evaluation contributing to our understanding of administration and organizational behavior in local settings can prove extremely useful in the transport and travel of crime policies. Local evaluations provide the systematic knowledge of institutions, practices, and value patterns that shape the implementation of crime policies, and, thus, help to accumulate "multisite local knowledge." Consequently, the global exchange of crime and criminal justice policies transforms the "what works" agenda into the agenda of "what works under which conditions," and why it works locally.

Applied research is increasingly identified as a major or even dominant site of knowledge production, and as profoundly changing the general mode of knowledge production. Applied research is embedded locally, and thus makes knowledge production more local. This transformation of inquiry and application has been conceptualized as a transition from (traditional) Mode I production of knowledge to Mode II (Gibbons, Limoges, Nowotny, Schwartzmann, Scott, & Trow, 1994). Gibbons and his colleagues conceptualize the emerging Mode II and the transition in terms of a coherent set of attributes. The relevant contrast between Mode I and Mode II is "between problem solving that is carried out following the codes of practice relevant to a particular discipline, and problem solving that is organized around a particular application" (Ibid., p. 3). Mode I describes the generally traditional context of knowledge production governed by the largely academic interests of a specific scientific community, with a separation of basic from applied research and linear relationships between them. It is organized in a disciplinary way, characterized by homogeneity of approaches, institutions, and controls of evidence and findings. Consequently, it is organized in a hierarchical way, which in particular affects the type and quality of control brought to bear on data and subject matter. In contrast, Mode II is "transdisciplinary," characterized by more heterogeneity; it is less hierarchical and more transient. Mode II is more accountable and reflexive, and it includes a wider, more temporary and heterogeneous set of practitioners and experts involved, who are collaborating on a problem defined in a specific and localized context.

As such, we recognize in Mode II production the typical characteristics of local knowledge production, which is situated in crime prevention projects in communities, and in programs implemented in criminal justice institutions. It is driven by particular local problems and strategies of problem solving, it draws on the expertise of both practitioners and citizens (as in community crime prevention programs), and it is based on the collaboration and knowledge-sharing mechanisms that evolve in this process. The production (and use) of local knowledge is shaped by a more diverse set of intellectual and social demands than was the case in the more traditional setting of applied science. The global travel of crime policies, thus, requires and encourages Mode II production of knowledge.

Mode II knowledge production is particularly important for multisite local knowledge. It increases the number of potential sites where knowledge can be created; it enhances awareness about the variety of ways in which advances in criminological theory and crime prevention can affect the public interest; it encourages problem solutions that do not arise mainly from the application of knowledge that already exists, but to the contrary from the integration of existing and new types of knowledge; it produces solutions comprising both empirical and theoretical knowledge, though these may be embedded in different institutional settings, and need to be linked and fed back into each setting differently. The efficiency of knowledge production in Mode II depends in particular on the interaction, feedback, and relationships between the institutional settings, and on the quality controls that can be established in such transient situations.

Mode I and Mode II are types of knowledge production, and can be only roughly related to universal and local knowledge. Basic science and problem solving were intertwined in many of the great discoveries of science, as, for example, in the work of Louis Pasteur, who started from basic research, but became more and more involved in problem solving in his later years, a context in which he made his most important basic scientific discoveries. This clearly points to the importance of problem solving for contributing to basic criminological inquiry, and the importance of local multisite knowledge to those crime policies that are traveling the globe with a claim to universality.

The context of Mode II knowledge production—local communities, criminal justice institutions, police unions, and national governments, just to name a few—is less stable than traditional settings of (mostly academic) knowledge production. It needs to be based on a diligent design of institutional links, networks of research, and problem solving. This, particularly, includes a set of quality controls that are adaptable to the "nonhierarchical," multisite, and transient context, and which help to deal with the vested interests and needs of politicians, experts, practitioners, and, ultimately, the public, in the field of crime prevention and criminal justice. Strategies of evaluation need to go beyond the audit model that is preferred by governments; this might involve fewer, but better, evaluations on the one hand, and a diversity of less stringent evaluative strategies on the other hand. Citizens may set up their own audits. Expert and practitioner reports might equally contribute to the overall framework within which the success of the adoption of a specific crime prevention measure is assessed, and avoid fads in crime prevention policies being adopted and, just as quickly, discarded again.

Local knowledge, however, is at once too complex and too important for the public interest to be left solely to a dialog between (government-sponsored) experts and practitioners. Alternative interpretations of data and outcomes need to be fed back not only within, but also outside the specific, localized context of problem solving. New institutional designs, mechanisms, and features of collaboration between criminologists, practitioners, and the public need to be developed that can fulfill this task. Local and multisite knowledge needs to be linked and networked, both vertically and horizontally. Flows of knowledge have to be balanced in order to feed local results back to the export site. The London Metropolitan Police would have profited hugely with their own crime prevention program from knowledge fed back to them from a remote community on the shores of the Amazon.

A Plea for Institutional Travel

Any import of crime prevention programs or technologies into the institutional/organizational framework of criminal justice initiates changes in the "rules of the game," and impacts on the underlying belief system. Simultaneously, the programs undergo a process of adaptation in the new environment. Understanding institutions—the local importing ones as well as exporting—is seminal in this process in order to avoid failure or counterproductive consequences. Tensions emerge between parochial mechanisms of crime and social control and the formal rule of law between cultural identities and universal practices and between local and universal knowledge. It is important to realize that the rule of law (and the institutions that are based on it) is a mechanism of governance by distance, not by proximity. This, however, allows institutions to function as linking mechanisms. The moderate success stories of institutional traveling, adaptation, and imagination reflect conditions where the new and old institutions fulfill their vital functions of linking people with each other and to institutions, and create trust and confidence in criminal justice institutions. The improvements gained might not directly be outcome-related, but they produced changes within the institutional field and of the rules of the game in which other strategies might be ultimately successful.

Institutional travel, it seems, is more promising than just the exchange of technologies and packages of crime prevention, and institutions should definitely not be left behind. It has competitive advantages over the travel of highly parochial- and community-based forms of crime prevention and social control, and the principled institutional change seems to have some advantages over a purely outcome-oriented import. Presently, much of institutional change and traveling is initiated and linked to international pressures, coercion, and bargaining in the transnational sphere. This type of traveling might not be the worst kind in criminal justice and crime prevention. The quest for fair, reliable, and impartial criminal justice institutions seems to be a universal one for humankind.

References

Bauman, Z., & May, T. (2001). *Thinking sociologically*, 2nd ed. Oxford: Blackwell.

Braithwaite, J. (2000). The new regulatory state and the transformation of criminology. In D. Garland & R. Sparks (Eds.), *Criminology and social theory* (pp. 47–70). Oxford: Oxford University Press.

Braithwaite, J. (2003). What's wrong with the sociology of punishment? *Theoretical Criminology, 7*, 5–28.

Braithwaite, J., & Drahos, P. (2000). *Global business regulation*. Cambridge: Cambridge University Press.

Braithwaite, J., & Drahos, P. (2002). Zero tolerance, naming and shaming: Is there a case for it with crimes of the powerful? *The Australian and New Zealand Journal of Criminology, 35*, 269–307.

Cohen, S. (1982). Western crime control models in the Third World: Benign or malignant? *Research in Law, Deviance and Social Control, 4*, 85–119.

Comaroff, J., & Comaroff, J. (2000). Millennial capitalism: First thoughts on second coming. *Public Culture, 12*, 291–343.

Comaroff, J., & Comaroff, J. (2003). Reflections on liberalism, policulturalism and ID-ology: Citizenship and difference in South Africa. *Social Identities, 9*, 445–474.

Dixon, B. (2004). Cosmetic crime prevention. In B. Dixon & E. van der Spuy (Eds.), *Justice gained? Crime and crime control in South Africa's transition* (pp. 163–192). Cullompton, U.K.: Willan.

Easterlin, W. (2001). Can institutions resolve conflict? *Economic Development and Cultural Change, 49*, 687–706.

Eck, J., & Maguire, E. R. (2000). Have changes in policing reduced violent crime? An assessment of the evidence. In A. Blumstein & J. Wallmann (Eds.), *The crime drop in America* (pp. 207–265). New York: Cambridge University Press.

Gibbons, M., Limoges, C., Nowotny, H., Schwartzmann, S., Scott, P., & Trow, M. (1994). *The new production of knowledge*. London: Sage.

Harcourt, B. E. (2001). *Illusion of order. The false promises of broken windows policing*. Cambridge, MA: Harvard University Press.

Hope, T. (2000). Inequality and the clubbing of private security. In T. Hope & R. Sparks (Eds.), *Crime, risk and insecurity* (pp. 83–106). London: Routledge.

Hope, T. (2001). Community crime prevention in Britain: A strategic overview. *Criminal Justice, 1*, 421–439.

Hope, T., & Karstedt, S. (2003). Towards a new social crime prevention. In H. Kury & J. Obergfell-Fuchs (Eds.), *Crime prevention. New approaches* (pp. 461–489). Mainz, Germany: Weisser Ring.

Johnston, L., & Shearing, C. (2003). *Governing security. Explorations in policing and justice*. London: Routledge.

Jones, T., & Newburn, T. (2003). The convergence of US and UK crime control policy: Exploring substance and process. In T. Newburn & R. Sparks (Eds.), *Criminal justice and political culture* (pp. 123–151). Cullompton, U.K.: Willan.

Karstedt, S. (2001). Comparing cultures, comparing crime: Challenges, prospects and problems for a global criminology. *Crime, Law and Social Change, 36*, 285–308.

Karstedt, S. (2003). Durkheim, Tarde and beyond: The global travel of crime policies. In T. Newburn & R. Sparks (Eds.), *Criminal justice and political culture* (pp. 16–29). Cullompton, U.K.: Willan.

Karstedt, S. (2004). Linking capital: "Institutionelle dimensionen sozialen kapitals." In F. Kessel & H-U. Otto (Eds.), *Soziale arbeit und soziales kapital. Zur kritik lokaler gemeinschaftlichkeit* (pp. 45–62). Wiesbaden: VS Verlag fuer Sozialwissenschaften.

Loader, I., & Walker, N. (2004). State of denial? Rethinking the governance of security. *Punishment and Society, 6*, 221–228.

Newburn, T., & Sparks, R. (2003). Criminal justice and political cultures. In T. Newburn & R. Sparks (Eds.), *Criminal justice and political culture* (pp. 1–15). Cullompton, U.K.: Willan.

North, D. C. (1996). *Where have we been and where are we going?* Economic History, Economics Working Paper Archive at WUSTL. St. Louis, MO: Washington University.

O'Malley, P. (2003). Globalising risk? Distinguishing styles of 'neoliberal' criminal justice in Australia and the USA. In T. Newburn & R. Sparks (Eds.), *Criminal justice and political culture* (pp. 30–48). Cullompton, U.K.: Willan.

O'Malley, P. (2004). *Risk, uncertainty and government*. London: Glasshouse.

Pitts, J. (1992). The end of an era. *The Howard Journal of Criminal Justice, 31*, 133–149.

Sampson, R. J., Raudenbusch, S., & Earls, F. (1997). Neighborhoods and violent crime: A multilevel study of collective efficacy. *Science, 277*, 918–924.

Stinchcombe, A. L. (2003). Cultures of discipline: Law teaches Hawaii to become a colony. *Law and Social Inquiry, 28*, 591–608.

Taylor, R. B. (2001). *Breaking away from broken windows*. Boulder, CO: Westview.

van Zyl Smit, D., & van der Spuy, E. (2003). Importing criminological ideas in a new democracy: Recent South African experiences. In T. Newburn & R. Sparks (Eds.), *Criminal justice and political culture* (pp. 184–208). Cullompton, U.K.: Willan.

Wacquant, L. (2003). Toward a dictatorship over the poor? *Punishment and Society, 5*, 197–205.

Worrall, A. (2004). What works and the globalisation of punishment talk. In G. Mair (Ed.), *What matters in probation* (pp. 327–345). Cullompton, U.K.: Willan.

The Italian Mafias and Migrant Smuggling

11

ARIJE ANTINORI

Contents

Italy and the Immigration Influx

Italy, due to its geopolitical profile in the Mediterranean area, symbolizes an imaginary hub that connects the richer states of the European Union (EU) to African and Arabic countries, people, and cultures. Because of this, Italy became a point of arrival for massive human migration flows from Africa and the Middle East. It is one of the preferred countries for illegal immigrants who wish to take up permanent residence or use Italy as a transit point en route to other countries in Central Europe.

The following brief sociohistorical reconstruction of human migration flows to Italy places the current migrant smuggling problem in context. The first wave of migrants, after the 1974 oil shock, resulted in the closing of borders in many European countries, such as France, Germany, and Britain. Migrants were diverted to Southern Europe and approximately 700,000 to 800,000 migrants entered Italy between 1984 and 1989. About half of these entered the country or overstayed without a proper permit. The migrants were mainly women who came from South America, the Philippines, the Cape Verde Islands, and other African countries.

As the flow accelerated in the 1980s, Italy and Germany became preferred locations for migrants. An increase in private care and domestic services added to the growth of small enterprises that advanced the spread of moonlighting, which represented an attractive option for many illegal migrants.

These migrants were predominantly drawn from the Maghreb area of Africa (Morocco, Tunisia, and Algeria).

Between 1986 and 1998, the Italian government decided to regularize the status of migrants and granted amnesty to those who were already present in Italy. The inefficiency of the state bureaucracy to deal effectively with the legalization of resident migrants gave rise to another massive wave of illegal entries. These migrants were predominantly from post-Soviet Bloc Eastern European countries, such as Romania, Bulgaria, Hungary, and others. In addition, Chinese migrants arrived in Italy and engaged in import–export businesses focusing on trade with China. The influx of people into Italy was further augmented by asylum seekers from countries experiencing conflict, notably from Southeast Asia.

The high presence of non-EU migrants in Italy led to the rise of almost xenophobic behavior by many citizens. Regulation of immigration at the EU institutional level gave rise to a very restrictive immigration policy in Italy. However, today, illegal migration into Italy is not only exploited by individuals and/or small criminal groups, but also is being orchestrated by a complex and well-settled Italian criminal network capable of influencing local social and political structures. It promises "off the books" employment with blatant disregard for human rights and is capable of trafficking illegal migrants across the country thereby eluding Italian police.

Main Regional Mafia Groups in Italy

Italian mafia groups originated as associated groups of criminals who wanted to profit from illegal and violent activities. To achieve this objective, mafia groups needed to operate in wealthy territories where it was possible to manage construction and market business.

If mafia territories expanded into poorer areas, this type of organized crime structure, unlike others, has the capability and the power to redirect its businesses to other more lucrative areas inside and/or outside Italy. However, even when it redirects its operation to other areas, mafia power does not cease in its territory of origin, but is preserved due to the availability of cheap labor that it is able to exploit. It operates similarly to multinational companies employing strategies involving winding up operations and relocating to underdeveloped and/or developing territories and countries.

In Italy, four native mafias can be found. They are characterized by their strong ties with geographical territory (Figure 11.1), social, and political systems at local level. The Cosa Nostra is based in the Sicilian island region of Southern Italy. It is considered the most ancient organized crime structure. It is very cohesive and has historical links with some Italian mafia families established in United States. It is built on an ancient and specific code of honor.

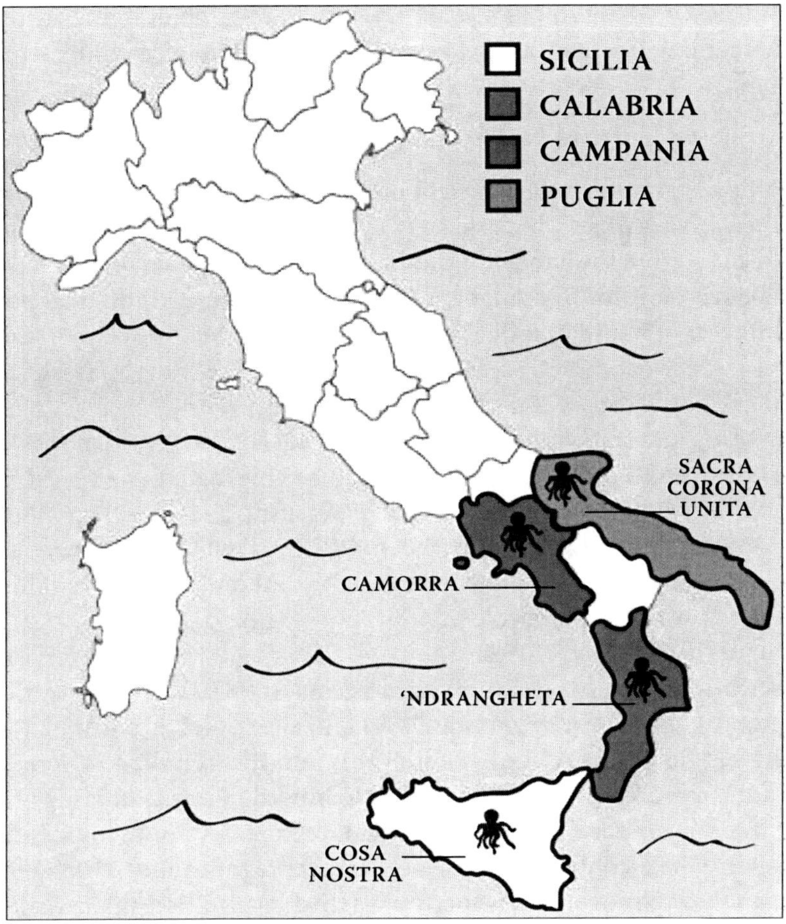

Figure 11.1 Main Regional Mafia Groups in Italy.

Camorra is based in the Campania region of Southwest Italy. It is not unitary, but atomized into about 15 clans. Each one of them autonomously exercises power in its own territory. It wields its power through the direct control of local trade and microcriminality.

Sacra Corona Unita is based in the Puglia region, Southeast Italy. It is the youngest mafia group and is characterized by the relatively young age of its leaders, who average around 35. It also has close relationships with the Albanian mafia to manage illegal activities in the Adriatic Sea, especially in the Balkan area due to the geostrategic location of Albania.

'Ndrangheta is based in the Calabria region of Southwest Italy. Currently, it is considered the most powerful and, perhaps, the most geographically wide-spread mafia. It has partnered with some of the best of Colombian drugs *cartellos* (cartels) to manage a considerable part of the transnational drug trafficking market, particularly related to cocaine. It is structured in a transnational network of many family "hermetically sealed compartments."

'Ndrangheta Culture and Structure

Etymology of the word *'Ndrangheta* on the one hand could be derived from the Greek *andragathía*, which means virility and bravery. On the other hand, it could come from the name of a geographical area between today's Basilicata and Calabria regions. 'Ndrangheta's symbolic, secret, and mystical power is due to its origin in myth, probably founded on *garduna*, which is Spanish for a secret society of the 15th century, and sea travel of three Spanish knights named Osso, Mastrosso, and Carcagnosso, who reached Calabria region in Italy to bring and spread the law of the secret society. Today, in the age of globalized postmodernity, 'Ndrangheta has to be considered as a very dynamic and flexible nonstate global actor capable of taking part in different business fields, only some of which are illegal. In this illegal context, it is necessary to analyze 'Ndrangheta, which is the most powerful Italian mafia organization that has, at present, a main role in migrant smuggling.

The term *'Ndrangheta* (or *Onorata Società* and *Picciotteria*) is used to describe the organized crime group from the Calabria region of Italy. 'Ndrangheta was born from small organized crimes groups that circulated in Reggio Calabria, the capital of this Southwest Italian region. Today, 'Ndrangheta represents the most powerful and dangerous organized crime group in both Italy and the Mediterranean region.

Italian police confirm that in the Calabria region about 150 mafia entities—called *cosche* or *'ndrine*—are now active locally. 'Ndrine networks are composed of about 6,000 mafia members linked to each other by strong family ties. 'Ndrangheta wields power in all regions using force and violent tactics to achieve political, economic, and social conditioning. Because of this, past Italian and foreign 'Ndrangheta affiliates had an annual meeting at Madonna di Polsi Sanctuary in the San Luca territory, in the heart of the Aspromonte mountains. Development and rise of 'Ndrangheta is inversely proportional to state presence in the territory, and their involvement manifests at different levels (Figure 11.2), notably:

1. Society and culture: People of local communities can perceive the rules of 'Ndrangheta as the only acceptable rules to organize and manage the territory, to give work to the many young unemployed, and to solve any kind of local conflicts.
2. Finance and economy: Many enterprises, particularly operating in the public works domain, are directly connected to 'Ndrangheta leaders. Cigarettes and tobacco, black market, cultivation, manufacture, trade,

distribution and sale of illegal drugs are controlled and managed by 'Ndrangheta families.

3. Law and order/safety and security: A state of fear and conspiracy of silence characterizes all 'Ndrangheta operations and activities. People who fight for freedom and legality, such as police operators, investigative journalists, law enforcement members, scholars and volunteers, are threatened. Those opposing the mafiosi are often killed because they are without state protection. Another way to exert criminal power and authority is corrupting civil servants and police officers at both the local and national level.

All of the above-mentioned effects give rise to a twisted and degenerate relationship with law and state authority. The state is perceived as an enemy that can hardly modify the core socioeconomic balance in reality based on the archaic "eye-for-an-eye" law and "law of the stronger."

It is necessary to point out that 'Ndrangheta is structurally different from other mafia organizations because its minimum entity is represented by the family unit. Then, all the strength of its operational tree is guaranteed by the blood tie. It can be proved by police force's intelligence activities that show how 'Ndrangheta affiliate marriages have an important symbolic and strategic meaning to joint criminal interests, but also to ratify peace agreements and to end blood feuds. Each family—named 'ndrina—holds the exclusive

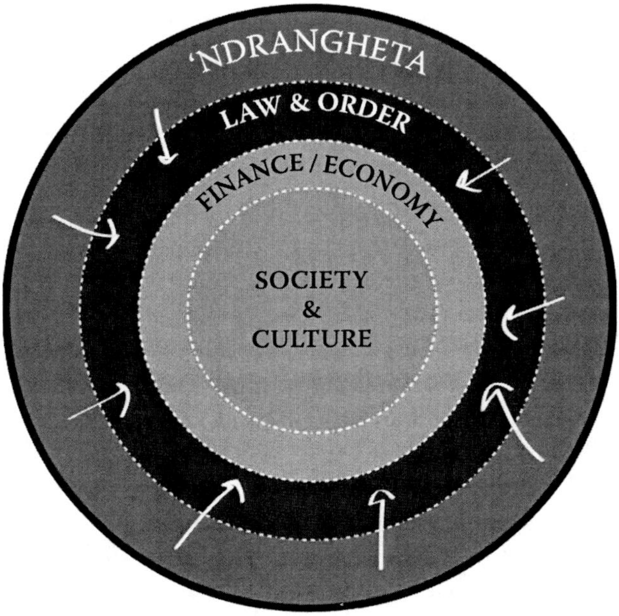

Figure 11.2 'Ndrangheta Multilevel Pervasive Conditioning.

control and use of power in its own territory and the role of each family member is deeply codified and ruled by 'Ndrangheta law.

A group of many 'ndrina located in the same geographical zone are referred to as *locali*—the local unit. Within the local unit can be found the boss who has "life and death" power over all members; sort of a post similar to the Secretary of the Treasury of a nation, or a Secretary of War, who has the authority to manage the settling of scores, conditions against rival clans, etc. All this behavior is supported by the never-ending use of extortion, intimidation, blitz operation, homicide, and massacre.

To understand the sociopsychological conditioning of 'Ndrangheta in the cultural framework of local social structures, it is important to analyze the affiliate's walk of life.

First, the affiliate's access is ruled by a rigorous rite called "baptism," which can be overlapped with the Christian Church religious rite, for example, in the event of a 'Ndrangheta boss's son. The adult affiliate can gain access by a semiesoteric oath in which he has to swear on Jesus Christ.

If the newcomer betrays a 'Ndrangheta group, a member of his family will be wounded or killed. All that has a strong pseudonormative meaning because it is almost impossible that a man can act against the safety of his family. This is the reason why, at the moment, there are so few 'Ndrangheta affiliates who turn informant. Police activities to counter this kind of mafia organization are very difficult. The rituality and involvement have a main role in mafia structure.

Each year, an important annual 'Ndrangheta meeting called *Santa* is celebrated in a secret place. All the bosses are involved in this pivot assembly, but only the bosses from Reggio Calabria district can participate in the election of *U Zianu* (the boss of bosses), the most important 'Ndrangheta man who represents the entire organization and who can be considered the guarantor of its rules, traditions, and reputation.

The up–down hierarchical profile of 'Ndrangheta is composed by seven ranks (Figure 11.3):

1. *Associazione:* Association; it is a collective body formed by all the powerful bosses who are reputed to make important resolutions about the clan's activities.
2. *Quintino:* It's the top individual rank. Only a few of 'Ndrangheta affiliates can reach this important rank. So, the group of Quintino—recognizable by a five-pointed star tattoo—can be considered as a kind of powerful oligarchy. New sub-*Quintino* ranks, such as *Quartino* and *Trequartino,* can be found.
3. *Vangelo* or *Vangelista:* Gospel; it is the affiliate who swears faithfulness by putting his hand on Gospel.

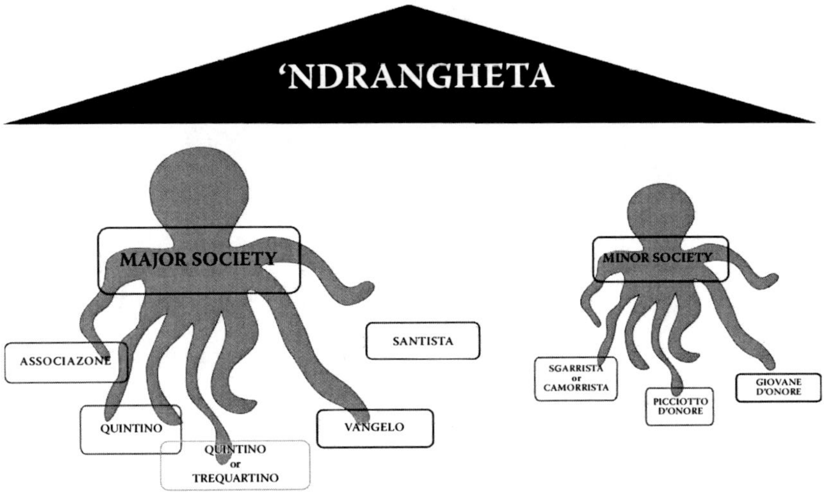

Figure 11.3 'Ndrangheta Structure.

4. *Santista:* It is the affiliate who has been accepted into *Santa* as recompense for his criminal ability.
5. *Sgarrista* or *Camorrista di sgarro:* This is the affiliate who has the job of collecting corruption payoffs.
6. *Picciotto d'onore:* This is the affiliate who works in a 'Ndrangheta group as a soldier.
7. *Giovane d'onore:* Honored young man who is the blood tie affiliate, the son of a 'Ndrangheta affiliate.

'Ndrangheta "Colonial" Strategy in Italy

Regarding the long-term strategy, tactical profile, and operative dimension of this criminal organization, it is important to underscore that 'Ndrangheta empowerment, strengthening, and expansion (Figure 11.4) began in the 1960s when some families went to Northern Italy where they initially engaged in kidnappings and operated extortion rackets, games of chance, and later specialized in arms and drug trafficking, usury, and trafficking of women for sexual exploitation throughout Eastern Europe during the 1980s and 1990s. Today, from the northern to the southern regions of Italy, it is possible to find the presence of 'Ndrangheta. It appears in one region after the other. In the Liguria region, 'Ndrangheta bosses use Genova and Massa Carrara harbors for illegal trading and criminal joint ventures with French organized criminal groups. In the Piemonte region, 'Ndrangheta use migration smuggling also to manage the entire business of drug trafficking from the Colombian *cartellos*. In the Lombardia region, 'Ndrangheta has cloned the same Piemonte criminal network, but here the peculiarity consists in increasing its money

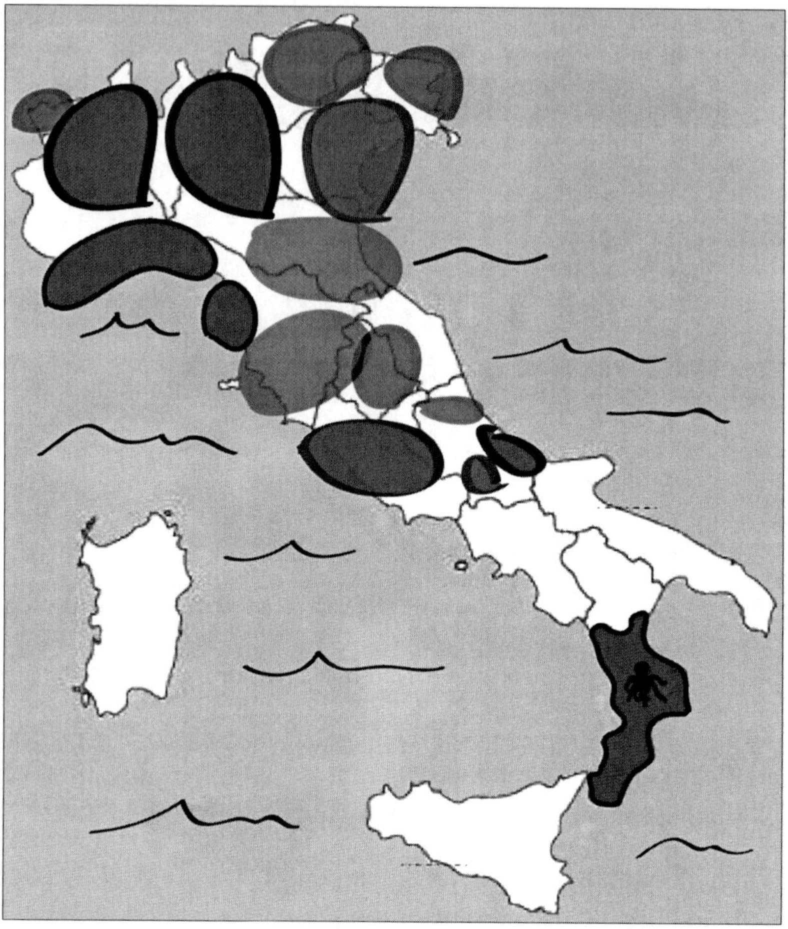

Figure 11.4 'Ndrangheta "Colonialism" in Italy.

and power thanks to the creation of a strong nexus with some leading figures of financial, banking, and institutional domain. In Valle d'Aosta, Trentino Alto Adige, Friuli Venezia Giulia, and Veneto regions, 'Ndrangheta has built a complex process of changing large amounts of money obtained from arms and drug trafficking. In the Emilia Romagna region, 'Ndrangheta has colonized many enterprises and manages migrant smuggling in the seaside area. In the Toscana region, 'Ndrangheta joins with minor criminal entities to control drug trafficking. In the Umbria region, it creates many midsized legal companies and "ghost companies" involved in money laundering. In the Lazio region, 'Ndrangheta controls many shops by *pizzo* (extorting protection money), especially in Rome where it manages drug trafficking. Here, just like in the Abruzzo and Molise regions, 'Ndrangheta creates companies to take part in public procurement.

'Ndrangheta and Immigration

Today, the relevance of the relationship between 'Ndrangheta mafia power and migration is given by one of the last well-articulated police operations in Italy. On February 3, 2010, D.D.A., Antimafia Distrectual Directior, of Reggio Calabria ordered the Polizia di Stato—Italian State Police, the Civil Police Force—to arrest 'Ndrangheta affiliates involved in aiding and abetting illegal immigration and migrant smuggling to Italy. This great police operation named *Leone* (Lion) showed that 'Ndrangheta has for the first time acted not just to exploit immigrants, but also to manage immigrant smuggling.

Regarding the organizational profile of this criminal structure, 32 'Ndrangheta affiliates and 35 Indian citizens formed a national network that permits migrants from India and Pakistan to illegally enter Italy. The modus operandi used by 'Ndrangheta is based on the release of fake employment contracts for migrants subscripted by obliging businessmen. These employment contracts have permitted migrants to receive regular visas to legally cross Italian borders.

In the same operation, the police have pointed out that the local 'Ndrangheta groups have demanded employers, usually Pakistan or Indian men, to pay about €10,000 to 18,000 for each employed migrant. This illegal business created an amount of €6,000,000 thanks to the vital partnership in crime of some Provincial Work Office of Reggio Calabria employers.

Moreover, in the last decade, but mainly in the past years, the relations between mafia groups, territories, and migrants has reached a high level of conflict. Indeed, Italy has been the territory of four important rebellions guided by Africans who want to go against mafia groups.

The first two rebellions were in the Campania region. The first one, during 1989, was in Villa Literno, a small town—characterized by a high mafia infiltration level—in the Caserta district. The second, in 2008, about 10 years later, in another riot, this one in Castelvolturno, a small center in Caserta hinterland, hundreds of Africans protested against the mafia domination and cried, "We are ready to die."

The territory where the riots took place is a very degraded area, where building without a planning permission is predominant, and it is considered to be one of the most populous African ghettos in the Campania region. The local streets are rampant with young Nigerian prostitutes, approximately 20 years of age; the countryside is inhabited by many African hired men; and an entire hotel (the Boomerang) has changed to a "ghost building," totally managed by drug addicted persons. The riot has transformed Castelvolturno into a "wild west town," where, during the Camorra blitz, Africans were killed. In particular, two workers from Togo, three from Ghana, and one from Liberia were killed by Camorra affiliates disguised as carabinieri (Italian military police) who use AK-47 Kalashnikov and 9 mm automatic guns.

The same day as the 2008 riot, not far from the first crime scene, an Italian local game room manager was killed by 60 bullets from the same weapons. Police think that the cause of the massacres was due to the Africans' reaction to Camorra's increasing extortion racket and/or to illegal drug trafficking. The members of one of the most violent Camorra clan (*Casalesi*) are thought to be the instigator of this criminal action. Previously, this clan may have shot some relatives of the president of the Nigerian Association in Campania, which is constantly committed to ending Camorra's exploitation of women prostitution.

The second two rebellions were in the Calabria region. During 1994, in Rosarno (Figure 11.5), a small town in the Reggio Calabria district, a young hired hand from the Ivory Coast was killed by a single rifle shot to chest. In 2008, in the same town, two young Italian 'Ndrangheta affiliates driving by in a car shot two African workers at a neglected paper mill. After a 16-hour a day job for the salary of €25 per day, about 400 South Africans —moonlighting hired men—living in the paper mill had begun a public protest against their abuse and exploitation. Only the intervention and mediation of some *Médecins Sans Frontières* (Doctors Without Borders) members stopped the

Figure 11.5 Rosarno.

African riot. It's important to clarify that many rioters were not clandestine, but just asylum seekers; people who escaped from a country embroiled in political, ethnic, and religious conflicts.

Behind the Rosarno Case

The so-called Rosarno Case can be shown as a series of riotous events that took place in January 2010, from the 8th to the 14th, in Rosarno, which is located in the Calabria region called the Plain of Gioia Tauro. Rosarno is the third highest Italian town in terms of density of immigrants. Since 2005, the town's administration has been placed under a commissioner because of 'Ndrangheta infiltration within. The same town has been the scene of similar incidents in the recent past, characterized by less social tensions, such as less manifestations of violence. The Rosarno Case involves numerous actors including the local community, immigrants community, institutions, humanitarian associations, media, police forces, and local and national politicians who constantly enter into the debate. Attention focused on the Rosarno events has progressively transformed the Rosarno Case from a local newspaper story into a national issue based on the debate about the capacity to ensure security in a territory historically "colonized" by the 'Ndrangheta presence. The same events have caused a deep thinking nationally of the relationship between immigration and xenophobic elements in contemporary Italian culture.

The revolt of migrants has brought to light the exploitation of immigration through illegal employment, moonlighting; not just a Calabria phenomenon, but a "stain" on all Italian society. In fact, the plight of African laborers was known for a long time. During the past few years, significant changes in agriculture policy within the European Union have had negative effects, striking the 'weak points' of the Rosario African immigrant workforce.

The long-term, sociocultural critical situation is given by the compression characterizing the economic territory of Calabria, the exploitation of migrants, on-going incidents of racist harassment, which they have been subjected to over the years, as well as poverty and social problems within the entire community of African laborers.

The increasing poverty, which characterizes all the above-mentioned territories, added to the spread of mafia power and control, increased the migrant smuggling and exploitation of illegal immigrants workforce, and has created a very serious situation of social tension. Every year, those that favor the explosion of violent riots don't often capture the media coverage. But, it's necessary to make clear that the causes of this tension have deep roots—at least 20 years in the past—and it's important to underline that African workers represent, in fact, Southern Italy agricultural economics.

They work every day from dawn to sunset in inhuman conditions, taking jobs that Italians don't want to do, eating nothing more than oranges for days. The criminal paradox is that their low salaries are not at all connected to agricultural market prices. However, the explosiveness of the African riots in a social, economic, cultural, and political context are strongly influenced and sometimes "indirectly ruled" by 'Ndrangheta. In fact, it has to be noted that Rosarno is considered the headquarter of 'Ndrangheta management level, so it's evident that the 'Ndrangheta's hidden role in urging more or less directly the riots is to destabilize the political local administration authority creating a national crisis matter. This key to the reading shows how 'Ndrangheta is powerful and capable of changing its strategy using tactics, which are similar to the terrorism traditional role, to weaken state authority.

It can be asserted that both African hired men and the all consumers who buy these products are involved in a "rotten" agricultural food chain where the fruits of nature are "fed" by the sweat and blood of illegal immigrants.

Conclusion

Roberto Saviano, Italian writer and famous author of the best-seller, *Gomorra*, affirms that Africans react to mafia organized groups because "they want to defend some rights that Italians want no more to defend." 'Ndrangheta power and pervasivity within some territories representing Italian society is so strong as to produce a vision of hand-to-mouth life in crime characterized by a loss of future projects, which causes a sort of "new nihilism" based on fear, living in a state of uncertainty, and spreading of mafia crime values, snuffing out young people.

Finally, it becomes sadly obvious that now 'Ndrangheta has reached the full power to overturn the balance between state and people in many regions, compromising the security all over Italy.

Bibliography

Aloise, S. (2010). Una pagina chiusa per sempre. *Le Monde, January 21, 2010.*

Antinori, A. (2009). L'activité des force de police dans la lutte contre le criminalité organisée de type mafieux en Italie. In *Cahiers de la Sécurité*, janvier-mars 2009 n. 7: Institut National des Hautes Etudes de Securite, France.

Antinori, A. (2010). *News in fiamme. Fatti e ipotesi sul Caso Rosarno.* In *Notizie da Babele* Dall'Osservatorio Carta di Roma, anno I luglio 2010: F.N.S.I., Federazione Nazionale Stampa italiana.

Ciconte, E. (1992). *'Ndrangheta, dall'Unità ad oggi*. Bari: Laterza Editore.

Condoluci, F. (2008). Rosarno, migranti in piazza. *Il Quotidiano della Calabria*, December 14, 2008.

Cosentino, R. (2009). Rosarno, dopo l'incendio dell'ex cartiera più disumana la condizione degli immigrati. *Redattore Sociale,* October 1, 2009.

Cosentino, R. (2010). Rosarno, la cronaca della guerriglia. *Redattore Sociale,* January 1, 2010.

Del Grande, G. (2009). Arance amare: Reportage da Rosarno, tra i braccianti immigrati. *Fortresse Europe,* January 1, 2009.

D.I.A.—Direzione Investigativa Antimafia. (2007–2009). *Relazione sull'attività svolta e sui risultati conseguiti.*

Donadio, R. (2010). La rivolta di Rosarno. *New York Times,* January 21, 2010.

Forgione, F. (2008). Commissione Parlamentare di Inchiesta sul Fenomeno della Criminalita Organizzata Mafiosa o Similare–XV Legislatura. Relazione Annual sulla 'Ndrangheta. Doc. Xxiii N.5. February 19, 2008.

Forgione, F. (2008). *'Ndrangheta. Boss, luoghi e affari della mafia più potente al mondo. La relazione della Commissione Parlamentare Antimafia.* Roma: Baldini Castoldi Dalai.

Gratteri, N., & Nicaso, A. (2008). *Fratelli di sangue.* Cosenza: Luigi Pellegrini Editore.

Gratteri, N., & Nicaso, A. (2008). *Il grande inganno.* Cosenza: Luigi Pellegrini Editore.

Iadeluca, F. (2007). *Criminalità organizzata e la 'ndrangheta in Calabria.* Roma: Gangemi.

Laquaniti, G. (2008). *Italia, basta uccidere i neri. Gazzetta del Sud,* December 14, 2008.

Lombardi, A., & Sperandio, G. (2007). *Africani a Rosarno. Carta,* February 1, 2007.

Lucentini, U. (2008). *La 'Ndrangheta è come Al Qaeda. Corriere della Sera,* February 20, 2008.

Lucentini, U. (2008). *I segreti dell'Ndrangheta nella relazione dell'antimafia. il Sole* 24.

Magro, A. (2006). *Un inferno chiamato Rosarno. Il Manifesto,* December 20, 2006.

Marotta, G. (2003). Straniero e devianza. Saggio di Sociologia criminale, CEDAM.

Nicaso, A. (2007). *'Ndrangheta, le radici dell'odio.* Reggio Emilia: Aliberti Editore.

Oliva Ruben, H., & Fierro, E. (2007). *La Santa.* Milano: Rizzoli.

Porqueddu, M. (2010). *Nei campi di Rosarno tornano gli immigrati fuggiti. Corriere della Sera,* January 20, 2010.

Rovelli, M. (2007). *Caccia al nero. Carta,* March 10, 2007.

Saviano, R. (2009). *Il coraggio dimenticato. La Repubblica,* May 13, 2009.

Tranfaglia, N. (1992). *Mafia, politica e affari 1043–1991.* Bari: Laterza.

IV

Police Leadership, Management, Education and Organization

Issues and Trends

Converging Corporatization? Police Management, Police Unionism, and the Transfer of Business Principles

12

PAT O'MALLEY AND STEVEN HUTCHINSON

Contents

> While I regard police unions as a disaster for the quality of policing, I have fairly good relations with senior police officers. Their role is in some ways comparable with mine as a private sector CEO. They have reporting relationships to police boards and authorities; they are assigned program goals; they have to devise business plans that are consistent with the goals laid out for them by their governing boards or authorities; they have to operate within a budget; and they face the hostility of unions who try to restrict their area of managerial discretion (McLeod, 2002, pp. 75–76).
>
> **Ross McLeod**
> *CEO of the Canadian security company Intelligard*

Introduction

What has emerged in countries such as Britain, the United States, Australia, and Canada is a convergence of public and private policing. Of course, this is not a new observation. It has been argued for some time that private sector police increasingly have been taking over many roles that public police traditionally have been assigned (e.g., Shearing & Stenning, 1983; Johnston, 1992).

This is particularly evident at the local level where foot patrols in many elite suburbs, public housing estates, and "mass private property" sites are most frequently carried out by private security (Shearing & Stenning, 1981; 1987; Loader, 1999). However, while it may epitomize some changes underway, this expansion of the private police domain should not be regarded as the only process at work. Nor should it be regarded as necessarily the most important. Some areas of security work now assumed to be associated with public police actually have a longer and closer nexus with private security. For the most part, crime prevention throughout the first three quarters of the 20th century was the preserve of private police (Shearing & Stenning, 1981; 1983). In the initial "watchman" phase, these were mostly in-house security officers (McLeod, 2002), but increasingly after World War II, private security operatives were contracted in, ringing the first alarm bells about the rise of private police (Draper, 1978). The massive and much trumpeted development of "community" crime prevention by public police, beginning in the 1970s, was really the first of a series of attempts by the public police to develop practices that formerly had been virtually a private security monopoly. It was also a harbinger of a new corporate consciousness exhibited by public police managers. The period since the 1970s is perhaps better regarded then not just as one in which private police have invaded the space of the public police, but equally one in which the public police have begun to carry out activities normally associated with private police. Primarily this involves adopting similar business principles and moving in organizational directions that produce a partial convergence with the private security industry (Johnston, 2000a; 2000b; Jones & Newburn, 1998).

This shift has been driven by a range of factors. The rise of the victim movement doubtlessly put pressure on public police and government to provide crime prevention services and to be more publicly accountable (Stanko, 1996). Demands for more public responsibility and participation, with respect to government, lie behind the development of community crime prevention regimes, such as Neighborhood Watch (O'Malley, 1992). Increasing cultural diversity has been associated with pressures to make public police more responsive to "micromarkets" for security (Reiner, 1992). But linking such disparate pressures has been a sustained change in the demands placed on public police by more business- and market-oriented neoliberal governments. Public police have had to do more with less and pay increased attention to the economic bottom line. Management and executive recruitment practices are increasingly streamlined, and new emphasis has been placed on professionalism (O'Malley, 1997). A customer orientation, frequently backed up by consumer satisfaction audits, has required police to become more market-oriented (McLaughlin & Murji, 1998; Etter, 1995). In one of the classic statements reflective of this view, to have a considerable impact in pushing Canadian policing toward the business model (Clarke, 2002), Normandeau and Leighton argue that:

> Police organizations in the future will, much like private organizations, pursue excellence. They will no longer be stagnant and assume that funding will be stable or constantly increasing and that the public will remain supportive but passive. Total quality service is now being demanded. Further quality service must now be delivered within the context of a lean department because fiscal constraints are expected to be ever present in the future. (Normandeau & Leighton, 1990, p. 1)

In this process, some activities have been outsourced or "civilianized," for example, bureaucratic work, operating red-light cameras, and the transport of prisoners. Various services are increasingly offered on a contract basis, notably the provision of security for private events. Other activities associated with a business and cost-effective rationality, such as the example of crime prevention and loss minimization above, have moved from the periphery toward the center of public policing (O'Malley, 1997). This has been a major source of the rising competition between public and private police, and reflects the fact that the public police are becoming more like corporations in terms of their organization, orientation, and activities.

Over a somewhat longer period, the private security sector has been undergoing changes that extend beyond the simple issues that have concerned many sociologists (relating to the number of private police and the ratio of this to the number of public police). While it is still the case that the large number of private police is dispersed among many small organizations (Jones & Newburn, 1998, p. 80), this does not explain several of the concerns that currently characterize the policing field. The organization, scale, and political resources of public police would allow them to marginalize and discredit such competition, and probably to have it regulated in ways that would stifle its competitiveness. Likewise, the capacity of most private security agencies to compete with police in the new marketplace has been marginal. However, since the 1960s, private security has itself evolved as a corporate sector composed of national and transnational, large-scale, and multifaceted businesses. Indeed, in the past 20 years, the dominance of the private security industry by larger well-established corporations has been increasing at a faster rate than ever (O'Connor, Lippert, Greenfield, & Boyle, 2004, p. 146). These organizations, including Group 4, Chubb, and Wackenhut, which employ tens of thousands of staff and have annual turnovers in the billions of dollars, bear little or no relation to the primitive small businesses of the "gumshoe" era (Johnston, 2000b). Private investigation and traditional forms of private security have been joined by the provision of "infotech" services, community building and management, fraud investigation, international policing and peacekeeping, and even operations linked with state security (Sheptycki, 1998; Johnston, 2000a, pp. 128–132). Such activities are coupled with sophisticated marketing techniques, occupational specialization, and highly paid executive management (Rigakos, 2002). Moreover, the management sector of private security has itself been affected by the spread of new managerial ideas, displacing traditional management models with leadership orientations that emphasize greater innovation, enterprise, and competitiveness (McLeod, 2002). One result has been a much more aggressive and enterprising orientation in the private security sector; a new form of business consciousness that has actively sought out new areas for growth, and has become more visibly competitive with public police.

Such changes in management in the private security sector are not independent of pressures exerted by a new age of business-oriented governments, and a transformation in the theory and practice of management more generally (Keat, 1991; Keat & Abercrombie, 1991). The "new managerialism" literature, epitomized by writers, such as Kanter (1990), Peters (1987), and Osborne and Gaebler (1993), was not only grasped by the business community, but also by neoliberal governments keen to reform both private and public enterprise. In this sense, the transformation of the police industry is more than simply the effect of the transfer of business principles to the public sector, although it may be referred to in such terms. It is equally the product of the government-stimulated transfer of generic enterprise principals to the entire sector of private and public government. It is this, especially, that gives the *entire* policing sector its major characteristic as a new industry—as a field in which new managerial principles govern regardless of the private or public designation of the service providers. In the following sections, we will argue that transfer of these principles has already been realized in much public police management policy and practice. However, another characteristic of the emerging new "industries" is that industrial relations have been replaced by human resource management, a process in which the old oppositions between management and labor are supposedly displaced by mutual enterprise. This is registered in most industries by the weakening and displacement of trade unionism (Turner, 1992; Davis, 1994), and will be seen to be most characteristic of the private security sector where unionized labor is frequently absent. Ironically, however, as public police managers have become corporate, a divide has opened up between the management and street level police that has strengthened, rather than diminished, the role of police unionism. In its turn, this failure to transfer new enterprise principles to the public police has been seen by some to set up obstacles to the further corporatization of the policing industry.

The Managerial Revolution

One of the clearest manifestations of the corporatization of policing has been the adoption or imposition of new public management as a guiding rationale. This has provided general formulae whereby all state agencies are to become enterprises in an effort to make them more responsive and accountable, to deliver greater efficiencies and more innovative outputs, while at the same time subjecting their fiscal regimes to cost minimizing and cost-benefit analyses. It is very clear that when these changes were first introduced, it was against the often vehement opposition of all levels of police, including senior police managers (Bayley, 1994; Fleming & Lafferty, 2000; Loader & Mulcahy, 2003, pp. 291–294). In part, this resistance reflected a legacy of the public police as a quasimilitary, quasiguild organization in which solidarities were crucial and were formed by the fact that all police, up to and including chief commissioners or chief constables, had come up through the ranks. The guild-like environment was most apparent in the apprenticeship system; officers learned the job in an empirical fashion on the streets, with theoretical education playing a relatively marginal role (O'Malley, 1997). Promotion came through a mixture of seniority and merit, but the importance of seniority and common entrance meant that senior managers were schooled in police-working culture. This did not mean that police rank and file were never in conflict with senior police officers; it is clear that in many police forces around the world, police associations and unions have frequently been directly in confrontation with police managers over issues, such as working conditions, pay, discipline, and promotions, the traditional concerns of the trade union movement (Finnane, 2002; Forcese, 1999). But rarely were these internal conflicts over what policing was about, what principles it should follow, and how it should be practiced. The police forces—senior officers and rank and file members—under such conditions retained militaristic solidarity against outside criticisms and attempts to increase external regulation and accountability.

This organizational characteristic of police solidarity was already being eroded in the 1980s, especially through pressures associated with the need to import expertise through horizontal appointments. However, as noted above, the transfer of new managerialism was still largely resisted by senior police managers who had achieved their rank through the traditional processes. In Britain, there was explicit resistance from the top echelons to making police "like a business" and, in the early 1990s, senior police warned that "a nonprofit-making, caring public service could not be judged by economic criteria used by ICI and Marks and Spencers," and that the British public would reject a police service that was "too efficient, too effective, too sophisticated" (quoted in McLaughlin & Murji, 1997, p. 95). As with the traditional bureaucracies that were also anathema to neoliberal governments, initial efforts to convert policing took the form of interventions that worked on senior management in a more or less coercive fashion. Among the first of these was direct economic pressure. That is, if police management was resistant, it could be brought to heel simply by providing limited budgets or by earmarking elements in budgets for tasks or procedures specified by government. For Mick

Palmer, the former Chief Commissioner of the Australian Federal Police, it was evident that:

> . . . police are under pressure to satisfy governments that they are cost effective and achieving the required results. Limited resources have already substantially impacted on policing as governments apply spending cuts. Police managers have been forced to achieve considerable savings through more stringent and controlled use of finance and other resources. "Lean and mean" has been the emphasis at management levels in addressing the demand to provide policing services at considerably reduced cost (Palmer, 1995, p. 7).

Certainly there was little that was novel about funding cuts. However, the thrust of this new generation of economic stringency was directed against police organization and management rather than merely at reducing government expenditure. As Fleming and Lafferty have argued, ". . . budgetary considerations forced police organizations to adopt program management schemes and to decentralize command. As responsibility for planning and budgeting was devolved to frontline managers, budgetary practices, once concerned solely with the management of police numbers, were refocused on the distribution of limited financial resources and operational outcomes" (Fleming & Lafferty, 2000, pp. 155–156). These techniques were soon matched with a battery of new instruments that didn't merely reflect business practice. Rather, they were designed precisely to effect the transfer of principles and practices from the business sector.

By now, the image of the audit, especially as a way of making agencies responsible to their customers, has become something that is almost taken for granted as a governmental technique (Power, 1994). But, what is not always recognized is that the audit is not merely a mechanism of accountability; equally, it is part of an assault on the inscrutable knowledge systems of "closed" institutions and professions. As Rose has indicated, audit is one means whereby a change is effected in the relations between expertise and government (Rose, 1996, pp. 54–55). The arcane knowledge of the professions and bureaucracies, including the military and the police, represented means of constituting "enclosures within which their authority could not be challenged" (p. 54). Whatever criticisms are offered from without have to be validated from within, or else be subject to the accusation that they are inexpert or politically motivated. In the case of police, this expertise was shared by rank and file and senior management who, thus, could find common cause in rejecting external criticisms and at the same time use their expertise to demand more autonomy and more resources. The characteristic of the new governmental techniques of audit, accountancy, marketing, budgetary disciplines, and so on, however, was that they were simultaneously expert, but transparent, critical, but neutral. They could be applied to police or to universities, to medical administration or to legal services in a way that does not challenge practitioners' expertise, but does, however, subordinate them to another set of governing categories. Thus, with respect to budgetary discipline, Rose suggests that:

> [m]aking people write things down, prescribing what must be written down and how, is itself a kind of government of individual conduct, making it thinkable according to particular norms. Budgetary discipline transforms the activity of the budget holder, increasing choices at the same time as regulating them and providing new ways of ensuring the responsibility and fidelity of agents who remain formally autonomous. Not merely in the setting of the budget, but in the very "budgetization" of the activity, the terms of calculation and decision are displaced and new diagrams of force and freedom are assembled. (Rose, 1996, pp. 54–55)

Audit, combined with other accounting technologies, ramped up the critical power of economic coercion by rendering such funding cuts expert rather than ignorant, and, at the same time, distanced governments from any accusation that they were interfering in the independence and professional expertise of the police. It was for such reasons, as McLaughlin and Murji point out, that in Britain "[v]irtually every Home Office policy document stresses that modernization will be achieved through constant auditing, priority and target setting, monitoring, evaluation, and inspection" (2001, p. 115). Criminal justice professionals, including senior police, are advised "that the capacity for audit and inspection will be developed to assess the performance of the criminal justice system as a whole; to provide assurance that it is operating economically and efficiently, and is achieving its aims and objectives effectively" (Ibid.). The position of any obdurate police management thus became scarcely tenable, for the transparency of the new criteria left them open to critiques of featherbedding, inefficiency, and rigidity that are difficult to fight from a traditional police knowledge base. However, for much the same reason, the adoption by management of these new managerialist techniques, or even their acceptance of these as valid, goes to the heart of police solidarity in a way that distances them from the rank and file in new ways. Management working with these principles and technologies was being disembedded from the traditional knowledge of the police guild; a first step in recreating police as a corporation (Loader & Mulcahy, 2003, pp. 240–241, 290–291).

The expansion of these new governmental techniques during the 1980s and 1990s, perhaps needless to say, was linked with new priorities for appointment and promotion into the top echelons of police forces. Over the course of a decade, promotion would come to senior officers who appeared meritorious in—and committed to—the new ways of managing (Davids &

Hancock, 1998, pp. 46–48). In turn, as the preferences of this generation of managers were put into effect, so training at universities and police colleges became more critical as entry procedures. Those adept at the abstract rather than the concrete knowledge associated with traditional rank and file policing were promoted or parachuted in through horizontal appointments (MacDonald, 1995). In their turn, elements of new managerialism and programs were inserted into themes of police training, as was the case with the Ontario "police learning system" and the Royal Canadian Mounted Police "CAPRA problem-solving model" (De Lint, 1998, pp. 270–271).

As a result, by the mid-1990s, the coercive mechanisms put in place to discipline management had themselves become a part of the equipment that a new generation of police managers were skilled at operating as a form of self-discipline. Through these techniques and procedures, key aspects of their own authority and organizational power were constituted. Increasingly, police managers were becoming generic "new" managers almost as much as they were police. For Rohl and Barnsley (the latter, the dean of the Australian Police Staff College), "truly efficient and effective policing would only be achieved when policing developed a professional culture underpinned by superior management practices and a commitment to corporate excellence" (1995, p. 253). This view is echoed everywhere, usually associated with a vision of the traditional structure of policing as a problem or obstacle to progress (see, e.g., Drennan, 2003, pp. 2–4). Thus, the view of the former chief commissioner of the New Zealand Police is that the military structure and monopoly privilege of police worked against essential reforms: "...whilst private companies were forced to adapt their leadership style in order to survive in a competitive environment, police organizations were slower to adapt. After all, the police tended to operate in a captive market in which law enforcement had been a growth industry." In such an environment, he ruefully noted, "it is unlikely that a strategic plan would have existed" (MacDonald, 1995, pp. 210–212). Likewise, the Australian Federal Police Commissioner argued that "the paramilitary style of police agencies, with its strict discipline, autocratic command, centralized decision making, and hierarchical structure" had become inadequate in the new environment and that "it was clear that a shift was required by senior management from control by issuing orders to the use of visionary leadership to motivate and direct the organization" (Palmer, 1995, p. 42).

It cannot be asserted that such expressions are merely statements of convenience, evidence only of police managers putting into print views that their political masters want to see. Not only is it clear that many openly embrace the language and ideas of new managerialism, but in some cases they have promoted such change in the face of government resistance (Etter, 1995, p. 302). Commissioner David Hunt of the South Australia Police notes that in response to a strategic analysis that was "...aimed at determining whether the existing functions contributed to achieving the department's mission and corporate [*sic*] goals..." (Hunt, 1995, pp. 60–61), seven functions were identified as marginal to providing core police services to the community (Ibid.). These included duties such as coronial investigations, the operation of speed cameras, the serving of warrants for nonpayment of fines and costs, and provision of prosecution services. For each function, Hunt states, "A review was undertaken and a business case prepared." However, the process of implementation was slowed by resistance from other government agencies. It was not given its head until a more ideologically compatible government was elected that established an audit review, put in place stringent cost-reductions, and "created a climate of change that was necessary for consideration of the department's proposals" (Ibid.).

It is fair to agree with Fleming and Lafferty that "... in a relatively short period these managerialist techniques came to dominate public and police administration... in most English-speaking countries today" (2000, p. 155), and even with Adlam's more cynical view that 'most forces have chosen to ape the corporate style of the multinational companies' (2002, p. 31). In this light, it is perhaps not surprising that many of this new generation of police corporate managers find themselves at best ambivalent about or hostile toward traditional police culture. It is at this point that understanding the process of transferring business principles to policing practice becomes a little more complex.

Police Unions and Police Culture

> As late as the 1960s, police chiefs had virtually unlimited power to run their department. Today police chiefs are severely constrained. Not only are many important issues subject to collective bargaining, but police unions exert enormous informal influence both within the department and in the community at large. Police unions are here to stay; we cannot ignore them. (William O. Douglas Institute, 1984)

One of the clearest areas of convergence between the corporate public police managers and their private counterparts is their view of police associations and trades unions as obstacles to "progress" (McLeod, 2002; Drennan, 2003). As suggested earlier, in part, this may reflect the new managerial vision in which the oppositional divide between managers and workers has been rendered obsolete and counterproductive. New managerialism has attempted to reconstitute "employees into entrepreneurs" (Rose, 1999, pp. 156–158). 'Workers' and 'employees' come to be replaced by 'partners', 'representatives', 'members'; and in the entrepreneurial organization '... there are no 'subordinates', only 'associates'' (Drucker, 1993, p. 108). It is not difficult to find this kind of discourse in police human relations publications (see, generally, Etter & Palmer, 1995; cf. De Lint, 1999). Whether or not any of this is translated into practice, either in the public or the private sectors of policing, is another question entirely.

While police managers were rapidly becoming corporatized during the 1990s, police associations were busy resisting the very kinds of changes to working relations, management practices, and police work that the reconstituted police executive promoted and sought to realize. The British Police Federation's successful struggles beginning in the early 1990s have probably received the most attention (McLaughlin & Murji, 1997; 2001). However, parallel examples can be found in other English-speaking countries, such as Canada, the United States, and Australia (e.g., De Lint, 1998; Kadleck, 2003; Finnane, 2002). There is then an apparent irony that, while new managerialism seeks to dissolve trade union consciousness and organization, the successful corporatization of police management has reinvigorated precisely these characteristics of police labor at a time when trade unionism generally has been in retreat. Two related conclusions are usually drawn from this observation. First, the continued corporatization of policing will be hindered or halted by a revitalized trade unionism (e.g., Vickers, 2000, p. 507), and second, this has entrenched a conservative police working culture that is dedicated to a vision that policing can only be learned on the streets (De Lint, 1999). The latter, in turn, is regarded as continually reinforced because the rank and file policing experience is formed on the streets and in relation to a largely unchanged set of experiential problems and dangers. Rather than managerial principles filtering down to the lower ranks, this interpretation suggests that police "low" culture will continue to be reproduced, change will be further resisted at the street level, and the transfer of the corporate model will fail (De Lint, 1999, pp. 145–146; 1998, p. 280). For many police managers, this cultural problem appears as linked to a larger issue, as by implication police union resistance and the resistance of a solidarist rank and file police culture are mutually reinforcing (Landa & Dillon, 1995, pp. 135–138; Palmer, 1995). As is discussed below, this has led many to argue that police unions have indeed become entrenched, and, thus far, have not adapted to the new environment in ways that have occurred elsewhere in the union movement. As Fleming and Lafferty concluded in their review of Australian police:

> ... [n]ew management techniques do not adapt readily to the police context. Police cultures articulate very different values (such as loyalty to fellow officers) from those articulated in new management techniques (such as individual performance and organizational accountability). This contradiction indicates a practical limitation to the effectiveness of organizational change practices. The implementation of new management techniques has produced a management division between senior police and rank and file officers ... it

> may be that a stronger "us and them" situation between police officers and their superiors is being created. Whereas once managers and police officers were members of a common, highly insular organizational culture, the restructuring processes have inaugurated a more formal employer–employee relationship. In such a situation, management will need to be very careful to avoid reigniting the very aspects of solidarity among the rank and file they sought to dismantle (Fleming & Lafferty, 2000, pp. 163–164).

Of course, this interpretation seems to run counter to Chan's work on transforming police cultures (1997; 2003). Chan argues, quite rightly, that accepting the existence of an "...all-powerful, homogeneous, and deterministic conception of police culture insulated from the external environment leaves little scope for cultural change.... A satisfactory reformulation of police culture should allow for the possibility of change as well as resistance to change" (Chan, 1997, p. 67). She suggests that efforts at change have failed partly because managerial attempts to deal with changing police culture have attempted only top-down methods of implementing reforms—for example, by promoting an abstract model of "professionalism" without providing a suitable organizational environment (1997, p. 154; 2003, pp. 314–315). This is borne out by Clarke's study of the Royal Canadian Mounted Police (RCMP), where management:

> ...assumed that members could easily adapt to a new service delivery model without education and within the current organizational structure. It was also believed that all administrative and operational support personnel would readily and willingly modify their policies and practices. We know this has not occurred...audit asserted that reform would have been more effective if the RCMP had, in fact, addressed organizational and structural concerns before downloading to the detachment and assuming frontline officers would quickly adapt (Clarke, 2002, p. 21).

At first sight, this account lays the blame for failure at the feet of poor management rather than an impervious police culture. The conclusion that Chan draws is that changed management will not fail because of an impervious culture, but because management has worked with a "mythic vision" of what police could do rather than one "based on what police can realistically do" (Chan, 2003, p. 316). One of the features of this analysis is that it detracts attention from the obsession with a police working culture, an analytical juggernaut that proceeds as if it has been demonstrated that this necessarily is a barrier to any effective reform of police. An alternative view, put forward by certain advocates of the private security sector is that the more critical problem is not the culture per se, so much as its nexus with police unionism (McLeod, 2002; Drennan, 2003).

For McLeod (2002), speaking as a private security executive, unionization has been the critical issue not just because it has entrenched, or expresses, a rigid culture. More important is that it prevents the realization of many of the goals of initiatives, such as community policing, that allow a better customer orientation and, thus, the development of a more responsive and accountable police. While it is not necessary to accept all of McLeod's (probably overstated) arguments, they provide an interesting counter to some received sociological truths. His claim may be summarized in the following statement:

> Adversarial police unions defend their members' working conditions in ways that prevent a large number of reforms. For example, it is unions that have resisted getting patrol officers out of their cars and onto foot patrol duties especially late at night when public demand for a police presence is at its greatest. It is the unions that resist market pressures for a responsive police that can get "down among the people" and listen to their needs, and that can provide a diverse array of services. It is unions that frustrate managers' attempts to institute and carry through business plans that would facilitate greater accountability, and so on.

Private security can provide for all of these needs, he suggests, because its labor is not unionized. It can more readily be required to respond to market pressures and management directives, and to work for considerably lower pay and under more stringent economic conditions (e.g., operating single-person cruisers). In short, this labor force is much more subordinate and compliant (Lippert & O'Connor, 2003). McLeod probably would not resist this last interpretation, but, for our purposes, the argument is interesting because it is evident that none of his claims make any reference to a police working culture as a problem. Indeed, as the fieldwork of Rigakos (2002) makes clear, most of the features of public police culture are abundantly evident among private security officers, and for much the same reasons. They confront dangerous situations where great reliance is placed on collegial support and solidarity. In this context, a macho self-image prevails. Moreover, in order to expedite their duties, they carry out activities that are often unauthorized or illegal, giving rise to occupational secrecy. This defensive culture is entrenched by the fact that they are constantly under critical scrutiny by management and the public, and are hostile to various tools that are put in place to monitor their performance according to the standards of management: management, and their audit tools are regarded as out of touch with the real needs of policing. In other words, the character of both public police and private security is very similar with respect to the level of organizational and cultural distance between management and the workforce. So, private security management is better able to achieve at least some of the ends sought by public sector management because it is in a better position to require a certain performance of its workforce, not simply because its workforce develops a specific working culture.

Converging Corporatism, Police Unions, and Segmented Police Markets

There is a clear irony in this analysis if we consider that in attempting to produce a postmodern organization in keeping with new managerial principles, public police management has unintentionally produced a classically modernist corporate structure. Structurally, the effect has been remarkable, because, as suggested above, the dominant 20th-century model of policing was guild-like. In most cases, this has virtually disappeared or at least been heavily modified. In turn, the current struggle between management and police labor, equally ironically perhaps, has accelerated the breakdown of premodern military and mercantilist elements in police organization, and made it more appropriate to engagement on a terrain where market principles are normal.

To the extent that public police officers find themselves in "normal" employment relations, their distance from their private sector counterparts is reduced. There is already a considerable interchange of personnel between the two sectors (Jones & Newburn, 1998, pp. 89–91). Private security officers usually aspire to membership of public police, senior public police are lured into private security management, and public police moonlight in the private sector on a contract basis (Rigakos, 2002). Educational and related differences between the sectors are beginning to narrow (O'Connor et al., 2004, p. 147; Micucci, 1995). Increasingly, public police pursue contract opportunities and often find themselves in direct competition with private security as well as other public police services. While this is not altogether new, changes in employment relations suggest that the comparisons have become more salient than before. This convergence does not so much suggest that differences between the public and private policing corporations are disappearing, as is sometimes argued, but rather that they are changing.

A common feature of modernist markets is that they break up into sectors according to the kinds of service provided and the labor costs they support. While critical of police unions, the private sector nevertheless recognizes exactly this. They often accept that their own service provision may be subordinate, picking up those tasks discarded or ignored by the expensive public sector, and adopting the role of "handmaiden" (McLeod, 2002). It is not difficult to see this occurring in practice, as public police focus on core tasks (often as a result of the economic coercions mentioned above), discarding such roles as the escorting of prisoners or the operation of red-light cameras. Equally, it is the private corporations that pick up these tasks (Lippert & O'Connor, 2003). Of course, there are many instances in which the unionized sector of the police labor market objects, and may succeed in fighting off such readjustments. The point is not that a slippery slope has been created and that public police must slide down it. Rather, it is that—while local conditions will affect these processes—we are looking at the kinds of segmented market arrangements that are characteristic of a large number of modernist industries, with a semimonopoly, unionized, high cost sector, and a competitive, nonunionized, low-cost sector.

In such markets, trade unions tend to be especially active and aggressive precisely because of the threat posed by the competitive sector. However, it cannot be assumed that, even where relations with management are hostile, police unionism will be frozen in a stance of rigid opposition forever. New generations entering the police service may no longer regard the managerial principles, and the competitive market structures associated with it, as alien or out of place. For better or worse, this environment has been becoming part of everyday life for two decades, reaching into many institutions, long enough for it to become fairly normal rather than new. Universities compete for students on television and on the World Wide Web. Former public utilities have been in private hands for the lifetimes of the new generation of recruits. The themes of enterprise, individual responsibility, and market competition are accepted, even embraced, by political parties on both sides of the spectrum. Only recently, the former chief administrator of the Ontario Provincial Police Association (1995) warned that police associations risk losing touch with their members as the education, gender, race, and values of new cohorts are changing rapidly (Drennan, 2003, p. 7). Police associations, Drennan suggests, face a situation in which traditional labor relations are no longer adequate to deal with a competitive market in policing, and have no choice but to embrace business principles. From this point of view, the time has come "to incorporate into the management of the police association the same values, practices, and culture that characterize the management of police services" (p. 3). This includes, for example, not only the use of marketing strategies to promote the superior quality of public police provision over private security, but more importantly to:

> ... be willing to sit down with management with a view to improving overall relations within the organization by supporting, with safeguards, such new initiatives as civilianization. Closing the door on the private security industry will be much easier if the police leadership sees that the police association is prepared to work with government (Drennan, 2003, pp. 143–144).

Indeed, this is not a startling shift, when considered in the broader context of contemporary trade unionism. Rather, as many have indicated (see the collections of essays edited by Gallie, Penn, & Rose, 1996, and Niland, Lansbury, & Verevis, 1994) there has been a general decline in adversarial relations and an increasing tendency for management and unions to collaborate in the face of changed—and more competitive—economic conditions. Unionization then, while appearing as an obstacle, in fact may be a medium of change.

Continued negotiation between union leaders and management, in turn, may produce unanticipated convergences simply because each side must engage with the terms of the other. Thus, McLaughlin and Murji have already detected that in Britain, where this process has proceeded farthest, "... the Police Federation, the focal point for the 'forces of conservatism' within the police, increasingly uses the language of managerialism to attack reforms, and to press its own case for more resources. Resistance to further managerialization tends to take place within a managerial framework" (McLaughlin & Murji, 2001, pp. 118–119). In this sense, even though unionization may appear antithetical to new managerialism, it may in certain respects be hastening the rate of change still farther away from the old military guild of public police, toward the formation of a public business corporation, and a privileged labor force, in a segmented policing market.

Conclusion

While the importance of police union resistance has certainly been registered in the contemporary policing literature, our argument puts a rather different slant on current policing. Many analysts rightly point to the increasing difficulties of distinguishing between private and public police, and to the emergence of hybrid security agencies (e.g., Johnston, 1992). This complexity has been dealt with by thinking in terms of networks, nodes, or even "extended families" of policing (Jones & Newburn, 1998; Johnston, 2003; Wood, 2004). It is not our intention to deny these complexities. However, focus on these points tends to submerge, or render only of secondary interest, certain key distinctions that are salient in the politics of policing, especially as these are identified by key participants. In particular, while the distinction between profit and nonprofit orientations has long been recognized in this field (e.g., Jones & Newburn, 1998, p. 213), the correspondence of this with the distinction between unionized and nonunionized labor has largely been passed over. Yet, this coupling has become particularly salient in the views of managers and rank and file, and corresponds to critical structural differences in the policing industry. No doubt it is not a sharp divide. It does appear, for example, that a considerable proportion of the in-house private security workforce is unionized (Micucci, 1995). Despite this, in our analysis, this "industrial" distinction appears central to understanding limitations in the transfer of business principles to public police, and represents an important divide within contemporary policing.

In its possible instabilities, as much as in its apparent rigidities, and due to a general lack of research and theorization on the topic, the issue of police unionism should perhaps be moved to the forefront of our analysis of contemporary transformations in policing. In this respect, we follow Shearing and Stenning's suggestion that the public/private distinction not be abandoned in the face of complexities, but rather we should "...explore the ways in which it has been successfully deployed to support political and economic orderings, and to see whether it cannot be fruitfully reframed as an analytically useful concept..." (Shearing and Stenning, 1987, p. 15).

References

Adlam, R. (2002). Governmental rationalities in police leadership: An essay exploring some of the 'deep structure' in police leadership praxis. *Policing and Society, 12*, 15–36.

Bayley, D. (1994). It's accountability, stupid. In K. Bryett & C. Lewis (Eds.), *Unpeeling tradition: Contemporary policing*. Melbourne: Macmillan.

Chan, J. (1997). *Changing police culture. Policing in a multicultural society*. Cambridge: Cambridge University Press.

Chan, J. (2003). *Fair cop: Learning the art of policing*. Toronto: University of Toronto Press.

Clarke, C. (2002). Between a rock and a hard place. RCMP organizational change. *Policing: An International Journal of Police Strategies and Management, 25*, 14–31.

Davids, C., & Hancock, L. (1998). Policing, accountability and citizenship in the market state. *The Australian and New Zealand Journal of Criminology, 31*, 38–68.

Davis, E. (1994). Trade unionism in the future. In J. Niland & R. Lansbury (Eds.), *The future of industrial relations*. London: Sage.

De Lint, W. (1998). New managerialism and Canadian police training reform. *Social and Legal Studies, 7*, 261–285.

De Lint, W. (1999). A postmodern turn in policing: policing as pastiche? *International Journal of the Sociology of Law, 27*, 127–152.

Draper, H. (1978). *Private police*. Harmondsworth, U.K.: Penguin Books.

Drennan, J. (2003). *Police leadership and labour relations*. Toronto: Edmond Montgomery.

Drucker, P. (1993). *Post-capitalist society*. New York: Harper Business.

Etter, B. (1995). Mastering innovation and change in police agencies. In B. Etter & M. Palmer (Eds.), *Police leadership in Australasia*. Sydney: Federation Press.

Etter, B., & Palmer, M. (Eds.) (1995). *Police leadership in Australasia*. Sydney: Federation Press.

Finnane, M. (2002). Police unions in Australia. A history of the present. *Current Issues in Criminal Justice, 12*, 5–19.

Fleming, J., & Lafferty, G. (2000). New management techniques and restructuring for accountability in Australian police organisations. *Policing: An International Journal of Police Strategies and Management, 23*, 154–168.

Forcese, D. (1999). *Policing Canadian society*, 2nd ed. Toronto: Prentice Hall.
Gallie, D., Penn, R., & Rose, M. (Eds.) (1996). *Trade unionism in recession*. Oxford: Oxford University Press.
Hunt, D. (1995). Strategic management in policing. In B. Etter & M. Palmer (Eds.), *Police leadership in Australasia*. Sydney: Federation Press.
Johnston, L. (1992). *The rebirth of private policing*. London: Routledge.
Johnston, L. (2000a). *Policing Britain. Risk, security and governance*. New York: Longman Press.
Johnston, L. (2000b). Transnational private policing. The impact of global security. In J. Sheptycki (Ed.), *Issues in transnational policing*. London: Routledge.
Johnston, L. (2003). From pluralisation to the police extended family. Discourses on the governance of community policing in Britain. *International Journal of the Sociology of Law*, *31*, 185–204.
Jones, T., & Newburn, T. (1998). *Private security and public policing*. Oxford: Oxford University Press.
Kadleck, C. (2003). Police employee organizations. *Policing: An International Journal of Police Strategies and Management*, *26*, 341–351.
Kanter, R. (1990). *When giants learn to dance*. London: Unwin Hyman.
Keat, R. (1991). Introduction: Starship Britain or universal enterprise? In R. Keat & N. Abercrombie (Eds.), *Enterprise culture*. London: Routledge.
Keat, R., & Abercrombie, N. (Eds.) (1991). *Enterprise culture*. London: Routledge.
Landa, D., & Dillon, H. (1995). Police accountability and external review of police conduct. In B. Etter & M. Palmer (Eds.), *Police leadership in Australasia*. Sydney: Federation Press.
Lippert, R., & O'Connor, D. (2003). Security assemblages: Airport security, flexible work and liberal governance. *Alternatives*, *28*, 331–358.
Loader, I. (1999). Consumer culture and the commodification of policing and security. *Sociology*, *33*, 373–392.
Loader, I., & Mulcahy, A. (2003). *Policing and the condition of England*. Oxford: Oxford University Press.
MacDonald, R. (1995). Skills and qualities of police leaders required of police leaders now and in the future. In B. Etter & M. Palmer (Eds.), *Police leadership in Australasia*. Sydney: Federation Press.
McLaughlin, E., & Murji, K. (1997). The future lasts a long time. Public police work and the managerialist paradox. In P. Francis, P. Davis, & V. Jupp (Eds.), *Policing futures. The police, law enforcement and the twenty-first century*. New York: St. Martin's Press.
McLaughlin, E., & Murji, K. (1998). Resistance through representation. Storylines, advertising and police federation campaigns. *Policing and Society*, *8*, 367–399.
McLaughlin, E., & Murji, K. (2001). Lost connections and new directions: Neo-liberalism, new public managerialism and the 'modernization' of the British police. In K. Stenson & R. Sullivan (Eds.), *Crime, risk and justice*. Portland, OR: Willan.
McLeod, R. (2002). *Parapolice. A revolution in the business of law enforcement*. Toronto: Boheme Press.
Micucci, A. (1995). The changing of the guard. The transformation of private security. *Journal of Security Administration*, *18*, 21–45.
Niland, J., Lansbury, R., & Verevis, C. (Eds.) (1994). *The future of industrial relations. Global challenges and changes*. London: Sage.

Normandeau, A., & Leighton, B. (1990). *A vision of the future of policing in Canada.* Ottawa: Solicitor General Canada.

O'Connor, D., Lippert, R., Greenfield, K., & Boyle, P. (2004). After the 'quiet revolution': The self-regulation of Ontario contract agencies. *Policing and Society, 14,* 138–157.

O'Malley, P. (1992). Risk, power and crime prevention. *Economy and Society, 21,* 252–275.

O'Malley, P. (1997). Policing, politics and postmodernity. *Social and Legal Studies, 6,* 363–381.

Ontario Provincial Police. (1995). *Strategic planning committee on police training and education.* Toronto: Ontario Provincial Police.

Osborne, D., & Gaebler, T. (1993). *Reinventing government.* New York: Penguin Books.

Palmer, M. (1995). The likely environment in the year 2000 and beyond. In B. Etter & M. Palmer (Eds.), *Police leadership in Australasia.* Sydney: Federation Press.

Peters, T. (1987). *Thriving on chaos: Handbook for a management revolution.* New York: Knopf.

Power, M. (1994). *The audit explosion.* London: Demos.

Reiner, R. (1992). Policing a postmodern society. *Modern Law Review, 55,* 761–781.

Rigakos, G. (2002). *The new parapolice. Risk markets and commodified social control.* Toronto: University of Toronto.

Rohl, T., & Barnsley, R. (1995). The strategic transformation of policing from occupational to professional status. In B. Etter & M. Palmer (Eds.), *Police leadership in Australasia.* Sydney: Federation Press.

Rose, N. (1996). Governing 'advanced' liberal democracies. In A. Barry, T. Osborne, & N. Rose (Eds.), *Foucault and political reason.* Chicago: University of Chicago Press.

Rose, N. (1999). *Powers of freedom: Reframing political thought.* Cambridge: Cambridge University Press.

Shearing, C., & Stenning, P. (1981). Modern private security: Its growth and implications. In M. Tonry & N. Morris (Eds.), *Crime and justice. An annual review of research.* Chicago: Chicago University Press.

Shearing, C., & Stenning, P. (1983). Private security: Implications for social control. *Social Problems, 30,* 493–506.

Shearing, C., & Stenning, P. (1987). Say 'cheese.' The Disney order that is not so Mickey Mouse. In C. Shearing & P. Stenning (Eds.), *Private policing.* London: Sage.

Sheptycki, J. (1998). Policing, postmodernism and transnationalisation. *British Journal of Criminology, 38,* 485–503.

Stanko, E. (1996). When precaution is normal: A feminist critique of crime prevention. In L. Gelsthorpe & A. Morris (Eds.), *Feminist perspectives in criminology.* Milton Keynes, U.K.: Open University Press.

Turner, L. (1992). *Democracy at work. Changing world markets and the future of labor unions.* London: Cornell University Press.

Vickers, M. (2000). Australian police management education and research: A comment from 'outside the cave.' *Policing: An International Journal of Police Strategies and Management, 23,* 506–525.

William O. Douglas Institute for the Study of Contemporary Social Problems. (1984). *The future of policing. A panel report.* Seattle: William O. Douglas Institute.

Wood, J. (2004). Cultural change in the governance of security. *Policing and Society, 14,* 31–48.

13

Evaluation of Motivating Incentives on Performance of Police Personnel at Tema Community 2

GERALD DAPAAH GYAMFI

Contents

Overview of Ghana Police Service

Historically, little is known about policing in Africa and many people believe that it was European colonial administration that introduced the idea of policing to the continent. However, Ghana's history reveals that prior to the colonial administration there were systems in place in the Ashanti kingdom that had their own police structures. The Ashanti Empire had road wardens, known as *Akwansrafo*, who were responsible for patrolling to enforce the laws guiding the jurisdiction of the kingdom, controlling the movement of travelers, collecting taxes, and defending the kingdom (Tankebe, 2008). These men were mobilized to fight the colonial administration in 1874 during the Sagrenti war. When the colonial administrators realized they were not able to withstand the forces from the Ashanti kingdom, they had to bring additional troops from the West Indies and 700 Hausa men from Nigeria for reinforcement. After the war, in 1894, the colonial administration's fighting force was left with only 400 men who were retained to serve the interest of the colonial masters. These remnants constituted the Gold Coast Constabulary under the Gold Coast Police Ordinance (1897), which was promulgated to empower them to use "brute force" on the people while defending the British administration. These men formed the Gold Coast Police Force. The size of the police force grew gradually from that time on. In 1970, Police Service Act 350(1) was passed that changed Ghana Police Force to Ghana Police Service.

After the independence of Ghana in 1957, the various governments set up commissions to try and improve the conduct of the police service and motivate the personnel. Most of the Commissions' reports were shelved and not acted on. For example, the 1971 Boyle's Commission Report recommended improvement in the salaries of policemen, improvement in police organizational structures, appointments into the service, and the promotion of the men; however, these recommendations were not fully adhered to. The 1992 Constitution of Ghana, 200(3), also sought to empower the police service to perform its traditional role of maintaining law and order. Despite all the recommendations supported by the 1992 Constitution, the police service personnel were among the most poorly motivated workers in Ghana.

For organizations to achieve a high level of performance and sustain employees, management should provide incentives that would bring employee satisfaction (Mullins, 1996). Motivating workers is about getting them to move in the direction one wants them to go in order to achieve a task (Armstrong, 1998). The factors for motivation touch on the physical and psychological needs of all people, such as money, security, shelter, recognition, fair treatment, and respect (Huczynski & Buchanan, 1991). Generally, there is a perception that civil servants seem to be more sensitive to monetary incentives than all other incentives (Mullins, 1996).

A study on police performance conducted in Russia showed that most of the police recruits thought corruption within the police service was justifiable and morally acceptable under certain circumstances, for example, when they were not well remunerated (Adrian & Lee, 2002). In Malaysia, when the police force was marred with corruption and underperformance, then President Datus Seri Najib increased their remuneration, promoted them on a time basis, provided logistics, and offered other incentives to enhance their efforts to fight crime. This brought about enormous improvement in their performance (see: http://thester.com.my/news/story.asp?file=2010).

Ghana police service statutory responsibilities, as enshrined in Article 200 (3) of the 1992 Constitution of Ghana, are to protect life and property and ensure maintenance of law and order throughout the territorial boundaries of Ghana. During the period of this study, the police were under severe criticism by both the local and international media for underperformance. According to Yanney (2005), it was reported that corruption in Ghana was so bad that one might think it had been institutionalized in the public sector and that police and prison officers were ranked as the highest bribe takers. A media report in December 2004 indicated that police officers in Ghana were among those perceived as being "especially corrupt." A Ghana Integrity Initiative (2005), the local representative of Transparency International, conducted a survey on institutions perceived to be highly affected by corruption indicated that 76.8% of respondents considered the Ghana police service as one of the top 10 most corrupt institutions in Ghana. Aning (2009) asserted that the police were corrupt because the government lacked the political will to implement the various reports on police service improvements, such as the Boyles Report (December, 1971), which addressed pay, welfare, appointments, and promotions.

Notwithstanding the perceived underperformance, Ghanaian policemen on peace missions abroad perform marvelously well. Even in Kosovo, some Ghana police personnel whose tour of duty had come to an end were requested to continue for another tour because of their positive performance. (S.C. Cowboy, leader of the U.N. Mission in Kosovo, on June 14, 2006) (retrieved from: www.policeoracle.com/forum/forum-posts.asp?TID=2053). The question that needs to be asked is: Why such impressive performance on missions abroad as opposed to that at home? This could be attributed to the fact that, when on mission abroad, the policemen are better motivated than when at post in Ghana. Various experts and the general public attribute the poor performance and unprofessionalism of the police to lack of motivation (Aning, 2009).

The public outcry on the lack of motivation and poor performance prompted this study that covered a 10-year period (1998–2008). During the period of the study, the Ghana Police Service was under severe criticism by the general public as a result of their poor performance in the country in general, giving rise to questions about the relevance of the "integrity" attached to their motto: Service with Integrity. The study, therefore, strived to find answers to those challenges and to determine whether "motivation packages" offered to police personnel had any significant impact on their performance and to suggest practical means of motivating the police to carry out their obligations with perfection.

Materials and Methods

In December 2009, a team of five members (including the author) was contracted to carry out a research study. The study was a descriptive, covering a wide range of the cross section of the Ghana police personnel at the Tema Community 2 Police Station in the Greater Accra region of Ghana, West Africa. The method and nature of collecting data involved both qualitative and quantitative techniques. The field work was undertaken within a period of 12 weeks.

In designing the instruments, experts from Ghana Police Service were consulted for more information on the structure of the police service at Tema Community 2 Police Station. This helped the team to stratify personnel based on ranks, departments, and gender. The population included all the police personnel in the Ghana Police Service (22,129). The sampling frame was 111 out of which 23 (20.7%) were selected from the following police units at the station:

- Criminal Investigation Unit (CID)
- Administration
- Motor Traffic Unit (MTTU)
- Patrols and Station Duties

The researchers selected respondents who were available at the study area, using a convenience sampling technique because this technique affords researchers the opportunity to sample respondents who may be present at the time of data collection for the study. A cross-sectional time dimension design was used to cover all the personnel at the various functional units to enable the team to select the subjects covering the personnel from various ranks and units.

For this study, a set of structured questionnaires consisting of items on motivation was administered to the police personnel at Tema Community 2. The subjects were to provide answers to the questions without any recourse to the team of researchers. The questions were mostly centered on how the personnel were motivated and whether there were some links between the motivating factors and their performance. Three weeks were used for pretesting of the questionnaire for the team to determine how responsive police personnel would be toward the questions, leaving time to make necessary amendments to the questions if the need arose. The pretesting during the pilot study took place in January 2010. To ensure reliability, the respondents were interviewed by the team on some of the questions already asked in the questionnaire. Nine weeks were devoted to the administration of the questionnaire and interviews of the subjects.

Observation was further used to reinforce the information gathered through the questionnaire, and interviews were conducted to establish an in-depth understanding of motivation and performance of the police at the station. During the observation period, the team looked out for certain factors, such as the kind of work the subjects were undertaking at the post, the difficulties encountered while at the post, briskness with which the personnel moved about their duties, and how quickly they responded to complaints that were lodged by victims.

Considering the sensitive nature of the study, respondents were assured of confidentiality and the team made sure that none of the respondents was victimized for providing information.

Results

All of the 23 subjects responded to the questionnaire from the units, as shown in Table 13.1. Out of the 23 respondents, 17.4% were from the CID unit, 34% were from the Motor Transport and Traffic Unit (MTTU), 21.7% were from Patrol and Station, and 26.1% were officers from the Administration Unit.

Ranking in the Ghana Police Service is done according to qualification, number of years of service, appointment, and promotion by the president of Ghana. The overall boss, the Inspector General of Police (IGP) is appointed by the president as the head of the service. The IGP is followed by commissioners of police, assistant commissioners of police (ACP), regional commanders, district commanders, chief inspectors, inspectors, sergeants, corporals, and constables in a hierarchical order. The respondents were of various ranks ranging from assistant commissioner of police to corporal, as indicated in Table 13.2.

Incentives are material items that are used to motivate personnel within an organization. The study showed that 56.5% of the respondents indicated that they had received some incentives, while 43.5% said they had never received any form of incentives apart from their pay since they joined the police service. Table 13.3 indicates the basis upon which the personnel were given incentives from the perspective of the respondents. There was the indication that incentives were only given based on position (46.2%) and number of years of service (53.8%), but not on overtime or performance.

Table 13.1 Departments (Units) of Respondents

Department	Frequency	Percentage (%)
CID	4	17.4
MTTU	8	34.8
Patrol and Station Duties	5	21.7
Administration	6	26.1
Total	23	100.0

Source: Field data (2010).

Table 13.2 Respondents Positions

Positions	Frequency	Percentage (%)
Commissioner	0	0.0
ACP	2	8.7
Inspector	8	34.8
Sergeant	4	17.4
Corporal	9	39.1
Total	23	100.0

Source: Field data (2010).

Table 13.3 Basis Upon Which Incentives Were Provided

Basis for Incentives	Frequency	Percentage (%)
Overtime	0	0.0
Position	6	46.2
Number of years of service	7	53.8
High performance	0	0.0
Total	13	100.0

Source: Field data (2010).

Table 13.4 Motivating Factors

Factors	Frequency	Percentage (%)
Decent accommodation	6	26.0
Utility bills	4	17.4
Transport allowance for operations	2	8.7
Kilometric allowances	5	21.7
Free uniforms	3	13.0
In-service training	3	13.0
Total	23	100.0

Source: Field data (2010).

Evidence produced by the study revealed that 76.9% indicated that the incentives had significant effect on their performance, while 23.1% concluded that the incentives had no effect on their performance. Normally, it is expected that incentives given to personnel are aimed at motivation and enhanced performance. However, the result received from the study showed that 15.4% of those who were motivated by the incentives were not sure whether the incentives really motivated them. Contrary, a significant number of them (61%) agreed that the incentives highly motivated them in the performance of their duties and functions, while 23.1% indicated that the incentives did not motivate them to any appreciable extent.

The results further revealed that in ranking the motivating factors, provision of decent accommodation (26%) came first, followed by kilometric allowance (21.7%), utility bills (17.4%), free uniforms and in-service training (13%), and transport allowance for operations (8.7%), which is shown in Table 13.4.

On the environmental conditions, none of the respondents was highly satisfied, 60.9% were somewhat satisfied, and 39.1% not satisfied at all. According to those who were not satisfied with the environment, they said their environment was unattractive as compared to the environment of other similar public institutions, such as the Custom, Excise, and Preventive Service (CEPS) and the Immigration Service.

Discussion

According to the 1992 Constitution of Ghana, Article 200 (3), the police service is entrusted with the mandate to protect life and property and ensure maintenance of law and order throughout the territorial boundaries of Ghana. With this mandate, the police men and women are expected to perform their duties with absolute diligence. The personnel are judged by the people of Ghana based on their performance. During the period of the study, the police were always under bashing from the public for misconduct and underperformance. These could be attributed to how personnel was motivated and developed (Mullins, 1996). The study showed that the majority of the police personnel were not happy with the incentives provided to motivate them, especially their accommodation facilities, allowances, and settlement of their utility bills. The remuneration package was not pleasing and, therefore, this could be a major factor that contributed to their misconduct and underperformance. It also could be deduced from the study that, because of the perception by the police that the incentives were not offered them based on their performance, the personnel were not exerting their maximum effort.

When police personnel are not motivated by the incentives offered them, they use their positions to indulge in corrupt practices. They justify corruption as proper behavior, which is consistent with the Russian study discussed earlier (Adrian & Lee, 2002). Based on this study, the dissatisfaction of police personnel with the incentives provided them could account for the corruption and poor performance of the police. It was established by the study that only 56.5% (against 43.5%) had ever received other incentives apart from their regular pay from the service. The implication of this is that where the personnel feel their services are not appreciated by those in command, they will resort to all forms of unprofessional practices, such as bribery. Further evidence of this is the excellent performance of police personnel when they are on UN missions abroad, for example, as in Kosovo in 2006. In Kosovo and elsewhere, police personnel are given incentives that give them the satisfaction and motivation to perform as identified by Stephen Canteen Cowboy, UN mission leader in Kosovo in 2006. According to Aning (2009), monetary incentives are more motivating to civil servants than any other incentive. An interesting aspect that this study revealed was that incentives were not offered the personnel for excellent performance and overtime performance, the incentives were rather given on the basis of number of years in service and the policeman's position. This could also account for the use of corrupt practices to extort money and indulge in other nefarious activities, as raised by both the local and international media.

Conclusions

Incentives have a positive effect in improving the performance of civil servants. However, this study has shown that most of the police personnel were not happy with the incentives offered to motivate them to perform with their maximum effort. It could also be deduced from the study that the allegations of corruption and underperformance of the police personnel could emanate from the fact that the personnel were not offered the necessary incentives, such as proper accommodation facilities and incentives for performance, to motivate them.

Recommendations

Based on the findings and analysis of the study, the following recommendations are essential to improve performance of the Ghana Police Service. There should be improvement in the incentive packages offered by the government of Ghana and the other stakeholders to boost the performance of the personnel. In addition to compensation, other necessary incentives should include the provision of good accommodation facilities, and logistics, such as vehicles and weapons, for them to function well. There should be a total reform of the police service to meet modern policing. The reform could be in the area of ICT (information and communications technology) and finance. These are necessary because the wages and the allowances offered were not adequate enough to compensate police personnel for the kinds of risks they take and services they provide to the nation. These provisions could help them avert the unprofessional practices, such as bribery and corruption, as perceived by the public.

There should be the provision of quality training for the personnel to keep them fit and abreast with modern policing, for instance, through international exchange programs. The unnecessary interferences from top government officials both within the service and outside should be curtailed when the personnel are carrying out their professional duties and functions as enshrined by the Police Service Acts and the 1992 Constitution of the Republic of Ghana.

Even though it is necessary for motivational incentives to be given on the bases of position and long-term service, it is equally important for the service to specially reward exceptional performance.

Acknowledgment

The following team members are acknowledged for their immense contributions toward the completion of this research work: Osei-Adu Juliet, Sakyiama Gladys, Torsu Ruth, and Ntem Louis.

References

Adrian, B., & Lee, R. (2002). Motivation and performance of police personnel. *Crime, Law and Social Change Journal, 38*(4), 357–372.

Aning, E. K. (2009). An overview of Ghana Police Service. *International Article, 4*(2).

Armstrong, M. (1998). *A handbook of personnel management.* London: Koga.

Ghana Integrity Initiative (2005). Institutions perceived to be highly affected by corruption. *The Voice of the People Survey.* Retrieved from www.tighana.org/giipages/publication/voice of the people.pdf.

Huczynski, A. A., & Buchanan, D. A. (1991). *Organisational behaviour.* New York: Prentice-Hall.

Mullins, L. J. (1996). *Management and organisational behaviour.* London: Pitman.

Tankebe, T. (2008). Colonialism, legitimation, and policing in Ghana. *International Journal of Law, Crime and Justice, 36,* 67–84. Retrieved from www.elsevier.com/locate/ijlcj

Yanney, P. (2005). Corruption in Ghana on the increase? *Accra Daily Mail.* June 5, 5.

Further Readings

Bratton, J., & Gold, J. (1999). *Human resource management: Theory and Practice.* London: MacMillan.

Brumbach, G. B. (1988). *Public personnel management.* London: Koga.

Busher, C. H., & Harter, S. P. (1980). *The role of the public library towards the achievement of a total functional adult education in Ghana.* Accra: Sonlife.

Cordner, W. R. (1989). *Introduction to police administration,* 2nd ed. London: Anderson.

Evans, J. R., & Lindsay, W. M. (1999). *The management and techniques of social research.* Mason, OH: South-Western Cengage Learning.

Kumekpor, T. K. B. (2000). *Research methods and techniques of social research.* Accra: Sonlife.

Lau, J. B., & Shani, A. B. (1992). *Behaviour in organisations,* Chicago: Irwin.

Macshane, S .L., & Gilnow, V. (2000). *Organisational behaviour.* London: McGraw Hill.

Mukhwan, W. (1978). Manpower planning for organization development. *Journal of Management Studies, 10*(1).

Vroom, V. H. (1992). *Management and motivation.* London: Penguin.

New Strategic Directions in Police Education

An Australian Case Study

14

DAVID BRADLEY

Contents

The Changing Nature of Police Work

Policing is a practice-based work discipline. It consists of a range of more or less evidence-based practices, along with a body of knowledge and skills, designed to achieve safety and justice outcomes. Police training and education (curricula) are the formal means by which policing practices are reproduced in new generations of officers.

Police work, like work generally, has experienced considerable change over recent years. This change has been generated by complex social, economic, and political changes; changes in science and technology; changes in laws, values, and standards; and changes in knowledge and understanding about the causes of crime and social disorder.

There is a strong evidence base for what we know about good police work in the modern era. First, there has been academically rigorous published research. The pioneering work of Banton (1964), Bittner (1970), and Muir (1977) provided the foundation for research in the modern era by

Fielding (1999) in the United Kingdom, and, most recently, by Chan (2003) in Australia.

Overall, the cumulative findings of this publicly available body of knowledge present a form of work under continuous change and growth in terms of its complexity and standards. Good policing, where it exists, is found to be intellectually demanding, increasingly taking the form of "knowledge" work, and requiring mastery of a range of multidisciplinary skills. High standards of general duties policing require substantial learning across a range of domains of practice, high level interpersonal and communications skills, and a demanding capacity to handle ambiguity and uncertainty, and take control across critical, complex, and sometimes dangerous situations.

This understanding of the nature of police work has been reinforced time and again by applied and vocationally centered research projects conducted on behalf of police services themselves, usually to help inform the design of police curricula. For example, in the United Kingdom during the 1980s, the work of the Centre of Applied Research in Education, (CARE) underpinned radical changes to both the British and New South Wales police initial training curriculum (New South Wales Police Board, 1986). In the 1990s in England and Wales, National Police Training (Her Majesty's Stationary Office (HMSO), 1995) commissioned a competency-based research report into the core general duties competencies, and a similar report was published in Canada (Ontario National Police Training, 1994). In Australia, three major competency-based studies have been completed: one in South Australia (South Australian Police Department, 1993), one in New South Wales (New South Wales Police Board 1995), and another by the then National Police Research Unit (see Bradley, 1996). The recently closed Australasian Centre for Policing Research also produced a substantial research-based job analysis of the work of general duty police officers (Kaczmarek and Packer, 1996).

Critique of Police Training

Police work, especially in contexts where it has been poorly, even illegally, conducted, also has come under scrutiny in other ways. In recent years. a number of commissions of inquiry into policing have been conducted in Australia: Neesham (1985) in Victoria, Fitzgerald (1989) in Queensland, and both Lusher (1981) and Wood (1997) in New South Wales. Collectively, although it was not the direct subject of their terms of reference (nor, arguably, of their expertise and capability, but such limits rarely restrict the curiosity and self-confidence of judges), these judicial investigations into police work nevertheless produced a critique of police training. Either indirectly or directly, police training was found to be systemically deficient everywhere.

All the Australian inquiries concluded that training was closed off from external knowledge bases and wider cultural values. They found police academy teachers struggling because they were poorly prepared to teach high-level complex skills, insulated as they were from basic teacher training, let alone the kind that is nurtured from knowledge of advances in adult learning and cognate subject-related research and development.

Generally, these investigations found that the builders and deliverers of the police core curriculum relied too much on rote learning and used assessment methods that did not bring about deep learning. They found skills taught in decontextualized ways, with recruits taught process and law, but not educated into the aims and outcomes of good policing. The academy experience also was found to encourage the subordination of new members into their lowly organizational status and as a result to be vulnerable to negative influences in the field.

Police academies did not endeavor to produce constables who could develop as autonomous, self-disciplined decision makers operating comfortably with high levels of discretion. Recruits were not adequately prepared to cope with the ambiguities and conflicts inherent in a great deal of police work, nor were they encouraged to develop as reflective learners. Most "real learning" was found to occur, not at the academy, but on the job and in the field, in informal and ad hoc ways. Training was generally not subject to rigorous and continuous evaluation. Academy budgets and resources were almost always insufficient or under threat.

From Lusher (1981) to Wood (1997), these judicial investigations into policing have placed significant weight on the connection between good policing and good police training. And, without exception, they called for changes in police training that would bring about a systemic connection between police training and the wider education system.

Neesham (1985) called for the import of nonsworn teaching skills into the academy and a civilian Dean of Studies. Lusher recommended formation of a Police Education Advisory Council containing strong higher education representation, an academy Board of Studies, a strong nonsworn as well as sworn faculty, and an eventual partnership between academy and a higher education body with recruit training based on a 2-year diploma in policing. Fitzgerald (1989) advocated a partnership between the academy and the universities where police recruits would "rub shoulders" with other university students. Despite the fact that in the 1980s and 1990s the New South Wales Police Service had developed strong university partnerships at senior constable, supervisory, and executive development levels, Justice Wood was heavily critical of what he found to be an insulated and control-focused recruit training program. He recommended that foundational police education become university-based and prerecruitment, with the Police Academy restricted to the provision of postrecruitment skills training (a law discipline model).

Responses to the Critique

Until the creation of a national police education body, responses by Australian governments and police forces to the judicial critique of police training were patchy and discontinuous, this despite the emergence during the early 1990s of an Australasian policing strategic commitment to what was called a "full professionalization of policing" (Australian Centre for Policing Research, 1997).

In Victoria, there was a partial and one-off implementation of Neesham's training recommendations, and no arrangements were developed to ensure the ongoing systemic continuous improvement of police education. Eventually, Victoria Police chose to become itself a Registered Training Organization accredited by the state vocational education body to award its own diplomas. In effect, this move served to inform the universities that Victoria Police would not be seeking partnerships with them.

In Queensland, the Criminal Justice Commission, through its Police Education Advisory Council, imposed a badly designed and flawed university/academy model of recruit training. A subsequent evaluation served to devalue the idea of a link to the universities, and the partnerships were abandoned, to be substituted by a reformed internal training system based on the New South Wales Police Recruit Education Program (PREP) (New South Wales Police Board, 1987). In Queensland, then, a move toward systemic university linkage is recommended, tried, found expensive and wanting, and not sustained.

Perhaps the most sustained long-term period of substantial police educational reform occurred during the 1980s and 1990s in New South Wales. There, a powerful and independent Police Board and its Police Education Advisory Council, initially linked recruit training to the higher education system through negotiating recognition of prior learning with those New South Wales colleges of advanced education delivering police-related studies. This linkage was strengthened by a well-funded scholarship scheme that enabled police to undertake cost-free university education in approved police-related courses.

Eventually, in New South Wales, formal partnerships between university providers and the academy were developed at the senior constable, supervisor, and executive development levels. Ironically, the latter two did not survive the Wood Royal Commission. However, the former, called the Constable Development Program, (CDP), did survive. Started in 1991, it paved the way for future radical and systemic educational reform in New South Wales.

The Constable Development Program resulted from a tendering process advertised throughout the Australian university system. The tender called for a replacement of the internal exam that was the educational prerequisite of promotion to senior constable by a 2-year-long university diploma in policing. The diploma was to be delivered through distance education through a partnership between academy and university teaching staff. Once in place, it became the only pathway to senior constable rank and above.

Charles Sturt University won the tender. The diploma started in 1991. It was taught by a team of police and university teachers who staffed a Center for Professional Development at the Police Academy. The diploma was available to all police officers. It was cost-free and supported by some limited study leave. Between 1991 and 1997 over 6,000 constables successfully completed the program. A version of the diploma also was provided for any senior constables and sergeants who wished to undertake it.

The Wood Royal Commission had recommended that New South Wales Police foundational education should take the form of a "preservice university qualification." This recommendation proved impracticable for a number of reasons. First, there was no policy mechanism through which either the federal government or any particular university could be required and funded to provide a professional policing course specific to the needs of the New South Wales Police Service. Second, even though two universities had already developed and were teaching a bachelor's of policing, no formal and robust policy mechanism existed through which the Police Service could ensure its needs were properly met by the curriculum and that only professionally suitable students were enrolled in the courses. Third, the university-based allocation of funding to the degrees was insufficient to guarantee provision of the numbers of police recruits required (some 500 per annum in the mid-1990s). Lastly, even if these problems could have been overcome, introduction of the scheme could have resulted in a 3-year-long lag in police recruitment, which, of course, would have been politically unacceptable. Some intermediary pathway was required, or even a different model better designed to meet the requirements of the police.

Rejecting the Wood recommendation, the NSW Police Service built upon its experience of partnerships with universities and invited tenders from the university system for an academy–university partnered diploma (associate's degree) in policing practice to replace its Police Recruit Education Program. Charles Sturt University won the tender partly because it was willing to invest a substantial level of its Educational Full-Time Study Equivalent Units (referred to as EFTSUs and representing the standard unit cost for universities that includes salary costs, support costs, and capital) budget into the diploma.

The diploma in policing practice commenced in 1997. It continues today. It is a flexibly delivered 18-subject-unit-strong university diploma. It is co-taught by the university and academy staff. Charles Sturt University created a School of Policing Studies, staffed by 24 academics and headed by an associate professor, at the Police College. Police College teachers of the diploma have to be accredited by the university. Teaching is shared equally between university and Police College, and co-operation between the two is required across all subject units.

The partnership with Charles Sturt does not prevent the New South Wales Police Service from doing business with other tertiary providers. Its nonexclusive nature allows graduates of policing from other universities to finish their preattestation training at the Police College alongside Charles Sturt University students.

The diploma in policing practice is structured and taught in a variety of ways. To enroll, applicants must satisfy the university that they possess the skills and experience to complete the course. Applicants also must satisfy the professional suitability criteria required from the New South Wales Police Service.

Enrolled students do not become employees of the service until half way through the diploma. Applicants are informed that enrollment and progress onto the course is not a guarantee of employment in the NSW Police Service.

Applicants who lack sufficient study skills, but who are otherwise acceptable, have the choice of enrolling onto the university's specially designed enabling course. Others deemed too young or immature for policing are encouraged to enroll in one of the full-time study policing degrees available in New South Wales.

Three versions of the diploma are available:

Version 1: This is the full mainstream diploma. It starts with an initial 14-week–long, full-time study "trimester," (the academic year is organized around three of these) at the Police College. Then, following a short break, students complete two field placements of 6 weeks each, one at a police station, and the other in a community organization. During this time, students are required to complete a further two subjects taught through distance education. Then, they return to the Police College for a further 14-week-long trimester of full-time study. On successful completion of all their first year subjects, and on condition that they have maintained their professional suitability, they are offered employment as probationary constables. After a short break, they return to the Police College for a week of preparation, and then start their 1-year-long period of probationary on-the-job training. During that year, they continue as students of the university, completing three more trimesters of distance education including a robust practicum of job performance assessment. At the end of the year, they qualify for the award of a diploma of policing practice.

Version 2: A second version of the diploma fast-tracks some already tertiary qualified students by giving them recognition of prior learning for a tertiary degree in policing or in a related/cognate discipline. These students attend a weekend orientation workshop followed by 6 weeks field experience at a police station. They then complete the preattestation trimester (during which they have to complete an additional subject unit covering areas of the first trimester curriculum that they need to understand) and then progress into the field-based second year.

Version 3: This third form of the diploma is designed for potential police recruits already in employment and with significant financial responsibilities. It makes it considerably easier for them to change to a police career. It allows enrolled students to complete Trimester One and Two subject units by distance education and to complete their police station field experience over weekends. Students then continue their studies at the Police College for the preattestation trimester.

A fourth pathway into policing in New South Wales is provided for the full-time study students of both Charles Sturt University's and the University of Western Sydney's bachelor of policing degrees wishing to become police officers. If they satisfy professional suitability criteria they are able to attend the Police College-based preattestation trimester and complete probationary training without further distance education. They still need to satisfy the on-the-job practicum requirements.

The Memorandum of Understanding between the Police Service and Charles Sturt University prescribes the way the diploma is organized and delivered. The various forms of the diploma and their overall governance are generically subsumed under the title "Constable Education Program" (CEP). The diploma is subject to the usual university regulations. However, its course committee and assessment committee membership is equally shared between senior police/police educators and the university's academy-located School of Policing Studies, with the faculty of Arts Dean of Studies presiding. All teachers in the School of Policing (some 24) are selected and appointed by joint university/Police Service panels. A board of management supervises the nonacademic administration of the CEP. The board has equal representation from university and Police Service (the vice chancellor and commissioner are ex officio members, but do not usually attend meetings). An independent, jointly appointed person chairs the board.

In contrast to the earlier, wholly Police Service-funded PREP, the CEP is funded from multiple sources. This makes it significantly more cost effective from a police agency perspective. First, because the diploma is a mainstream university course, it is part-funded through the university's budget (most of which comes from the Commonwealth government). Second, in their first year and/or during their full-time studies, students are not employed by the Police Service. They must meet police-set professional suitability criteria, but are not guaranteed police employment. This significantly reduces police costs. However, a Police Service-funded and university-administered scholarship scheme provides a means-tested scholarship for all of the students.

The 500 students who board at the academy are charged at cost for bed and board (students have the choice of making their own living arrangements).

Until changes made to university funding by the Federal Department of Education and Training in December 2004, all students accrued HECS (higher education contribution scheme) liability for the diploma subjects. HECS funding is no longer available for police vocational undergraduate study (this can change, but only if more than one police employer requires university-based police education to at least undergraduate degree level). In New South Wales, there is an agreement to reserve sufficient university places for NSW police force recruitment requirements (the employers' reserved places scheme). And, the current agreement between the university and police is that students only have to pay a fee equivalent to HECS (at a nondiscounted level). Also, because students are employed as probationary constables during the second year of the diploma, they can claim tax rebates on the fees they have to pay.

The Police Service provides 50% of the training staff as well as police training customized premises for use by the university faculty and support staff, including the Police College library. The library benefits from a funding stream through the normal EFTSU formula. The university pays the Police Service the salary equivalents for the weighted subject units taught by Police College university-accredited teachers and trainers. Field teaching officers, too, are trained by the university and accredited for their coaching roles. The university also pays the costs of the community organization placements, and for the teaching materials taught by its staff. These arrangements significantly reduce university costs. Indeed, despite the recent changes that eliminated HECS funding for police vocational university education, the robust partnership and sharing between university and Police Service allowed a feasible fee-based funding arrangement to sustain the diploma at levels that make it accessible to all students.

The CEP successfully met the need for high recruitment numbers over the period 1997 to 2002 and beyond, eventually delivering an annual figure of no less than 1,500 successful attestations. When student numbers exceeded the numbers covered by the original agreement, a top-up per capita fee was paid by the Police Service.

Currently, police diploma holders who "cash in" their diploma by electing to complete a bachelor of policing degree are fully reimbursed their HECS payments, at the up-front level, by the New South Wales Police Service Tertiary Scholarship System. Arrangements are currently being made for the educational prerequisite for promotion to senior constable to be changed to a bachelor of policing, so eventually having all sworn officers professionally qualified at the full degree level.

Other Australian states have not chosen the university-based recruit education path. In contrast to New South Wales, they have taken a minimalist higher educational pathway, one suggested, but not required, by the Vocational Education Accrediting Board (VETAB) competency model developed by the Australasian Police Educational Standards Council (APESC). The (below undergraduate capability standards) core competency profile for operational policing is set at the diploma level.

Some police academies, including Victoria's, as part of the larger police agency, have become VETAB-accredited Registered Training Organizations (RTOs). This licenses them to teach and award VETAB-accredited courses. Nearly 1,000 Victoria Police members have qualified for the award of the Diploma in Public Safety (Policing). Quite recently, Victoria Police incorporated a university diploma into its 2-year-long probationary training period. This was delivered by Deakin University's Department of Police Studies. The diploma ran for only a brief period before it was ended on cost grounds.

The Victoria Police Academy's current recruit curriculum standards, assessment methods, teaching, and facility standards are required to meet VETAB-set standards and these are subject to some monitoring and inspection by the appropriate VETAB-1 body. The curriculum is organized through 10 levels of assessed training. The first 7 of these are met through the 20-weeks-long, academy-based, preattestation residential training.

During their 2 years of probationary on-the-job training, students complete levels 8, 9, and 10 of the diploma, each of which is supported by a 1-week-long residential workshop. Students' competency requirements are assessed through supervisory reports and the contents of an "evidence-based portfolio." Successful graduation with the diploma is a prerequisite for progressing beyond probationary status. Some 1,000 officers have so far met the requirements for award of the diploma.

Differences Between the University and RTO Models: Numbers, Costs, and Quality

A number of risk-associated features of these two types of programs deserve comparative attention.

Managing Recruitment Targets

In principle, any model for police recruit training must be capable of meeting the establishment strength requirements of policing set by the government or police authority within police jurisdictions.

These requirements can vary over the short term. In the longer term, police recruitment targets in Australia have grown progressively, matching population growth. It is reasonable to expect a similar pattern over the medium-to-long term future.

Generally, it might be expected that the RTO model would provide police forces with a better capability to cope with radical variations in recruitment numbers over the short term. A sudden cessation in the need for recruitment (as happened for a 6-months-long period in New South Wales over the 1987–2002 period) saw the police teaching staff there complete a much-needed period of curriculum redevelopment. The university model would be more difficult to manage in such circumstances. Arguably, though, the university model might provide pressure upon governments to provide more stability in the long term police recruitment planning process.

What has been the New South Wales experience? There, the university model has been given a severe testing in terms of its ability to cope with very large numbers. The results demonstrate a robustness that would certainly have severely tested the academy-exclusive model. Prior to the Charles Sturt University partnership, recruitment onto PREP began to show evidence of crisis. A large pool of qualified applicants began to dry up, and it became increasingly difficult to maintain recruit-entry educational standards. These difficulties carried through to severely test assessment standards. In contrast, meeting a tripling of recruitment numbers to over 1,500 per annum, the university model has met these, raised entry academic standards, and met the higher university-required nonnegotiable degree level standards of learning and assessment. By 2005, some 3,000 people who satisfy university and police entry requirements were queuing to get onto the diploma in policing practice.

All this provides some evidence that, unless police forces move toward the university model, they will be driven backward toward early school-leaver cadetship schemes in order to recruit required numbers. This is because the traditional blue-collar workforce from which police recruited has shrunk dramatically in the globalized, postindustrial developed world. One large Scottish police force, faced with an inability to compete with the knowledge and service industries for well-educated employees has had to reinvent its long-since abandoned cadetship scheme to mop up early school-leavers (low in education, low in maturity and life experience, and low in occupational aspiration).

In contrast, in New South Wales, currently, a pool of 3,000 qualified and professionally suitable applicants wait entry into the university diploma in policing. This success in meeting big number targets was achieved despite a rise in attrition rates during training. Under the closed academy training model, attrition rates ran from between 3 and 4%. With the university model, these rates ran between 10 and 12%. This difference stems from a number of causes. Under the conventional police training model, with recruits employed from the start of their training, a great deal of pressure was placed on getting as many as possible through the program. Failure (on academic as against behavioral grounds) was unacceptable.

The university model allows closer scrutiny of students over an extended period of time before their employment, and it is much easier to detach students from their studies than it was to dismiss employed trainees operating under industrial awards monitored by police unions. Dismissing under-achieving recruits proved almost impossible because the Industrial Commission operated on the basis that once someone was employed the Police Service became responsible for their competency. And, a highly drilled, rote-learning, multiple choice assessment system was able to "crunch the numbers" more efficiently than a university-run course.

The university model also has enabled the New South Wales Police to better meet its diversity recruitment standards. It has comfortably met the 50% target for female recruits, and could probably exceed it if that was required. The enabling entry programs, which will soon include one for aboriginal persons, are particularly supportive of recruitment from culturally and language diverse (CALD) groups. Arguably, one of the more important barriers to CALD group police recruitment is that their families encourage their offspring to aspire to professional, university-based careers. This, perhaps, suggests why the university police education model has proved more popular with these groups than the conventional police training system it replaced.

Costs

In principle, and as a counter to an otherwise dependency-encouraging work culture, it is desirable for would-be police students to meet some of the costs of their vocational education, but the overall cost and funding arrangements should not prevent any suitable persons from entry.

Cost, per se, was not a factor in the strategic decision to choose the university pathway in New South Wales. However, the university model has emerged as a much less costly option than the model it superseded, and, these days, value for money is becoming a more compelling requirement in the public sector (one estimate puts the cost savings in New South Wales since the university course started at well over $40 million).

Because the federal government funds the state-based universities, the Australian university model spreads costs across both federal and state governments, and it requires a contribution from those wishing to join the police profession. This multiple sourcing strengthens police training in a number of ways. It takes some pressure off the police-provided budget. It significantly reduces the cost of police teacher salaries. And, especially for metropolitan-based police academies, it can take pressure off academy usage by enabling the relocation of at least part of student training to a university campus, with the additional (cultural) benefit of having them mix with other university students.

In terms of value for money, the university model also allows better management of student time. When training is wholly equated with paid employment based on industrial awards, there are significant constraints on the amount of study that can be required of employee-students. In New South Wales, PREP allowed for no more than 35 hours of rostered learning per week. Under the CEP, students are required to invest a significant amount of their own time in studying. Also, the university model allows for far more flexible ordering of study times and sessions. Finally, when people are required to invest considerable personal resources to gain entry into an occupation, it is generally the case that perceptions of the status and social worth of that occupation rise.

Quality Assurance

In principle, any model should guarantee that the quality and content of the vocational education meet the Police Service's requirements on a continuing developmental basis.

Because of the nature of their educational requirements, both RTO and university models are superior to the nonhigher educational courses they replaced. Both set minimum tertiary educational standards that must be independently monitored and met in terms of curriculum, assessment, teaching standards, and work-based learning.

However, the university model is at a higher Australian Qualifications Framework quality level than the RTO model. The diploma in policing practice is the equivalent of an associate's degree. This means that students must demonstrate graduate generic and technical capabilities in order to progress to graduation.

Also, the university model has the advantage of being able to draw upon the considerable support structures and processes that a university institution, unlike the typical police academy or college, offers: library, educational information technology, teaching and learning support, counseling, sports and other club-based activity, student unions, enabling programs, student counseling, and so on. The RTO model cannot provide such benefits, which are only available through partnerships between police and educational organizations.

In cultural and disciplinary terms, a close working relationship with an actual higher education institution also opens up police education to a diverse and challenging environment. It enables the applied discipline of general practice policing to be exposed to, and benefit from, other cognate and scientifically and technologically relevant applied disciplines. Law, computer science, forensic science, communications skills, psychology, urban, civic and neighborhood studies are all becoming increasingly important to policing.

The university partnership model makes it easier and more likely that the policing body of knowledge is not just kept up to date, but developed to "leading edge" standards. Evidence-based policy and practice is better sustained and disseminated within the university model than under the "organizational do it yourself" RTO. Also, the university model allows police students to mix, socially, intellectually, and culturally, with other novitiate professionals, with all that that might entail in terms of their professional growth and networking.

Perhaps most importantly of all, in the long-term police strategic time frame, the university model ensures something that no other model can do: The continuous intellectual nourishment of foundational police education. This is because a mainstream-delivered university course requires police faculty members not only to reproduce best practice knowledge and skills through teaching and learning, but also to undertake peer-reviewed research in their disciplinary field (i.e., in the applied discipline of general policing).

Policing will only develop a comprehensive, robust, and evidence-based set of practices, knowledge, and skills when a significant number of sworn practitioner/researchers with higher order, research-based qualifications engage in sustained, long-term research with the aim of extending and improving their discipline's body of knowledge and skills. Until now, Australian policing has not benefited from such research. Rather, it has had to rely upon research work carried out by nonpolice academics, usually in non-Australian settings, or, locally, taking what it can from ad hoc, more or less relevant, discontinuous research partnerships. As Reiner (1998) has pointed out, academic research on policing has generally focused upon what have been seen as the twin deficits of integrity and accountability. The knowledge deficit in policing has largely been ignored except as something that criminology could fix if police were more amenable to its direction.

And, of course, the university model of foundational police education will act like the tide that raises all the ships. If general practice police training is organized at associate and undergraduate degree levels, then higher level training (e.g., investigation, intelligence, negotiation skills, and specialist operational safety and practice) invites positioning at the postgraduate certificate, diploma, master's, and doctoral levels. It is no accident that Charles Sturt University has created a graduate school of policing, (not police management), funded by a 200 full-time EFTSU budget, and dedicated to the development and delivery of advanced police education and training (what was unintended was that, with such a significant amount of the police curriculum devoted to applied ethics, Charles Sturt University ended up with one of the largest departments of philosophy in Australia).

The final advantage of the university model may seem to some as "cosmetic" or credentialist in nature: the higher standing in the community that university education provides occupations. But, how others regard them affects how the members of an occupation see themselves. In this respect, it is salutary to look at the experience of the most recent occupation to relocate its training to the university—nursing. Ten years after nurse education entered the university system, not only did applied research into better nursing practices increase significantly (representing an increase in evidence-based practices), but nursing experienced a large rise in occupational self-esteem.

For any occupation credibly to call itself a profession, or claim to be on the road to becoming one, nothing less than the university route will do. Arguably, only the university model sends an unmistakable message to the community, to the media, to prospective police officers, and to government about the need for an autonomous and strong professional police occupation that effectively discharges its mandate while embracing the highest standards of competence and integrity.

Modern policing has to work closely with communities, private and public agencies as well as with the rest of the criminal justice world. All of these enjoy strong educational institutional linkages. Police officers, across the board, are required to work more closely, both within and outside their own organization, with other professional networks. Police life in the 21st century seems certain to become more complex, unpredictable, and fast-changing. Relocation of police education to the university system will help an occupation of immense social importance better discharge its mandate.

Conclusion

Arguably, the public police are vulnerable to failing to meet the rising standards encouraged by social change. The public police now constitute but one node in a wider network of security and policing agencies and partnerships, many of whose members are professionally educated. If policing, an emergent profession, is to meet the challenge, then the VETAB relationship is best seen as a transitional stepping stone moving us toward the university-located full professional model. There are major strategic, organizational, and operational reasons for the relocation of foundational police education to the university sector. We know it is possible to achieve it without threat to a number of important principles. All that is required is the political will and police leadership vision. Well, perhaps these constitute a rather daunting challenge in most, if not all, police jurisdictions?

References

Australian Centre for Policing Research. (1997). *Strategic directions in Australasian policing.* Adelaide: Australian Centre for Policing Research.

Banton, M. (1964). *The policeman in the community.* London: Tavistock.

Bittner, E. (1970). *The function of police in modern society.* Washington, D.C.: U.S. Government Printing Office.

Bradley, D. (1996). Contemporary police education. In P. Wilson & D. Chappell (Eds.), *Australian Policing: Contemporary issues*, 2nd ed. London: Butterworths.

Chan, J. (2003). *Fair cop: Learning the art of policing Toronto*. Buffalo, London: University of Toronto Press.

Fielding, N. (1999). *Joining forces: Police training, socialisation and occupational competence*. London, New York: Routledge.

Fitzgerald, G. E. (1989). *Report of a commission of inquiry pursuant to orders in council*. Brisbane: Government Printer.

Her Majesty's Stationary Office. (1995). *Draft competency report on the work of uniformed officers*. London: HMSO.

Kaczmarek, A., & Packer, J. (1996). *Defining the role of the general duties constable: A job analysis*. Adelaide: National Centre for Police Research.

Lusher, E. A. (1981). *Report of the commission to enquire into the New South Wales Police Administration*. Sydney: NSW Government Printer.

Muir, K. W., Jr. (1977). *Police: Street corner politicians*. Chicago: Chicago University Press.

Neesham, T. (1985). *Final report of the committee of inquiry*. Melbourne: Victoria Police Force.

New South Wales Police Board. (1986). *The interim police education and training advisory council*, 2nd Report (incorporating the first). Sydney: New South Wales Police Board.

New South Wales Police Board. (1987). *The police recruit education program course documentation*. Sydney: Police Board.

New South Wales Police Board. (1995). *The domains of police practice*. Sydney: New South Wales Police Board.

Ontario National Police Training. (1994). Report.

Reiner, R. (1998). Process or product? Problems of assessing individual performance. In J-P. Brodeur (Ed.), *How to recognize good policing*. Washington, D.C.: Police Executive Research Foundation/Sage Publication.

South Australian Police Department. (1993). *Aboriginal-related study of general duties community constables*. Adelaide: University of South Australia.

Oversight Mechanism for Law Enforcement
The Experience of Bangladesh

15

TAPTUN NASREEN

Contents

Introduction

This chapter is a result of a study that identifies features of an effective oversight framework for law enforcement agencies applying Transparency International's (TI) graphical metaphor the "Greek temple" model to explain an oversight mechanism (Transparency International, 2001) in the national integrity system. The study explains the emergence of oversight agencies for law enforcement accountability and examines a suitable and effective oversight framework. It develops a theoretical framework to analyze the mode, where cooperation from all stakeholders is required for the effectiveness of the agency. Drawing from documentary and secondary data analysis, the study analyzes the major strengths and weaknesses of the proposed model and identifies the key challenges by critically examining functions, structure, strategies, and performance that ensure that members of law enforcement agencies are made more accountable for their actions. Finally, the study explores the oversight mechanism for police accountability in Bangladesh.

Since ancient times, the question of who will guard the guardians has been debated. Different schools argued on different methods of police accountability. But, the procedure for handling complaints against police emerged as the principal means of ensuring police accountability. Establishment of oversight agency has been designed to check police corruption and misconduct. The history of civilian oversight identifies the linkage of police, political parties, and the government power that created the environment for police corruption and misconduct. To eradicate the problem, developing countries are now moving to the democratic culture emphasizing public demand and trust in policing. But, the countries with a democratic culture and far away from such kind of checks and balances systems have demanded to control the coercive power of police. Countries with a colonial inheritance are now under popular pressure to establish oversight mechanisms for policing.

The police in Bangladesh are struggling to improve professionalism, transparency, and responsiveness. The police also felt that they themselves are overworked, overloaded, and unappreciated. Also, there are constraints of logistics, technologies, and transportation support. Moreover, salaries for the police are low and sometimes they adopt corrupt practices in order to meet expenses. Poor organizational roles and excessive paperwork or red tape is a factor that hinders police in doing a job well. However, the reform program is continuing to improve performance and morale, which is improving the image of the police. Establishment of new units and considering new policies for strategic development are now the new paradigm of policing in Bangladesh. Police leaders also have voiced their concern about the complaint-handling process against police.

It is argued that a powerful statute with adequate resources is essential for an effective and independent oversight body. The strong operational mandate needs to provide an accountability mechanism so that complainants get fair treatment in a complaint-handling process involving members of law enforcement agencies. To do so, an oversight agency must be accountable under Parliamentary oversight for the independence and for the checks and balances in the system. The study suggests developing a reactive–proactive preventative approach that ensures an effective law enforcement oversight agency.

National Integrity System: The Greek Temple Model

An integrity system is judged to be an essential concern for a democratic society (Walker, 2001; Bayley, 1985). In this system, a set of institutions and their processes ensure that public power is used for public purposes. This concept has been developed by TI, which has identified some strategies and elements for building a robust framework of a national integrity system. TI defines this by using the "Greek temple" graphical metaphor where all the pillars are the parts of the integrity system.

The Greek Temple metaphor provides a coordinated framework within government agencies dealing with the integrity system (Pope, 2008). Here, the temple is considered an integrity system supported by a series of pillars, each being an individual element with different strengths. There are three round balls—peace and security, rule of law, and sustainable development—resting on the flat roof. If one pillar weakens, an increased load is thrown onto one or more of the others. If several pillars weaken, their load will ultimately slope, so that the round balls roll off. The temple also needs sustained foundations that include people's awareness and values. According to Pope (2008), a concrete "national integrity system" requires proper identification of gaps and weaknesses in the governance system. It is consistent with an interrelationship program among these pillars to keep the building standing in an integrity system.

This mutually strengthening integrity system ensures a structure where people work for the public interest. The Organization for Economic Cooperation and Development (OECD, 1996) defines this integrity system as an "ethics infrastructure" that is a set of rules, institutions, and practices. This process is set to guide, manage, and enforce good conduct in the public sector. This can be a combination of laws, institutions, and management mechanisms that help prevent corruption and promote integrity in the public service. A supportive environment is fundamental to obtaining transparency and accountability in this combination. In order to prevent corruption and promote good governance, organizations need to identify good practices and work out standards for developing a sound framework.

In a democratic society, accountability works to minimize each agency or function from malpractice through the classic theory of "checks and balances" (Schedler, 1999; Terrill, 1990). This mutual relationship of accountability assists minimizing corruption in the broad area of institutions and keeps them accountable to each other (Mulgan, 2003). The main aspect of accountability is the focus on expected standards in exercising public power. Cooperation and interdependence of institutions within a supportive environment can ensure an effective integrity framework.

Accountability for a Law Enforcement Body

Accountability is a symbol of good governance both in the public and private sector. Generally, the concept of accountability denotes that a person who exercises power and authority must abide by laws and be accountable for the exercise of power. This emphasizes more the behavior of actors so that actors are accountable for their actions. Accountability, responsibility, and answerability are distinct concepts, though they are often related. Accountability is a situation where a person is required or expected to justify work. But, it also refers to a case when a person is responsible for some activity. Brown (2008) defines accountability as the obligation to answer for a responsibility conferred by laws and procedures. Moreover, accountability may require giving an answer to justify "actor work to the recipient" (Uhr, 1993) or "implementing new policies" (Petterson, 1991).

However, the accountability process "expresses the continuing concern for checks and oversight, for surveillance and institutional constraint on the exercise of power" (Schedler, 1999, p. 13). Thus, it is not a way of removing or weakening power, rather it acts to ensure that power is exercised in a transparent way according to the rules. In this process, those exercising public power must be answerable, responsive, and transparent. Transparency and accountability are related for sound public administration. So, accountability is supposed to be part of the professional behavior of law enforcement officials (Goldsmith & Lewis, 2000; Lewis & Prenzler, 1999). In this way, integrity is driven by the accountability that bridges the gap between citizens and government and helps to ensure public confidence in government.

Questions arise about the use of coercive power by law enforcement officials, as it is a function risking corruption for power or money or both (Costigan, 2004). Sometimes peer group influence or strong loyalty among officers may involve them in corruption (Prenzler, 2000). The Fitzgerald Report (Fitzgerald, 1989) in Queensland, Australia, revealed that law enforcement maintained connection between entrenched police corruption and inadequate institutional protections against public sector misconduct.

A significant issue raised by the community is that law enforcement agencies need to be aware that it is a coercive force that they use against civilians (Stone, 2007). Over the past few decades, the focus on accountability of individuals (Shacklock, 2007) has shifted to an occupational or organizational one (Ekenvall, 2003) that involves performance and provides service to the public. It emphasizes that personal integrity and, at the same time, organizational integrity are needed in an accountability framework.

Accountability Mechanism: Emergence of Oversight Agencies

Recent literature on the integrity of law enforcement agencies has been concerned with misconduct, complaints processes, and improvement of integrity (Lewis & Prenzler, 1999; Goldsmith & Lewis, 2000; Prenzler & Ransley, 2002). To achieve lawfulness and legitimacy, Bayley (2002) suggested controlling police power and making them subject to accountability mechanisms. Initially the police opposed the establishment of external independent oversight mechanisms (Miller, 2002). However, the demand from citizens and routine misconduct by police officers made the police establish an internal oversight body (Prenzler, 2000). This oversight body is a monitoring system that is designed to ensure that law enforcement agencies are accountable for their actions. The main function of the agency is to establish the principle of accountability in promoting integrity and curbing corruption.

Designing an Effective Oversight Body

Scholars argue about a more concrete, pragmatic review of the effectiveness of an oversight body (Brereton, 1999), but what constitutes an ideal oversight model is a matter of examination in a particular context. Arguments for an independent oversight body have often been focused on the effectiveness of such an oversight body in addressing complaints, misconduct, or broader police policy. The main task of oversight is to supervise, control, and coordinate operations; achieve people's confidence on service delivery and discourage malpractice. However, the most important task of the oversight is to set up a balance between organization independence and public expectation.

Experts in this field have classified different models of oversight agencies. It is noted that there are variations in size, role, powers, functions, and strategies in agencies. Some entities are responsible for receiving and investigating complaints, some deal only with serious corruption and misconduct.

Some models are generalist and some are specialist governed by statute. An agency whose jurisdiction extends to all public sector officials is referred to as belonging to the generalist model. An agency that oversees police or any special agency activities alone is referred to as belonging to the specialist model.

Kerstetter (1985, cited in Lewis, 1999) identified three models of civilian oversight: (a) civilian review, (b) civilian input, and (c) civilian monitor. Civilian review has the power to investigate, determine, and recommend punishment. The second model confines civilian involvement to the receipt and investigative stages of the complaints process and recommends disciplinary action to the police authority. In the last model, police do the investigation and the oversight body supervises the investigation to ensure that it is fair and just.

Goldsmith's six ideal type categories of oversight bodies are in between "exclusive control by police" and "exclusive control by civilians." The Police Assessment Resource Centre (PARC, 2005) of Canada created a new conceptual framework for categorizing police oversight models. These three categories are: (a) review and appellate models, (b) investigative and quality assurance models, and (c) evaluative and performance-based models. Review and appellate models can only review the completed file and cannot conduct independent investigations or hearings, or subpoena witnesses or documents. Generally, these bodies cannot make policy recommendations based on their review of completed internal investigations. An investigative and quality assurance model is independent with significant power over the conduct of internal investigations. Evaluative and performance-based models investigate the performance of the investigation.

McDevitt, Farrell, and Andresen (2005, cited in Greene, 2007) identified four models of oversight:

1. Fully external investigation and review model.
2. Internal review conducted by the police with external review conducted by others.
3. The use of professional monitors, ombudspersons, auditors who are external to the police, but work with police.
4. Hybrid of the first three models.

Every oversight model has a certain range of power. Each of the models has weaknesses and strengths. There are also potential advantages and disadvantages of each oversight model. Different oversight bodies work in different ways. But, their sustainability or success depends on various determinants. One institution can be effective for complainants, but may not be acceptable to law enforcement agencies or the community. The mission and vision of these models are to investigate complaints against law enforcement agencies in a transparent and independent way.

Consideration for a Sustainable Model

Selecting the most appropriate model for an oversight process requires analysis of the structure, powers, functions, and strategies of the oversight body. However, to create a specialized structure of civilian oversight, it needs to emphasize strengthening capability, resources, and greater independence in decision making (Lewis, 1999). A good source for the purpose of identifying strengths could be the examination of governing legislation, and consulting government and agency documents, and reports from different bodies related to the oversight body. From this aspect, the research proposes some characteristics for a model considered for independent oversight.

Legislation

An independent body that is responsible for complaints investigation, monitoring, and reviewing needs a values mandate to give strong support for its actions (Lewis, 1991). The legislations "provide accountability to ensure that complainants get fair treatment while preserving appropriate protection for subject officer" (Lewis, 1991, p. 152) and, simultaneously, to oversight agency work according to the law. Stenning (2000) stressed clear goals and criteria in a particular field of legislation. It may be said that if the legislation is strong, the oversight body is also strong.

There are arguments about the correct structure and power for law enforcement oversight. Bayley (1985) added some crucial points, such as flow of correct information, fairness, and speed in effective accountability mechanisms. Reporting power is another important criterion for a powerful body. Moreover, strengthening the role of effective leadership is vital in securing confidence of other stakeholders (Prenzler, 2004). Equally, skilled persons with integrity are necessary to run an efficient investigation. In many cases, the capacity of oversight agencies is determined by the staffing and financial resources available (Brown & Head, 2005; 2008). Smith's research (2005) shows that education and training play an important role in developing skills in the staff of an integrity agency.

Quality of investigations is also essential in operational integrity (Prenzler, 2000). Moreover, an oversight body should work impartially and objectively, and according to the merits of specific complaints (Beattie & Weitzer, 2000). Additionally, protection of witness is also an effective step for a strong oversight body, which assists in the investigation process. This can be on a short-term or long-term basis, depending on special needs.

Partnership Among Institutions in the Integrity System

Nowadays, partnership has become an important principle of government policies. In a partnership, every partner brings to the relationship a set of skills, abilities, and experience that, when worked together and carried out competently, achieve a much better result than if each of the partners had acted on their own (Pesce, 2008). The principle of a partnership relationship is that "collective effort" among agencies makes the oversight result more successful, receiving this "co-creating value." This relationship can avoid instances of duplication through systematic communication with other agencies (Commonwealth of Australia, 2009). In a partnership approach to oversight, an entity can seek advice from other agencies, which can be a powerful tool for oversight agency (Stewart, 2008). This model can help managers to develop and implement a cohesive, focused relationship management strategy. It is the coordination approach that an independent oversight body needs if it is to see itself as being in a partnership with other agencies.

Accountability Process

As the research has discussed above concerning accountability, the oversight mechanism itself needs to be accountable for checks and balances in the distribution of power. Oversight bodies need coercive power to tackle corruption and maladministration, but at the same time the body should be accountable to the Parliament. An actor with capability and integrity can regulate this well-managed system (Commonwealth of Australia, 2009). In this system of checks and balances, the procedure can be made more accountable. Thus, personal as well as organizational accountability help to produce a well-balanced oversight model.

A Proactive Approach

The proactive approach is concerned with the reduction and prevention of misconduct and recommends change in the organization. Organizational insight from conventional analysis of the "rotten apple" theory of police misconduct applied to organization responsibility has brought about change in the perception of integrity processes (Palmer, 1992). The oversight body explores the problem proactively through investigation, data collection, and analysis, and focuses the organization as a whole (Millar, 2002). Research and specific corruption prevention strategies, such as capacity building through identification of problematic systems within an organization, make the system effective. Nevertheless, Walker found lack of research on oversight activities and effectiveness of oversight agencies (2001, p. 184).

The policy review function is an important aspect of citizen oversight. A proactive body has the capacity to take any action and can review policy and procedure of the oversighted agencies (Lewis, 1996). This process is designed to serve a preventive function by identifying problems and recommending corrective action (Walker & Kreisel, 1996). It can be an effective information tool for oversighted bodies to identify the problems and initiate corrective action. In order to develop the structure of the oversight body, Brereton (2000) suggests engaging in research and policy development. This can minimize the causes of citizen complaints by offering change in officers' attitude and community perception.

Performance Measurement

Performance measurement can be applied to the practice of oversight agencies in order to assist in determining their performance and effectiveness, and also in providing public accountability of the agency itself (Prenzler & Lewis, 2005). However, there are disagreements among experts about which measures are appropriate for the performance of an independent oversight body to ensure that an oversighted agency operates with integrity (Lewis & Prenzler, 1999; Brereton, 2000; Livingston, 2004).

Oversight agencies need to be involved in complaint investigations, review, complainant satisfaction, and prevention measures (Brereton, 2000). Prenzler and Lewis (2005) propose setting a standard time line to complete complaint investigations. Walker (2006, p. 20) accordingly supports development of appropriate performance measures and sponsoring of independent research. There is a need to ensure that oversight bodies themselves are performing properly for desired outcomes. Moreover, Prenzler and Lewis (2007) recognize the merit of the performance aspect of an oversight agency and suggest publicizing that performance. The performance of the accountability mechanism depends on powers and resources for effective oversight.

Another argument is that performance measurement of civilian oversight is difficult as the oversight agency plays a preventative role, which should not concentrate on measuring the outcome by statistics only. There are other determinants for increase or decrease in complaint numbers. However, it is suggested that the number of complaints and investigations cannot provide instructions on behavior. Moreover, longitudinal study and observation of other variables need to be considered. Brereton (2000) argues for more solid empirical assessment of performance such as numbers and types of complaints and timeliness of the address. The success of oversight can be measured in part by audits reports, reviews, and surveys to ascertain that the complaints process is transparent and its feedback contributes to improve the process.

Challenges for the Oversight Body

Challenges are identified in the literature that oversight bodies struggle with impediments such as insufficient budgetary appropriations, lack of police cooperation, and political interference (Lewis, 1999; Brown & Head, 2008; Brown, 2008). Lack of resources inevitably undermines the effectiveness and damages support for the oversight process (Smith, 2005; Millar, 2002). The Queensland's Police Complaints Tribunal is an example of this (Lewis, 1999). Oversight mechanisms are sometimes overburdened. Sometimes change of government and lack of well-established support can lead to a poor result. Thus, commitment for an effective mechanism is indeed necessary to increase integrity in law enforcement.

Government Cooperation

In an integrity system, government has an important role in effective oversight practice (Lewis, 1999; Goldsmith & Lewis, 2000). Terrill (1990) argues that government's "inactivity and inattentiveness" can often obstruct the ability of the oversight body to be effective. Lewis (2000) suggests the need for a serious commitment of the government to maintain effectiveness of civilian oversight policies. She pointed out the negative symbiotic relationship between police and government, which creates an incentive for governments to pay mere "lip service" in police accountability issues. So, continuity and support for resources from government is an important aspect for an effective oversight body.

Political Will

Political support is crucial for establishing and sustaining effective civilian oversight (Millar, 2002). Police usually operate in a political environment. Analysis by Chan (1997) on changing police culture revealed that law enforcement members see their role as protectors of their political masters as they are inherently political. This argument also is supported by the research by Prenzler (2000). Thus, a political role is essential for achieving change in police culture. Again, when there is a change of government, the new government tries to shelve the efforts of the previous government and establish some new form of model to replace the previous one (Prenzler & Lewis, 2005). This has been evident in Australia as well.

Law Enforcement Cooperation

Cooperation among law enforcement agencies with the oversight body is one of the significant factors that can affect the performance of oversight

(Goldsmith & Lewis, 2000). It has been recognized that noncooperation from a police department negatively affects the oversight mechanism (Walker, 2001; Lewis, 1999). This strong unwritten code of brotherhood encourages police to cover up corruption activities. Millar (2002) argues that lack of a collaborative and partnership environment between law enforcement agencies and oversight bodies can undermine the effectiveness of oversight and challenge its legitimacy.

Significantly, an attitude of mutual respect and a reasonable working relationship are considered necessary for an effective police oversight body relationship (Walker, 2001). This change of culture must come from inside the organizations (Chan, 1997). Similarly, change in the law may have some impact on behavior and that a wider impact could be achieved through further modification of the rules. To change police practice, therefore, an attack upon police "occupational and cooperative culture" may be necessary (Chan, 1997). Therefore, the need for more deliberate strategies for coordination of integrity policies is obvious in the accountability process.

Public Support

A fundamental principle of democratic theory is securing and maintaining public consent for the activities of the state. In this regard, any government agencies, including oversight agencies, need to be justified in the eyes of the public, so that citizens can see those agencies operating efficiently and effectively, and seeking legitimacy.

It is evident as well that the success of oversight depends on the public awareness of the complaints handling process and a transparent investigation system. Another study concludes that the existence of oversight agencies can promote greater public confidence in the police (Buren, 2007). Citizens have more confidence in complaint investigations when they are conducted by an agency outside the police department (Prenzler, 2004; Livingston, 2004; Landau, 1996; Perez, 1994). It is urged that people know the existence of such an agency.

Evaluation of the Model

The review of the literature summarizes a theoretical framework (Figure 15.1) of an oversight model for law enforcement agency. From the literature, a more relevant explanation of an effective law enforcement oversight process emerges in the figure, which requires a sound legislative foundation, skilled personnel to administer it, public confidence in it, a reasonable level of commitment and cooperation on the part of law enforcement organizations and the commitment of political support, and, finally, adequate resources for full and effective implementation of the process.

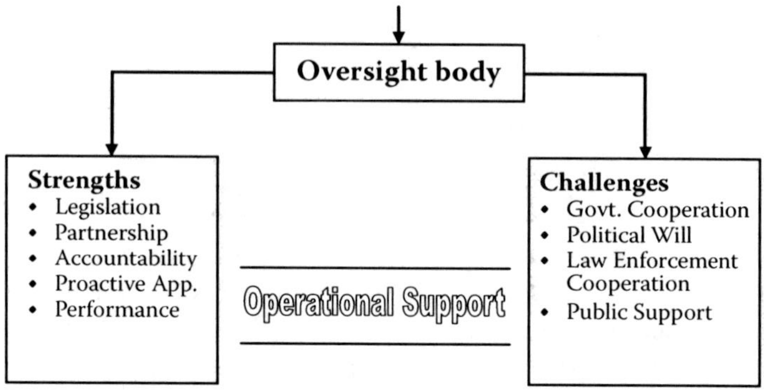

Figure 15.1 Law Enforcement Oversight Model.

Moreover, they should have the power to conduct investigations from the beginning of the case and have the ability to monitor police investigations into serious and sensitive allegations of misconduct, and be able to investigate or review complaints by police against other police. Policy review also requires careful examination of all these aspects of oversight.

Context of Bangladesh Police

Bangladesh, a developing country of the southern Asia, has a history of colonial heritage. So, the foundation of today's Bangladeshi police administration can be traced back to the British colonial period. The British tried to establish the police in the subcontinent to prolong their subjugation and economic extortion. Eventually, the police were separated from ordinary people and were engineered solely for the service of the colonial masters (Mishra, 1989). Although the primal concern of the police is to help collect revenue and to maintain law and order through implementation of the law, it gradually expanded its grip on the other sectors. However, the British were highly successful in using the police as a very effective tool of colonial administration.

Colonial Legislation

Since the journey of policing in undivided India, impact of the attitude, behavior, and the culture of the colonial police continue inherently. From British rule to the Pakistan era, the police were used against the people's will to support political masters the same way. After 39 years of independence for Bangladesh, the police organization is still run by the same Police Act of 1861 and "The Police Regulation of Bengal of 1943." Even the major criminal laws like the Penal Code of 1860, the Evidence Act of 1872, and the Criminal Procedure Code of 1898 are the product of the colonial era. The Police Act

1861 does not explain the people's right (Huda, 2008), rather the Act was designed by the colony to keep the people bound to obeying the colonial rule. From the British era to independent Bangladesh, police have acted almost the same way (Shahjahan, 2008), implementing their coercive power.

Police Coercive Power

It is said that police in Bangladesh have lot of stories about the use of their coercive power. From various media reports and TI, it was revealed that police corruption typically involves using their status as police officers to obtain wrongful gains or benefits. Sometimes lower-level police use power to grant immunity from police action to certain citizens or peers, and demand cash payment in return for protection against police action. Often, they keep weapons or drugs that are confiscated from suspects. It was very common that the police use abusive or deceptive means in interrogation of subjects. The police have the ability to detain, arrest, and use force when necessary. Police accountability is thus of paramount concern to the public.

Police Corruption

In addition, police have been given the power to deny human rights and civil liberties to the citizens. In this unwholesome environment, police become corrupted and treat citizens in a degraded way (Huda, 2008). Besides, by profession policing is the high-risk occupation involving corruption for power or money or both (Prenzler, 2000). Many times police engaged in corruption because of their poorly paid status (Karzon, 2006). They also work 13 to 18 hours a day, which is almost double the working hours of the government employees. Besides, they do not get leave or are they compensated for extra work. Transparency International Bangladesh has several times identified Bangladesh police as the most corrupted department (2001). In most cases, people have to bribe the police for a favor. Thus, the poor status and the greed for money make the Bangladesh police corrupt (Shahjahan, 2008). Citizens have accepted it as a part of their daily life experience (Lewis, 1996). The reason for such helplessness is the presence of corruption in almost all levels of government (World Bank, 1996).

Relation Between Police and Politics

Historically, police in many countries have performed a variety of nonpolice administrative duties (Lewis, 1999). The diversity of their functions serves to enhance their importance to governments. Bayley (1985) identified this general way in which police and political power are knotted with each other.

Government can use the police as a first line of defense against the opponent. In addition, by maintaining the legacy of British and Pakistani regimes, the police of Bangladesh remain busy giving the opposition a hard time (Karzon, 2006). Moreover, a major hurdle to accountability lies with the Police Act of 1861 that overemphasizes the constabulary functions of the police against the professional aspect of crime control, making amendment of the Act an important consideration (Huda, 2006).

Organizational Structure and Lack of Accountability

Bangladesh police have three tiers of entry. Lower-level police entry is Constables, the middle level is Subinspectors, and the supervisor level is Assistant Superintendent of Police (ASP). The Public Service Commission recruits the ASPs. The lower stratum of police is the majority who are unskilled or not well trained. Their behavior and exposure are sometimes questionable by the community (Karzon, 2006). This is evident that the insufficient departmental mechanism in policing is running out. Huda (2006) suggested that an officer-based organization can provide a public-friendly, service-oriented policing with internal accountability that can enhance competence.

Public Awareness

The common person's impression of the police is not a good one in Bangladesh. Fear of police discourages the public to lodge complaints against the police. The people prefer to avoid going to police stations for fear of harassment and other various forms of repression (Asian Human Right Commission, 2008). However, developing a trust between the force and the people is needed for any democratic policing. The public is aware nowadays about the role of police in performing their duties. For professional and institutional police, public participation in policing is very important (Huda, 2008). Experts and scholars are making valuable suggestions about the policing, which is a positive trend for Bangladesh Police.

Pressure From Media and Society

Use of excessive force, brutality, misconduct, and corruption of police are now regular news items in the media. Some of the incidents are getting a great deal of attention. International organizations also pressured the government of Bangladesh to investigate these allegations of deaths and torture of victims while in police custody (Amnesty International, 2002; Commonwealth Human Rights Initiative, 2007). Scholars also stressed concern for the improvement of the individual behavior in the police reform process.

Traditional Approaches of Misconduct

Traditional approaches of misconduct mainly focus on individual misconduct. These remedies rarely focus on systematic changes within law enforcement agencies. It is desirable to shift from this "rotten apple theory" of misconduct where an individual person is responsible for systematic organizational change. Experts on criminology argued for such mechanisms where whole organizations need to take some initiatives to build up police accountability (Goldsmith & Lewis, 2000; Bayley, 2002). Funding for a service-oriented and people-friendly police force is now in extensive demand from today's society. The police administration became concerned, aware of their responsibility for citizens' welfare (Huda, 2008; Shahjahan, 2008). To do that, the police organization has taken steps to control coercive power and made the police more friendly to the community.

Current Police Accountability System in Bangladesh

The current police accountability system in Bangladesh is controlled by state laws and, at the same time, by internal regulations. Higher police personnel are subject to the public service laws and regulations and the lower level personnel are directed by the police internal set of laws. Besides these, the Anti-Corruption Commission Act 2004 and the general laws are applicable if needed.

A plethora of rules and regulations were framed by the government to prevent public officials from unwanted behavior and actions. The Government Servants (Conduct) Rules 1979, and the Government Servants (Discipline and Appeal) Rules 1985 are among the rules that have provisions against delinquent officers for inefficiency, misconduct, corruption, and subversive activities. There are special provisions for certain members of police force. The Police Officers (Special Provisions) Ordinance 1976 is a different type of ordinance where courts' jurisdiction was barred. The duty and responsibility of the police are explained in the PRB of 1943. Police also are governed by the Armed Police Battalions Ordinance (1979) and relevant Metropolitan Police Acts.

Police headquarters, headed by Inspector General of Police (IGP), largely controls the police. The entire unit is accountable to the IGP through their respective unit leaders. Finally, the police are accountable to the Ministry of Home Affairs. The Parliamentary Committee on Law and Order oversees the entire law and order situations in the country.

Complaints Against Police: The Way Investigation Works

The internal disciplinary approach of Bangladesh police deals with misconduct of individual police officials. In this process, after receiving a complaint against a policeman, the authorities engage an investigator to investigate the complaints. It is prescribed that only the senior officer of the alleged policeman can conduct a disciplinary inquiry. If the person is found guilty, the investigator then suggests a punishment. The accused can appeal the case. This investigation process can be initiated by the police or by the public. In some cases, the government may direct the police to inquire into the matter. Sometimes, the court can direct the police to take disciplinary action against the accused policeman. If the complaint is a criminal offense, the policeman will be prosecuted under the criminal law and, simultaneously, will be subject to the disciplinary process.

The investigation system against senior-level personnel is different, according to the Government Servants (Discipline and Appeal) Rules 1985. It is a prolonged investigation process. The violations of any clause of the Government Servants (Conduct) Rules 1979 are considered as misconduct and are subject to be punished under the rule of 1985. The accused may apply to the president for preview of the order. According to the Police Officers (Special Provisions) Ordinance 1976, police authority frame charges against the offender and serve a show-cause notice, which had to be replied to by the offender within seven to ten working days. The accused person can go for a hearing of the case. If the authorities find the accused guilty, the penalty will be imposed upon within 20 days. This procedure is lengthy and the accused can manage the investigation in series of steps to his/her favor.

Therefore, the development of Police Internal Oversight (PIO) has emerged to curb corruption and increase efficiency in policing. The senior-level police awareness of the need for police control and performance development played an important role in developing an internal oversight model for confidence in police–community relations in Bangladesh.

Police Internal Oversight Model

PIO explained the reasons for establishment of such a body, saying that "the absences of good governance and endemic corruption have led to the diversion and misallocation of resources, which blatantly stand in the way of ensuring social justice and economic equity" (Police Internal Oversight, 2009). So, as a responsive police to the people's aspiration, PIO was established to revamp the Bangladesh police.

Police Internal Oversight is headed by a Deputy Inspector General of the police headquarters and is directly accountable to the IGP. All the units of Bangladesh police fall under the surveillance of PIO (Figure 15.2).

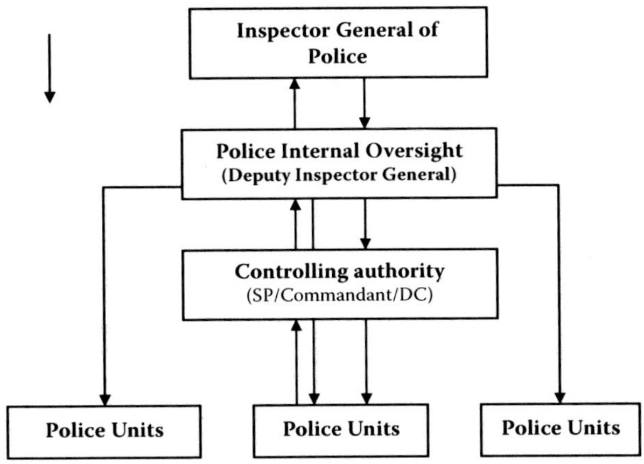

Figure 15.2 PIO Mechanism in Bangladesh.

There are three major levels in PIO functioning: (a) Policy and Administration, (b) Inquiry and Implementation, and (c) Observation and Reporting. The first level is the highest level stationed at Police Headquarters, which organizes training for the newly recruited agents and is responsible for administration, logistic issues for smooth functioning. Field-level agents work mostly undercover. They send reports to the policy and administration level. After examining the report, this level sends it to the Unit Chief (at a level minimum to a Superintendent of Police) to take necessary steps in accordance with the PIO Operational Manual, Part-1. A copy of the same report is sent to the superior authority for records and to reflect the issue in the Annual Confidential Report of the officer. The Unit Chief endorses the report and forwards it to the officer who is the senior officer of the accused for inquiry. This officer then returns a report with recommendations.

On the basis of the inquiry report, Unit Chief disposes of the issue either by enforcing the Criminal Procedure Code or by departmental procedure by issuing a warning letter to the alleged to be more alert in the future. Whatever the result is or action that has been taken, this is to be forwarded to PIO headquarters with a copy to the superior authority of the Unit Chief.

Within this short period of time, it has become a successful medium of "policing over the policing." The PIO has received 124 complaints against the police, 86 complaints against civilians, 129 suggestions, and 84 e-mails with information for investigation (up to January 21, 2011).

Key Challenges for Bangladesh Police

The fundamental challenge for any oversight body is to achieve the support and confidence of law enforcement agencies, Parliament, and the public.

Besides, factors that immensely undermine the internal disciplinary system are illegitimate political interference and a lack of professional senior police management will to properly implement systems. Political influence on senior management may refuse to punish a perpetrator who has produced what they consider to be a result, no matter how illegal the means or unjust the outcome. Huda (2008) wrote that most of the governments are not interested in maintaining effective oversight policies, thus, keeping colonial legislation for police operations.

Recently, some media revealed that sometimes political leaders acting in favor of the accused person are putting pressure on the senior level officials to act in favor of the political leaders' arguments. Perhaps the strongest criticism of internal police investigations is that the officers investigating these reports have an inherent inability to conduct impartial investigations, which has been discussed above. Questions may arise whether these investigators are skilled to do so or willing to do so in a professional manner. It is also a fact that the leadership of police (including the police chief and his assistants) is honest and willing to organize and committed to uphold the police accountability mechanism.

One of the key challenges is the coordination and cooperation of the oversight body in investigations. It is argued that cooperation from all corners is indispensable for police integrity including political support. Shahjahan (2008) argues that government commitment and powerful political leaders interfering less in the police job can make an accountable and professional police force. Intellectuals argued to curtail the political government's control over police and make it a pro-people organization (*The Daily Star*, July 8, 2007). They suggested changing the traditional mindset of policing and move toward proactive policing.

It is also noted that the success of police substantially depends on community cooperation with the respect of law. Consequently, the system that was established needs to be transparent. Investigation process needs to be reliable and acceptable to the community. Steps need to render the police professionally competent, operationally neutral, functionally cohesive, and organizationally responsible for all their action (Huda, 2008). There must be a will to implement the system comprehensively. It noted that an internal discipline system is largely viewed as biased in favor of the police. The perception of police brotherhood and the "silent blue curtain" contribute to this lack of public trust. In many cases, the inquiry officer may also tend to favor the accused police officer rather than the complainant (Lewis, 1996). In addition, internal investigations may be less likely to result in favorable results for claimants.

Conclusion

From the above discussion, it is evident that Bangladesh lacks any independent oversight model, rather the police of Bangladesh are controlled by a plethora of rules and a newly established internal oversight body. It can be said that starting of such an accountability model is a ray of hope for people-friendly policing. In order to establish a service-oriented police service, a corruption-free force is indispensable. The process has been started to make corruption punishable irrespective of the level of authority and power. Some fundamental institutional and policy reforms have been started as well through Police Reform Programs. These include concrete progress made toward community-oriented policing.

This new police accountability arrangement, which is applied to all officers irrespective of their rank, can ensure a good community partnership policing where police become a trusted partner rather than a feared tool of the state. A new dimension in the Bangladesh police, accountability mechanism, ensures that the members of Bangladesh Police are more accountable for their actions. Though the objective of the accountability needs to be more proactive, it is at least a starting point to the journey of developing the notion of democratic policing in Bangladesh.

The research concludes that there are advantages and disadvantages in all models of oversight agencies, but the crucial factors in terms of effectiveness are the appropriate resources and performance of the staff. This oversight body could be a successful one if the government demonstrates good will by providing adequate support. And, such support must not be for political benefit. The study thus concludes that strong power aligned with adequate resources can still position the model as an effective law enforcement oversight agency.

References

Amnesty International. (2002). *Bangladesh: Accountability needed in 'Operation Clean Heart.'* Retrieved from: www.amnesty.org.uk/news-details.asp?NewsID=12860 (accessed Jan. 15, 2012).

Asian Human Right Commission. (2008). Bangladesh: Empty rhetoric will not improve Bangladeshi police. Retrieved from: www.humanrights.asia/news/ahrc-news/AHRC-STM-051-2008 (accessed January 1, 2012).

Bayley, D. H. (2002). Law enforcement and the rule of law. *Criminology and Public Policy*, *2*,133–154.

Bayley, D. H. (1985). Police in political life. In *Patterns of policing: A comparative international analysis*. David H. Bayley (Ed.). New Brunswick, NJ: Rutgers University Press.

Beattie, C., & Weitzer, R. (2000). Race, democracy and law: Civilian review of police. In A. Goldsmith & C. Lewis (Eds.), *Civilian oversight of policing: Governance, democracy and human rights.* Oxford, U.K.: Hart Publishing.

Brereton, D. (2000). Policing and crime prevention. In D. Chappell & P. Wilson (Eds.), *Crime and the criminal justice system in Australia.* Sydney: Butterworths.

Brereton, D. (1999). *Evaluating external oversight bodies.* Paper presented at the 1999 IACOLE World Conference, September 5–9, Sydney.

Brown, A. J., and Head, B. W. (2008). Consequences, capacity and coherence: An overall approach to integrity system assessment. In B. W. Head, A. J. Brown, & C. Connors (Eds.), *Promoting integrity evaluating and improving public institutions.* Aldershot, U.K.: Ashgate Publishing.

Brown, A. J., & Head, B. W. (2005). Institutional capacity and choice in Australia's integrity systems. *Australian Journal Public Administration, 64*(2), 84–95.

Brown, A. J. (2008). Towards a federal integrity commission: The challenge of institutional capacity-building in Australia. In B. W. Head, A. J. Brown, & C. Connors (Eds.), *Promoting integrity evaluating and improving public institutions.* Aldershot, U.K.: Ashgate Publishing.

Buren, B. A. (2007). *Evaluating citizen oversight of police.* New York: LFB Scholarly Publishing LLC.

Chan, J. B. L. (1997). *Changing police culture: Policing in a multicultural society.* Cambridge: Cambridge University Press.

Commonwealth of Australia. (2009). *Inquiry into law enforcement integrity models.* Paper presented to the Parliamentary Joint Committee on ACLEI, February, Canberra, Australia.

Commonwealth Human Rights Initiative. (2007). *Feudal forces: Democratic nations: Police accountability in Commonwealth South Asia.* Retrieved from: http://www.humanrightsinitiative.org/publications/police/feudal_forces_democratic_nations_police_acctability_in_cw_south_asia.pdf (accessed April 22, 2010).

Costigan, F. (2004). *Is corruption a concern?* Address to AGM of Transparency International Australia, November 2003. (reprinted in *TI Australia News,* no. 37).

Ekenvall, B. (2003). Police attitudes towards fellow officers' misconduct: The Swedish case and a comparison with the USA and Croatia. *Journal of Scandinavian Studies in Criminology and Crime Prevention, 3*(2), 210– 232.

Fitzgerald, G. (1989). *Report of a Commission of Inquiry pursuant to orders in Council.* Brisbane: Government Printer.

Goldsmith, A., and Lewis, C. (2000). *Civilian oversight of policing: Governance, democracy and human rights.* Oxford, U.K.: Hart Publishing.

Greene, J. R. (2007). Make police oversight independent and transparent. *Criminology and Public Policy, 6*(4), 747–754.

Huda, M. N. (2006). Conceptualising police reform. *The Daily Star,* July 8. https://docs.google.com/viewer?a=v&q=cache:uE-XMwjR5WkJ:www.prp.org.bd/Media/8July08.pdf+Nurul+huda+2006+IGP&hl=en&pid=bl&srci (accessed January 15, 2012).

Huda, M. N. (2008, January 1). Reforming omnipotent police and omniscient politicians. *The Daily Star*, Dhaka.

Karzon, S. H. R. (2006, October 14). Bangladesh police: Existing problems and some reform proposals, the law and our rights. *The Daily Star*, no: 258. Retrieved from http://www.thedailystar.net/law/2006/10/02/index.htm (accessed March 27, 2009).

Landau, T. (1996). When police investigate police: A view from complainants. *Canadian Journal of Criminology*, July, 291–315.

Lewis, C. (1991). Police complaints in Metropolitan Toronto: perspectives of the public complaints commissioner. In A. J. Goldsmith (Ed.), *Complaints against the police: The trend to external review.* Oxford, U.K.: Clarendon Press.

Lewis, C. (1996). *Independent oversight of complaints against the police: Problems and prospects.* (Research paper no. 30) Brisbane: Griffith University, The Centre for Australian Public Sector Management.

Lewis, C. (1999). *Complaints against the police: The politics of reform.* Sydney: Hawkins Press.

Lewis, C. (2000). The politics of civilian oversight: Serious commitment or lip service? In A. Goldsmith & C. Lewis (Eds.), *Civilian oversight of policing: Governance, democracy and human rights.* Oxford, U.K.: Hart Publishing.

Lewis, C., & Prenzler, T. (1999, December). *Civilian oversight of police in Australia: Trends and issues in crime and criminal justice.* Canberra: Australian Institute of Criminology.

Livingston, D. (2004). The unfulfilled promise of citizen review. *Ohio State Journal of Criminal Law, 1*, 653–669.

Miller, J. (2002). *Civilian oversight of policing: Lessons from the literature.* Paper presented at the Global Meeting on Civilian Oversight of Police, Los Angeles, May 5–8. Online at: http://www.vera.org/download?file=93/Civilian%2Bovesight.pdf (accessed April 14, 2009).

Mishra, H. K. (1989). *Bureaucracy under the Mughals.* Delhi: Amar Prakashan, pp. 36–41, 73–78.

Mulgan, R. (2003). *Holding power to account: Accountability in modern democracies.* Basingstoke, New York: Palgrave McMillan.

OECD. (1996). *Annual Report 1996.* Retrieved from: http://www.globalcompetitionforum.org/regions/europe/Norway/AnnualReport1996.pdf (accessed April 17, 2009).

Palmer, M. (1992). Controlling corruption. In P. Moir and H. Eijkman (Eds.), *Policing Australia.* South Melbourne: Macmillan.

PARC. (2005). *Review of national police oversight models.* http://www.parc.info/citizen_oversight_of_police.chtml (accessed April 22, 2009).

Perez, D. W. (1994). *Common sense about police review.* Philadelphia: Temple University Press.

Pesce, A. (2008). *Human resources partnership model.* http://www.pesceassociates.com/pdfs/MicrosoftWord-PartnershipModel.pdf (accessed April 20, 2009).

Petterson, W. E. (1991). Police accountability and civilian oversight of policing: An American perspective. In A. J. Goldsmith (Ed.), *Complaints against the police: The trend to external review.* Oxford, U.K.: Clarendon Press.

Police Internal Oversight. (2009). Retrieved from http://www.pio.gov.bd/releases.php (accessed December 25, 2010).

Pope, J. (2008). National integrity systems: The key to building sustainable, just and honest government. In B. W. Head, A. J. Brown, & C. Connors (Eds.), *Promoting integrity: Evaluating and improving public institutions*. Aldershot, U.K.: Ashgate Publishing.

Prenzler, T., & Lewis, C. (2007). Police oversight agencies: Measuring effectiveness. In B. W. Head, A. J. Brown, & C. Connors (Eds.), *Promoting integrity: Evaluating and improving public institutions*. Aldershot, U.K.: Ashgate Publishing.

Prenzler, T., & Lewis, C. (2005). Performance indicators for police oversight agencies. *Australian Journal of Public Administration, 54*, 2, June.

Prenzler, T., & Ransley, J. (2002). *Police reform: Building integrity*. New South Wales: Hawkins Press.

Prenzler, T. (2004). Stakeholder perspectives on police complaints and discipline. *Australian and New Zealand Journal of Criminology, 37*(1), 85–113.

Prenzler, T. (2000). Civilian oversight of police: A taste of capture theory. *The Centre for Criminal Justice and Studies, 40*, 659–674.

Schedler, A. (1999). Conceptualizing accountability. In L. Diamond, M. F. Plattner, & A. Schedler (Eds.), *The self-restraining state: Power and accountability in new democracies*. Boulder, CO: Lynne Rienner Publishers.

Shacklock, A. (2007). *Assessing integrity and anti-corruption mechanisms using the national integrity system assessment methodology*. Paper presented at the Australian Public Sector Anti-Corruption Conference, Sydney, October.

Shahjahan, A. S. M. (2008). Police reforms in Bangladesh strengthening police reform. Retrieved from http://www.adb.org/Documents/Books/Strengthening-Criminal-Justicesystem/chap03.pdf (February 24, 2010).

Smith, R. (2005). Mapping the New South Wales public integrity system. *Australian Journal of Public Administration, 64*(2), 54–61, June.

Stenning, P. C. (2000). Evaluating police complaints legislation: A suggested framework. In A. Goldsmith & C. Lewis (Eds.), *Civilian oversight of policing: Governance, democracy and human rights*. Oxford, U.K.: Hart Publishing.

Stewart, C. (2008, May 19). National anti-graft body left toothless. *The Australian*. Retrieved from: http://www.theaustralian.news.com.au/story/023720117-5001561,00.html (accessed April 17, 2009).

Stone, C. (2007). Tracing police accountability in theory and practice: From Philadelphia to Abuja and Sao Paulo. *Theoretical Criminology, 11*(2), 245–259.

Terrill, R. J. (1990). Alternative perceptions of independence in civilian oversight. *Journal of Police Science and Administration, 17*(2), 77–83.

The Daily Star (2007). Curbing political control must for police reform. July 8. 5(113), 1.

Transparency International. (2001). *The National Integrity System: Concept and practice*. (Country Studies Overview Report) Berlin: Transparency International.

Uhr, J. (1993). Redesigning accountability. *Australian Quarterly, 65*, 1–16, Winter.

Walker, S., & Kreisel, B. W. (1996). Varieties of citizen review. *American Journal of Police, 15*(3), 65–88.

Walker, S. (2006). Alternative models of citizen oversight. In J. C. Perino (Ed.), *Citizen oversight of law enforcement*. Chicago: American Bar Association Publishing.

Walker, S. (2001). *Police accountability: The role of citizen oversight*. Belmont, CA: Wadsworth-Thomas Learning.

World Bank. (1996). *Secured transactions: The power of collateral*. Retrieved from www.worldbank.org/fandd/english/0696/articles/0150696.htm - 21k (accessed April 22, 2010).

Conclusion
The Global Environment of Policing

16

Contents

Reforming police is one of the key challenges of contemporary policing and governance (Brodeur, 2010; Manning, 2010; Fleming & Wood, 2006). A few years ago, Stenning and Shearing (2005), drawing on work a decade earlier arguing that the 1990s represented a "watershed" period in policing reform (Bayley & Shearing, 1996), outlined what they believed to be the key opportunities, drivers, and challenges to reforming police. In their analysis, they identified a range of internal and external factors shaping the reform process, more or less "facilitating" or "hastening" reform (2005, p. 168). They concluded that we can be both optimistic and pessimistic about the potential for police reform. Reform is quite possible even in circumstances of entrenched and seemingly unchangeable *bad* policing arrangements and practices (*our term*), while, on the other hand, the same applies to *good* policing arrangements—they should never be assumed to be so good as to protect against reforms that are less progressive in the sense of undermining democratic, human-rights respecting, and community-based policing. Many of the chapters in *Global Environment of Policing* offer different aspects of good and bad, and different internal and external forces shaping policing reform.

The wide-ranging collection of chapters that comprise *Global Environment of Policing* address worldwide public policing issues from the academic and practitioner perspectives. These perspectives are not mutually exclusive. Many practitioners embody Dilip Das's ideal of *Police Leaders as Thinkers* and demonstrate a keen awareness of the academic literature and critical issues. K. S. Dhillon, Luis Fernandez, and Taptun Nasreen all provide insightful critiques of policing issues in their respective countries. By the same token, many of the academics who have contributed to this collection also have extensive practitioner experience. These include Dilip Das, editor and founder of IPES, and contributors Michael Berlin, David Bradley, and John Eterno.

Five broad themes emerge from these chapters. Four of these themes are captured by the four parts of this book. Articles focusing on these themes are grouped together in each of the four parts of this book. These include (Part I) Policing, Crime Control, and the Community; (Part II) Policing, Politics, and Democracy; (Part III) Policing: Global Challenges; and (Part IV) Police Leadership, Management, Education, and Organization: Issues and Trends. A fifth common theme arises from Susanne Karstedt's chapter, Creating Institutions: Linking the 'Local' and the 'Global' in the Travel of Crime Policies. However, merely because an article focuses on one theme does not mean that it does not address the other themes. To a certain extent, placement in a particular section is somewhat problematic. Most articles address at least two or more of the above themes, so the question is one of emphasis. For example, while Berlin focuses on the evolution of community policing in the United States and Eterno focuses on zero tolerance and crime control strategies, both also address the role of politics in relation to these strategies. On the other hand, Dellasoppa focuses more on social, cultural, economic, and political aspects influencing adoption or implementation of these strategies. Frühling explores community policing programs in Brazil and Columbia as well as the Latin American context in which they arose. Issues of politics and governance are virtually unavoidable and arise in all of the sections.

Understanding the Local Context

We begin with the fifth theme, first. While each of the four themes have universal implications, the framework in which they are applied and should be understood is local. Karstedt devotes her chapter (10) to the issue of diffusion of Western community policing and crime control strategies to other parts of the world. She argues convincingly that successful policy transfer and implementation of best practices must take into account social, cultural, political, and institutional factors at the receiving end to be successful. Dellasoppa echoes this theme when he states that "policing in the developing countries and, specifically in Brazil, cannot be analyzed by simple comparisons or by 'importing ideas' from developed countries. Strong differences between economical, political, social, and cultural systems must be seriously taken into account." He takes the inquiry a step farther when he notes the decay of the efficiency of the traditional Weberian concept of legitimate violence in developed countries and raises the question of "what happens with the Weberian formula in countries where the monopoly of legitimate force was *never* obtained by the state" (emphasis added).

Karstedt's principles and Dellasoppa's arguments apply not just to transfers between countries or continents, but to local and regional differences within the same country. Berlin's discussion of community policing in the United States notes substantial local differences in history, culture, politics, and problems between jurisdictions within the same country. Frühling notes the tendency toward decentralization of policing in Latin America from the national to the state or provincial and local levels.

Similarly, although the focus is on contemporary problems and issues, the context is historical. This is apparent in articles as diverse as Berlin's on community policing in the United States, Dhillon's on police accountability in India, Fernandez's on policing in Portugal, and Palmer's and Bradley's on memorials and police education in Australia.

The first section of the book, Policing, Crime Control, and the Community, addresses contemporary Western policing strategies, community policing and zero tolerance (Compstat/crime control), and their application in the United States, Latin America, and Europe. Berlin's chapter examines the evolution of policing in the United States, focusing on the origins of community policing in the early 1980s, its growth and development over the next 15 years, subsequent decline from the late 1990s to the mid-2000s, and nascent transformation in recent years. He indicates that rising crime and increasing complaints against the police led to implementation of community policing, but that even 30 years later there is no common definition of community policing. Berlin sets forth his own framework for defining community policing at five levels: (a) philosophy: principles and values; (b) proactive programs and activities; (c) changes in patrol and enforcement strategies; (d) changes in management and organization; and (e) changes in training. While the idea of defining community policing in terms of elements or multiple levels is not new (e.g., Manning (1989); Cordner (2001)), his framework benefits from conceptual simplicity and ease of application. He argues that his framework clearly demonstrates the mechanism by which community policing is intended to improve police–community relationships, but that the specific mechanisms by which community policing would reduce crime are not clear.

Rising crime coupled with increased citizen complaints and dissatisfaction with local police were primary factors that contributed to the development of community policing in the United States. While community policing generally appeared to improve police–community relationships in the many jurisdictions, these improved relationships did not necessarily result in reduced crime. Berlin indicates that given the broad diversity of American communities, the U.S. model of local control and local politics and personalities makes it very difficult to compare community policing efforts between police agencies and reach general conclusions.

The inability of community policing to reduce crime provided a window of opportunity for the introduction of new policing strategies to reduce crime. For Berlin, the decline of community policing is tied, at least in part, to its apparent inability to reduce crime in many jurisdictions. The explosive growth of Compstat (COMParative (or COMPuter) STATistics), zero tolerance, and aggressive enforcement approaches and their apparent success in reducing crime in New York and elsewhere coincided with the decline of community policing.

Compstat and zero tolerance are discussed at length by John Eterno in Chapter 3. While zero tolerance appeared successful in reducing crime, it gave rise to increasing numbers of complaints against the police. Balancing community service and enforcement approaches is a critical issue democratic societies must address. Eterno describes the balance in terms of crime control and due process approaches and the values of Compstat and CPR (courtesy, respect, and professionalism). The values of CPR—to maintain a high standard of integrity, value human life, respect the dignity of each individual, and render services with courtesy and civility—are intended to promote a culture of professionalism, balance the values of the crime control approach, protect lives and property, enforce the law, and fight crime both by preventing it and aggressively pursing violators.

Frühling and Dellasoppa demonstrate the need to balance community policing and crime control approaches is not unique to the United States. Dellasoppa suggests that for nation–states now under the influence of "that complex process of globalization, multiculturalism, marginalization, and increasing income differences," this task is even far more difficult than in developed nations. In addition to decentralization discussed briefly above, Frühling cites democratization and increasing crime rates as driving police reforms in Latin America. This sets the stage for both crime control and community policing in Latin America.

Police and Politics

Politics and policing are inextricably intertwined in both developed and developing nations. The nature and extent of political involvement varies considerably between and within nations. Under the U.S. model of local control of policing, politics plays both explicit and subtle roles in cities and counties across America. As Berlin indicates, the decision to implement community policing or Compstat is often a policy decision accomplished through the appointment of police chiefs or commissioners by elected officials, typically mayors or county executives, occasionally city manages, or city and county councils. Local criminal justice policies are frequently election issues in the United States. Candidates may and often include issues concerning community policing or Compstat in their election campaign platforms. Public safety or "law and order" must be balanced with respect for civil and human rights and control of police abuse. Eterno addresses this issue in Chapter 3 discussed above.

Frühling and Dellasoppa discuss the impact of democratization on policing in Latin America. Democracy in Latin America opened the door to both criticism of the police and sharply rising crime. Complaints of police corruption, inefficiency and abuse became increasingly vocal at the same time crime and violence increased substantially. As public expectations of the police grew, their legitimacy declined. Community policing and curbing police abuse appeared to be pitted against crime control.

The first formally evaluated experience in Latin America took place in Copacabana, Rio de Janeiro, in 1994. While this initiative was short-lived, it was followed by similar programs in many other cities throughout Brazil (Muniz, Larvie, Musumeci, & Freire, 1997, pp. 197–214). This experiment and the ones that followed confronted similar obstacles. First, the demand for crime control and the parallel call for a drastic reduction in police abuse have been perceived as somewhat contradictory by significant sectors of public opinion, which brought about an early end to many of the reform initiatives (Frühling, 2001). Second, increased crime and fear placed pressure on the police to show short-term results in circumstances that require long-range efforts. Finally, the institutional modernization required faces significant obstacles within the police given the large numbers of police members involved, serious financial difficulties, and a highly regulated, centralized administration. While police in developed countries tend to enjoy higher levels of legitimacy, community policing in industrialized countries experiences obstacles similar to those described by Frühling in Latin America.

Portugal, generally associated with the developed nations of Western Europe, also underwent democratization in the 1970s. Democratic reform of policing followed in the 1980s and 1990s, resulting in the creation of the General Inspectorate of Internal Administration (GHIA), which provided external oversight of the police and movement toward community policing. Fernandez's discussion of the evolution of policing in Portugal spans almost 700 years. He details periods of increasing and declining democratization and on-going tension within and between police organizations. He explores the tension between centralized command and operational decentralization (more on this in the discussion of organization and management issues section), which for Portugal raises issues concerning local–national relationships and military–civilian police personnel. Palmer suggests that nations that "maintain inquisitorial-oriented legal systems may find stronger practices or remnants of the military" than common law legal systems. This raises interesting questions concerning the "paramilitarization" of police in many developed countries, documented in the United States even prior to the terrorist attacks of 9/11.

K. S. Dhillon raises the issue of partisan politics in India. Dhillon begins discussion in his chapter with a quote from David H. Bayley: "The rule of law in modern India, the frame upon which justice hangs, has been undermined by the rule of politics." Dhillon raises concerns that partisan politics threatens Indian policing and Indian society. He argues that "the Indian police have been acting in a partisan manner for several decades now and getting increasingly politicized, ... is no longer a secret and ... that all political parties, whether secularist, leftist, centrist, or rightist in orientation, freely and shamelessly indulge in politicalization of governmental institutions and agencies, more particularly those charged with enforcement functions." He further argues that this threatens the rule of law and "equitable enforcement of public order."

While U.S. policing history provides ample evidence of the role of partisan politics during the "political era" of the 1800s, political influence on policing has largely, although certainly not completely, evolved along policy lines suggested by Berlin. Civil service reform and the professionalization of the police during the "reform era" played a major role in the transition. An Indian National Police Commission (NPC) was formed in 1977, studied the issues, and made recommendations for updating the organization, structure, and functioning of the Indian police. Dhillon indicates that for political reasons, these reforms were never implemented. He argues that police reform in India is essential and requires popular accountability, legal accountability, and functional transparency. He suggests that police must move away from their traditional crime fighting approach to promote and be part of social change. It is unclear the extent to which this goal was accomplished in developed countries, even where it was attempted. An interesting issue to consider is why some nations have not experienced the same levels of partisanship and corruption and the extent that national cultures and values have been important factors.

Kempa explores police accountability from a somewhat different perspective, incorporating accountability of "nonstate" policing and hybrid policing by examining the work of the Independent Commission on Policing in Northern Ireland (the Patten Commission). While the recommendations of the report were not fully endorsed and implemented as Kempa indicates, the report made an important contribution to deliberation on new frameworks for the democratic accountability of policing.

Recent Developments

The third section of the book, Global Challenges (Part III), incorporates a wide range of issues from cybercrime, to police memorials as a mechanism of building public support and legitimacy, to the transfer of crime control policies and immigrant smuggling. Additional issues, such as the impact of terrorism on civilian law enforcement, arise in the context of other chapters, such as community policing and crime control.

Wall explores cybercrime in the context of evolving technology. He indicates that modern policing has always had a relationship with technology, citing the industrial revolution that resulted in sweeping migration from rural to urban settings and the development of the police as an all-purpose service agency. More recent technological innovations could be said to include the automobile, telephone, radio, and computers, all of which have had significant impacts on policing from "routine preventative patrol" to Compstat and crime mapping. Wall argues that the Internet and three different levels of cybercrime arising from it are raising fundamental questions concerning the structure, role, and strategies of police agencies. According to Wall, more than simply greater knowledge and capacity are necessary to counter the growing threat of cybercrime. He suggests that nodal networks and partnerships are critical if law enforcement is to be successful in meeting public expectations and overcoming legal, practical, and technological challenges posed by cybercrime. His discussion of partnerships parallels the concept of partnership raised by Berlin in the context of community policing—on a global as opposed to a local scale. Wall, himself, proposes a "neo-Peelian paradigm across a global span" to improve police effectiveness and legitimacy.

Palmer addresses the issue of legitimacy from a different perspective—the construction of police memorials dedicated to "representing" police officers killed in the line of duty. This approach to police reform centers on alternative ways of garnering police support and legitimacy, mirroring, more or less, the practices that have been associated with war memorialization. In this sense, there has been a global movement toward memorializing police that is significantly different to past practices. Memorialization has become openly public, seeking to engage at a communal level to enhance public support and understanding of the sacrifices of police personnel, emphasizing the danger of police work, and acting as a counter-narrative to the critiques of police work emanating from various enquiries into police malpractice, use of force, and police killing citizens. While still at the early stages of his research into this global phenomenon the tentative conclusions seek to open a new field of policing research.

Karstedt takes Palmer's discussion of global process a step farther. She argues that information technology and exchange of knowledge have facilitated the transfer of knowledge and policies, but that criminal justice institutions are "thoroughly local and parochial." She discusses barriers to transferability and argues that understanding local and exporting institutions is critical and adapting policies of the new environment is critical. Dellasoppa and Frühling discuss issues in the context of Latin America and Brazil and conclude that complex processes of globalization, multiculturalism, marginalization, and increasing income differences shape and complicate the need for police reform and the nature of the reforms.

Antinori examines the growing role of organized crime in migrant smuggling in the Mediterranean and its impact on Europe. He traces the flow of migrant smuggling from its origins following the oil shock of 1974 and the different Italian organized crime grounds involved in migrant smuggling. He discusses the extent of illegal North African migration to Southern Italy and the beneficial impact it has on agricultural productivity, despite the low wages paid to African workers.

Police Reform

The fourth and final section of the book, Police Leadership, Management, Education, and Organization: Issues and Trends (Part IV), explores police leadership, management, education, and integrity from a variety of perspectives in the developed and developing world.

O'Malley and Hutchinson argue that as a result of the growth of private security there has been an increasing convergence of public and private policing in many industrialized countries. At the same time, they indicate increasing political pressure on senior police leaders to demonstrate that they are efficient and effective. As a consequence of these and other factors, there has been a transfer of business principles to policing that has impacted leadership, management, and unions. Not surprisingly, in the face of these new demands and a competitive market, public police unionism has increased. The unexpected benefits of this have been that unions have appeared to have adopted the language of managerialism and rather than serving as an obstacle to reform may be helping to facilitate it.

Gyamfi explores issues concerning the use of incentive to motivate officers and increase police performance and integrity in a nonunion, resource-scarce environment typical of many developing countries, in this case, Ghana. Students sampled a small group of police personnel from a community police station in the capital and found that police believed that incentives could have significant impact on their performance, particularly decent accommodations, food allowances, and assistance with utility payments. However, the study also found that none of the respondents was highly satisfied, 60.9% were somewhat satisfied and 39.1% were not satisfied. The researchers concluded that the lack of incentives contributed to poor performance and corruption and that an improved incentive package was essential. Other recommendations included "total reform of the police service," quality training, curtailed government interference, and rewards for exceptional performance.

In his chapter, Bradley examines the issue of police training in Australia and examines two conflicting models, the university model and the Registered Training Organization based on three criteria: managing recruitment targets, costs, and quality assurance. Bradley considers the university training model superior and argues that it provides the best pathway for the future of the police profession. The extent to which police training should follow a collegiate, "academic" model as opposed to a high stress, papa-military model also has been the subject of debate in the United States and many European countries. In the United States, where the university model is in the minority, many agencies attempt to combine aspects of both models.

Finally, Nasreen's chapter explores a developing country with limited resources, Bangladesh. The author proposes a national integrity system based upon a Greek Temple model, with institutional pillars supporting key goals on the temple roof. Nasreen argues an effective oversight agency with a strong legislative mandate is critical to ensure integrity and she explores a variety of approaches in use in different countries. Factors that contribute to the success of an effective oversight body include government cooperation, political will, law enforcement cooperation, public support, and adequate resources. She indicates that appropriate resources and performance of the staff are critical to the effectiveness of oversight agencies.

References

Bayley, D., & Shearing, C. (1996). The future of policing. *Law & Society Review, 15*(1), 19–41.

Brodeur, J. P. (2010). *The policing web.* New York: Oxford University Press.

Cordner, G. W. (2001). Community policing: Elements and effects. In R. G. Dunham & G. P. Alpert (Eds.), *Critical issues in policing: Contemporary readings* (pp. 493–510). Prospect Heights, IL: Waveland Press.

Fleming, J., & Wood, J. (Eds.) (2006). *Fighting crime together: The challenges of policing and security networks.* Sydney: University of New South Wales Press.

Fruling, H. J. (2001). *La reform policial y el proceso de democratizacion en America Latina.* Santiago, Chile: Centro de Estudios para el Desarrollo.

Manning, P. K. (1989). Community policing. In R. G. Durham & G. P. Alpert (Eds.), *Critical issues in policing contemporary readings* (pp. 451–468). Prospect Heights, IL: Waveland Press.

Manning, P. K. (2010). *A review of policing in a changing world.* Boulder, CO: Paradigm Press.

Muniz, J., Larvie, S. P., Musumeci, L., & Freire, B. (1997). Resistencias e dificuldades de um programa de policiamento comunitário. *Tempo Social, 9*(1), 197–214.

Stenning, P., & Shearing, C. (2005). Reforming police: Opportunities, drivers and challenges. *Australian and New Zealand Society of Criminology, 38*(2), 167–180.

Index

G

H

I

N

O

P

T

U

V

W

Z

IPES History

The International Police Executive Symposium was founded in 1994. The aims and objectives of the IPES are to provide a forum to foster closer relationships among police researchers and practitioners globally; to facilitate cross-cultural, international, and interdisciplinary exchanges for the enrichment of the law enforcement profession; and to encourage discussion and published research on challenging and contemporary topics related to the profession.

One of the most important activities of the IPES is the organization of an annual meeting under the auspices of a police or educational institution. To date, meetings have been hosted by

- The Canton Police of Geneva, Switzerland (Police Challenges and Strategies, 1994)
- The International Institute of the Sociology of Law in Onati, Spain (Challenges of Policing Democracies, 1995)
- Kanagawa University in Yokohama, Japan (Organized Crime, 1996)
- The Federal Police in Vienna, Austria (International Police Cooperation, 1997)
- The Dutch Police and Europol in The Hague, The Netherlands (Crime Prevention, 1998)
- Andhra Pradesh Police in Hyderabad, India (Policing of Public Order, 1999)
- The Center for Public Safety, Northwestern University, Evanston, Illinois (Traffic Policing, 2000)
- (A special meeting was co-hosted by the Bavarian Police Academy of Continuing Education in Ainring, Germany, University of Passau, Germany, and State University of New York, Plattsburgh, to discuss the issues endorsed by the IPES in April 2000.)
- The Police in Poland (Corruption: A Threat to World Order, 2001)
- Police of Turkey (Police Education and Training, 2002)
- The Kingdom of Bahrain (Police and the Community, 2003)

- British Columbia, Canada (Criminal Exploitation of Women and Children, 2004), co-hosted by the University College of the Fraser Valley, Abbotsford Police Department, Royal Canadian Mounted Police, the Vancouver Police Department, the Justice Institute of British Columbia, Canadian Police College, and the International Centre for Criminal Law Reform and Criminal Justice Policy
- Prague, The Czech Republic (Challenges of Policing in the 21st Century, 2005)
- Turkish National Police (Local Linkages to Global Security and Crime, 2006)
- Dubai Police (Urbanization and Security, 2007)
- Cincinnati, Ohio (Police Without Borders: Fading Distinction Between Local and Global, 2008), City of Cincinnati Police and the Ohio Association of Chiefs of Police
- Ohrid, Republic of Macedonia (Policing, Private Security, Economic Development and Social Change, 2009)
- Valletta, Malta (Tourism, Strategic Locations, and Major Events: Policing in an Age of Mobility. Mass Movement and Migration, 2010)
- Karlskrona, (Blekinge County), Sweden (Contemporary Issues in Public Safety & Security, 2011)
- New York City (Economic Development, Armed Violence, and Public Safety, 2012)

The majority of participants of the annual meetings are usually directly involved in the police profession. In addition, scholars and researchers in the field also participate. The meetings comprise both structured and informal sessions to maximize dialogue and exchange of views and information. The executive summary of each meeting is distributed to participants as well as to a wide range of other interested police professionals and scholars. In addition, a book of selected papers from each annual meeting is published through Prentice Hall, Lexington Books, Taylor & Francis Group, and other reputable publishers.

Closely associated with the IPES is the *Police Practice and Research: An International Journal (PPR)*. The journal is committed to highlighting current, innovative police practices from all over the world; providing opportunities for exchanges between police practitioners and researchers; reporting the state of public safety internationally; focusing on successful practices that build partnerships between police practitioners and communities, as well as highlighting other successful police practices in relation to maintaining order, enforcing laws, and serving the community. For more information, visit our website: www.ipes.info.

IPES Board of Directors

A Not-for-Profit (501 [3c]) organization with a Special Consultative Status with the UN, it is administered by a Board of Directors consisting of the following:

President: Dilip Das
Email: dilipdas@ipes.info
6030 Nott Road, Guilderland, NY 12084, USA
Tel (802) 598-3680—Fax (410) 951-3045

Vice President: Etienne Elion
Email: ejeej2003@yahoo.fr
Case J-354-V, OCH Moungali 3, Brazzaville, Republic of Congo
(Ex French Congo)
Tel 242 662 1683—Fax 242 682 0293

Treasurer/Secretary: Paul Moore
Email: Paul@ipes.info
P.O. Box 1611, West Monroe, LA 71294, USA
Tel (318) 322-5300—Fax (318) 340-1021

Directors

Rick Sarre
Email: rick.sarre@unisa.edu.au
P.O. Box 2471, Adelaide, 5001, South AUSTRALIA
Tel 61 8 84314879 (h)—61 8 83020889—Fax 61 8 83020512

Tonita Murray
Email: Tonita_Murray@hotmail.com
73 Murphy Street, Carleton Place, Ontario K7C 2B7 CANADA
Tel: 613 998 0883 (w)

Snezana (Ana) Mijovic-Das
Email: anamijovic@yahoo.com
6030 Nott Road, Guilderland, NY 12084, USA
Tel (518) 452 7845—Fax (518) 456 6790

Andrew Carpenter
Email: carpenter@un.org
The Pier, 1 Harborside Place, Apt 658, Jersey City, NJ 07311, USA
Tel (917) 367-2205—Fax (917) 367-2222—Cell (347) 721-1104

Paulo R. Lino
Email: paulino2@terra.com.br
111 Das Garcas St., Canoas, RS, 92320-830, BRAZIL
Tel 55 51 8111 1357—Fax 55 51 466 2425

Rune Glomseth
Email: Rune.Glomseth@phs.no
Slemdalsveien5, Oslo, 0369, NORWAY

Mustafa Ozguler
Email: Mustafaozg@hotmail.com
1849 Algonquin Place, Kent, Ohio 44240, USA
Tel 330 389 0187

Maximillian Edelbacher
Email: edelmax@magnet.at
Riemersgasse 16/E/3, A-1190 Vienna, AUSTRIA
Tel 43-1-601 74/5710—Fax 43-1-601 74/5727

A. B. Dambazau
Email: adambazau@yahoo.com
P.O. Box 3733, Kaduna, Kaduna State, NIGERIA
Tel 234 80 35012743—Fax 234 70 36359118

IPES Institutional Supporters

1. Fayetteville State University (Dr. David E. Barlow, Professor and Dean), College of Basic and Applied Sciences, 130 Chick Building, 1200 Murchison Road, Fayetteville, North Carolina 28301, Tel 910-672-1659, Fax: 910-672-1083, dbarlow@uncfsu.edu
2. Department of Social Sciences (Dr. Bankole Cole), 226 Lipman Building, The University of Northumbria at Newcastle, Newcastle-upon-Tyne, NE1 8ST, United Kingdom, Tel: +44 (0)191 227 3457, bankole.cole@northumbria.ac.uk
3. National Institute of Criminology and Forensic Science (Kamalendra Prasad, Inspector General of Police), MHA, Outer Ring Road, Sector 3, Rohini, Delhi 110085, India, Tel: 91 11 275 2 5095, Fax: 91 11 275 1 0586, kprasadindia@hotmail.com
4. Defendology Center for Security, Sociology and Criminology Research (Valibor Lalic), Srpska Street 63,78000 Banja Luka, Bosnia and Herzegovina, Tel and Fax: 387 51 308 914, lalicv@teol.net
5. The Faculty of Criminal Justice and Security (Dr. Gorazd Mesko), University of Maribor, Kotnikova 8, 1000 Ljubljana, Slovenia, Tel: 386 1 300 83 39, Fax: 386 1 2302 687, gorazd.mesko@fvv.uni-mb.si
6. Abbotsford Police Department (Bob Rich, Chief Constable), 2838 Justice Way, Abbotsford, British Columbia V2 T3 P5, Canada, Tel: 604-864-4809, Fax: 604-864-4725, bobrich@abbypd.ca, swillms@abbypd.ca
7. Department of Criminal Justice, North Carolina Central University, 301 Whiting Criminal Justice Bldg., Durham, North Carolina 27707 (Dr. Harvey L. McMurray, Chair), Tel: 919-530-5204, 919-530-7909, Fax: 919-530-5195, hmcmurray@nccu.edu
8. University of the Fraser Valley (Dr. Darryl Plecas), Department of Criminology & Criminal Justice, 33844 King Road, Abbotsford, British Columbia V2 S7 M9, Canada, Tel: 604-853-7441, Fax: 604-853-9990, Darryl.plecas@ucfv.ca
9. National Police Academy, Japan (Suzuki Kunio, Assistant Director), Police Policy Research Center, 183-8558: 3-12-1 Asahi-cho Fuchu-city, Tokyo, Tel: 81 42 354 3550, Fax: 81 42 330 1308, PPRC@npa.go.jp

10. Royal Canadian Mounted Police (Gary Bass, Deputy Commissioner, Pacific Region), 657 West 37th Ave., Vancouver, British Columbia V5Z. 1K6, Canada, Tel: 604 264 2003, Fax: 604 264 3547, gary.bass@rcmp-grc.gc.ca
11. Eastern Kentucky University (Dr. Robin Haarr), Stratton Building 412A, Stratton Building, 521 Lancaster Avenue, Richmond, Kentucky 40475, Tel: 859-622-8152, robin.haarr@eku.edu
12. The Faculty of Law, University of Kragujevac, Serbia (Prof. Branislav Simonovic), Str. Jovanba Cvijica 1, Kragujevac, Serbia 34000, Tel: 381 34 306 580, Fax: 381 34 306 546, simonov@eunet.rs
13. Cyber Defense & Research Initiatives, LLC, PO Box 86, Leslie, Michigan 49251 (contact James Lewis), Tel: 517 242 6730, lewisja@cyberdefenseresearch.com
14. Audiolex (contact Dr. Kate J. Storey-Whyte), 9-10 Old Police Station, Kington, Hereford, Herefordshire HR53DP, United Kingdom, Fax: 44 154 423 1965, Mobile: 44 7833 378 379, cj@audiolex.co.uk
15. The Department of Criminal Justice, Molloy College, 1000 Hempstead Avenue, PO Box 5002, Rockville Center, New York 11571-5002 (contact Dr. John A. Eterno, NYPD Captain-Retired), Tel: 516-678-5000, ext. 6135, Fax: 516-256-2289, jcterno@molloy.edu
16. The Senlis Council, Center of Excellence on Public Safety (George Howell), Rua Maria Queteria, 121/305, Ipanema, Rio de Janeiro, RJ 22410040, Brazil, Tel: 55 21 3903 9495, Cell: 55 21 8156 6485, howell@senliscouncil.net
17. The Department of Applied Social Studies, City University of Hong Kong (Dr. Li, Chi-mei, Jessica, Lecturer), Tat Chee Avenue, Kowloon Tong, Hong Kong, Tel: 2788 8839, Fax: 2788 8960, jessica@cityu.edu.hk
18. University of Maine at Augusta, College of Natural and Social Sciences (Professor Richard Mears), 46 University Drive, Augusta, Maine 04330-9410, Rmears@maine.edu
19. Office of the Commissioner South Australia Police (Commissioner Mal Hyde), Adelaide, South Australia Police, 30 Flinders Street, Adelaide, South Australia 5000 Australia, Tel: 08 8204 2871, Fax: 08 8204 2322, mal.hyde@police.sa.gov.au
20. University of New Haven (Dr. Richard Ward, Criminal Justice), 300 Boston Post Road, West Haven, Connecticut 06516, Tel: 203 932 7260, rward@newhaven.edu
21. International Police Association, Illinois (Kevin Gordon), 505 N. 10th Street, Mascoutah, Illinois 62258, Treasurer@ipa-usa.org
22. UNISA, Department of Police Practice, Florida Campus, Cnr Christiaan De Wet and Pioneer Avenues, Private Bag X6, Florida, South Africa 1710, Tel: (011) 471 2116, cell: 083 581 6102, Fax: 011 471 2255 (Setlhomamaru Dintwe, Dintwsi@unisa.ac.za)

23. Justice Studies Department, San José State University, 1 Washington Square, San José, Ca 95192-0050 (Dr. Mark E. Correia, Chair and Associate Professor), Tel: 408-924-1350, mcorreia@casa.sjsu.edu
24. Australasian Institute of Policing (Ian Lanyon), P.O. Box 99. Pascoe Vale South, Victoria, 3044, Australia, Tel: 61-3-986-58208, Fax: 61-3-986-68325, Cell: 61-9-144-6614, ian.lanyon@aipol.org
25. Department of Psychology, Mount Saint Vincent University (Dr. Stephen Perrott), Department of Psychology, Mount Saint Vincent University, 166 Bedford Highway, Halifax, Nova Scotia, Canada B3M 2J6, Tel: 902-457-6337, Stephen.perrott@mvsu.ca
26. Kaplan University, Houston (Cliff Roberson, LLM, Ph.D., Managing Editor, *Police Practice & Research: An International Journal*), Tel: 713-703-6639 or AIM: Roberson37, 16307 Sedona Woods Lane, Houston, Texas 77082-1656, managingeditorppr@gmail.com